Springer Proceedings in Business and Economics

Springer Proceedings in Business and Economics brings the most current research presented at conferences and workshops to a global readership. The series features volumes (in electronic and print formats) of selected contributions from conferences in all areas of economics, business, management, and finance. In addition to an overall evaluation by the publisher of the topical interest, scientific quality, and timeliness of each volume, each contribution is refereed to standards comparable to those of leading journals, resulting in authoritative contributions to the respective fields. Springer's production and distribution infrastructure ensures rapid publication and wide circulation of the latest developments in the most compelling and promising areas of research today.

The editorial development of volumes may be managed using Springer Nature's innovative EquinOCS, a proven online conference proceedings submission, management and review system. This system is designed to ensure an efficient timeline for your publication, making Springer Proceedings in Business and Economics the premier series to publish your workshop or conference volume.

This book series is indexed in SCOPUS.

Evgeny Kuzmin · Geoffrey M. Hodgson ·
Laura Bravi · Yuliya Lavrikova
Editors

Searching for Developmental Alternatives in Economic Theory

Proceedings of the 2024 Euro-Asian Symposium on Economic Theory (EASET), Ekaterinburg, Russia, June 26–28

Springer

Editors
Evgeny Kuzmin
Department of Regional Industrial Policy and Economic Security
Institute of Economics of the Ural Branch of the Russian Academy of Sciences
Yekaterinburg, Russia

Laura Bravi
Department of Economics, Society, and Politics
University of Urbino
Urbino, Pesaro-Urbino, Italy

Geoffrey M. Hodgson
Institute for International Management
Loughborough University
London, UK

Yuliya Lavrikova
Institute of Economic of the Ural Branch of the Russian Academy of Sciences
Yekaterinburg, Russia

ISSN 2198-7246 ISSN 2198-7254 (electronic)
Springer Proceedings in Business and Economics
ISBN 978-3-031-91158-3 ISBN 978-3-031-91159-0 (eBook)
https://doi.org/10.1007/978-3-031-91159-0

This Springer imprint is published by the registered company Springer Nature Switzerland AG
The registered company address is: Gewerbestrasse 11, 6330 Cham, Switzerland

About this Book and Keywords

This book presents selected papers from the Euro-Asian Symposium on Economic Theory, held by the Institute of Economics of the Ural Branch of the Russian Academy of Sciences (Ekaterinburg, Russia) on June 26–28, 2024. Continuing the tradition of fostering scholarly dialogue, the conference focused on advancing theoretical insights and practical solutions to contemporary challenges in economic science.

The main topic of the 2024 Symposium is "Searching for Development Alternatives". Reflecting the dynamic shifts in the global economic landscape, this theme encourages to reexamine established paradigms. Researchers were invited to critically examine existing models and explore forward-looking strategies to address pressing economic and social challenges.

The book is structured into four sections, each addressing key aspects of modern economic discourse. They delve into the evolution and resilience of industrial ecosystems and investigate the fundamental nature of money; the complexities of achieving justice and efficiency in economic development are addressed, examining income disparities, the convergence of economies, and social aspects within economic mechanisms.

The contributions featured in this book offer a synthesis of theoretical models and empirical analyses, bridging the gap between academic inquiry and practical application. This collection is a valuable resource for researchers, policymakers, and practitioners seeking innovative solutions to navigate the complexities of today's economic systems.

Keywords. Economic Theory · Economic Policy · Justice · Inequality · Economic Analysis

Headliners

- Expanding the Horizons of Economic Theory at the Crossroads of Paradigms
- Bridging Theoretical Insights and Practical Solutions for Contemporary Economic Challenges
- Discussing Development Alternatives Amid Economic Shifts

Contents

About the Editors

Geoffrey M. Hodgson is Emeritus Professor in Management at Loughborough University London. He is an Editor-in-Chief at the *Journal of Institutional Economics*, and the author of several books includes *The Wealth of a Nation* (2023), *Liberal Solidarity* (2021), *Is Socialism Feasible?* (2019), *Is there a Future for Heterodox Economics?* (2019), *Conceptualizing Capitalism* (2015), *From Pleasure Machines to Moral Communities* (2013) and *Darwin's Conjecture* (with Thorbjoern Knudsen, 2010). He was ranked in 2023 by Research.com "Best Scientists in Economics and Finance" as #18 in the UK and #155 globally. His website is www.geoffreymhodgson.uk.

Laura Bravi has a Ph.D. degree in "Economics and Business Management" (Summa cum Laude) at the University of Urbino Carlo Bo, Italy, where she is now Assistant Professor in International Marketing in the bachelor degree course and Integrated Business Logistics in the master degree course at the University of Urbino. Her research areas and teaching activities are concentrated on Quality Management Systems and sustainable business practices, Supply Chain Management and the enabling technologies of Industry 4.0 and 5.0. She is author of several publications of international relevance. She also collaborates with an Italian Accredited Laboratory for quality tests for the wood furniture sector in Pesaro, Italy, as for quality accreditation and quality tests.

Dr. Yuliya Lavrikova is the Director of the Institute of Economics of the Ural Branch of the Russian Academy of Sciences. She is a member of the international Eurasian business and economic community (USA, Netherlands, Turkey), the Association of Russian geographers and social scientists. She has over 150 scientific publications, including over 30 monographs. Research interests: theoretical and methodological aspects of the strategy of balanced territorial and sectoral development, strategic directions for the development of sectoral complexes, institutions of spatial development, sustainable, and safe socio-economic development of regions.

Evgeny Kuzmin is a researcher at the Department of Regional Economic Policy and Economic Security at the Institute of Economics of the Ural Branch of the Russian Academy of Sciences. He serves as a reviewer for several high-impact international journals, including the Journal of Cleaner Production, PLOS ONE, Sustainability (Switzerland), Heliyon, Business Strategy and the Environment, among others. He has authored over 150 scientific publications. He has participated in the execution of more than ten research projects (grants) funded by the Russian Foundation for Basic Research, the Russian Humanitarian Scientific Foundation, the Russian Science Foundation, and the Ministry of Education and Science of Russia. His research interests encompass risk and uncertainty, economic crises, sustainability, public-private partnerships, industrial policy, economic growth, and entrepreneurship.

Editorial: Exploring New Horizons of the Economic Thought in the Changing Reality

Yuliya Lavrikova[1], Geoffrey Hodgson[2], Olga Buchinskaia[3](✉), Evgeny Kuzmin[4], and Laura Bravi[5]

[1] Institute of Economics of the Urals Branch of the Russian Academy of Sciences, 29 Moskovskaya Street, 620014 Ekaterinburg, Russia
lavrikova.ug@uiec.ru

[2] Institute for International Management, Loughborough University London, 3 Lesney Avenue, The Broadcast Centre, Here East, Queen Elizabeth Olympic Park, London 20 3BS, UK
g.hodgson2@lboro.ac.uk

[3] Center of Economic Theory, Institute of Economics of the Ural Branch of the Russian Academy of Sciences, 29 Moskovskaya Street, 620014 Ekaterinburg, Russia
gto2000@list.ru

[4] Department of Regional Industrial Policy and Economic Security, Institute of Economics of the Ural Branch of the Russian Academy of Sciences, 29 Moskovskaya Street, 620014 Ekaterinburg, Russia
kuzmin.ea@uiec.ru

[5] Department of Economics, Society, Politics, Carlo Bo University of Urbino, 61029 Urbino, Italy
laura.bravi@uniurb.it

Abstract. This chapter summarizes the best research from the 11th Euro-Asian Symposium on Economic Theory (EASET-2024), held from June 26–28, 2024, by the Institute of Economics of the Ural Branch of the Russian Academy of Sciences. The editors highlight the trends and conditions driving the research, with a focus on current economic challenges and future development prospects. Chapter's contributions and key conclusions are summarized, demonstrating the variety of approaches presented. The review provides insight into recent advances in economic theory and their practical implications for economic policy.

Keywords: Economic theory · Economic development · Social transformation

During the 20th century, mainstream economic trends like neoclassical economics, new Keynesianism, and new institutionalism dominated Western, and by the end of the century, Russian economic thought. Yet, these trends began to show paradoxes and contradictions, which questioned the fundamental tenets of neoclassical doctrines and led to the mainstream's inability to withstand them. Kosieme et al. [1] identify the following comparatively recent failures of the mainstream:

E. Kuzmin et al. (Eds.): EASET 2024, SPBE, pp. 1–8, 2025.
https://doi.org/10.1007/978-3-031-91159-0_1

1. *The Lucas Paradox.* According to some neoclassical ideas, capital flows from countries with an excess of capital to countries with a shortage of capital. A similar movement should take place with a highly skilled workforce. However, in reality, financial capital is concentrated in rich countries [2], as is the migration flow of highly skilled workers [3], which contradicts theoretical expectations.
2. *The controversial nature of the environmental Kuznets curve.* Initially, mainstream theory assumed that the anthropogenic environmental burden first increases with economic growth, but then decreases with capital accumulation, forming an inverted parabola. Later it was proven that the quality of the natural environment does not depend linearly on the level of income [4] and this dependence cannot be considered universal and applicable to all cases [5].
3. *Criticism of the invisible hand of the market.* Critics have questioned the postulate that an individual's pursuit of self-interest benefits society, citing works that show the negative impact of inequality on economic growth [6, 7] and the standard of living [8, 9]. These studies have shown that excessive inequality can hinder sustainable development and create social and economic problems. There is evidence [10, 11] that excessive inequality leads to lower consumer demand, lower economic growth, deeper social gaps, and ultimately weakens political stability and increases social tension. An important contribution came from Saez & Zucman [12], who analyzed the dynamics of the tax burden and its connection to economic injustice. Additionally, R. Barro [13] linked the growth of inequality to the deterioration of long-term development prospects.
4. *Refutation of the theory of income equalization in the long term.* T. Piketty [14] showed that the distribution of income and wealth in the long term not only does not smooth out but also shows a tendency to increase inequality. He argued that the concentration of wealth in the hands of a minority is a systemic phenomenon driven by the structural features of the capitalist economy. Other researchers [15–17] have further documented the growing global wealth stratification. In addition, Solow [18] has shown that that technological progress and globalization can exacerbate inequality.

These and other examples show the significant challenges facing mainstream economic thought and the need to find alternative approaches that can adequately reflect the complexity of the modern world.

These trends are pushing the mainstream to adopt less dogmatic approaches, gradually moving away from the strict dominance of the neoclassical paradigm in favor of a more flexible and realistic economic theory. The emergence of new economic thought has been shaped by such factors as the frequent global economic crises, particularly the 2008 crisis, which prompted economists to reevaluate existing models and seek new approaches to financial risk management. Additionally, escalating environmental issues have driven the need to integrate environmental protection and social responsibility into economic policy. These challenges have sparked greater interest in behavioral economics, systemic resilience, and the development of sustainable economic models.

These issues led participants of the 11th Euro-Asian Symposium on Economic Theory (EASET-2024) to explore ways to improve economic systems. The symposium attracted researchers from various countries and served as a platform for discussing emerging trends in economic research, such as digitalization, the green economy, and social justice.

One of the topics discussed was the concept of industrial ecosystems. *E. Kuzmin, G. Rakhimova, and H. Nasirova (Chapter 2)* provide a comprehensive overview of theoretical approaches to the study of industrial ecosystems, their role in technological development, and key characteristics that distinguish them from other models of industrial connectivity. The authors outline four key approaches to understanding industrial ecosystems, shedding light on their formation and functioning. They also structure the attributes of these ecosystems, highlighting their role in stimulating innovation. Special focus is given to how ecosystems connect with technological niches to drive radical innovations that can transform socio-technical regimes. This paper provides a theoretical foundation for further study and practical tools for implementing industrial ecosystems across different contexts.

The rapid digitalization of the economy and the growing role of network structures have created new opportunities and challenges, necessitating the adaptation of both theoretical foundations and practical tools for economic analysis. In this context, the sustainability of enterprises and regional economic systems has become especially important. *V. Yakimova, S. Pankova, and S. Khmura (Chapter 3)* have shown that the amplitudes of decline and recovery can be used to assess the resilience of business ecosystems in border regions affected by the COVID-19 pandemic and sanctions pressure. Their results show that industrially oriented ecosystems turned out to be the most sensitive to shocks, while export-oriented systems showed significant fluctuations in income. As a strategy for ensuring sustainability, the authors propose the development of local value chains, stimulating innovation and strengthening network communication between ecosystem participants. Thus, V. Yakimova, S. Pankova and S. Khmura confirm the need to create adaptive management mechanisms that can quickly respond to external changes, minimize the negative effects of shocks and ensure the sustainable development of business ecosystems.

When considering the sustainability of regional economic systems, it's crucial to highlight the role of digital technologies as a key driver of innovation and adaptation to modern challenges. In *Chapter 4, E. Aydarkina, T. Laskova, A. Nikitaeva, and D. Laskova* examine the impact of digitalization on business innovation in a Russian region. Through scientometric analysis, the authors explore the relationship between business model innovations, digital technologies, and the concept of Industry 4.0. Their findings show that digital technologies act as catalysts for transitioning to innovative business models. Additionally, the authors identify priority areas for innovation in business models and the factors influencing their successful implementation.

These aspects align well with the findings of *Z. Ermakova and S. Fomin (Chapter 5)*, whose research focuses on developing an effective internal planning system for industrial holdings. Illustrating this with the example of a specific company, the authors demonstrate how systematically identifying and eliminating losses in the planning process can boost productivity and organizational sustainability. Their paper emphasizes the importance of implementing a unified, integrated planning system that optimizes resources, reduces losses, and ensures long-term enterprise sustainability.

These studies collectively show that, across economic sectors, introducing innovative technologies, optimizing business processes, and developing modern management systems are crucial for enhancing the sustainability and competitiveness of both individual enterprises and regional economic systems.

The research provides valuable insights for analyzing the broader issues that support sustainable economic development.

The fundamental question of whether economic equilibrium is achievable continues to spark lively discussions among economists from both orthodox and heterodox schools of thought. In their study, *S. Casagrande and B. Dallago (Chapter 6)* offer a new perspective on this problem. Examining extensive theoretical material and using the tools of chaos theory, the authors argue that traditional economic debates about the presence or absence of equilibrium are misleading, as they ignore the systemic nature of economic dynamics. Instead, they propose the concept of economic harmony, which assumes that all elements of the system must be coordinated and ordered, creating a harmonious unity. According to the authors, harmony is essential for the survival and sustainable development of a system. Economic harmony is achieved when the interaction between the system's components is focused and balanced, minimizing conflicts and creating a synergistic effect. However, as Casagrande and Dallago highlight, modern economic realities are far from harmonious: the selfish interests of certain social groups, coupled with political and economic imbalances, disrupt the system's coherence and impede the transition toward sustainable development, ultimately threatening its integrity.

The study by *M. Nosova and N. Tyukavkin (Chapter 7)* further contributes to the discussion on the sustainability of economic systems and their social dimensions. The authors trace the evolution of the concept of "justice" from antiquity to the present and examine its relationship with efficiency. They propose using additional indicators—such as process and target equity—to better assess equality. These indicators focus on the availability of public services, the removal of barriers for vulnerable groups, and their access to these services. This approach is particularly important in light of the growing social and economic imbalances, which call for a reassessment of resource allocation strategies. The study advances both the theory and practice of sustainable economic management by demonstrating how social and economic objectives can be harmoniously integrated to achieve broader societal well-being.

A. Pasynkov and E. Zakharchuk (Chapter 8) examine the socio-economic aspects of resource allocation by analyzing household income structures and levels using municipal data within the context of territorial accounts. Focusing on the Ural Federal District of Russia, their study highlights that income from wage labor is the primary component for municipalities in the region. However, they also identify significant regional disparities in the share of wages, influenced by both geographical location and the local economic structure. The authors observe a marked increase in labor incomes in northern territories. While the income structure in urban and rural areas is generally similar, it is primarily shaped by the administrative division of municipalities. These patterns are attributed to the specifics of Russia's spatial development, where the concentration of business activity in large cities impacts incomes in smaller towns and rural areas.

A. Steblyanskaya, A. Pasynkov, and Z. Jiandong (Chapter 9) explore regional development factors by comparing interregional differences in household incomes between

Russia and China. This study expands on the spatial development issues discussed in the previous chapter. The authors examine the main sources of income and standards of living in both countries, revealing significant differences in household income structures and regional characteristics. They also compare incomes based on purchasing power parity and analyze national differences in the ratio of average to minimum wages. Special focus is given to how these factors contribute to economic inequality in both nations. The study highlights China's success in reducing inter-regional disparities through comprehensive government policies, such as infrastructure development, entrepreneurship support, and efforts to equalize economic conditions across regions. The authors suggest that Russia could benefit from adopting China's strategies to address regional imbalances in economic development.

N. Kosolapova, A. Nikitaeva, O. Dolgova, D. Gridnev, and A. Fedorova (Chapter 10) use cluster analysis to study the socio-economic development of Russian regions, focusing on behavioral patterns, resilience to change, and transitions between clusters over time. Their findings show that regions with strong economic specialization tend to be more stable, while regions with less specialization are more vulnerable to internal and external shocks. The authors offer recommendations for enhancing strategic management at the regional level and developing sustainable economic models tailored to regional characteristics. This paper provides insights into regional economic dynamics through systemic economic theory and endogenous development approaches.

Regional imbalances and their impact on sustainable development must also consider environmental challenges, which increasingly shape economic policy. In *Chapter 11, F. Murmura, G. Pierli, and L. Bravi* explore the EU's environmental policies aimed at greening the economy. A survey of Italian citizens reveals a significant awareness gap regarding environmental issues and responsible institutions. This information gap, stemming from limited access to environmental and economic policy data, undermines citizens' participation in environmental initiatives and diminishes their effectiveness.

In contrast to the focus on regional inequality, an important area of research is the analysis of mutual trade and its impact on the convergence of economic development levels across countries. This question is addressed by *E. Andreeva and A. Ratner in Chapter 12*, where they examine the relationship between trade flows and economic convergence in the CIS countries. Using 25 years of extensive statistical data, they present a methodology for evaluating interrelationships between countries, considering both raw and non-raw components of trade. By conducting a comparative analysis with econometric methods, the authors uncover deeper patterns, demonstrating that trade is a key mechanism for equalizing economic development levels.

The previously discussed issues of regional inequality and the mechanisms for addressing them are further explored through the study of social factors, such as the impact of technological progress, human capital, and labor mobility on economic processes.

E. Kuzmin and B. Ummatov (Chapter 13) contribute to the discussion about human capital as a factor of sustainability and competitiveness of economic systems. The authors highlight the differences between human resource management and human capital, focusing on the strategic approach. The study offers a typology of human capital management strategies, analyzes their key characteristics, accents and attributes. This paper offers a theoretical framework for further research in the field of strategic human capital management.

The discussion on strategic human capital management, introduced in the previous chapter, is further developed in the study by *E. Kuzmin and U. Yakubova (Chapter 14)*. They propose a conceptual framework for assessing and classifying human capital mobilization reserves, evaluating them according to employee qualifications, readiness for new tasks, the ability to replace key specialists, and the time required for training. Additionally, the authors identify strategies to enhance the efficiency of human capital utilization.

The impact of technological development on the transformation of family structures is explored by *E. Tukhtarova and N. Neklyudova (Chapter 15)*. Using the Ural region of Russia as a case study, the authors analyze how changes in technological patterns over the past 250 years have influenced family demographics. Their research shows how the shift from an agrarian economy to a mining and metallurgical industry led to smaller family units, replacing the traditionally larger families with high birth rates. The authors argue that Russia's long-standing catching-up economic development has created significant intergenerational gaps, reduced human capital levels, and led to an imbalance between industrial relations and the family institution. They call for a new economic model that considers regional specifics and addresses family-related challenges, integrating cultural and social aspects to strengthen the family unit. The authors also stress the importance of adapting public policy to the evolving technological and economic environment to maintain and enhance human capital.

Continuing the discussion of social aspects within the economic mechanism, *N. Logacheva, A. Uskova, and J. Salomatova (Chapter 16)* present an innovative approach to analyzing intraregional labor migration using social media data. Focusing on several Russian cities, the authors demonstrate how social network data can provide insights into the gender and age structure of intraregional labor migration. The results reveal significant regional variations in migration processes, shaped by the unique economic and social characteristics of each city. The authors identify key drivers of intraregional migration, including the pursuit of better working conditions, housing availability, infrastructure, and educational and career opportunities. The study emphasizes the role of intraregional migration in socio-economic development, both in enhancing the labor potential of large cities and in addressing imbalances within agglomeration systems. By highlighting the value of big data, the paper broadens the context of human capital studies and offers new avenues for adapting migration management to modern challenges and local labor market specifics.

Another important area of analysis gaining significant scholarly attention is financial markets. In line with this trend, the following section focuses on the nature of money, along with the specifics and prospects of the derivatives market.

In his study of the nature of money, *V. Islamutdinov (Chapter 17)* applies chaos theory to demonstrate that money serves as the universal equivalent of negentropic supply (orderliness) in the economic system. From this perspective, the material content of money becomes secondary, as its true essence lies in its negentropic nature, which enables money to maintain order and structure in the economy. Islamutdinov argues that the source of this negentropic nature is a universal and impersonal trust in the institutions that ensure the stability of the monetary and banking systems. He reframes money's traditional functions — unit of account, medium of exchange, and store of value—through a negentropic lens, offering an explanation for how the monetary system can remain stable amid chaotic economic dynamics. However, the author also addresses challenges within the negentropic framework, particularly the difficulty of measuring the supply of negentropy and the subjective entropy in the behavior of economic agents. This subjective entropy can erode trust in the institutional foundation of money, undermining its negentropic function.

Building on previous discussions of tools and mechanisms supporting economic system stability, *E. Karov, P. Soloviev, and K. Krinichansky (Chapter 18)* examine the use of derivatives to hedge interest rate risk in the securities market. They classify the experience of launching long-term interest rate futures in different countries, revealing fundamental differences in the structure of these derivatives compared to traditional futures. These differences stem from variations in underlying assets, regulatory environments, market liquidity, and participant preferences. The authors emphasize that universal approaches used in major financial centers may not be suitable for local markets, particularly in developing economies. They further highlight the pivotal role of institutional infrastructure in fostering the successful development of the derivatives market. Thus, the study underscores the importance of creating tailored financial instruments for risk management, especially in light of the growing instability in capital markets.

The 11th Euro-Asian Symposium on Economic Theory highlighted diverse approaches and tools for studying modern economic systems. Participants stressed the need for an interdisciplinary view to address challenges like globalization, digitalization, social inequality, and environmental issues. Their findings show the importance of revising traditional economic models to adapt to changing realities. In conclusion, the symposium emphasized that future economic development requires focusing on systemic changes and the interdependence of global and local processes. The studies in this book expand economic theory and offer practical solutions for these challenges.

References

1. Coscieme, L., et al.: Overcoming the myths of mainstream economics to enable a new wellbeing economy. Sustainability **11**(16), 4374 (2019). https://doi.org/10.3390/su11164374
2. Lucas, R.: Why doesn't capital flow from rich to poor countries? Am. Econ. Rev. **80**(2), 92–96 (1990)
3. Bailey, A., Mulder, C.H.: Highly skilled migration between the Global North and South: gender, life courses, and institutions. J. Ethn. Migr. Stud. **43**(16), 2689–2703 (2017). https://doi.org/10.1080/1369183X.2017.1314594
4. Wagner, M.: The environmental Kuznets curve, cointegration, and nonlinearity. J. Appl. Economet. **30**(6), 948–967 (2015). https://doi.org/10.1002/jae.2421
5. Husnain, M.I.U., Haider, A., Khan, M.A.: Does the environmental Kuznets curve reliably explain a developmental issue? Environ. Sci. Pollut. Res. **28**, 11469–11485 (2021). https://doi.org/10.1007/s11356-020-11402-x
6. Persson, T., Tabellini, G.: Is inequality harmful for growth? Am. Econ. Rev. **84**(3), 600–621 (1994)
7. Goda, T., Onaran, Ö., Stockhammer, E.: Income inequality and wealth concentration in the recent crisis. Dev. Change **48**(1), 3–27 (2017). https://doi.org/10.1111/dech.12280

8. Wilkinson, R.G.: Unhealthy Societies: The Afflictions of Inequality. Routledge (2002). https://doi.org/10.4324/9780203421680
9. Wilkinson, R., Pickett, K.: The spirit level: why equality is better for everyone. Penguin (2010)
10. Atkinson, A.B.: Inequality: what can be done? Practice **40**(2), 289–292 (2016)
11. Stiglitz, J.E.: The Price of Inequality: How Today's Divided Society Endangers Our Future. W. W. Norton & Company (2012)
12. Saez, E., Zucman, G.: The Triumph of Injustice: How the Rich Dodge Taxes and How to Make Them Pay. W. W. Norton & Company (2019)
13. Barro, R.J.: Inequality and growth revisited (No. 11). ADB Working Paper Series on Regional Economic Integration (2008). https://hdl.handle.net/11540/1762
14. Piketty, T.: Capital in the Twenty-First Century. Harvard University Press (2014). https://doi.org/10.4159/9780674369542
15. Milanovic, B.: Global Inequality: A New Approach for the Age of Globalization. Harvard University Press (2016). https://doi.org/10.4159/9780674969797
16. Seery, E., Caistor Arendar, A.:. Even it Up: Time to End Extreme Inequality. Oxfam International (2014)
17. Atkinson, A.B., Piketty, T.: Top Incomes: A Global Perspective. Oxford University Press (2010)
18. Solow, R.M.: Perspectives on growth theory. J. Econ. Perspect. **8**(1), 45–54 (1994). https://doi.org/10.1257/jep.8.1.45

Theory of Economic Ecosystem Development

Industrial Ecosystem Framework: A Literature Review

Evgeny Kuzmin[1](✉), Guzalbegim Rakhimova[2,3], and Hatidje Nasirova[2]

[1] Institute of Economics of the Ural Branch of the Russian Academy of Sciences, 29 Moskovskaya Street, 620014 Ekaterinburg, Russia
kuzmin.ea@uiec.ru

[2] Department of Accounting and Auditing, Tashkent Institute of Irrigation and Agricultural Mechanization Engineers" National Research University, 39 Kori Niyazi Street, Tashkent 100000, Uzbekistan

[3] Department of Science and Rating, Diplomat University, 1 Sayilgoh Street, Tashkent 100047, Uzbekistan

Abstract. Amid growing competition and accelerating technological progress, the concept of industrial ecosystems is getting increasingly important in enhancing the efficiency and sustainability of industrial development. This study presents a literature review on industrial ecosystems, their role in technological development, and key characteristics that differentiate them from other models of cooperation and industrial connectivity. We distinguish between four possible ways to interpret the phenomenon of industrial ecosystems, namely as a localized complex, an integrated formation, a network organization, and a self-organizing system. On this basis, we clarify and systematize blocks of industrial ecosystems' attributes related to the conditions for their formation and a block of resultant attributes conveying their specific character. The research shows that technology niches can act as starting points for the formation of industrial ecosystems by providing support for radical innovation. Our analysis also demonstrates that the innovative component of industrial ecosystems drives technological progress through the creation of innovative value chains. Industrial ecosystems are a new organizational form that goes beyond traditional industrial structures. They play a key role in increasing the resilience of economic systems in the face of global challenges. Theoretical significance of the article lies in systematization of knowledge about industrial ecosystems, which creates the basis for further research in this field. The research findings will be useful for establishing the research framework.

Keywords: Industrial ecosystem · Technological development

JEL Classification: L16 · O14

1 Introduction

Accelerating globalization and intensifying competition make the issue of increasing industrial efficiency especially acute [1–5]. One of the promising approaches to solving this problem is the development of industrial ecosystems [6–9]. The concept of

E. Kuzmin et al. (Eds.): EASET 2024, SPBE, pp. 11–29, 2025.
https://doi.org/10.1007/978-3-031-91159-0_2

industrial ecosystems is based on analogy with natural ecosystems and assumes interdependent relationships between participants [10] in the production process. According to Shmeleva [11], industrial ecosystems are a localized complex of organizations, business processes, innovative projects and infrastructure elements that has the capacity for sustainable autonomous functioning based on a closed cycle of utilizing resources, products and production-technological systems. Through integration and interaction of ecosystem participants within a single platform aimed at achieving common goals, such entities effectively redistribute material and non-material flows, thus minimizing external dependencies and reducing costs through internal capabilities. The key elements that secure the autonomy and long-term resilience of industrial ecosystems are flexibility and adaptability to changes in the external environment and market needs. They are achieved through introduction of innovative technologies, the development of digital infrastructure and creation of strong cooperative ties that help strengthen competitive advantages and make the resource use more efficient.

An industrial ecosystem can also be viewed as a complex network of various interacting actors [12]. Each of these actors plays a specific part in the creation, exchange and consumption of resources, knowledge and technologies, while building a system of interdependent connections and cooperative relations. This formation organically combines the features of clusters, holdings, financial-industrial groups, technology parks, and business incubators [13].

The recent interest of researchers and practitioners in the phenomenon of industrial ecosystems is conditioned by its significant potential for transforming traditional approaches to industrial production organization. Despite the growing popularity of this topic, the literature still lacks a unified understanding of what an industrial ecosystem is; there are numerous questions left unresolved concerning the mechanisms of industrial ecosystems' formation and functioning, their key features and contribution to technological development. The diversity of research approaches that has emerged against this background requires their systematization and in-depth analysis, which will make it possible to identify promising areas for further study. In this regard, our article represents a review of the literature on industrial ecosystems and their role in technological development.

The results of this study deepen the understanding of the concept of industrial ecosystems. By combining disparate approaches and interpretations, we provide the theoretical foundation of the concept of industrial ecosystem, which contributes to the formation of a unified scientific ground. The highlighted lines of interpretation create the basis for further analysis of industrial ecosystems' nature. Key attributes of industrial ecosystems identified in the work and their classification allow us to enrich the understanding of the mechanisms of ecosystems' formation and functioning. Establishing a connection between industrial ecosystems and technological niches adds to the study of innovation processes, expands the boundaries of these phenomena and their role in the evolutionary change of socio-technical regimes in today's conditions. The named directions for future research outline the promising areas for developing the concept of industrial ecosystems.

2 Interpretation of the Industrial Ecosystem

Interpretations of the industrial ecosystem vary significantly according to the context. This is partly due to the complexity and multifaceted nature of the phenomenon, which encompasses economic, social, environmental and technological aspects. Having analyzed the existing definitions, we identified several key lines of interpretation of this term (Fig. 1).

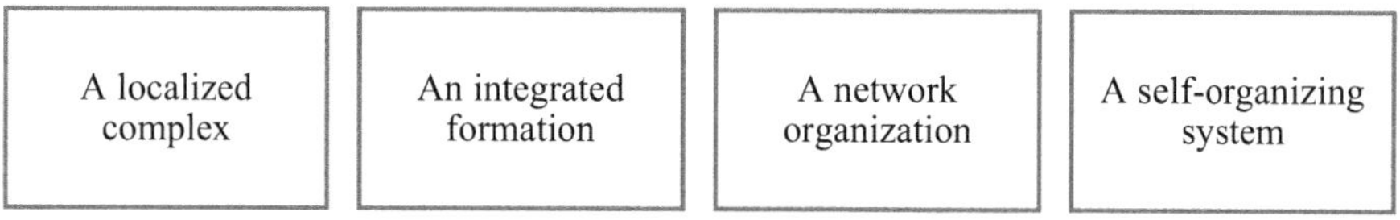

Fig. 1. Lines of interpretation of the industrial ecosystem.

Industrial ecosystems as a localized complex mostly represent geographically limited sets of organizations, business processes, innovative projects and infrastructure facilities capable of long-term autonomous functioning due to the closed cycle of using resources, products and production-technological systems [14]. In such ecosystems, enterprises and other participants interact within a limited area, which makes them similar to clusters [15]. This facilitates the efficient exchange of production potential, while minimizing external dependencies and reducing costs. This approach focuses on spatial concentration and coordination of participants, which allows of processes optimization and innovative development stimulation. Localization promotes closer cooperation by stimulating conditions for synergy and increased competitiveness. Proponents of this approach emphasize the significance of territorial proximity and integration of industrial ecosystem participants. Gamidullaeva [16] views a cluster as a localized ecosystem and proposes system mechanisms for integrating regional space based on optimizing the interaction between industrial cluster actors. Mochalova et al. [17] design an ecosystem diagram based on the principles of a circular economy, where an industrial enterprise, an industrial cluster and an industrial ecosystem are explored through the prism of interconnected elements of a localized complex [18]. For example, waste generated by one enterprise can be used as raw material by another, which helps boost resource efficiency. At that, regional specialization allows creating unique competence centers that guarantee a high concentration of knowledge and technology in a specific field of activity. Such centers play a key role in enhancing the competitiveness of a region by encouraging innovative development and strengthening its economic potential. Publications on regional economics and sustainable development underscore that regional specialization contributes to the efficient use of its natural, labor, and infrastructure resources [19]. In addition, regional specialization creates closed value chains and stimulates cooperation between economic actors [20, 21]. Such competence centers also play an important part in the development of human capital as they provide opportunities for professional growth, training and introduction of advanced technologies, which makes the region more resilient to economic and social challenges.

In practice, the industrial localized complex approach is used in a number of successful models. One of the examples is the Kalundborg Eco-Industrial Symbiosis (Denmark), a localized ecosystem in which businesses exchange resources and by-products, thus creating a closed production cycle [22]. Another example is the numerous industrial parks, in particular the technology parks of Shenzhen (China) [23], which function as localized ecosystems bringing together high-tech enterprises and research institutions. Thus, the localized complex approach to studying industrial ecosystems emphasizes the importance of geographical concentration and integration of participants in production to achieve sustainable and innovative development.

Within the *integrative approach*, industrial ecosystems are seen as sustainable socio-economic entities. This approach concentrates on the comprehensive integration of various elements and participants to reach synergies and enhance the competitiveness of each of them. Enterprises, research institutes, educational centers and other structures are united into a single system, thus bringing about not purely horizontal but vertical multi-level integration. The participants interact to attain common goals, such as innovative development and increased productivity. Their cooperation helps reduce costs and optimize production processes and ensures sustainable development through the integration of various resources and competencies. In this vein, we can see that Kleiner [13] proposes a concept of an "industrial future" based on the leading role of industrial ecosystems that combine features of various organizational forms, although it is not obvious that these are entities of different levels and functional affiliations, but they create a socio-economic system with its inherent complexity. An example of such an integrative approach is the Bavarian automobile cluster [24], which includes enterprises, educational and research centers united by a common mission. Hence, the integrative approach stresses the importance of a comprehensive combination of various elements and participants within the industrial ecosystem to achieve the goals of innovative development.

The *network approach* regards industrial ecosystems as complex networks of interacting actors, such as industrial enterprises, suppliers, consumers, research and educational institutions, and other infrastructure organizations [25, 26]. This approach highlights the dynamic connections and interactions between the participants [27, 28]. Actors are connected by various types of relationships, including cooperation, competition and coopetition [29]. The central element that bands together actors in an industrial ecosystem is the anchor organization, which is most often a large industrial enterprise or group of enterprises. This organization acts as an integrator that coordinates participants' actions and creates a single space for interaction [16, 30, 31]. This interconnectedness provides flexibility and adaptability. Flexibility is achieved through decentralized management and the ability to redistribute resources and functions among network participants [32]. The network approach emphasizes the importance of resource circulation, exchange of knowledge, technologies and best practices among ecosystem participants. In this context, Titova and Ziglina [33] analyze the points of contact characteristic of industrial ecosystems and industrial clusters. However, they concentrate their scrupulous attention on differences between these forms and note that the industrial ecosystem also incorporates consumers and participants may belong to unrelated types of economic activity. The authors conclude that industrial ecosystems are an evolutionarily more advanced form of industrial associations compared to clusters. A similar position was expressed earlier by Smorodinskaya [34], who discussed the advantages of the ecosystem approach in innovation policy, the fundamental differences between innovation clusters and other types of networks, and the role of the triple helix mechanism (cooperation between research/educational institutions, business, and the state) in ensuring macroeconomic sustainability. Thus, the network approach underlines the dynamic interactions and connections between participants in industrial ecosystems, which contributes to their flexibility, adaptability and innovative development.

Self-organizing systems are structures capable of organizing themselves without centralized control due to internal interactions between the system's elements. In the context of industrial ecosystems, this approach focuses on the ability of such systems to independently form sustainable and efficient structures through the interaction of various participants. Zheltenkov [35] examines the theoretical foundations and methodological approaches to establishing self-organizing control systems in industry. He notes the role of decentralized management and adaptability in improving the efficiency of industrial organizations. According to numerous studies, such systems are characterized by spontaneous orderliness, resilience and the ability to adapt with no external control involved. The self-organizing system approach falls within an interdisciplinary concept at the intersection of economics, systems analysis, and management theory.

For an ecosystem to function effectively, there is a need for understanding the dynamics of interactions between its elements, where each organization or individual can contribute to the activities of other participants. Thus, an ecosystem is not just an aggregate of elements, but a complex network of relationships supported by coordination processes. Complementarity and interdependence of participants are key characteristics of ecosystems, which determines their ability to co-create value through interactions within a system-level architecture [36–38]. In this context, an ecosystem is defined as a group of participants with varying degrees of multilateral, non-universal complementarity that is not fully hierarchically controlled [10]. This also suggests that managing them requires special mechanisms to facilitate voluntary interaction and resource exchange. Moreover, the multifaceted and non-universal complementarity of participants means that different elements of the ecosystem have certain properties that are valuable only if combined with other elements. At the same time, the integration of diverse resources and competencies becomes a fundamental condition for building a sustainable value chain.

As a rule, industrial ecosystems self-organize around the exchange of resources (materials, energy, waste, etc.) between participants, thus creating closed production cycles [13]. This encourages the implementation of the circular economy principles [39, 40]. At that, each participant in the system strives to optimize its activities within the ecosystem's overall functionality (local optimization) through flexibility in resource allocation.

Each element of the industrial ecosystem is to certain extent autonomous [16, 41, 42], which allows it to quickly respond to changes in the external environment and market conditions. In such a system, participants are able to make decisions at the local level in the absence of a single decision-making center. Instead, governance is exercised primarily through horizontal links between the participants [43]. The system develops evolutionarily, thanks to the constant exchange of knowledge, technologies and experience between its elements. Enterprises independently determine their participation strategy based on their own goals and capabilities. Ultimately, from the position of the self-organizational approach, an industrial ecosystem is a decentralized, dynamic system of interconnected participants that independently forms its structure and processes through internal interaction, exchange of resources, knowledge and technologies. It exhibits emergent properties, namely the collective activity of participants creates new qualities and outcomes that exceed the contribution of each individual element.

Thus, each of the approaches highlights particular features of industrial ecosystems, which expands their research and applied potential. Despite different emphasis, all the approaches converge in understanding the industrial ecosystem as a dynamic and flexible structure embracing numerous participants. The basis of all the approaches is a certain synergy that allows ecosystem participants to achieve more than they could if operated in isolation.

3 Systematization of the Industrial Ecosystem's Attributes

Having revealed the conceptual difference between the industrial ecosystem and other models of cooperation and industrial connectivity (such as industrial symbiosis, cluster, network, technology park, industrial park, eco-industrial park, eco-industrial network, special economic zone) [44], we can identify a number of fundamental attributes of this concept (Table 1). Different approaches to their study emphasize both common features and unique aspects.

The review of industrial ecosystems' attributes has shown that a combination of many factors is required for them to emerge, including technological integration of participants and shared access to resources/technologies, and these conditions provide the basis for their formation. In this abstract shape, production ecosystems are multi-level and multi-component structures united on the basis of a network organizational design and functioning on the principles of collaboration.

The results of the industrial ecosystem's functioning are manifested in its distinctive characteristics. The combination of the above factors results in industrial ecosystems exploiting dual economies of scale – through both the comprehensive scope of the solutions (products/services) offered and the resulting savings in the use of resources, infrastructure and technologies. Ecosystems, to a greater extent than other forms of industrial cooperation, appear to have come closer to solving the fundamental problem of the ever-growing efficiency. Their ability to integrate participants from different industries and value chains levels stimulates intense innovation activity, which makes ecosystems key drivers of modern industrial development. This is achieved through synergy effects, closed production cycles, process optimization, and more rational use of resources. Obviously, industrial ecosystems are superior to traditional forms of cooperation due to their flexibility, scalability and adaptability.

Table 1. Attributes of the industrial ecosystem.

Type of attributes	Attributes	Description
I. *Attributes related to the conditions for the industrial ecosystem's formation*		
1.1. Structural	Multiple components	Different types of participants: enterprises, suppliers, consumers, research and educational institutions, and other infrastructure organizations [16, 33, 45–48]
	Network-based organizational design	Transition from traditional hierarchical and linear management models to network structures, where the main principle is horizontal coordination and interaction between participants [40, 45, 49–53]
	Self-organization	The ability of its participants to independently build and develop internal links, interaction mechanisms and processes without centralized management [12, 27, 51, 54–56]
	Infrastructure	A combination of material and non-material (including digital) resources that enable interaction between participants and the functioning of the ecosystem [57–60]
1.2. Organizational	Autonomy	The ability to function independently of external support due to self-regulation; the attribute reflects a high level of self-sufficiency [54, 61–63]
	Self-regulation	Ecosystem actors participate in decision-making and coordination of actions through horizontal relationships (organizational bridges); it is a prototype of collective management [64–67]
	Network collaboration	Network collaboration reflects interactions between actors in an industrial ecosystem [16, 68–70], the nature of which is based on partnership, trust, cooperation and mutual assistance and includes various forms of relationships [71] – from cooperation and co-opetition (a combination of competition and cooperation) to constructive competition
	Cyclical knowledge	The process of circulation of knowledge, information and innovative ideas (generation-exchange-activation-return of values to the ecosystem) among participants, which serves as the driving force for development [11, 72, 73]. Knowledge plays the role of a key resource, analogous to energy in biological or physical systems, which fuels interactions and development of new projects, technologies and solutions

(*continued*)

Table 1. (*continued*)

Type of attributes	Attributes	Description
	Transboundariness	The transboundary nature of industrial ecosystem processes means the ability of the ecosystem to go beyond geographical, administrative and national boundaries by uniting participants and resources from different regions and countries [16, 74–76]. This attribute reflects the global nature of the modern economy, where production, innovation and business processes are integrated at the international level forming transnational networks
1.3. Functional	Chain multiplier effect	One project becomes an incentive for starting new initiatives, thus expanding the ecosystem's sphere of influence. The new project can create infrastructure solutions (production facilities, logistics hubs, digital platforms) that will be used by other participants in the ecosystem [77–79]
	Synergy	Participants working together produce better results rather than working individually [80–82]. The synergy effect is due to sharing resources, knowledge exchange, cooperation and creation of new opportunities that would be unattainable for participants in isolated settings
	Resource self-sufficiency and cyclicality [circularity]	Joint generation and use of innovative, information, intellectual and other resources. Developing closed cycles through waste recycling and resource reuse [83–88]
1.4. Technological	Technological integration	The attribute suggests the unification of technologies, processes, data and systems of ecosystem participants to create a single technological space. Participants can effectively interact, exchange information, optimize production processes and accelerate the implementation of innovations [44, 89, 90]
	Interoperability	Introducing common standards, platforms and innovative solutions for all the participants to work effectively. Various systems (devices, software, etc.) used by ecosystem participants or even consumers (clients) harmonize with other systems without additional adjustments [91–93]
	Digitalization	Introducing digital technologies and tools to optimize processes and participants' interaction and enhance the efficiency of the entire system. This includes data usage, automation, integration of digital platforms and the development of digital infrastructure to regulate production, logistics, analytics and coordination processes [94–96]

(*continued*)

Table 1. (*continued*)

Type of attributes	Attributes	Description
II. *Resultant attributes conveying the specific character of industrial ecosystems*		
2.1. Functional	Innovativeness	The key aspects of innovativeness in the industrial ecosystem are the creation of an innovative environment, collective generation of innovations, technology transfer, and infrastructure support. Ecosystem participants are able to generate, introduce and disseminate new ideas, technologies, products, processes and business models that create competitive advantages. This attribute reflects the key role of innovation in the transformation of the production system amid changes in external situation and market conditions [97–99]
	Self-development	The system and its participants can independently initiate improvement, adaptation and transformation processes without external intervention. This attribute shows the dynamic nature of the ecosystem, where internal interactions, knowledge sharing and innovative activity act as the basis for continuous growth and evolution [64, 100]
	Flexibility and adaptability	The attribute reflects the dynamic nature of the industrial ecosystem, which can adapt to market, technological, economic and environmental challenges. The system can quickly and effectively respond to changes in the external and internal environment, adjust its processes, resources and interactions to achieve sustainability and maintain competitiveness [16, 18, 33, 40, 101]
	Economic sustainability	The ability of the system and its participants to function stably, develop and generate value in the long term [102, 103]
	Value-based customer focus	The priority of creating value for customers through the adaptation of products, services, processes and interactions. The attribute helps create unique value for consumers, improves interaction between participants and stimulates innovative development, which makes the ecosystem more attractive to customers and partners [25, 102, 104, 105]
	Resource efficiency	The use of all types of resources (material, energy, human and information) is optimized to achieve maximum productivity and minimize losses. Ecosystem participants exploit resources rationally, reduce their excess consumption, costs and negative impact on the environment [11, 47, 106]

(*continued*)

Table 1. (*continued*)

Type of attributes	Attributes	Description
	Integrated (comprehensive) coverage	This attribute reflects the complex nature of the industrial ecosystem, its ability to create interconnected solutions that cover various aspects of the activities of both participants and customers (consumers), providing them with a comprehensive solution (product, service) or a number of interconnected products [33, 81]. These solutions are aimed at meeting special and multifaceted needs. However, it is possible that in some cases the ecosystem may focus on highly specialized products or services that meet the needs of a specific market segment [107]
2.2. Organizational	Global integration	The attribute demonstrates the ability to be included in international (regional) value added chains. The industrial ecosystem can successfully engage in value added chains and interact with participants from different countries, providing access to resources, technologies, markets and knowledge [46, 108, 109]
	Cross-sectoral interaction	By interacting, various industries bring together knowledge, technology and expertise to create breakthrough solutions [110, 111]. Cross-sectoral collaboration enables the development of products and services that meet stringent customer and market requirements

4 Industrial Ecosystem vs. Technological Niche

The relationship between technological development and industrial ecosystem necessitates clarifying the principal outcome of the latter. Above, we have highlighted that industrial ecosystems create a comprehensive solution (product/service) that covers various aspects of the activities of ecosystem participants and clients (consumers). This comprehensive coverage is at odds with the fundamental characteristic of a technological niche as a proxy mechanism that explains industrial transformation through the introduction of innovative technologies. In this context, a technological niche is a certain space for experiments, where innovations are supported to overcome barriers that exist in the dominant technological system (regime). Technological niches form the micro-level at which radical innovations emerge. In the early stages of their existence, these innovations are unstable with low productivity. It is such niches that create conditions for experiments, knowledge accumulation and testing of new solutions. Niches, therefore, act as incubation cells protecting innovations from competitive pressures [112–114]. Berkhout et al. [115] emphasize that the multi-level perspective (MLP) approach is to a certain unilinear in that it tends to "unduly to emphasise processes of regime change which begin within niches and work up, at the expense of those which directly address the various dimensions of the socio-technical regime or those which operate 'downwards' from general features of the socio-technical landscape" [Ibid., p. 62]. Thus, technological niches play a key role in shaping sustainable innovation paths and act as catalysts for the transition to new technological regimes.

According to Smith, Stirling and Berkhout [116], change in a socio-technical regime is the result of the interaction of two key processes, namely a change in selection pressures exerted on the regime and the coordination of resources available both within and beyond the regime to adapt to these pressures. Selection pressures include economic factors (competition, taxation, regulations) as well as broader political and social changes at the landscape level (such as demographic shifts). A significant influence is exerted by pressure coming from below – from innovative niches, which are not yet stable enough to form a new regime but are already creating conditions for its transformation.

Within the multi-level perspective approach, technological niches and socio-technical regimes are viewed as similar types of structures that differ mainly in size and degree of stability [117]. Both of these structures are similar to organizational fields, i.e., communities of interconnected actors. Socio-technical regimes are characterized by large and stable communities with established and institutionalized relationships [118]. In contrast, technology niches are smaller, less structured and unstable communities that are in the process of becoming established. Both regime and niche communities are united by a set of rules that coordinate their actions. In the case of regimes, these rules are stable, clearly formulated and based on historical practice. Niche innovations are characterized by instability of rules, which are in a state of dynamic formation and adaptation. They have the potential to transform into full-fledged socio-technical regimes as the networks that support their development grow and the rules and norms associated with them become stabilized and institutionalized [71]. These differences highlight the importance of niches as space of experimentation and innovation that can transform existing regimes and facilitate the transition to new socio-technical systems.

Coming back to the design of industrial ecosystems, it is worth noting that their ability to provide interconnected solutions addressing complex and multidisciplinary needs is not strictly limited. Industrial ecosystems are presumably quite flexible in choosing the focus of their activities, which is determined by internal resources and competencies and by external market demands. In some cases, an ecosystem may concentrate on highly specialized products or services that meet the needs of certain niche market segments [119]. At the same time, narrow specialization can be combined with close coordination between ecosystem participants, which facilitates adopting integrated solutions even in highly specialized areas. Thus, the industrial ecosystem demonstrates flexibility and customer focus by varying its emphasis from broad-based strategies to niche ones depending on conditions and opportunities.

However, the conceptual understanding of the industrial ecosystem still gravitates towards a broad, comprehensive and integrated coverage of the solutions created, rather than those demanded in a narrow circle. Such an ecosystem suggests not just developing individual products or services, but working out holistic, complementary solutions that generate added value for all stakeholders. The effectiveness of an industrial ecosystem is determined by its ability to integrate diverse resources, knowledge and competencies, thus contributing to the creation of sustainable and innovative value chains. We can conclude that the theoretical closeness between the technological niche and the industrial ecosystem is weakening, although it is not completely lost. Technological niches focus on developing innovations on a limited scale, which is typical of the early stages of the innovation process. The industrial ecosystem operates at a more mature level, where the accent is on scaling innovations. Therefore, niches can be considered as the first stage of ecosystems' formation providing the basis for their subsequent expansion. Hence, technological niches and industrial ecosystems can be perceived as elements of a single evolutionary process that reflects different development stages of socio-technical systems.

The innovation component of industrial ecosystems plays an important part in technological development. Against the backdrop of the diverse models of cooperation and industrial connectivity, ecosystems appear as a new organizational form that goes beyond traditional industrial structures. They concentrate around interconnected processes of co-creation, use and exchange of knowledge, technologies and resources. Their key peculiarities, embodied in multi-component nature, network self-organization, increased autonomy, resource self-sufficiency and cyclicality, interoperability, technological integration, cross-border collaboration and other abovementioned attributes, allow accelerating innovation processes, adapting to rapidly changing market environment and using resources more efficiently. The ecosystem approach opens up new opportunities for sustainable development, increased competitiveness and creation of added value for all stakeholders. Through this approach, ecosystems stimulate conditions for accelerated dissemination of innovations, reduced costs, and improved adaptability to shifts in the global competitive environment. Thus, innovative activity within industrial ecosystems not only boosts technological progress, but also transforms business models and approaches to organizing production; industrial ecosystems become not only a driver of technological progress, but also a key element of sustainable economic growth.

5 Conclusion

Our review has shown that the concept of industrial ecosystems is a promising organizational form that promotes innovation development and economic sustainability. Having systematized research approaches to understanding industrial ecosystems, we clarified their key differences and common features. Four main lines of interpretation of industrial ecosystems have been identified, namely as a localized complex, an integrated formation, a network organization, and a self-organizing system. Each of these interpretations focuses on different aspects of ecosystems' formation and functioning, which together allows outlining the definition of industrial ecosystem in economic science. On this basis, we have identified the blocks of industrial ecosystems' attributes related to the conditions for their formation and a block of resultant attributes conveying their specific character.

The study substantiated that the innovative component of industrial ecosystems plays an important role in technological development. Ecosystems emerge as a new organizational form that goes beyond traditional industrial structures. They have a key part in accelerating technological progress, creating innovative value chains and increasing the resilience of economic systems in the face of global challenges. Particular attention is paid to the role of technological niches, which act as a launching pad for radical innovations, which are then scaled up within more mature ecosystem structures.

The conducted analysis reveals the following promising areas for future studies: research into the role of platform technologies (digital platforms) in creating new business models within ecosystems; assessment of industrial ecosystems' contribution during the transition to sustainable production models; development of methodological approaches to industrial ecosystems' formation in various contexts; study of the stages of industrial ecosystems' life cycle. These and other areas open up broad opportunities for further research that will not only deepen the theoretical understanding of industrial ecosystems, but also create practical tools for their successful implementation.

Conflict of Interest. The authors declare that the research was conducted in the absence of any commercial or financial relationships that could be construed as a potential conflict of interest.

Credit Author Statement. E.K.: Conceptualization, Data Curation, Formal Analysis, Methodology, Project administration, Validation, Visualization, Writing – original draft, Writing – review & editing. G.R.: Formal Analysis, Visualization, Writing – review & editing. H.N.: Formal Analysis, Visualization, Writing – review & editing.

References

1. Skobelev, D.O.: Industrial policy for improving resource efficiency and achieving sustainable development goals. J. New Econ. **21**(4), 153–173 (2020). https://doi.org/10.29141/2658-5081-2020-21-4-8
2. Garnov, A.P., Garnova, V.Y.: Clustering the economy: methods to improve the effectiveness of state industrial policy. Vestnik Russ. Econ. Univ. Named After G.V. Plekhanov **6**(90), 110–117 (2016)
3. Romanova, O.A.: Industrial policy: evolution of implementation mechanisms. Modern Compet. **6**, 32–44 (2008)
4. Romanova, O.A., Ponomareva, A.O.: Industrial policy: new realities, issues of formation and implementation. Econ. Soc. Changes: Facts Trends Forecast. **13**(2), 25–40 (2020). https://doi.org/10.15838/esc.2020.2.68.2
5. Starikov, E.N.: Industrial policy: Approaches to formation and implementation management. Ural State Forest Engineering University, Yekaterinburg (2017)
6. Kleiner, G.B.: The economy of ecosystems: a step into the future. Econ. Rev. Russ. **1**(59), 40–45 (2019)
7. Astafyeva, O.E.: Features of the functioning of industrial enterprises and complexes in modern economic conditions: structural changes and prospects for industrial development. Univ. Bull. **2**, 95–100 (2023)
8. Evseeva, M.V., Starikov, E.N., Voronov, M.P.: The level of technological development in industrial regions: an ecosystem approach. Manager **12**(3), 13–30 (2021). https://doi.org/10.29141/2218-5003-2021-12-3-2
9. Burström, T., Lahti, T., Parida, V., Wincent, J.: Industrial ecosystems: a systematic review, framework and research agenda. Technol. Forecast. Soc. Chang. **208**, 123656 (2024). https://doi.org/10.1016/j.techfore.2024.123656
10. Jacobides, M.G., Cennamo, C., Gawer, A.: Towards a theory of ecosystems. Strateg. Manage. J. **39**(8), 2255–2276 (2018). https://doi.org/10.1002/smj.2904

11. Shmeleva, N.V.: Methodological approaches to assessing the resource efficiency of industrial ecosystems. Models Syst. Netw. Econ. Technol. Nat. Soc. **1**(45), 70–84 (2023). https://doi.org/10.21685/2227-8486-2023-1-4
12. Gamidullaeva, L.A., Tolstykh, T.O., Shmeleva, N.V.: Methodology for comprehensive assessment of industrial ecosystem potential in the context of sustainable regional development. Models Syst. Netw. Econ. Technol. Nat. Soc. **2**, 29–48 (2020)
13. Kleiner, G.B.: Industrial ecosystems: a look into the future. Econ. Rev. Russ. **2**, 53–62 (2018)
14. Soldak, M.A.: Industrial ecosystems and technological development. Econ. Ind. **4**(88), 75–91 (2019)
15. Koscheev, D.A., Tretyakova, E.A.: The phenomenon of industrial clusters: a system-agglomeration approach. J. Econ. Theory, **2**(17), 451–465 (2020). https://doi.org/10.31063/2073-6517/2020.17-2.17
16. Gamidullaeva, L.A.: Industrial cluster of the region as a localized ecosystem: the role of self-organization and collaboration factors. π-Economy **16**(1), 62–82 (2023). https://doi.org/10.18721/JE.16105
17. Mochalova, L.A., Eremeeva, O.S., Podkorytov, V.N.: Circular economy ideas in the practice of industrial ecosystems in Russia. J. New Econ. **25**(1), 87–109 (2024). https://doi.org/10.29141/2658-5081-2024-25-1-5
18. Korhonen, J.: Four ecosystem principles for an industrial ecosystem. J. Clean. Prod. **9**(3), 253–259 (2001). https://doi.org/10.1016/S0959-6526(00)00058-5
19. Rastvortseva, S.N., Snitko, L.T.: Regional specialization and agglomeration effects in the Russian economy. Econ. Soc. Changes: Facts Trends Forecast **13**(3), 46–58 (2020). https://doi.org/10.15838/esc.2020.3.69.4
20. Kostygova, L.A.: European experience of industrial modernization based on interregional cooperation. Eurasian Sci. Bull. **11**(4), 37 (2019)
21. Polyanskikh, E.A.: Theoretical foundations of the cluster approach in regional economic development. Philos. Soc. Commun, **2**, 147–156 (2011)
22. Kalundborg Symbiosis Surplus from circular production (n.d.). https://www.symbiosis.dk/en/. Accessed 19 Nov 2024
23. Gorod-Site: How technoparks are created around the world (2017). https://www.rbc.ru/photoreport/29/05/2017/592c383c9a7947f73d623765. Accessed 19 Nov 2024
24. Automotive Cluster (n.d.). https://www.bayern-innovativ.de/en/page/automotive-cluster. Accessed 19 Nov 2024
25. Molchan, A.S., Tolstykh, T.O., Nadaenko, A.Y.: Principles of ecosystem formation and development and their influence on industrial management strategies. Sustain. Dev. Econ. **1**(41), 124–128 (2020)
26. Stanczyk, S.: Organisational ecosystem and stakeholders view. In search of epistemological logic in management. Int. J. Econ. Bus. Res. **14**(3/4), 268–283 (2017). https://doi.org/10.1504/IJEBR.2017.087498
27. Tolstykh, T.O., Shmeleva, N.V., Agaeva, A.M.: Methodology for assessing the maturity level of economic security of enterprises in industrial ecosystems. Region: Syst. Econ. Manage. **4**(51), 126–143 (2020)
28. Erzhenkian, B.A.: Enterprises and ecosystems: a comparative analysis of characteristics. J. Econ. Regul. **11**(4), 44–56 (2020)
29. Vazhenin, S.G., Sukhikh, V.V.: The potential of competitive collaboration of companies in the reindustrialization of Russia. Econ. Rev. Russ. **4**, 71–82 (2014)
30. Adner, R.: Ecosystem as structure: an actionable construct for strategy. J. Manage. **43**(1), 39–58 (2017). https://doi.org/10.1177/0149206316678451
31. Grumadaite, K., Jucevicius, G.: Strategic approaches to the development of complex organisational ecosystems: the case of Lithuanian clusters. Sustainability **14**(23) (2022). https://doi.org/10.3390/su142315697

32. Leng, J., et al.: Towards resilience in Industry 5.0: a decentralized autonomous manufacturing paradigm. J. Manuf. Syst. **71**, 95–114 (2023). https://doi.org/10.1016/j.jmsy.2023.08.023
33. Titova, N.Y., Ziglina, V.E.: Differences and similarities between the concepts of "industrial clusters" and "industrial ecosystems." Vestnik Astrakhan State Tech. Univ. Ser.: Econ. **3**, 7–16 (2021). https://doi.org/10.24143/2073-5537-2021-3-7-16
34. Smorodinskaya, N.V.: Network innovation ecosystems and their role in driving economic growth. Innovations **7**(189), 27–33 (2014)
35. Zheltenkov, A.V.: Self-organizing management systems in industrial organizations: theory and methodology of creation (Doctoral dissertation). Moscow (2002)
36. Adner, R., Kapoor, R.: Value creation in innovation ecosystems: how the structure of technological interdependence affects firm performance in new technology generations. Strateg. Manage. J. **31**(3), 306–333 (2010). https://doi.org/10.1002/smj.821
37. Kapoor, R.: Ecosystems: broadening the locus of value creation. J. Organ. Des. **7**(1), 1–16 (2018). https://doi.org/10.1186/s41469-018-0035-4
38. Kapoor, R., Lee, J.M.: Coordinating and competing in ecosystems: how organizational forms shape new technology investments. Strateg. Manage. J. **34**(3), 274–296 (2013). https://doi.org/10.1002/smj.2010
39. Lowe, E.A.: Creating by-product resource exchanges: strategies for eco-industrial parks. J. Clean. Prod. **5**(1–2), 57–65 (1997). https://doi.org/10.1016/S0959-6526(97)00017-6
40. Zhu, J., Ruth, M.: Exploring the resilience of industrial ecosystems. J. Environ. Manage. **122**, 65–75 (2013). https://doi.org/10.1016/j.jenvman.2013.02.052
41. Wareham, J., Fox, P.B., Cano Giner, J.L.: Technology ecosystem governance. Organ. Sci. **25**(4), 1195–1215 (2014). https://doi.org/10.1287/orsc.2014.0895
42. Tolstykh, T., Shmeleva, N., Gamidullaeva, L., Krasnobaeva, V.: The role of collaboration in the development of industrial enterprises integration. Sustainability **15**(9), 7180 (2023). https://doi.org/10.3390/su15097180
43. Aarikka-Stenroos, L., Ritala, P.: Network management in the era of ecosystems: systematic review and management framework. Ind. Mark. Manage. **67**, 23–36 (2017). https://doi.org/10.1016/j.indmarman.2017.08.010
44. Tolstykh, T., Shmeleva, N., Gamidullaeva, L.: Evaluation of circular and integration potentials of innovation ecosystems for industrial sustainability. Sustainability **12**(11), 4574 (2020). https://doi.org/10.3390/su12114574
45. Bystrov, A.V., Tolstykh, T.O., Radaykin, A.G.: Cross-industry ecosystem as an organizational-economic model for the development of high-tech industries. Econ. Manage. **26**(6), 564–576 (2020)
46. Pudovkina, O.E.: Formation of a digital ecosystem for industrial cooperation based on advanced digital platforms in the context of reindustrialization. Vestnik Univ. **9**, 41–48 (2020)
47. Korhonen, J., Snäkin, J.P.: Analysing the evolution of industrial ecosystems: concepts and application. Ecol. Econ. **52**(2), 169–186 (2005). https://doi.org/10.1016/j.ecolecon.2004.07.016
48. Lu, C., Rong, K., You, J., Shi, Y.: Business ecosystem and stakeholders' role transformation: evidence from Chinese emerging electric vehicle industry. Expert Syst. Appl. **41**(10), 4579–4595 (2014)
49. Plakhin, A.E., Kochergina, T.V., Selezneva, M.V.: Directed distribution of income asymmetry as a method of managing an industrial ecosystem. Sci. Works Free Econ. Soc. Russ. **234**(2), 154–176 (2022). https://doi.org/10.38197/2072-2060-2022-234-2-154-176
50. Popov, E.V., Simonova, V.L., Tikhonova, A.D.: The structure of industrial ecosystems in the digital economy. Manage. Russ. Abroad **4**, 3–11 (2019)
51. Ashton, W.S., Chopra, S.S., Kashyap, R.: Life and death of industrial ecosystems. Sustainability **9**(4), 605 (2017). https://doi.org/10.3390/su9040605

52. Morris, Z.B., Weissburg, M., Bras, B.: Ecological network analysis of urban–industrial ecosystems. J. Ind. Ecol. **25**(1), 193–204 (2021). https://doi.org/10.1111/jiec.13043
53. Tsujimoto, M., Kajikawa, Y., Tomita, J., Matsumoto, Y.: A review of the ecosystem concept—towards coherent ecosystem design. Technol. Forecast. Soc. Change **136**, 49–58 (2018). https://doi.org/10.1016/j.techfore.2017.06.032
54. Glukhov, V.V., Babkin, A.V., Shkarupeta, E.V., Plotnikov, V.A.: Strategic management of industrial ecosystems based on the platform concept. Econ. Manage. **27**(10), 751–765 (2021)
55. Guo, Z., Zhang, Y., Liu, S., et al.: Exploring self-organization and self-adaption for smart manufacturing complex networks. Front. Eng. Manage. **10**, 206–222 (2023). https://doi.org/10.1007/s42524-022-0225-1
56. Chertow, M.R.: Dynamics of geographically based industrial ecosystems. In: The Dynamics of Regions and Networks in Industrial Ecosystems, pp. 27–42. Edward Elgar Publishing, Cheltenham (2009). https://doi.org/10.4337/9781848449374.00010
57. Shkarupeta, E.V., Dudareva, O.V., Filatova, M.V., Bekkiyev, A.Y.: Methodology for sustainable development of industrial ecosystems. Bull. Voronezh State Univ. Eng. Technol. **82**(4), 377–382 (2020)
58. Mityakov, E.S., Mityakov, S.N.: Methodological approach to analyzing the efficiency of regional industrial ecosystems. Econ. Reg. **20**(3), 836–850 (2024)
59. Shi, Y., Lu, C., Hou, H., Zhen, L., Hu, J.: Linking business ecosystem and natural ecosystem together—a sustainable pathway for future industrialization. J. Open Innov.: Technol. Mark. Complex. **7**(1), 38 (2021). https://doi.org/10.3390/joitmc7010038
60. Bobryshev, A.D., Tumin, V.M., Savelyev, A.V., Alenina, E.E., Trifonov, V.A.: Place of infrastructure in the innovation ecosystem of industry. In: International Scientific and Practical Conference Strategy of Development of Regional Ecosystems "Education-Science-Industry" (ISPCR 2021), pp. 37–43. Atlantis Press (2022). https://doi.org/10.2991/aebmr.k.220208.006
61. Filimonov, I.V.: The digital economy ecosystem: problems of subject identification. Innov. Inves. **6**, 51–58 (2020)
62. Thomson, L., Kamalaldin, A., Sjödin, D.: A maturity framework for autonomous solutions in manufacturing firms: the interplay of technology, ecosystem, and business model. Int. Entrep. Manage. J. **18**, 125–152 (2022). https://doi.org/10.1007/s11365-020-00717-3
63. Frandsen, T., Raja, J.Z., Neufang, I.F.: Moving toward autonomous solutions: exploring the spatial and temporal dimensions of business ecosystems. Ind. Mark. Manage. **103**, 13–29 (2022). https://doi.org/10.1016/j.indmarman.2022.03.004
64. Tolstykh, T.O.: Ecosystem model of organizational design for the innovative development of industrial enterprises. Proc. Southwest State Univ. Ser.: Econ. Sociol. Manage. **10**(3), 65–74 (2020)
65. Gunningham, N., Rees, J.: Industry self-regulation: an institutional perspective. Law Policy **19**(4), 363–414 (1997). https://doi.org/10.1111/1467-9930.t01-1-00033
66. Chaoxian, G., Wei, H.: Industrial organization in the digital economy era: evolution and effects. China Econ. **19**(4), 15–36 (2024)
67. Shkarupeta, E., Kalmykova, T., Serebryakova, N.: Cenological approach in industrial ecosystem research in transition to Industry 5.0. E3S Web Conf. **371**, 03054 (2023). https://doi.org/10.1051/e3sconf/202337103054
68. Tolstykh, T.O., Shmeleva, N.V., Gamidullaeva, L.A., Krasnobaeva, V.S.: The role of collaboration in the development of industrial enterprises' integration. Models Syst. Netw. Econ. Technol. Nat. Soc. **1**(45), 5–36 (2023)
69. Yang, Z., Chen, H., Du, L., Lin, C., Lu, W.: How does alliance-based government-university-industry foster cleantech innovation in a green innovation ecosystem? J. Clean. Prod. **283**, 124559 (2021). https://doi.org/10.1016/j.jclepro.2020.124559

70. Benitez, G.B., Ayala, N.F., Frank, A.G.: Industry 4.0 innovation ecosystems: an evolutionary perspective on value co-creation. Int. J. Prod. Econ. **228**, 107735 (2020). https://doi.org/10.1016/j.jclepro.2020.124559
71. Ashton, W.: Understanding the organization of industrial ecosystems: a social network approach. J. Ind. Ecol. **12**(1), 34–51 (2008). https://doi.org/10.1111/j.1530-9290.2008.00002.x
72. Kirillova, E.A., Dli, M.I., Kakatunova, T.V., Epifanov, V.A.: Transformation of the triple helix model in the formation of innovative ecosystems in the industry. Discussion **1**(110), 16–30 (2022)
73. Engez, A., Leminen, S.: Urban living lab as a circular economy ecosystem: advancing environmental sustainability through economic value, material, and knowledge flows. Sustainability **13**(5), 2811 (2021). https://doi.org/10.3390/su13052811
74. Titova, N.: Industrial ecosystems and clusters as tools for implementing sustainable development goals. Azimuth Sci. Res.: Econ. Manage. **10**(4), 271–274 (2021)
75. Hewett, K., Hult, G.T.M., Mantrala, M.K., Nim, N., Pedada, K.: Cross-border marketing ecosystem orchestration: a conceptualization of its determinants and boundary conditions. Int. J. Res. Mark. **39**(2), 619–638 (2022). https://doi.org/10.1016/j.ijresmar.2021.09.003
76. Cappellano, F., Makkonen, T.: Cross-border regional innovation ecosystems: the role of non-profit organizations in cross-border cooperation at the US-Mexico border. GeoJournal **85**(6), 1515–1528 (2020). https://doi.org/10.1007/s10708-019-10038-w
77. Kirillova, E.A.: Ecosystemal nature of transformations in modern industrial systems based on open innovations. Sci. J. ITMO Univ. Ser.: Econ. Environ. Manage. **3**, 42–49 (2022)
78. Tashenova, L.V., Babkin, A.V., Zinina, M.G.: Analysis of the state and development of industrial clusters in Russia. Innov. Clust. Digit. Econ.: Driv. **147** (2018)
79. Klimanov, V.V., Budaeva, K.V.: Growth points as an element of strategic planning in Russian regions. Reg. Stud. **3**, 99–106 (2017)
80. Plakhin, A.E., Ogorodnikova, E.S., Blinkov, I.O.: Study of inter-subject interaction effects among participants in the industrial ecosystem. Bull. Altai Acad. Econ. Law **7–2**, 276–281 (2022). https://doi.org/10.17513/vaael.2331
81. Tretyakova, E.A., Freyman, E.N.: Ecosystem approach in modern economic research. Manage. Issues **1**(74), 6–20 (2022). https://doi.org/10.22394/2304-3369-2022-1-6-20
82. Henriques, J., Ferrão, P., Castro, R., Azevedo, J.: Industrial symbiosis: a sectoral analysis on enablers and barriers. Sustainability **13**(4), 1723 (2021). https://doi.org/10.3390/su13041723
83. Babkin, A.V., Shkarupeta, E.V., Polshchikov, T.I.: Concept of effective sustainable ESG development of industrial ecosystems in the circular economy. Econ. Rev. Russ. **1**(75), 124–139 (2023)
84. Titova, N.Y.: Industrial symbiosis in a circular economy. Bull. Astrakhan State Tech. Univ. Ser.: Econ. **4**, 44–50 (2021). https://doi.org/10.24143/2073-5537-2021-4-44-50
85. Maksimtsev, I.A., Rekord, S.I.: Transformation of mineral resource production chains in modern conditions. Bull. St. Petersburg State Univ. Econ. **6**(138), 9–14 (2022)
86. Pizzi, S., Leopizzi, R., Caputo, A.: The enablers in the relationship between entrepreneurial ecosystems and the circular economy: the case of circularity.com. Manage. Environ. Q.: Int. J. **33**(1), 26–43 (2022). https://doi.org/10.1108/MEQ-01-2021-0011
87. Harala, L., Alkki, L., Aarikka-Stenroos, L., Al-Najjar, A., Malmqvist, T.: Industrial ecosystem renewal towards circularity to achieve the benefits of reuse: Learning from circular construction. J. Clean. Prod. **389**, 135885 (2023). https://doi.org/10.1016/j.jclepro.2023.135885
88. Pietrulla, F.: Circular ecosystems: a review. Clean.Circ. Bioecon. **3**, 100031 (2022)

89. Davidenko, L.M., Bespaly, S.V., Bekniyazova, D.S.: Resource paradigm for building a digital format industrial ecosystem. Bull. Belgorod Univ. Cooper. Econ. Law **1**, 58–68 (2020). https://doi.org/10.21295/2223-5639-2020-1-58-68
90. Boyer, J., Kokosy, A.: Technology-push and market-pull strategies: the influence of the innovation ecosystem on companies' involvement in the Industry 4.0 paradigm. J. Risk Finan. 23(5), 461–479 (2022). https://doi.org/10.1108/JRF-12-2021-0193
91. Akatkin, Y.M., Karpov, O.E., Konyavsky, V.A., Yasinovskaya, E.D.: Digital economy: conceptual architecture of the digital industry ecosystem. Bus. Inform. **4**(42), 17–28 (2017)
92. Mylnik, A.V., Golov, G.R.: Conceptual foundations for the development of digital ecosystems in the modern economy in the context of the Fourth Industrial Revolution. Proc. Free Econ. Soc. Russ. **240**(2), 392–406 (2023). https://doi.org/10.38197/2072-2060-2023-240-2-392-406
93. Côté, R.P., Smolenaars, T.: Supporting pillars for industrial ecosystems. J. Clean. Prod. **5**(1–2), 67–74 (1997). https://doi.org/10.1016/S0959-6526(97)00016-4
94. Soldak, M.O.: Industrial ecosystems and digitalization in the context of sustainable development. Econ. Ind. **4**(92), 38–66 (2020). https://doi.org/10.15407/econindustry2020.04.038
95. Nikitaeva, A.Y., Serdyukov, R.D., Fedosova, M.N.: Regional drivers for the development of digital ecosystems in industrial enterprises. Reg. Econ. South Russ. **9**(3), 100–112 (2021). https://doi.org/10.15688/re.volsu.2021.3.9
96. Sjödin, D., Parida, V., Visnjic, I.: How can large manufacturers digitalize their business models? A framework for orchestrating industrial ecosystems. Calif. Manage. Rev. **64**(3), 49–77 (2022). https://doi.org/10.1177/00081256211059140
97. Fadeykina, N.V., Malina, S.S.: Development of theoretical concepts of the categories "ecosystem" and "innovation ecosystem." Siberian Finan. School **2**, 103–111 (2021)
98. Gawer, A., Cusumano, M.A.: Industry platforms and ecosystem innovation. J. Prod. Innov. Manage. **31**(3), 417–433 (2014). https://doi.org/10.1111/jpim.12105
99. Xiaohua, L., Feng, L.I.U.: Industrial ecosystem and the development of strategic emerging industries. China Econ. **8**(6), 48 (2013)
100. Tolstykh, T., Gamidullaeva, L., Shmeleva, N.: Elaboration of a mechanism for sustainable enterprise development in innovation ecosystems. J. Open Innov.: Technol. Mark. Complex. **6**(4), 95 (2020). https://doi.org/10.3390/joitmc6040095
101. Ashton, W.S.: The structure, function, and evolution of a regional industrial ecosystem. J. Ind. Ecol. **13**(2), 228–246 (2009). https://doi.org/10.1111/j.1530-9290.2009.00111.x
102. Vishnyagova, E.A., Solovyova, I.A.: Ecosystem as a mechanism for sustainable industrial development. Bull. South Ural State Univ. Ser.: Econ. Manage. **16**(1), 62–76 (2022)
103. Lowe, E.A., Evans, L.K.: Industrial ecology and industrial ecosystems. J. Clean. Prod. **3**(1–2), 47–53 (1995). https://doi.org/10.1016/0959-6526(95)00045-G
104. Classen, M., Friedli, T.: Value-based marketing and sales of industrial services: a systematic literature review in the age of digital technologies. Proc. CIRP **83**, 1–7 (2019). https://doi.org/10.1016/j.procir.2019.02.141
105. Daneshvar Kakhki, M., Nemati, H.R.: Value-based view of firms enabled by data analytics: aligning suppliers for customer value creation. Enterp. Inf. Syst. **16**(1), 105–140 (2022). https://doi.org/10.1080/17517575.2020.1856419
106. Fan, J., Hu, S., Chen, D., Zhou, Y.: Study on the construction and optimization of a resource-based industrial ecosystem. Resour. Conserv. Recycl. **119**, 97–108 (2017). https://doi.org/10.1016/j.resconrec.2016.05.016
107. Popov, E.V., Simonova, V.L., Zyryanov, A.S.: Evolution of business ecosystems in industry: from the classical type to digital. Digit. Econ. Inform. **5**(3), 341–360 (2024). https://doi.org/10.18334/ide.5.3.121748

108. Nyström, M., Jouffray, J.B., Norström, A.V.: Anatomy and resilience of the global production ecosystem. Nature **575**(7781), 98–108 (2019). https://doi.org/10.1038/s41586-019-1712-3
109. Das, A., Dey, S.: Global manufacturing value networks: assessing the critical roles of platform ecosystems and Industry 4.0. J. Manuf. Technol. Manage. **32**(6), 1290–1311 (2021). https://doi.org/10.1108/JMTM-04-2020-0161
110. Andersen, A.D., Mäkitie, T., Steen, M., Wanzenböck, I.: Integrating industrial transformation and sustainability transitions research through a multi-sectoral perspective. SSRN (2024). https://doi.org/10.2139/ssrn.4766925
111. Mayorova, K.S., Balashova, E.S.: Digital transition of industrial enterprises into a "smart" ecosystem. Russ. J. Ind. Econ. **14**(4), 433–444 (2021)
112. Schot, J.W.: The usefulness of evolutionary models for explaining innovation: the case of the Netherlands in the nineteenth century. History Technol. **14**, 173–200 (1998). https://doi.org/10.1080/07341519808581928
113. Kemp, R., Schot, J., Hoogma, R.: Regime shifts to sustainability through processes of niche formation: the approach of strategic niche management. Technol. Anal. Strat. Manage. **10**, 175–196 (1998). https://doi.org/10.1080/09537329808524310
114. Schot, J., Geels, F.W.: Strategic niche management and sustainable innovation journeys: theory, findings, research agenda, and policy. Dyn. Sustain. Innov. Journeys 17–34 (2013)
115. Berkhout, F., Smith, A., Stirling, A.: Socio-technological regimes and transition contexts. In: System Innovation and the Transition to Sustainability: Theory, Evidence and Policy, pp. 48–75. Edward Elgar Publishing (2004). https://doi.org/10.4337/9781845423421.00013
116. Smith, A., Stirling, A., Berkhout, F.: The governance of sustainable socio-technical transitions. Res. Policy **34**, 1491–1510 (2005). https://doi.org/10.1016/j.respol.2005.07.005
117. Geels, F.W., Schot, J.: Typology of sociotechnical transition pathways. Res. Policy **36**(3), 399–417 (2007). https://doi.org/10.1016/j.respol.2007.01.003
118. Vargo, S.L., Wieland, H., Akaka, M.A.: Innovation through institutionalization: a service ecosystems perspective. Ind. Mark. Manage. **44**, 63–72 (2015). https://doi.org/10.1016/j.indmarman.2014.10.008
119. Adamides, E.D., Mouzakitis, Y.: Industrial ecosystems as technological niches. J. Clean. Prod. **17**(2), 172–180 (2009). https://doi.org/10.1016/j.jclepro.2008.04.003

The Phenomenon of Resilience in the Evolutionary Development of Russian Entrepreneurial Ecosystems

Vilena Yakimova[1(✉)], Svetlana Pankova[1,2], and Sergey Khmura[1]

[1] Amur State University, 21 Ignatievskoe Highway, 650027 Blagoveshchensk, Russia
vilena_yakimova@mail.ru

[2] Orenburg State University, 13 Victory Avenue, 460018 Orenburg, Russia

Abstract. In the regional studies of entrepreneurial activity, the ecosystem approach provides a means to identify factors that affect the behavior of business structures under shocks triggered by various reasons. The present work aims to clarify the nature of resilience, test the hypothesis about its cyclical nature, and assess it in different types of entrepreneurial ecosystems in border regions of Russia. In the study, the authors propose a theoretical four-phase model of the ecosystem resilience cycle. The two main characteristics—amplitudes of a downturn and an upturn—were identified; these characteristics were used to compare the resilience of ecosystems in border regions following the COVID-19 pandemic and increased sanctions in 2022. The study of the constructed cycles revealed that the sanctions caused a greater shock than the pandemic. Industrial ecosystems were found to be more susceptible to shocks than other ecosystems. Over the study period, export-oriented ecosystems exhibited greater revenue variation (26% to 74%), while for import-dependent ecosystems, revenue ranged from 13% to 63%. Foreign-invested ecosystems experienced severe shocks, with their revenue ranging from 15% to 98%. Despite this, the studied ecosystems show high resilience due to government support, reorientation to the markets of friendly countries, diversification of production, and increased intrasystem communication.

Keywords: Resilience · Entrepreneurial ecosystem · Sustainability · Economic cycles

JEL Classification: P51 · R11

1 Introduction

Since the third decade of the 21st century, the economy has experienced a cascading alternation of downturns and upturns. As a result, various types of shocks have intensified: geopolitical, financial, demographic, technological, etc. The problem is that they reduce the robustness of businesses and ecosystems. At the same time, some ecosystems recover quickly and seamlessly from crises, while others experience recovery problems,

E. Kuzmin et al. (Eds.): EASET 2024, SPBE, pp. 30–44, 2025.
https://doi.org/10.1007/978-3-031-91159-0_3

severe recessions, and rising. Strategies for increasing profitability and lean production are no longer effective and lead to unbalanced ecosystems. The inadequacy of classical theories in explaining ecosystem survival led to the development of a theory of ecosystem resilience. Despite studies of shock states of economies, most theoretical approaches view the country's economy as a whole, while mesocosystems are insufficiently studied. Therefore, the study of regional ecosystems' ability to recover from shocks and return to equilibrium becomes relevant. From a resilience perspective, it is important to study the effects of two types of shocks: those caused by COVID-19 and sanctions, and assess the impact of anti-crisis and anti-sanctions policies.

The purpose of the work is to clarify the essence of resilience, test the hypothesis of its cyclical nature and measure it in different types of entrepreneurial ecosystems in the border regions of Russia. Business units in Russia, with a structure and characteristics inherent in ecosystems, manifest their qualities differently from other countries. This determines the choice of our research object - regional entrepreneurship ecosystems operating in the Russian Federation.

The subject of study are ecosystems of border areas, as they can show the impact of COVID-19 and sanctions shocks accompanied by restrictions on cross-border cooperation with neighboring countries. The objectives of the study include identifying the essence of resistance and measuring cyclic development in various types of ecosystems in border regions.; To assess the impact of resilience on the development of ecosystems with foreign investment and export-oriented or import-dependent systems is a challenging task.

2 Literature Review

The ecosystem approach is a recognized area of research for entrepreneurial structures in various locations (regional, national, international). Prospects for the development of this approach in relation to European ecosystems are revealed by a study by Swedish and Dutch scientists [1]. According to Pittz [2], the success of an ecosystem depends on heterogeneous values, history, economy, and culture of a particular location. The author makes this conclusion based on the example of six North American ecosystems and their structural components. It is not appropriate for developing countries to fully adopt the experience of developed countries' entrepreneurial ecosystems due to differences in resources, institutions, and incomplete structures, as confirmed by scientists from the UK and China.

In the theory of economic cycles, shocks are defined as "independent impulses of wave dynamics that trigger forward and backward communication processes," which results in the ecosystem entering a cyclical state [3]. When shocks occur, entrepreneurial activity declines and economic growth slows down. While previously studied economic cycles were long-term in nature, the modern cycles are characterized by multi-effects resulting from a combination of one-time and slow shocks of different natures [4]. The resistance to the post-pandemic shock has been studied in business structures in various regions, including China [5], Europe [6] and North America [7]. In the period of recovery from post-pandemic shocks, the Russian economy was affected by sanctions. The contradictory nature of the current situation also manifests itself in the need for digital transformation under the technological embargo [8]. The nature of such shocks and tools for restoring entrepreneurial ecosystems under the new conditions are relevant and understudied issues. It also remains to be resolved why some ecosystems are more resilient to crises and shocks, while others experience long periods of severe downturns and upturns.

Since conventional theories cannot explain modern cycles and their nature, the theory of ecosystem resilience has been developed, which is based on evolutionary economics and complexity theory. Resilience as a property of ecosystems was considered by several authors [3, 9]. An industrial ecosystem is a geographically distributed network of industrial clusters or their symbioses intended to improve resource efficiency and mitigate negative environmental impacts [10]. As a result of the mutually beneficial allocation of resources and the partnership of actors, a new value is created.

From the perspective of complexity theory, the ecosystem develops nonlinear network connections between agents and their groups, whose behavior is difficult to predict under shocks. The heterogeneous nature of entrepreneurial ecosystems is the cause of their constant evolution and transformation, as well as self-development and generation of new ideas and products. The external environment of ecosystems yields new economic strategies and drives businesses to dynamic changes and new forms of interaction [11]. Thus, one of the incentives for ecosystem evolution is digitalization, which makes it possible to overcome shortages of some resources in a region [12]. Despite the fact that theoretical approaches to the evolution of entrepreneurial ecosystems are based on the assumption that entrepreneurs have equal access to resources, participation and support [13], business development is unequal. In the context of evolution, conventional systems transform connections: from linear in the third technological paradigm to network and intersectoral (digital, nano-, and biotechnologies) in the modern economy [8].

In the ecosystem theory, the evolutionary approach was developed from the perspective of co-evolution [14], change in stages (from creation to decay), and qualitative changes at each stage [15]. However, these processes were observed only under a stable external environment. Studies on economic cycles evaluated the effects of shocks depending on their origin and magnitude at the macro- and mesoeconomic level, the degree of distortion, and the period required to recover equilibrium. The synchronization of macroeconomic instability, shifts in technological paradigms, and other shocks with increasing robustness of the ecosystem was not considered. In this connection, the theory of ecosystem resilience requires an in-depth study.

The concept of "resilience" was used in 2010–2015 in the strategic and policy documents of the UN, OECD [16], and other international organizations as a new approach to ensuring economic security. We believe that resilience can be viewed from the perspective of four approaches.

First, resilience is a property of an ecosystem that characterizes self-organization, efficient use of resources, control over their use, and the transformation of mechanisms for flexible response to shocks. Resilience is "the ability of systems to plan preparation, counter-, and absorption measures against a wide range of diverse shocks, as well as measures intended for rapid recovery from shocks and flexible adaptation" [17]. An ecosystem is resilient if it has the integrity to withstand disturbances.

Second, resilience is viewed from the perspective of genoeconomics and maximizing opportunities to avoid a crisis. An ecosystem initially possesses intrinsic adaptive properties, inherent structural features, and a given evolutionary trajectory. The genetic code of a territory is "hereditary memory" determined by the region's predisposition to processes caused by internal and external factors [18]. Resilience is enhanced by the uniqueness of resources, regional policy, capital, and reputation, as well as organizational and functional complexity. Intrinsic adaptive properties, high diversification, and large businesses that are less sensitive to shocks are important [19]). A rapid post-shock growth is possible with high innovation potential and high-tech production. Ecosystems oriented toward the cybernetic approach and the use of digital technologies exhibit high resilience [20, 21]. However, authors often fail to explain the differences between the categories of "robustness" and "resilience," while the return to a state of equilibrium is considered possible through self-development, activation of accumulated reserves, and even emotional support from founders [22], with no emphasis on the role of the state.

Third, from the perspective of the theory of cycles, resilience is a dynamic feature representing a transition state following a shock to the phase of resistance and recovery [9]. This approach allows the categories "robustness" (developed prior to a shock) and "resilience" (post-shock state) to be distinguished. Resilient systems can return to their previous state and identify new growth trajectories [23]. Contrary to the previous approach, it is assumed that an ecosystem cannot independently transition to recovery and growth without institutional changes. Growth requires resources, intellectual potential, as well as scientific and technological potential [23].

Resilience should be understood as the ability of the system to cope with variability and extreme events, overcome shocks, adapt to new conditions, and return to the initial state [24]. Zhironkin et al. [19] propose a certain criterion of resilience: a system can withstand shocks if the recovery phase after the shock is less than two years. Shishkina [25] adheres to the process approach and characterizes resilience as a set of actions "to withstand, anticipate, prevent, resist, and absorb shocks, as well as to react and adapt to them and recover under external influences." Thus, the theory of economic cycles provides a promising procedural basis for assessing resilience—the speed of recovery and the degree of resistance.

Fourth, resilience is the ability to withstand systemic risks, in which a local shock that disrupts only one link leads to dysfunction and generates a ripple effect of cascading disruptions in the ecosystem as a whole. Roundy et al. [26] define resilience as the result of the interaction between the diversity of structural components in an ecosystem and their cohesion around shared values and activities. When considering ecosystems that are transnational corporations, resilience manifests itself at five levels: individual, organizational, ecosystem, institutional, and global [27]. Disruptions have structural consequences and disrupt inter-agent network communication between elements. In this sense, resilience is compensation for systemic risks. Sanctions imposed on a single business system can cause disruptions in global value chains. Unpredictable changes affect commodity, financial, and resource markets on which the ecosystem is dependent. There may be disruptions of export and investment projects, import shortages, as well as price and interest rate hikes. A resilient ecosystem transforms dynamically, adapting to new markets, changing the roles of agents in the ecosystem, and developing new business models.

3 Methods and Data

Researchers most often use trend estimation and dynamics analysis to identify the state of resilience. The procedural framework includes pre-shock assessment, behavior prediction, as well as integration of historical assessment and prospective evaluation [17]. From a dynamic perspective, socio-economic indicators are estimated at each cycle stage [3]. An analysis revealed that the study of dynamics and construction of time series are the main methods, as they provide a means to measure the speed and extent of shock propagation. Resilience is assessed as the economy's speed (growth rate) of return to equilibrium. Factor analysis and identification of correlations are used to study the effects of resilience.

Researchers consider the following indicators: employment and unemployment; production and consumption patterns; inflation; production volumes; investment and credit availability; industrial composition and its diversification; GDP; openness of the economy; and innovation activity [17, 28]. In order to analyze entrepreneurial ecosystems, it is necessary to use the total amount of revenue received from the main activities of all actors in the ecosystem as a basic indicator.

The study is based on analyzing the phases of cyclical behavior. A cycle refers to "a set of interrelated phenomena and processes that form a complete circle of development" and "progressive development of a socio-economic system" [28]. Cyclicity manifests itself in the tendency of business activity to oscillate around the trend, while external environment factors determine phase oscillations. Cycles can be of the accelerated and decelerated type.

The cycle consists of recurring phases. The growth phase is characterized by increased entrepreneurial and social sentiment and the accumulation of human capital, which prompts the population to start new businesses, thus expanding the entrepreneurial ecosystem. The shock state is characterized by a decline in indicators to the critical minimum (min). Upon reaching the critical minimum, the ecosystem begins to return to the normal state (Fig. 1).

Recovery periods imply a state of resistance to shocks (*k1*), in which the system uses proactive measures, builds up reserves, and becomes flexible. The institutional and external environment of the ecosystem fosters growth-oriented change. The ecosystem begins to resist disruptions and shocks, eliminate functional disturbances, and delay structural changes. Here, resistances include increased competition in the market, decreased quality of education, and increased cost of resources. In the recovery phase (*k2*), reserves are activated, and additional measures are implemented to restore flexibility. The third phase (*k3*) can be described as the phase of renewal driven by innovation, digital transformation, and structural changes. In the fourth phase (*k4*), the ecosystem accelerates the production volume growth, which indicates the complete adaptation of the ecosystem to the new conditions and structural transformations. The ecosystem is considered ready to be restructured and has a defined growth trajectory.

Regression analysis and the construction of polynomial equations allow us to study cyclical fluctuations, evaluate past events, identify cycles and integrate historical changes

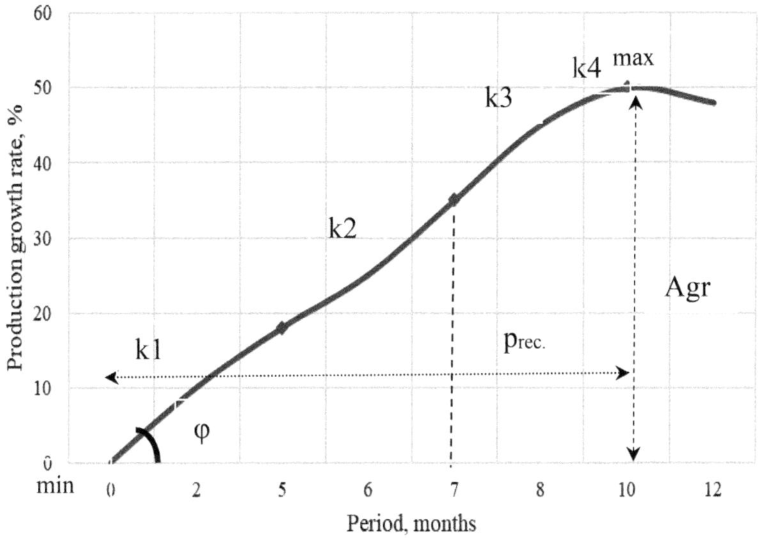

Note: *k1* – initial phase; *k2* – growth phase; *k3* – phase of accelerated growth; *k4* – maximum growth phase; *Agr* – amplitude of growth; φ – angle at the start of oscillations (oscillation phase), $p_{rec.}$ – period of recovery (resilience); *min* – minimum downturn, *max* – maximum upturn.

Fig. 1. Theoretical model of ecosystem resilience.

with future estimates. This method helps us measure the speed and extent of shock propagation, depth of recessions and rises, as well as estimate the rate of economic recovery or the return of the economy to equilibrium. Polynomial graphs enable us to compare cyclical patterns between ecosystems, identify resilient ones and describe their features.

The theory of oscillations uses the following parameters for characterization: amplitude (*A*), period, cyclic frequency, phase, and initial phase. Cyclicity is assessed according to growth rate and variability (coefficient of variation, *v*). Amplitude is characterized by the greatest deviation from the state of equilibrium (maximum or minimum value) of an oscillating quantity. Amplitude differences help to determine which shocks had a greater impact on ecosystems:

$$\Delta Ad = Ad1 - Ad2 \tag{1}$$

where *Ad1* – amplitude of the downturn during the first shock period (e.g., coronavirus), *Ad2* – amplitude of the downturn during the second shock period (e.g., sanctions);

$$\Delta Agr = Agr1 - Agr2 \tag{2}$$

where *Agr1* – amplitude of growth during the first shock period (e.g., coronavirus), *Agr2* – amplitude of growth during the second shock period (e.g., sanctions).

As the empirical base, the study uses entrepreneurial ecosystems located in border regions. Such ecosystems are most susceptible to change since both the COVID-19 period and the sanctions regime were accompanied by restrictions on cross-border cooperation with neighboring states. Therefore, the selected ecosystems can be used for the analysis of resilience. These ecosystems include priority development areas (PDAs), clusters, special economic zones (SEZs), industrial parks, and corporate networks, which exhibit cooperation, competition, and joint activities. The initial sample consisted of 763 communities that conform structurally to the ecosystem approach (clustering principles, network structures, support institutions, availability of a socio-cultural component and access to markets). At the same time, we identified both artificially created ecosystems and naturally occurring ones. Natural ecosystems form based on corporations and form value chains, developing according to the principle of self-organization. Artificial ecosystems are structures with state support, such as industrial parks and clusters.

To identify the key features among them, we reduced the sample by excluding units with a period of operation less than 3 years and a small number of enterprises. Next, we tracked signs of joint activities and the execution of a joint product. As a criterion, we chose the property of co-competition, which allowed us to reduce the sample to 194 ecosystems. We assessed the presence of similar activities, partnerships, and cooperation among the selected units. At the next stage, we selected ecosystems whose actors have foreign investments - 18%, including those with participation from a border country - 4%. Ecosystems with foreign investment from unfriendly countries are of particular interest, as the risk of collapse increases. We have identified such ecosystems in the Kaliningrad, Leningrad, Samara, Chelyabinsk regions and the Primorsky Krai. These ecosystems depend on imports and are export-oriented. To identify these factors with foreign trade transactions, we used ImportGenius as a source of statistical data. Ecosystems that are dependent on exports are located in Kursk, Kaliningrad and Pskov, and in Karelia. As examples for assessing resistance, we selected those with the largest number of factors and highest income.

The selected ecosystems are divided into the following types: foreign-invested ecosystems and ecosystems conducting export and import operations with unfriendly countries. The study hypothesis assumes that under systemic risks, ecosystems of different types exhibit similar features of resilience.

4 Results

The difference between the 2020 and 2022 crisis manifestations lies in the fact that the COVID-19 restrictions were imposed globally, and sanctions were primarily targeted at Russia. The 2020 crisis led to a drop in demand, supply disruptions, production disruptions, and high financial risks. The reduced demand resulted in a cascading decline in productivity in the industry, specifically the energy industry and mining operations. Economic growth slowed down and GDP declined. The service sector shrank, while the demand for digital technologies for online sales and remote interaction increased. In a closed economy, the way out of the crisis was to increase local production and reduce dependence on exports and imports. The number of low-margin businesses increased, which resulted in the need for subsidies and institutional support. During shocks, a significant role of state institutions in regulating ecosystem performance was noted.

The anti-COVID and anti-sanctions measures differed significantly. In 2020, the Central Bank of Russia maintained a low key rate. The monetary policy was aimed at increasing the purchasing power of the population and stimulate entrepreneurial activity. For ecosystems, this means facilitated access to resources and markets. The anti-COVID (recovery) measures included regulatory easings: a moratorium on business audits by regulatory agencies; extended timeframe for submitting reports, and an expedited procedure for registering small and medium-sized business entities in the register. Financial support measures were implemented: incentive payments and concessional lending for companies that retain their staff.

Conversely, in 2022 the key rate was high enough to ensure control over inflation expectations and prevent hyperinflation. Difficulties arose with the repatriation of foreign currency earnings from exports, as well as a foreign trade turnover imbalance due to the restricted access of Russian companies to certain goods and technologies. In order to ensure resilience, the focus of anti-sanctions measures was shifted to financial support: import substitution programs, including the lease of state-owned land plots without tendering for such projects; subsidies; concessional lending for highly localized projects.

For an empirical analysis, we constructed the cycles of the largest entrepreneurial ecosystems, estimating the revenue growth rate of all actors in the ecosystem (Y axis). Figure 2 shows the dynamics of this indicator over the period 2019 to 2023.

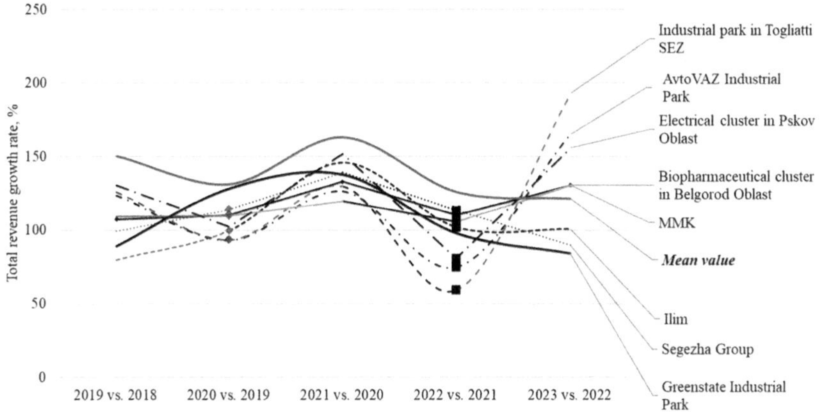

Note: The mean value is calculated for all ecosystems included in the sample (22 systems).

Fig. 2. Cycles on the example of individual large ecosystems.

On the example of the AvtoVAZ ecosystem, we obtained polynomial trends:

$$Y = 15.65X_4 - 181.3X_3 + 728.41X_2 + 742.29 \tag{3}$$

Assuming the mean value, the polynomial model is as follows:

$$Y = 9.19X_4 - 111.78X_3 + 466.33X_2 + 559.82 \tag{4}$$

Quartic polynomials mean that there are four extrema: two growth phases and two decline phases. The coefficients for the factor in the model for AvtoVAZ mean greater fluctuations as compared to the mean values. Smaller cycle fluctuations indicate a mitigation of the COVID-19 and sanctions restrictions. High fluctuations show a more rapid and dynamic recovery period. Of note is that steep upturns mean that the ecosystem has to use more resources to recover. The cycles suggest that sanctions were a more profound shock for border ecosystems than the COVID-19 period. A deeper downturn and recovery are noted. The most vulnerable ecosystem in the COVID-19 period was the AvtoVAZ ecosystem. Conversely, the Greenstate Industrial Park oriented toward digital technologies showed an upward trend in this period.

The cycle of the biopharmaceutical cluster in Belgorod Oblast differs from the mean. No downturn was observed in 2020, which indicates resilience to COVID-19 restrictions. This fact can be attributed to the specifics of the cluster and the medical orientation of its main actors. The 2022 decline was caused by the imposition of sanctions, specifically the restriction of access to certain drugs, as well as difficulties in financial transactions with unfriendly countries. The 2023 growth can be attributed to the policy of import substitution and localization of pharmaceutical production in the face of sanctions risks. This suggests that in 2022 this cluster was in its initial phase (*k1*), while growth phases *k2* and *k3* were observed in 2023.

For border ecosystems, the main shock consisted in the restrictions on international and cross-border cooperation. The increased global tensions transformed global chains and international institutions. The post-sanctions period is characterized by innovation policy strengthening and selective support of certain industries.

Table 1 summarizes the main indicators for analyzing ecosystems in which an actor receiving foreign investment is present. The indicators of variability are calculated, and amplitudes are compared.

The ecosystems include both homogeneous and heterogeneous systems. The heterogeneous systems are those that have been recently established, are in the process of gaining residents and defining development strategies, as well as exhibiting sectoral diversification. Homogeneous systems constitute either a group of companies or have a strong sectoral focus (woodwork, automobile production, etc.). A high coefficient of variability is noted for Zabaikalye PDA, Verkhny Ufaley PDA, Moglino Park, and Atlantis Holding. This coefficient shows general dynamics of intermittent growth, indicating a low susceptibility to shocks. In general, it can be noted that this type of ecosystem practically did not experience a decline in the COVID-19 period, while in 2022, most ecosystems experienced a decline in sales revenue as a result of sanctions and withdrawal of foreign capital from the financial system of actors in ecosystems. The biggest downturn under sanctions is observed in Togliatti SEZ and AvtoVAZ since these ecosystems are also sensitive to export and import supplies.

The main specialization of Greenstate Industrial Park is production and logistics. The development of this park is significantly impacted by sanctions risks, which can be seen in the negative trend in 2022–2023. This can be attributed to the large number of residents from unfriendly countries and the withdrawal of foreign companies from the Russian market. The decline can be explained by a reduction in logistical capabilities in the western part of Russia due to the reduced trade turnover with unfriendly countries located near the park.

Noteworthy is the policy of the Ilim Group in terms of resilience and mitigating the impact of external factors. The Ilim Group included the International Paper Company, an American company that sold all its ownership interests in Ilim to the ultimate Russian

Table 1. Resilience assessment of foreign-invested entrepreneurial ecosystems.

Ecosystem type	Coefficient of revenue variation for 2018–2023	2019 vs. 2018	Ad (2020 vs. 2019)*	2021 vs. 2020	Ad (2022 vs. 2021)*	2023 vs. 2022	2022 vs. 2020	ΔAd	ΔAgr
Kostomuksha PDA	0.66	119	151	205	158	84	325	−7	121
Atlantis Holding	0.78	by 3 times	by 4 times	190	104	140	198	248	50
Zalesye agricultural holding	0.46	88	151	129	135	124	175	16	5.1
Levoberezhny Industrial Park	0.15	125	70	99	121	82	119	−50	17
Greenstate Industrial Park	0.22	89	128	138	98	84	134	31	54
Ilim	0.18	80	100	146	102	101	149	−2.4	45
Moglino Industrial Park	0.77	18	97	175	178	145	by 3 times	−81	30
AvtoVAZ Industrial Park	0.23	124	93	126	75	165	94	18	−39
Industrial park in Togliatti SEZ	0.25	126	93	130	59	193	77	34	-63
Verkhny Ufaley PDA	0.86	by 7 times	150	by 4 times	95	141	by 4 times	55	227
MMK	0.26	110	110	119	105	131	126	4.4	−11
Zarinsk PDA	0.57	107	152	255	95	79	241	57	176
Transbaikal PDA	0.98	157	172	114	by 4 times	143	464	−235	−29

Note: * Periods of systemic shocks

beneficiaries. The company actively trades on the international financial market using yuan loans, thus mitigating currency risks related to the dollar and euro and reducing the interest rate for borrowing.

Thus, the group of ecosystems receiving investment from unfriendly countries is in shock, which corresponds to phase *k1*. Most ecosystems are the least robust to adverse external factors while showing good dynamics of adaptation to the current conditions. For stabilization and transition to the growth phase, it is possible to reprioritize to deal with companies from friendly countries, while sales can be redirected to domestic markets.

It is recommended to use import substitution tools, as well as to buy existing production facilities in foreign jurisdictions (Table 2).

Table 2. Results of assessing the resilience of export-oriented entrepreneurial ecosystems.

Ecosystem type	Coefficient of revenue variation for 2018–2023	2019 vs. 2018	Ad 2020 vs. 2019*	2021 vs. 2020	Ad 2022 vs. 2021*	2023 vs. 2022	2022 vs. 2020	ΔAd	ΔAgr
Segezha Group	0.26	99	114	139	113	90	158	0.3	49.2
Kondopoga PDA	0.53	106	134	101	193	120	195	−59	−18.7
Cluster of wood processing industry in Leningrad Oblast	0.74	117	87	by 3 times	84	83	by 3 times	3.4	256
Industrial electrical cluster of Pskov Oblast	0.34	131	102	152	80	156	122	22	−4.4

Note: * Periods of systemic shocks

The common behavioral patterns of export-oriented systems are weakly identified, with revenue growth frequently observed during crises. Industrial ecosystems showed the ability to recombine resources in a crisis, changing export and import policies. The government incentive policy included a series of measures designed to develop industries with a high value-added ratio. Most ecosystems adapted themselves, mitigating the impact of the pandemic and sanctions. The growth phase is characterized by industrial development, technological changes, and business profitability.

Segezha Group is one of the most marginal ecosystems due to the previous close contacts with unfriendly countries. Adapting to the new conditions, the company redirected exports to China. Also, Segezha increases the complexity of the system by embracing digital transformation. In the cluster of Leningrad Oblast, a significant decrease in the financial performance of a resident from one industry is compensated by a smaller decline or increase in the performance of an actor from another industry.

Table 3 presents a resilience assessment of import-dependent ecosystems.

Cluster ecosystems are the most import-dependent. During downturns, the policy of financial support and import substitution were effective. As can be seen from the resilience analysis data, most ecosystems experienced no problems with economic recovery, with sales growth during periods of general macroeconomic downturns. Given production chains, the emergent nature of the system increases, and cooperative ties improve,

Table 3. Results of assessing the resilience of import-dependent entrepreneurial ecosystems.

Ecosystem type	Coefficient of revenue variation for 2018–2023	2019 vs. 2018	Ad 2020 vs. 2019*	2021 vs. 2020	Ad 2022 vs. 2021*	2023 vs. 2022	2022 vs. 2020	ΔAd	ΔAgr
Regional innovation cluster in Volgograd Oblast	0.36	112	142	122	115	115	141	26	7.0
Biopharmaceutical cluster in Belgorod Oblast	0.33	107	110	133	110	131	146	0	2.2
Borovsky Industrial Park	0.42	123	173	131	109	104	143	64	28
Cluster of electronic devices, materials, and components in Belgorod Oblast	0.13	101	91	135	95	77	128	−3.2	58
South Urals instrument-making cluster	0.67	116	114	139	139	186	193	−24	−47

Note: * Periods of systemic shocks

which indicates the increased maturity of the ecosystem. The actors work together to solve problems and find ways to minimize the impact of adverse external factors.

Common manifestations of shock states for entrepreneurial ecosystems are as follows:

- all actors in the ecosystem are affected at the beginning and end of the crisis;
- unstable geopolitical situation and dependence on the situation in world markets;
- effective government support measures and ecosystem mechanisms to restore internal ties, recombine resources, switch markets, and search for new partners.

5 Conclusion

The conducted study proved that resilience is a property of entrepreneurial ecosystems, which differs from robustness in the dynamic and cyclic nature of its manifestation. Ecosystem robustness is preventive in nature, protecting systems from internal and external influences. Resilience helps to accept risks caused by various factors and return the system to the state of economic equilibrium, restoring its efficient and effective performance. In addition to internal resources developed by the ecosystem, a significant role in maintaining resilience can be played by institutional factors and government support.

The amplitudes of the decline and growth stages inherent in the revenue indicators under systemic shocks can vary significantly depending on the homogeneity of the entrepreneurial ecosystem, its specialization, geographic location, orientation to innovative activities, export orientation, dependence on imports, and other reasons. A behavior analysis of different ecosystems during the resilience cycle revealed their ability to quickly adapt to shocks associated both with the pandemic and sanctions. Some ecosystems were not adversely affected by the COVID-19 restrictions and showed robustness to the impact of sanctions.

The study suggests that a number of strategies should be outlined to ensure the resilience of regional entrepreneurial ecosystems:

- diversification in cases where adverse impacts may affect the most sensitive actors, but the overall losses for the system are minimal, and the impact of the shock is insignificant;
- configuration of networks and chains, change of supply sources, flexibility and recombination of resources;
- structural shifts and changes aimed at increasing the provision of services since the service sector is less procyclical;
- proactive planning to overcome the ripple effect;
- leader's strategy in which the focal firm of the ecosystem takes on the function of resource mobilization, developing tools to restore the ecosystem;
- buildup of buffer assets available to each actor in the ecosystem, as well as improvement in the interactive and network communication between actors;
- increasing ecosystem complexity and transition to innovation-based development;
- digitalization using analytical algorithms and big data to reduce disruption risks and sensitivity to external challenges.

Acknowledgements. This article was prepared by the research through the grant of the Russian Science Foundation № 23–28-00044 on the topic «Conceptual model of a regional entrepreneurial ecosystem in a digital environment», https://rscf.ru/project/23-28-00044/.

References

1. Alvedalen, J., Boschma, R.: A critical review of entrepreneurial ecosystems research: towards a future research agenda. Eur. Plan. Stud. **25**(6), 887–903 (2017). https://doi.org/10.1080/09654313.2017.1299694
2. Pittz, T.G.: Ballasts of the entrepreneurial ecosystem. Technovation **138**, 103113 (2024). https://doi.org/10.1016/j.technovation.2024.103113
3. Smorodinskaya, N.V., Katukov, D.D.: Resilience of economic systems in the era of globalization and sudden shocks. Bull. Inst. Econ. Russ. Acad. Sci. [Vestnik Instituta ekonomiki Rossiiskoi akademii nauk] **5**, 93–115 (2021). https://doi.org/10.52180/2073-6487_2021_5_93_115
4. Akberdina, V.V.: System resilience of industry to the sanctions pressure in industrial regions: assessment and outlook. J. New Econ. **23**(4), 26–45 (2022). https://doi.org/10.29141/2658-5081-2022-23-4-2

5. Yang, H., Tang, M., Chao, X., Li, P.: Organizational resilience in the COVID-19: a case study from China. J. Manage. Organ. **27**(6), 1112–1130 (2021). https://doi.org/10.1017/jmo.2021.59
6. Acciarini, C., Boccardelli, P., Vitale, M.: Resilient companies in the time of Covid-19 pandemic: a case study approach. J. Entrepr. Public Policy **10**(3), 336–351 (2021). https://doi.org/10.1108/JEPP-03-2021-0021
7. Zarowsky, Z., Rashid, T.: Resilience and wellbeing strategies for pandemic fatigue in times of COVID-19. Int. J. Appl. Pos. Psychol. **8**, 1–36 (2023). https://doi.org/10.1007/s41042-022-00078-y
8. Konobeeva, A.B., Esakov, V.A., Markova, O.V.: Technological structure in the life cycle of the economy. Bull. Moscow Finan. Legal Univ. MFUA [Vestnik Moskovskogo finansovo-yuridicheskogo universiteta MFYuA] **1**, 7–21 (2022). https://doi.org/10.52210/2224669X_2022_1_7
9. Romanova, O.A., Sirotin, D.V., Ponomareva, A.O.: From the economy of resistance to a resilient economy (using the example of an industrial region). AlterEconomics **19**(4), 620–637 (2022). https://doi.org/10.31063/AlterEconomics/2022.19-4.4
10. Gamidullaeva, L.A.: Regional industrial cluster as a localized ecosystem: The role of self-organization and collaboration factors. π-Economy **16**(1), 62–82 (2023). https://doi.org/10.18721/JE.16105
11. Kleiner, G.B.: Ecosystem economics: a step into the future. Econ. Rev. Russ. [Ekonomicheskoe vozrozhdenie Rossii] **1**(59), 40–45 (2019)
12. Marquardt, L., Harima, A.: Digital boundary spanning in the evolution of entrepreneurial ecosystems: a dynamic capabilities perspective. J. Bus. Res. **182**, 114762 (2024). https://doi.org/10.1016/j.jbusres.2024.114762
13. Brush, C., Edelman, L.F., Manolova, T., Welter, F.: A gendered look at entrepreneurship ecosystems. Small Bus. Econ. **53**, 393–408 (2019). https://doi.org/10.1007/s11187-018-9992-9
14. Spigel, B., Harrison, R.: Toward a process theory of entrepreneurial ecosystems. Strateg. Entrep. J. **12**(1), 151–168 (2018). https://doi.org/10.1002/sej.1268
15. Dedehayir, O., Makinen, S.J., Ortt, R.: Roles during innovation ecosystem genesis: a literature review. Technol. Forecast. Soc. Chang. **136**, 18–29 (2018). https://doi.org/10.1016/j.techfore.2016.11.028
16. OECD, SIDA: Resilience Systems Analysis: Learning and Recommendations Report. OECD Publishing, Paris (2017)
17. Myslyakova, Yu.G.: Economic resilience of industrial regions: Innovative aspect. Econ. Manage. [Ekonomika i upravlenie] **28**(12), 1242–1251 (2022). https://doi.org/10.35854/1998-1627-2022-12-1242-1251
18. Animitsa, E.G., Novikova, N.V.: Trends in economic dynamics of Russia's classic old industrial region: the case of the Sverdlovsk oblast. J. New Econ. **23**(2), 64–79 (2022). https://doi.org/10.29141/2658-5081-2022-23-2-4
19. Zhironkin, S.A., Taran, E.A., Aleshina, O.G.: The economy's resilience to shocks at the macro- and meso-levels: typology and conditions. Tomsk State Univ. J. Econ. 61, 225–249 (2023). https://doi.org/10.17223/19988648/61/15
20. Allal-Chérif, O., Guaita-Martínez, J.M., Sansaloni, E.M.: Sustainable esports entrepreneurs in emerging countries: audacity, resourcefulness, innovation, transmission, and resilience in adversity. J. Bus. Res. **171**, 114382 (2024). https://doi.org/10.1016/j.jbusres.2023.114382
21. Oliveira, W.P., Guimarães, M.R.N., Silva, J.E.A.R.: Ecosystems, strategy, and resilience: four empirical cases in the COVID-19 crisis. J. Eng. Tech. Manage. **67**, 101734 (2023). https://doi.org/10.1016/j.jengtecman.2023.101734

22. Li, X., Zhang, M., Liu, W., Wang, Z.: The impact of entrepreneurial co-founders' support on founders' entrepreneurial resilience in the high-tech industry: The roles of perceived digital technology and perceived failure-tolerant climate. Technol. Forecast. Soc. Change **202**, 123320 (2024). https://doi.org/10.1016/j.techfore.2024.123320
23. Malkina, M.Yu.: Resilience of Russian regional economies to the 2020 pandemic. Spat. Econ. [Prostranstvennaya ekonomika], **18**(1), 101–124 (2022). https://doi.org/10.14530/se.2022.1.101-124
24. Nikulkina, I.V., Zolotov, E.Yu.: The influence of income tax preferences on the resilience of economic systems in the Arctic regions. Creat. Econ. [Kreativnaya ekonomika] **7**, 3023–3040 (2021). https://doi.org/10.18334/ce.15.7.112361
25. Shishkina, E.A.: Formation of a sustainable infrastructure of the region: Approaches to defining and assessing the ecosystem: the role of factors of self-organization and collaboration. π-Economy **16**(1), 62–82 (2023). https://doi.org/10.18721/JE.16105
26. Roundy, P.T., Brockman, B.K., Bradshaw, M.: The resilience of entrepreneurial ecosystems. J. Bus. Ventur. Insights **8**, 99–104 (2017). https://doi.org/10.1016/j.jbvi.2017.08.002
27. Napier, E., Liu, S.Y.H., Liu, J.: Adaptive strength: Unveiling a multi-level dynamic process model for organizational resilience. J. Bus. Res. **171**, 114334 (2024). https://doi.org/10.1016/j.jbusres.2023.114334
28. Khomenko, E.B.: Economic cycles: the content of basic concepts and the impact on the industrial development of the economies of regions and industries of Russia. Bull. Udmurt Univ. Ser. Econ. Law [Vestnik Udmurtskogo universiteta. Seriya Ekonomika i pravo] **1**, 97–103 (2023). https://doi.org/10.35634/2412-9593-2023-33-1-97-103

The Role of Digital Technologies in the Business Model Innovations: The Regional Case

Ekaterina E. Aydarkina, Tatiana S. Laskova, Anastasia Y. Nikitaeva, and Daria S. Laskova(✉)

Department of Information Economics, Southern Federal University, 105/42 Bolshaya Sadovaya Street, 344006 Rostov-on-Don, Russia
{eeaydarkina,tslaskova,aunikitaeva,laskova}@sfedu.ru

Abstract. The research aims to analyze the potential of digital solutions in business model innovations and an assessment of the empirical experience of digitalization of organizations in the Rostov region of Russia. This region was chosen due to a relatively high level of socio-economic development and digital transformation, as well as a fairly typical regional profile for the specified country. The study was conducted on the basis of theoretical analysis and a questionnaire survey of company executives. The research has shown that digital solutions have a significant role in business model innovation. With regard to enterprises and organizations in the Rostov region of Russia, the study showed that most managers understand the need to change business models due to digital transformation, but cutting-edge technologies are only minimally utilized, and a small number of participants in the survey plan to completely change the business models of their organizations. This made it possible to determine the importance of greater dissemination of the digital economy technologies themselves and attention to ecosystem innovations of business models for integrating resources and neutralizing possible risks.

Keywords: Business model innovation · Digital transformation · Industry 4.0 · Innovation factors · Risks

JEL classification: O12 · O 14 · M15

1 Introduction

Stable functioning, successful development, and often the survival of business entities in any sphere of economic activity are closely linked to their ability to innovate business models. This stems from multiple contributing factors. First of all, innovations in the modern economy are at the heart of competitiveness, and business model innovations, on the one hand, allow for a higher level of return compared to product or process innovations [1, 2]. On the other hand, they themselves act as some kind of renewable competitive advantage [3]. The business model in its modern interpretation is largely associated with the spread of Internet technologies at the end of the last century and the

E. Kuzmin et al. (Eds.): EASET 2024, SPBE, pp. 45–66, 2025.
https://doi.org/10.1007/978-3-031-91159-0_4

emergence of innovative revenue generation mechanisms [3, 4] and can be considered a strategic asset to ensure the competitive advantages and efficiency of the organization in new realities [2, 5].

Along with this, the current economic situation in the global context is characterized by a noticeable reduction in the life expectancy of enterprises and organizations, rapid technological progress, the emergence of new risks and opportunities associated with Industry 4.0, and a sharp increase in the level of uncertainty and complexity of the environment, necessitating a demand for increased adaptive potential of economic actors. All this determines the importance of finding new, effective business models in the new reality and ways to build (or reconfigure) them. The significant potential of such business model innovations, according to the results of accumulated research, is embedded in cutting-edge technologies of Industry 4.0 and digital transformation [6–17]. Nevertheless, there are certain difficulties and limitations in the innovation of business models based on digital solutions. Firstly, investments in digital technologies do not always provide innovative transformations of business models and give noticeable positive effects [8, 18–20]. Secondly, the mechanism of digital innovation transformation in business entities remains not fully understood [13, 16, 21]. Thirdly, it is necessary to clarify the drivers and limitations of business model innovation in the context under consideration in order to understand what decisions need to be made and what management impacts should be implemented to ensure business model innovation. In addition, it is important to take into account the different effectiveness of using digital technologies to innovate business models in different organizations and in different environments. In this regard, this study is aimed both at considering universal aspects associated with a theoretical analysis of the potential of digital solutions in business model innovations and directly at evaluating the empirical experience of digitalization of activities in thematic connection with business model innovations of business entities in the Rostov region of Russia to formulate conclusions and proposals in this area. This region was chosen for analysis for several reasons. Firstly, the region demonstrates a high level of business activity of enterprises and occupies one of the leading positions in digital transformation in the country. Secondly, this region is characterized by a large regional quota for the implementation of the Federal Management Training Program for Enterprises and organizations of the National Economy, which makes it possible to conduct a survey in a group of trained business leaders and obtain a significant empirical data slice. Thirdly, the Rostov region is a typical agro-industrial region with high indicators of socio-economic development and digital transformation of the regional economy. This makes it possible to extend the findings to a wider range of similar regions. Accordingly, such a construction of logic will make it possible to connect the key trends identified based on the theoretical analysis with the practice of their implementation in a specific economic system.

2 Literature Review

Over the past decade, research on business model innovations, including those based on digital solutions, has become widespread.

In this study, the traditional definition of the business model is taken as the basis. A business model is a brief description of how and why a company operates [22]. As David

J. Teece notes, the business model formulates logic, data, and other evidence supporting a value proposition for the customer, as well as a viable revenue and cost structure for the enterprise providing this value [23].

In its most general form, the business model consists of three interrelated components: value creation, value capture, and value delivery [24, 25].

The most widespread scheme of business model components was proposed by A. Osterwalder and Y. Pigneur [26].

Business model innovation is defined as the process of identifying the need for a new business model and designing (redesigning), evaluating, and implementing it to create value for both the company and target customers [27].

Many researchers note that the prerequisites for business model innovations are largely related to the conditions that are being formed in the market in connection with Industry 4.0 [28–33]. These conditions include increased competition in the market, variability of market requirements, shortening the life cycle of innovations and products, increasing complexity of products and processes, changing the nature of relations between business entities, etc. Among the main prerequisites for the innovation of business models, researchers include:

- networking and reduction of industry barriers;
- flexibility and personalization;
- individualization of mass production (mass customization);
- territorial localization of production;
- the emergence and spread of smart goods and services;
- fragmentation of value chains;
- globalization and decentralization of production;
- integrated production systems and automation, etc. [28].

The technological possibility of the emergence of digital platforms has opened up new prospects for the transformation of business models [33]. And here we are talking not only about platforms for interaction between producers and consumers. Development of inter-organizational collaboration has a strong impact on the digital maturity of small businesses [34].

For a deeper dive into the subject of business model innovations, a scientometric analysis of relevant publications based on the system data from Lens.org was conducted. According to the relevant keywords "business model innovations," 225 511 publications were found. The dynamic of their distribution by year is shown in Fig. 1.

The analysis of the dynamic of publications indicates the growing attention of researchers to the topic of business model innovations, as well as the overall significant number of research papers on relevant areas. At the same time, the analysis of the research areas shows that the three leading areas are business (74,973 publications), computer science (61,439 papers), and economics (49,560 publications) (Fig. 2).

This allows us to conclude that business model innovations are currently directly related to Industry 4.0 digital technologies. For further analysis of the relationship between digital technologies and business model innovations, the term "digital" was added to the original keywords, and the query took the following form: business AND

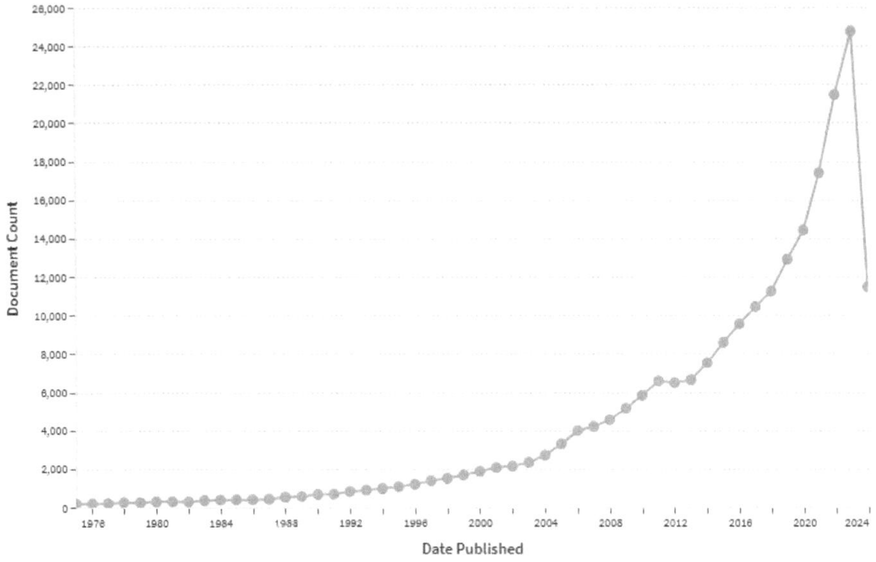

Fig. 1. Dynamics of publications on the subject of business model innovations. Source: Lens.org

Fig. 2. Areas of research on business model innovation. Source: Lens.org

model AND innovation AND digital. In this case, the broadest formulation was intentionally used, which allows us to meaningfully cover both digital innovations of business models and innovations of business models using digital technologies (Fig. 3). This allowed us to establish that the number of publications decreased almost tenfold when the search was narrowed (amounting to 27,793 works), but at the same time, from 2014–2015, we can talk about an exponential increase in their number.

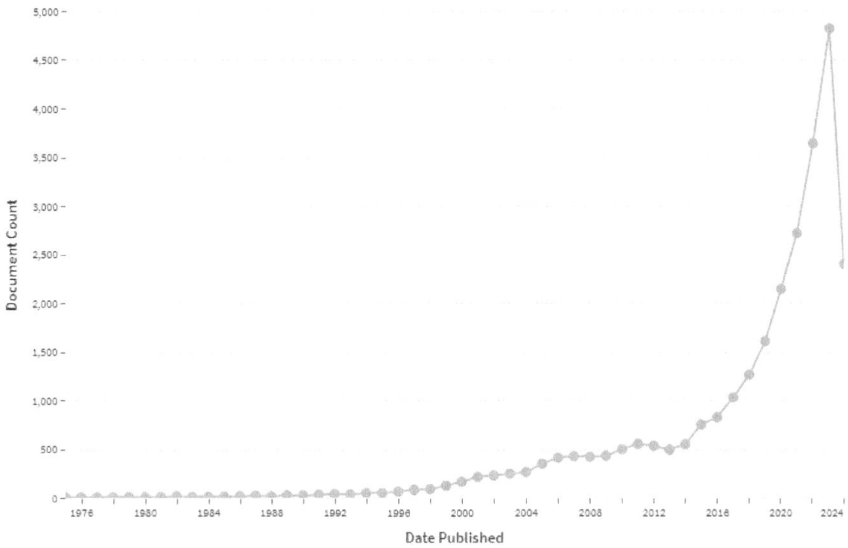

Fig. 3. Dynamics of publications on the topic of digital business model innovations. Source: Lens.org

With this in mind, the clustering of terms on digital business model innovations was further carried out, and a network map was built using the VOSviewer software product. The analysis was carried out on 1,000 publications selected by relevance. The network map reflecting the selected clusters and the date of publication is shown in Figs. 4 and 5. The analysis of changes in the popularity of terms over time revealed a shift in the focus of researchers' attention from studying the essence, types, and various components of new business models (or their various reconfigurations), their properties, and cutting-edge technologies (first of all, artificial intelligence and big data) to considering data and the relationship of economic actors as semantic the core of business model innovation in digital realities.

The content analysis of publications on business model innovations showed that, in most cases, the reconfiguration and regeneration of business models are associated with the new technological capabilities of Industry 4.0 [35]. Digital technologies are either the core of business model innovations (for example, in the case of digital platforms and ecosystems) or act as integrators, provided that they play a supporting role in building new business models (for example, within the framework of trends in servitization, circular economy, etc.), contributing to the convergence of the physical and digital worlds and connecting people, objects, and information. Moreover, digitalization can indeed become a driving force for business model innovation, for example, with the introduction of closed-loop economic models [36].

Research containing instrumental developments (various matrices, ontologies, morphological tables) showing the potential and effects of various cross-cutting digital technologies (blockchain, artificial intelligence, the Internet of Things, big data, and cloud technologies) in innovating business models, their structural components, or functional

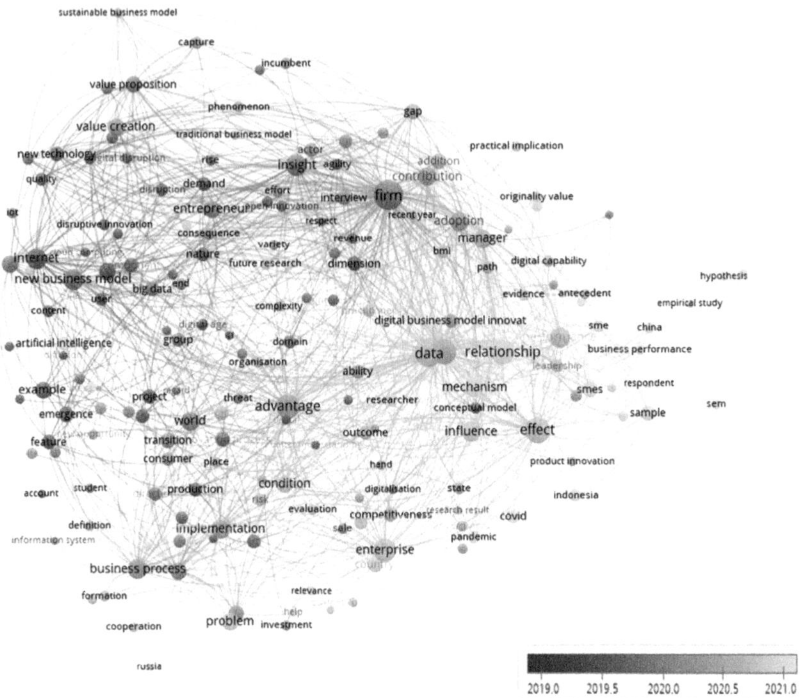

Fig. 4. Network map of terms for digital business model innovations. Compiled according to: data Lens.org using the VOSviewer software.

areas has become widespread in the scientific field [37–42], as well as what is required in the organizational and managerial plan to realize this potential.

However, despite the large number of studies in the subject area under consideration, as noted by WenJun Huang and Takeyasu Ichikohji [43], despite the rapid growth of research on the phenomenon of business model innovation, their study and theoretical justification are still at a preliminary and rather confusing stage since different theoretical approaches are used in different work platforms, levels of analysis, and scales of research, which leads to contradictions and inconsistencies in terms of factors, processes, types, barriers, and results of business model innovations. In turn, a number of empirical studies indicate limited or implicit positive effects of the use of digital technologies in business model innovations [8, 18–20]. Along with this, it is necessary to take into account country-specifics in terms of both the development and dissemination of digital technologies and the quality of the innovation landscape. This is due to the fact that some studies show the indirect impact of digital transformation on the innovation of business models. The nature of such influence is largely determined by cultural factors and other country factors and policies in the relevant field [44–47].

In Russia, the modern development of information technologies makes them an obligatory part of the internal environment and business processes of any organization. The challenges of the external environment, one of which was the coronavirus pandemic, acted as an impulse to accelerate the pace of integration of information technologies into

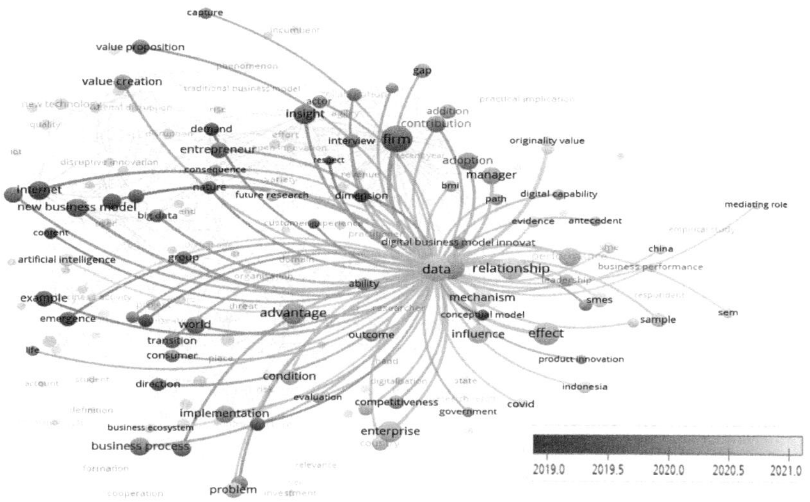

Fig. 5. Network map of terms for digital business model innovations with activation of the "data" point. Compiled according to: data Lens.org using the VOSviewer software

the business models of domestic companies. In the domestic economy, if before 2019, the processes of digitalization and information technology were mainly the competence of IT specialists, then with the beginning of the pandemic and after its completion, digital solutions started integrating into all elements of domestic organizational business models.

On the one hand, this situation is conditioned by the infrastructural conditions and the needs of the market and its subjects. The digitalization of business processes has become perceived not as a competitive advantage but as a state of competitive parity. For most industries, the integration of information technology into the activities of organizations is considered a key success factor.

On the other hand, this situation is related to the fact that managers of domestic organizations began to feel an imbalance between the market infrastructure, the needs of target audiences, and the traditional business models they use. Moreover, information technology has become perceived by them as a means to increase competitiveness. The digitalization of business processes contributes to increased flexibility, efficiency of activities, level of service, cost reduction, greening of business, unification, and efficiency of the process of interaction with consumers, partners, and suppliers.

Another contributing factor to the integration of information technologies is state policy, which considers this process a tool to increase the digital competitiveness of the country and its business entities in the global market.

The next factor contributing to the strengthening of the potential of digital technologies in the innovation of business models is the transformation of consumer needs. The coronavirus pandemic has generated high consumer loyalty to remote and virtual interaction with sellers and manufacturers of products and services. Another catalyst for this process was the tendency of society towards remote communication through various technologies and devices.

In general, the theoretical analysis made it possible to determine that digital technologies have significant potential for business model innovations. However, its practical implementation is closely linked, not only with theoretical research but also with how business entities perceive the connection between digitalization and digital transformation and business model innovations.

3 Methodology and Research Methods

The methodological basis of the study was the theoretical provisions of the concepts of business models, innovative economic development, digital economy and Industry 4.0. The relationship of the designated areas was studied through a scientometric analysis of publications corresponding to the topics, according to the system Lens.org. The articles were selected for the period 1975 to 2021 according to the criteria of correspondence of the abstract and keywords to the direction of theoretical propositions. Based on the analysis of the categories used in these publications, queries were generated using network maps and a search was conducted for scientific papers reflecting the interaction of theoretical concepts. This choice has formed a layer of publications that are most suitable for the topic of this study. A content analysis was conducted on them.

To determine the empirical component, a questionnaire was developed and conducted [35]. The questionnaire was created for 35 questions about the transformation of business models of various types of organizations in the new economic conditions. The structure of the questionnaire consisted of four sections: "acquaintance" - information about the field of activity of the organization; "impact of digital transformation" - the functioning of the organization under the influence of new digital and intelligent technologies; "innovations in the business model" - exposure to changes in the business model and mechanisms for implementing changes in the elements of the business model; "threats of changing the business model using digital technologies" are the visible risks of applying the achievements of digital transformation to the business model of an organization. The condition for the respondent's participation in the survey was his managerial position, where the most complete strategic information about the organization is concentrated, it is necessary to make innovative management decisions and have a sufficiently high level of awareness about the digital economy and business models. Due to the importance of the information received in relation to organizations, the survey was conducted anonymously without identifying specific organizations. The statistical significance of the respondents' answers was achieved by creating a sample based on students and graduates of the Federal Management Training Program for Enterprises and organizations of the National Economy (in Rostov region), which provides the appropriate "input" requirements contained in the methodological recommendations, curriculum and competence matrix of the specified educational program. The Rostov region was chosen for this part of the empirical analysis for several reasons. This is a region with a high level of socio-economic development and digital transformation. In addition, all the interviewed business leaders belong to the specified region; respectively, they operate in a common regional environment. In addition, the Rostov region is a typical region in terms of its development for Russia as a whole.

To confirm the results of the survey with real data and the results of content analysis, a statistical analysis of additional indicators provided by the information base of the Rosstat was carried out: income from digital changes in the business model, the cost of training personnel in digital technologies and the activity of adopting intelligent technologies in organizations. The data collected from the survey results and statistical analysis were organized into fourteen variables that were included in the cluster analysis. Clustering was carried out using the STATISTICA software product using the K-means method, that is, each observation belongs to the group to the center of which it is closest. For the correctness of the results, a standardization procedure was applied to reduce the disparate indicators to one unit of measurement.

Such a variety of working methods made it possible to study the topic of this study in the most correct and in-depth way.

4 The Practice of Business Model Innovations Based on Digital Solutions: The Experience of the Rostov Region

An analysis of the process of integrating information technologies into the economic activities of Russian business allowed us to notice the unevenness of this process.

During the research, a questionnaire was developed and a survey was conducted of the heads of 143 organizations operating in the Rostov region. When forming the sample, graduates of the Federal Program for Training Managerial Personnel for Enterprises and Organizations of the National Economy under the President of the Russian Federation were selected: managers and owners of enterprises of various spheres and scales of activity (for the study, it was important to get the opinion of decision-makers and those with a sufficiently high level of awareness about the digital economy and new business models, which is ensured in the sample by the corresponding "input" requirements of the specified educational program, its curriculum, and the competence matrix). 127 questionnaires were sent out for graduates of the 2019–2021 years of study. The specified data collection period is fixed at the given time interval for three reasons. Firstly, it is up to and including 2021 that the data in the network map built within the framework of scientometric analysis is used. For the possibility of comparing theoretical and empirical data, the same upper bound of the time interval is fixed. Secondly, adding new data to the array in 2022 and 2023 would reduce the possibility of using them, since during this time the situation can change for companies involved in the survey at the first stages. Thirdly, a number of threats and challenges that have arisen for the Russian economy since 2002, in particular in connection with sanctions restrictions, could affect the choice (or change) of priorities and the redistribution of resources. In this paper, the innovations of business models based on the use of the potential of digital technologies are considered from a strategic perspective. 85 heads of enterprises and organizations returned completed questionnaires.

The fields of activity of the organizations whose representatives participated in the survey are shown in Fig. 6.

As for the scale of activity of the organizations studied, 38.8% of them belong to large businesses, 35.3% to medium-sized businesses, and 25.9% to small businesses. The respondents were company owners (21.2%), top managers (23.5%), senior managers

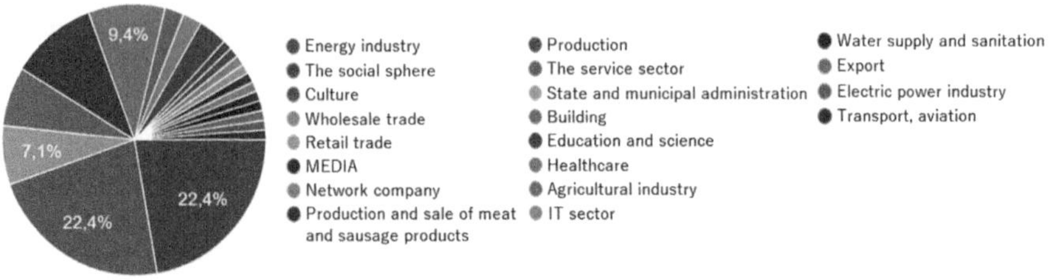

Fig. 6. Percentage of companies participating in the survey by field of activity.

(16.5%), and 38.8% line managers. Such coverage of all levels of the organizational management hierarchy allows for a comprehensive assessment of the integration of digital solutions into the enterprises and organizations under study.

The size of the enterprises whose representatives participated in the survey is shown in Fig. 7.

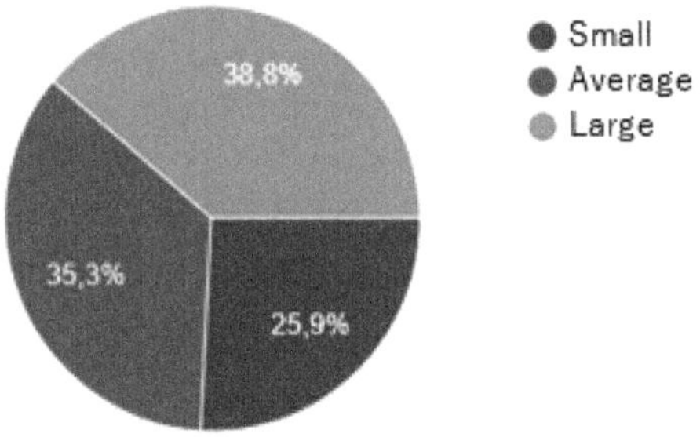

Fig. 7. Scale of activity of enterprises and organizations of respondents.

In the course of the study, it was found that 91.8% of respondents agreed that the global digital transformation and the transition to an information society have an impact on the functioning of the organization in which they work. More than 60% of respondents feel the serious impact of digital transformation on business processes and the functioning of the companies in which they work. It is important to note that 64.7% of the respondents implemented the restructuring of business models, taking into account this influence (Fig. 8). At the same time, 58.8% of respondents indicated that these changes were related to the integration of digital solutions into the activities of companies.

If we consider the implemented changes in the context of the structural elements of the business models of the organizations under study, the results were distributed as follows (Fig. 9).

The diagram indicates that over half of all changes targeted restructuring business processes. One-fifth of all innovations are related to the value proposition for consumers. Resources and the profit formula were recognized as elements that are less susceptible to change. The managers of the companies under study were also asked how significant the changes that had already been implemented were. The assessment was carried out on a 7-point scale (where 1 is the minimum degree of significance and 7 is the maximum degree of significance). The results are shown in Fig. 10.

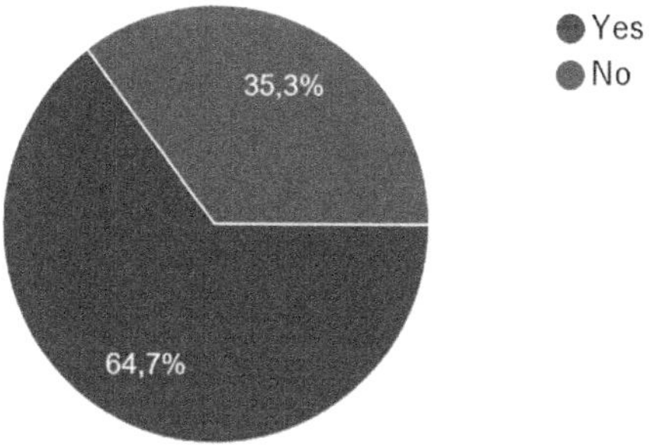

Fig. 8. The results of the answers to the question "Has digital transformation forced you to change anything in the business model of your company/enterprise/institution?"

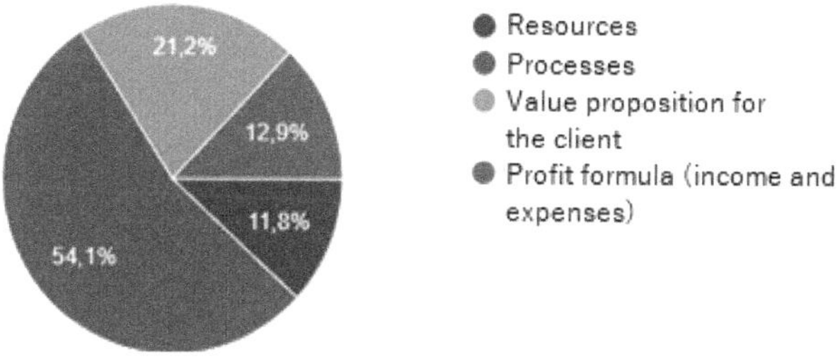

Fig. 9. Elements of the business models of the studied organizations in which the changes were implemented

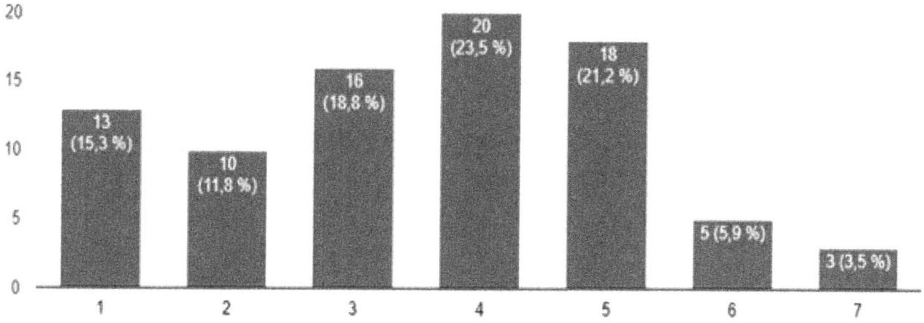

Fig. 10. Assessment of the significance of implemented changes on a 7-point scale.

Based on the presented results, it can be concluded that managers of regional organizations currently, although they feel the impact of digital transformation on the functioning of the companies they manage, are in no hurry to implement a radical and significant restructuring of existing business models. According to the survey results, 37.6% of respondents indicated that the implemented changes were not solely related to digital transformation but rather were dictated by internal, infrastructural, and market needs. As for the prospects for the development of the studied regional enterprises, 62.4% of the surveyed managers said that they see the need to change existing business models in the near future. An assessment of promising changes in the context of business model elements is presented in Fig. 11.

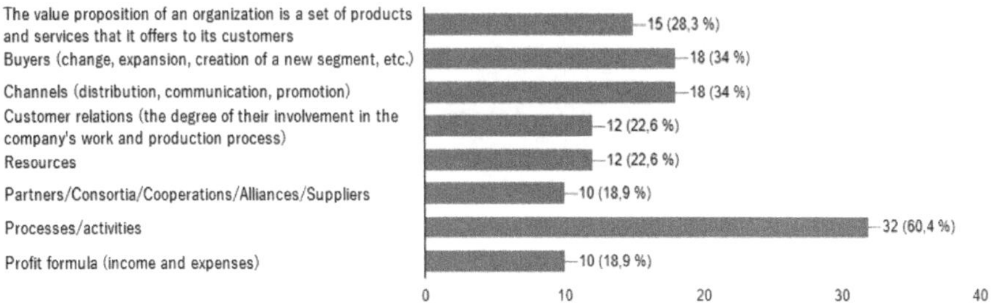

Fig. 11. Planned changes in business models in the context of the element structure.

It can be seen from the figure that business processes are the leader of transformation, as well as in the system of already implemented changes. The second place is occupied by interaction with consumers, channels, and products and services. The least common answers regarding the restructuring of business models are related to issues of relationships with customers and other environmental actors, resource provision, costs, and profit generation. Less than 5% of the respondents plan to implement a complete restructuring of each of the considered elements (and the entire business model). It can be assumed that this situation is due to the risks that may arise in the process of changing elements of business models using digital technologies, including threats related to information security, high costs of digitalization, increasing dependence on equipment, increasing barriers to exiting the industry, etc. (Fig. 12).

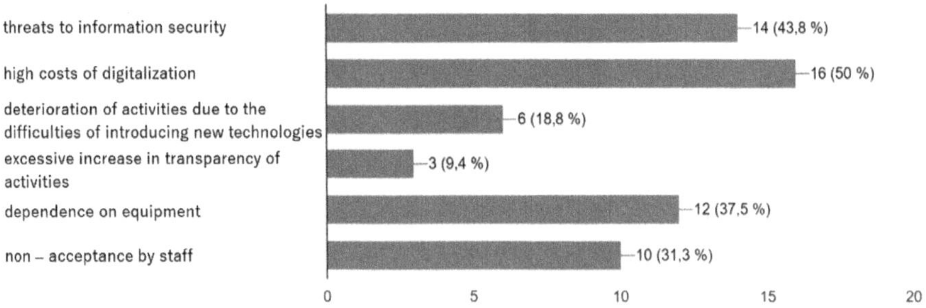

Fig. 12. Assessment of the importance of risks of digital business model innovations

The main reasons for the sluggish pace of business model innovations based on digital transformation were: high costs, threats to information security, dependence on equipment, and staff rejection. As for the effects that managers plan to receive in the process of implementing changes, they can be presented as follows (in descending order of importance for respondents):

1. performance improvement;

2. increasing profitability;
3. increasing competitiveness;
4. cost reduction;
5. expanding market share;
6. expanding the scope of activities;
7. improving the adaptability and manageability of the business;
8. increasing customer loyalty;
9. entering new sales markets;
10. reducing the time to bring a new product to market.

It is important to note that 7.5% of the surveyed managers do not expect to receive significant effects from the implementation of the modernization of the elementary structure of business models under the influence of digital transformation. The respondents were also asked to answer the question of what is necessary for the successful implementation of the planned changes and restructuring of organizational business models, taking into account the specifics of the digital economy. The distribution of responses is shown in Fig. 13.

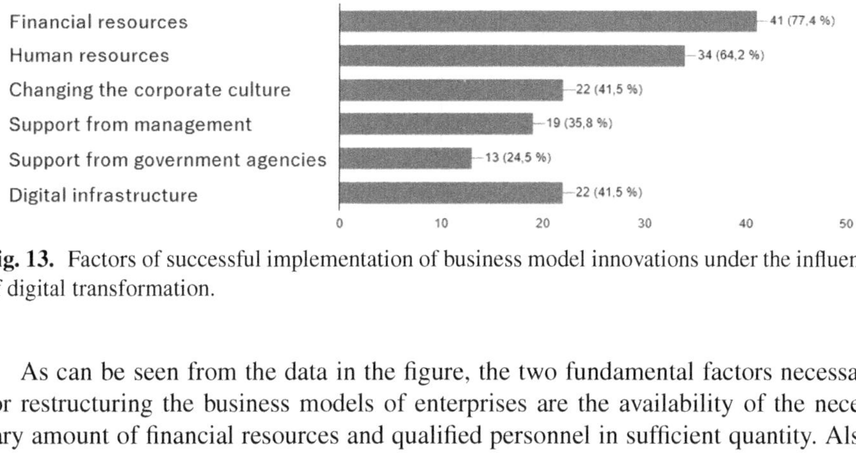

Fig. 13. Factors of successful implementation of business model innovations under the influence of digital transformation.

As can be seen from the data in the figure, the two fundamental factors necessary for restructuring the business models of enterprises are the availability of the necessary amount of financial resources and qualified personnel in sufficient quantity. Also, important conditions for the successful implementation of changes are considered: the availability of the necessary digital infrastructure throughout the territory of the presence and functioning of the organization and all its counterparties, including consumers, suppliers, partners, etc.; adapting the corporate culture and subordinating it to the needs of the information economy and digital integration; and comprehensive interest in the support of owners and top management of organizations in the implementation of these changes. It is interesting to note that only a quarter of the respondents highlighted the support of public authorities in this area as a necessary element for successful business model innovations in the context of digital transformation. As noted in the theoretical part of the study, scientists closely associate business model innovations with end-to-end technologies of Industry 4.0. During the study, the degree of practical use of cross-cutting technologies in the activities of business entities participating in the survey was assessed (Fig. 14).

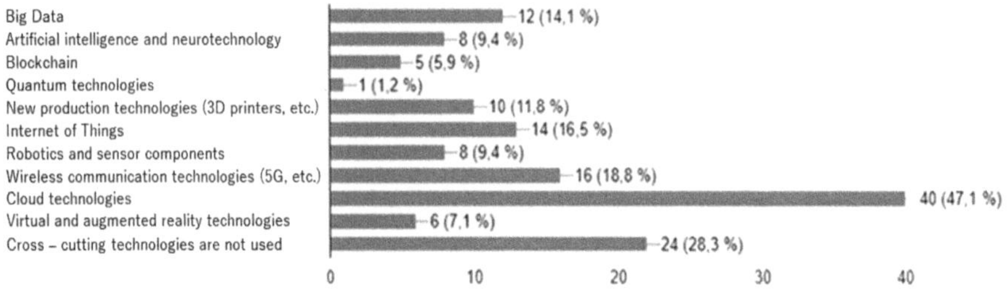

Fig. 14. Cutting-edge digital technologies used in the organization.

To study the relationship between the size and scope of the organization's activities and the cutting-edge technologies of Industry 4.0, based on the information base of the Rosstat and an anonymous survey of representatives of the management of enterprises and organizations in the Rostov region, a cluster analysis was implemented using the STATISTICA software. Common metric indicators are the scale of the organization, the scope of the field of activity in which the organization operates, the position of the organization, and the average age of the organization's staff. To consider the aspect of the impact of digital transformation on the organization, information was selected on the integral impact of digitalization on the sphere of functioning of the organization, the volume of implemented digital technologies in the organization, and their impact.

The effect of digital transformation is assessed through a prism of indicators on income from digital changes in the business model, the cost of training personnel in digital technologies, and a number of characteristics of the activity of adopting cross-cutting technologies both as a whole and separately for wireless communications and cloud technologies, the Internet of Things, Big data, artificial intelligence, and neurotechnologies. Due to the peculiarities of using cluster analysis technology, the indications of the questionnaire, where there is a multiple response, were analyzed separately according to the indicator of the adoption of end-to-end technologies in the organization. The data modernization increases the number of observations to one hundred and forty-three, improves the quality of cluster formation, and allows you to keep the results of the survey relevant. Clustering was carried out according to fourteen indicators using the K-means method, in which each observation belongs to the cluster to the center of which it is closest. For the correctness of the results, a procedure for normalizing variables was applied, reducing variously measurable data to one unit of measurement by expressing these values in terms of a ratio to a certain value reflecting certain properties of a particular feature: one standard deviation (Table 1).

The optimal format for dividing into clusters fell into three groups, and the decision to correlate observations (they are depersonalized, since the survey was conducted anonymously due to the confidentiality of information about organizations, and are indicated by the conditional number of the survey sheet C_No) in them was acquired during three repeated recalculations of clusters. To demonstrate the resulting cluster structure, a graph of the average values for each cluster was used (Fig. 15).

The graph shows that the clusters are quite diverse and do not duplicate each other. Based on it, we note that group 3 included all the extreme values of observations, the

Table 1. Results of the clustering procedure.

Number of variables	14
The number of observations is	143
The number of observations by the	K-means method
PD has been deleted	line by line
Number of clusters	3
The solution was obtained after	3 iterations

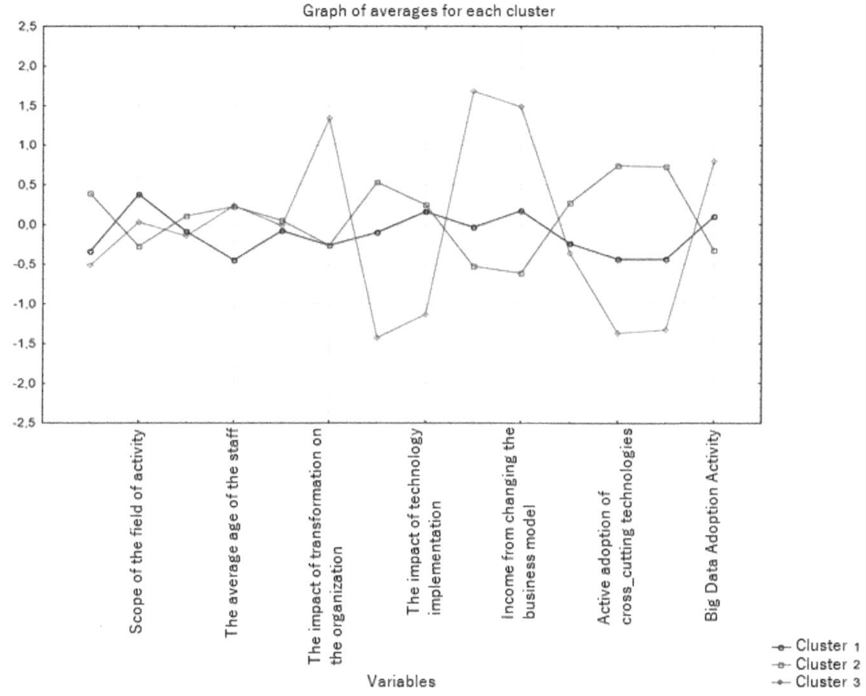

Fig. 15. A graph of the average values for each cluster.

explanation of which is associated with the possibility of falling into this cluster of organizations whose business models differ from the total range of data and/or the use of cutting-edge technologies in the digital economy differs from general practice (Table 2).

A study of the 23 organizations in Group 3 shows that all of them are large or medium-sized companies engaged in large-scale static production. According to the results of the survey of respondents conducted initially to collect data, most of these organizations do not use cutting-edge technologies in their core activities, which is not even compensated by interest in the possibilities of Big Data, and the rest (C_7, C_18, C_37, C_63, C_64,

Table 2. Observations included in the third cluster.

Observations	The distance to the cluster 3 center	The use of digital technologies
C_3	0.822428	Cutting-edge technologies of the digital economy are not used
C_4	0.706812	Cutting-edge technologies of the digital economy are not used
C_7	0.764998	Cloud technologies are used
C_8	0.781003	Cutting-edge technologies of the digital economy are not used
C_11	0.833083	Cutting-edge technologies of the digital economy are not used
C_18	1.146876	Cloud technologies are used
C_19	0.926769	Cutting-edge technologies of the digital economy are not used
C_25	0.859294	Cutting-edge technologies of the digital economy are not used
C_27	0.960349	Cutting-edge technologies of the digital economy are not used
C_37	0.708335	Cloud technologies are used
C_38	0.756842	Cutting-edge technologies of the digital economy are not used
C_39	1.078689	Cutting-edge technologies of the digital economy are not used
C_44	1.145836	Cutting-edge technologies of the digital economy are not used
C_62	0.979704	Cutting-edge technologies of the digital economy are not used
C_63	0.941338	Cloud technologies are used
C_64	0.954390	Cloud technologies are used
C_68	1.229010	Cutting-edge technologies of the digital economy are not used
C_80	1.043677	Cutting-edge technologies of the digital economy are not used
C_81	1.066305	Cloud technologies are used
C_82	0.849266	Cloud technologies are used
C_117	1.221560	Cutting-edge technologies of the digital economy are not used

(*continued*)

Table 2. (*continued*)

Observations	The distance to the cluster 3 center	The use of digital technologies
C_118	1.114106	Cutting-edge technologies of the digital economy are not used
C_132	0.964395	Cutting-edge technologies of the digital economy are not used

C_81, and C_82) use cloud technologies only to build communication between employees of different departments or branches. As a result, the profit of the business model does not apply to the cost of training employees in new technologies. The organizations included in the cluster are influenced by transformation in the category of production processes; therefore, the transformation of the business model of such organizations proceeds along the lines of technological innovations in production and does not require cardinal comprehensive digitalization measures. More important for increasing competitiveness and survival as a result, here is the procedure for reducing the business cycle of products by making changes to the techniques used by the organization. In Group 1, the use of wireless communications, cloud technologies, and Big Data is more dynamic and balanced compared to the previous group and affects 49 organizations (Table 3).

Table 3. Part of the elements of the first cluster

Observations	The distance to the cluster 1 center	The scale of the organization's activities
C_1	0.937708	Large
C_2	0.906214	Large
C_6	0.697780	Large
C_9	0.646133	Large
C_10	0.686196	Large
C_12	0.795608	Large
C_13	0.804872	Large
And then similar data on observations		

These large companies represent the public and municipal administration, education and science, healthcare, construction, manufacturing, and IT sectors and successfully exploit the potential of end-to-end technologies, including the Internet of Things, blockchain, artificial intelligence, robotics and sensors, and virtual and augmented reality technologies. The payment of significant personnel training costs is reflected in the consequent increase in profitability from the use of "digitalized" business models. The activities of the organizations in this group are focused on improving the quality of resources. Avoiding the risks associated with the leakage of information and human resources becomes an important point at which the work of all elements of the business model is aimed. Representatives of this cluster recognize the need for digital transformation of their business model components and use the potential of technologization for effective resource management. The most numerous is cluster 2, in which the averages in terms of "end-to-end technology adoption activity" and "wireless and cloud technology adoption activity" are represented by high positive values, which means that such digital economic opportunities play an important role for organizations in this group (Table 4).

Table 4. Components of the second observation cluster.

Observations	The distance to the cluster 2 center	The prevailing information and communication technology in the organization
C_5	0.531472	The use of 4-G communication technology prevails
C_16	0.837993	The use of 5-G communication technology prevails
C_17	0.757881	The use of 4-G communication technology prevails
C_22	0.736923	The use of 4-G communication technology prevails
C_23	0.714361	The use of 4-G communication technology prevails
C_24	0.799525	The use of 4-G communication technology prevails
C_26	0.920896	The use of 5-G communication technology prevails
And then similar data on observations		

The small and medium-sized organizations that make up the observations of this group operate in the fields of agriculture, industrial production, culture, and services. 4-G and 5-G technologies, individual components of robotics, neurotechnology, and blockchain, and various cloud resources are actively and extensively used here to improve the efficiency of the business model. For the organizations in this cluster, two elementary blocks of the business model are the most valuable: promotion channels and buyers. Therefore, digitalization in this cluster is used to improve the effectiveness of tasks such as increasing market share, reducing costs, expanding activities, and more. The transformational impact of the introduction of digital technologies is changing the mechanisms of interaction with customers in such organizations, both reducing logistics chains to meet customer needs as soon as possible and increasing work on the psychological aspects of improving customer experiences from interacting with the organization.

5 Conclusions

The conducted research has shown that digital technologies play an important role in business model innovation, contributing to the emergence of completely new types of digital business models as well as their reconfiguration and regeneration, covering individual structural components. At the same time, in order to develop specific management decisions in practice, it is important to understand how the management of business entities assesses the need for business model innovations based on and through digital technologies, factors, and barriers to their practical implementation. The analysis conducted on the example of enterprises and organizations in the Rostov region showed that the management of business entities recognizes the need to transform business models but implements such innovations using digital solutions rather conservatively. This is partly due to the limited use of Industry 4.0 end-to-end technologies in the region (more than a quarter of respondents do not use end-to-end technologies in their activities at all). In this regard, it is important for the management of organizations to consider issues of digital transformation and the expansion of the influence of digital technologies in Industry 4.0 and business model innovations. It is advisable to take into account not just the possibility of changing individual components of business models but also the growing importance of platforms and ecosystems and the need for coordination with the use of digital capabilities of business models by various entities to implement their innovations from the standpoint of a systematic and holistic approach. To implement this approach in practice, it is necessary to build up digital competencies and attract digital talents. This will enable the integration of digital transformation strategies and business model innovations. The implementation of this approach will make it possible to integrate resources for greater dissemination of end-to-end technologies and neutralize the risks of their isolated application. Along with this, the identification of ways and priorities of business model innovations may be partially based on the results of cluster analysis performed in the study. Cluster analysis made it possible to correlate the use of end-to-end technologies of the digital economy with the size of enterprises, their sphere of activity, and form of ownership, since these factors are significant both in terms of risk attitude and volume of resources and capabilities related to development goals and digital innovations of business models.

References

1. Lindgardt, Z., Reeves, M., Stalk Jr., G., Deimler, M.:. Business model innovation: when the game gets tough, change the game. In: Deimler, M., Lesser, R., Rhodes, D., Sinha, J. (eds.) Own the Future (2012). https://doi.org/10.1002/9781119204084.ch40
2. Chesbrough, H.: Business model innovation: it's not just about technology anymore. Strateg. Leadersh. **35**(6), 12–17 (2007). https://doi.org/10.1108/10878570710833714
3. Geissdoerfer, M., Pieroni, M.P.P., Pigosso, D.C.A., Soufani, K.: Circular business models: a review. J. Clean. Prod. **277**, 123741 (2020). https://doi.org/10.1016/j.jclepro.2020.123741
4. Wirtz, B. W., Schilke, O., Ullrich, S.: Strategic development of business models: implications of the Web 2.0 for creating value on the internet. Long Range Plan. **43**(2–3), 272–290 (2010). https://doi.org/10.1016/j.lrp.2010.01.005
5. Casadesus-Masanell, R., Ricart, J.E.: From strategy to business models and onto tactics. Long Range Plan. **43**(2–3), 195–215 (2010). https://doi.org/10.1016/j.lrp.2010.01.004

6. Dolgova, O.I., Nikitaeva, A.Yu.: Business model innovations: digitalization, easement, and customization in the activities of industrial companies. Drucker's Bull. **6**(44), 4–16 (2021). (in Russia). https://doi.org/10.17213/2312-6469-2021-6-4-16
7. Nikitaeva, A.Yu., Kiseleva, N.N.: Reconfiguration of business models of industrial enterprises: vectors of increasing sustainability in the new realities. Vestnik Volgogradskogo gosudarstvennogo universiteta. Ekonomika [J. Volgograd State Univ. Econ.] **23**(1), 110–120 (2021). (in Russia). https://doi.org/10.15688/ek.jvolsu.2021.1.9
8. Ancillai, C., Sabatini, A., Gatti, M., Perna, A.: Digital technology and business model innovation: a systematic literature review and future research agenda. Technol. Forecast. Soc. Change **188**, 122307 (2023). https://doi.org/10.1016/j.techfore.2022.122307
9. Böttcher, T.P., Weking, J., Hein, A., Böhm, M., Krcmar, H.: Pathways to digital business models: the connection of sensing and seizing in business model innovation. J. Strateg. Inf. Syst. **31**(4), 101742 (2022). https://doi.org/10.1016/j.jsis.2022.101742
10. Coskun-Setirek, A., Tanrikulu, Z.: Digital innovations-driven business model regeneration: a process model. Technol. Soc. **64**, 101461 (2021). https://doi.org/10.1016/j.techsoc.2020.101461
11. Foss, N.J., Saebi, T.: Fifteen years of research on business model innovation. J. Manage. **43**, 200–227 (2017). https://doi.org/10.1177/0149206316675927
12. Gregori, P., Holzmann, P.: Digital sustainable entrepreneurship: a business model perspective on embedding digital technologies for social and environmental value creation. J. Clean. Prod. **272**, 122817 (2020). https://doi.org/10.1016/j.jclepro.2020.122817
13. Kohtamäki, M., Parida, V., Oghazi, P., Gebauer, H., Baines, T.: Digital servitization business models in ecosystems: a theory of the firm. J. Bus. Res. **104**, 380–392 (2019). https://doi.org/10.1016/j.jbusres.2019.06.027
14. Kotarba, M.: Digital transformation of business models. Found. Manage. **10**(1), 123–142 (2018). https://doi.org/10.2478/fman-2018-0011
15. Kronblad, C., Pregmark, J.E.: Responding to the COVID-19 crisis: the rapid turn toward digital business models. J. Sci. Technol. Policy Manage. 1–17. https://doi.org/10.1108/JSTPM-10-2020-0155
16. Teece, D.J.: Profiting from innovation in the digital economy: enabling technologies, standards, and licensing models in the wireless world. Res. Policy **47**(8), 1367–1387 (2018). https://doi.org/10.1016/j.respol.2017.01.015
17. Verhoef, P.C., et al.: Digital transformation: a multidisciplinary reflection and research agenda. J. Bus. Res. **122**(889), 901 (2021). https://doi.org/10.1016/j.jbusres.2019.09.022
18. Gebauer, H., et al.: How to convert digital offerings into revenue enhancement: conceptualizing business model dynamics through explorative case studies. Ind. Mark. Manage. **91**, 429–441 (2020). https://doi.org/10.1016/j.indmarman.2020.10.006
19. Leinwand, P., Mani, M.M.: Digitizing isn't the same as digital transformation. Harv. Bus. Rev. **26** (2021). https://hbr.org/2021/03/digitizing-isnt-the-same-as-digital-transformation
20. Volberda, H.W., Khanagha, S., Baden-Fuller, C., Mihalache, O.R., Birkinshaw, J.: Strategizing in a digital world: overcoming cognitive barriers, reconfiguring routines and introducing new organizational forms. Long Range Plan. **54**(5), 1–18 (2021). https://doi.org/10.1016/j.lrp.2021.102110
21. Foss, N.J., Saebi, T.: Business models and business model innovation: between wicked and paradigmatic problems. Long Range Plan. **51**, 9–21 (2018). https://doi.org/10.1016/j.lrp.2017.07.006
22. Johnson, M., Christensen, C., Kagermann, H.: Reinventing your business model. Harv. Bus. Rev. **86**(12), 50–59 (2008)
23. Teece, D.J.: Business models, business strategy and innovation. Long Range Plan. **43**, 172–194 (2010). https://doi.org/10.1016/j.lrp.2009.07.003

24. Iheanachor, N., David-West, Y., Umukoro, I.O.: Business model innovation at the bottom of the pyramid – a case of mobile money agents. J. Bus. Res. **127**, 96–107 (2021). https://doi.org/10.1016/j.jbusres.2021.01.029
25. Massa, L., Tucci, C.L., Afuah, A.: A critical assessment of business model research. Acad. Manage. Ann. **11**, 73–104 (2017). https://doi.org/10.5465/annals.2014.0072
26. Osterwalder, A., Pigneur, Y.: Business Model Generation: A Handbook for Visionaries, Game Changers, and Challengers. John Wiley and Sons (2010)
27. Bachmann, N., Jodlbauer, H.: Iterative business model innovation: a conceptual process model and tools for incumbents. J. Bus. Res. **168**, 114–177 (2023). https://doi.org/10.1016/j.jbusres.2023.114177
28. Ibarra, D., Ganzarain, J., Igartua, J.I.: Business model innovation through Industry 4.0: a review. Proc. Manuf. **22**, 4 (2018). https://doi.org/10.1016/j.promfg.2018.03.002
29. Santarsiero, F., Carlucci, D., Schiuma, G.: Driving digital transformation and business model innovation in tourism through innovation labs: an empirical study. J. Eng. Tech. Manage. **74**, 101841 (2024). https://doi.org/10.1016/j.jengtecman.2024.101841
30. Fang, T.M., Ahmad, N.H., Halim, H.A., Iqbal, Q., Ramayah, T.: Pathway towards SME competitiveness: digital capability and digital business model innovation. Technol. Soc. **79**, 102728 (2024). https://doi.org/10.1016/j.techsoc.2024.102728
31. Paiola, M., Grandinetti, R., Kowalkowski, C., Rapaccini, M.: Digital servitization strategies and business model innovation: the role of knowledge-intensive business services. J. Eng. Tech. Manage. **74**, 101846 (2024). https://doi.org/10.1016/j.jengtecman.2024.101846
32. Marcon, É., Le Dain, M.-A., Frank, A.G.: Designing business models for Industry 4.0 technologies provision: changes in business dimensions through digital transformation. Technol. Forecast. Social Change **185**, 122078 (2022). https://doi.org/10.1016/j.techfore.2022.122078
33. Veile, J.W., Schmidt, M.-C., Voigt, K.-I.: Toward a new era of cooperation: How industrial digital platforms transform business models in Industry 4.0. J. Bus. Res. **143**, 387–405 (2022). https://doi.org/10.1016/j.jbusres.2021.11.062
34. Foguesatto, C.R., Frare, A.B., Wegner, D., Mitregra, M., Rodrigues, R.A.B.: You will never stand alone: the role of inter-organizational collaboration and technological turbulence in shaping small business' digital maturity. J. High Technol. Manage. Res. **35**(2), 100518 (2024). https://doi.org/10.1016/j.hitech.2024.100518
35. Nikitaeva, A.Yu., Laskova, T.S., Aydarkina, E.E., Amiri, L.P.: Digital transformation of business models: theoretical prerequisites and practical implementation in the Rostov region. In: International May Conference on Strategic Management – IMCSM22, vol. XVIII, no. 1, pp. 47–55 (2022). https://drive.google.com/file/d/1wcrG5Hbo7AArG4BOUzopNfEIIM60H0Fh/view
36. Neligan, A., Baumgartner, R.J., Geissdoerfer, M., Schöggl, J.-P.: Circular disruption: digitalisation as a driver of circular economy business models. Bus. Strateg. Environ. **32**(3), 1175–1188 (2023). https://doi.org/10.1002/bse.3100
37. Godavarthi, B., Narisetty, N., Gudikandhula, K., Muthukumaran, R., Kapila, D., Ramesh, J.V.N.: Cloud computing enabled business model innovation. J. High Technol. Manage. Res. **34**(2), 100469 (2023). https://doi.org/10.1016/j.hitech.2023.100469
38. Haaker, T., Ly, P.T.M., Nguyen-Thanh, N., Nguyen, H.T.H.: Business model innovation through the application of the Internet-of-Things: a comparative analysis. J. Bus. Res. **126**, 126–136 (2021). https://doi.org/10.1016/j.jbusres.2020.12.034
39. Lee, J., Suh, T., Roy, D., Baucus, M.: Emerging technology and business model innovation: the case of artificial intelligence. J. Open Innov.: Technol. Mark. Complex. **5**(3), 44 (2019). https://doi.org/10.3390/joitmc5030044

40. Sjödin, D., Parida, V., Kohtamäki, M.: Artificial intelligence enabling circular business model innovation in digital servitization: conceptualizing dynamic capabilities, AI capacities, business models, and effects. Technol. Forecast. Soc. Chang. **197**, 122903 (2023). https://doi.org/10.1016/j.techfore.2023.122903
41. Schlecht, L., Schneider, S., Buchwald, A.: The prospective value creation potential of Blockchain in business models: a Delphi study. Technol. Forecast. Soc. Chang. **166**, 120601 (2021). https://doi.org/10.1016/j.techfore.2021.120601
42. Yang, Y.: Business ecosystem model innovation based on Internet of Things big data. Sustain. Energy Technol. Assess. **57**, 103188 (2023). https://doi.org/10.1016/j.seta.2023.103188
43. Huang, W., Ichikohji, T.: A review and analysis of the business model innovation literature. Heliyon **9**, e17895 (2023). https://doi.org/10.1016/j.heliyon.2023.e17895
44. Malewska, K., Cyfert, S., Chwiłkowska-Kubala, A., Mierzejewska, K., Szumowski, W.: The missing link between digital transformation and business model innovation in energy SMEs: the role of digital organisational culture. Energy Policy **192**, 114254 (2024). https://doi.org/10.1016/j.enpol.2024.114254
45. Kolade, O., Oyinlola, M., Ogunde, O., Ilo, C., Ajala, O.: Digitally enabled business models for a circular plastic economy in Africa. Environ. Technol. Innov. **35**, 103657 (2024). https://doi.org/10.1016/j.eti.2024.103657
46. Lafuente, E., Sallan, J.M.: Digitally powered solution delivery: the use of IoT and AI for transitioning towards a solution business model. Int. J. Prod. Econ. **277**, 109383 (2024). https://doi.org/10.1016/j.ijpe.2024.109383
47. Laudien, S.M., Reuter, U., Garcia, F.J.S., Botella-Carrubi, D.: Digital advancement and its effect on business model design: qualitative-empirical insights. Technol. Forecast. Soc. Change **200**, 123103 (2024). https://doi.org/10.1016/j.techfore.2023.123103

Digitalization of Internal Planning in Industry

Zhanna A. Ermakova[1(✉)] and Semyon G. Fomin[2]

[1] Orenburg Branch of the Institute of Economics of the Ural Branch of the Russian Academy of Sciences, 11 Pionerskaya Street, Orenburg 460000, Russia
56ermakova@mail.ru

[2] Institute of Economics of the Ural Branch of the Russian Academy of Sciences, 29 Moskovskaya Street, Ekaterinburg 620014, Russia

Abstract. The importance of internal corporate planning for sustainable and dynamic development of an enterprise is significant, leading to the current focus on selecting planning mechanisms and tools, methods of digitalization of planning processes and the formation of such systems that ensure adequate response of the entire functionality of the enterprise to the challenges of the external environment. The authors in this paper utilized general scientific cognitive methods and EPC methodology (event-driven process chain), alongside questionnaires and economic analysis. The object of the study was the engineering holdings of Russia. The following results were identified: methodologies for developing an end-to-end planning system in the holding; the requirements and characteristics of the digital planning environment; a model of the planning system and its modification. The findings and results of the study are applicable for developing internal corporate planning frameworks based on digitalization and achieve greater planning depth, modify individual elements of the planning system considering industry specifics.

Keywords: Planning system · Enterprise · Digitalization · Industry

JEL Classification: L23 · M11 · O21

1 Introduction

The relevance is confirmed by both the long-term intensity of scientific research on planning and digital transformation in industry [1–5], and the applied demand through development programs at the corporate and state levels [6–8]. According to surveys of top managers and leaders of the professional planning community, digitalization of industry and planning has been among the top 10 development trends for more than 5 years in a row ASCM [9, 10].

The scientific challenge is to establish an internal corporate planning system that effectively integrates strategic and tactical management at the holding level and relative independence of enterprises at the operational level; secondly, meets the requirements of modern technological trends, has the ability for long-term development through the

E. Kuzmin et al. (Eds.): EASET 2024, SPBE, pp. 67–84, 2025.
https://doi.org/10.1007/978-3-031-91159-0_5

integration of new technologies; thirdly, quickly adapts to changes in the external environment, ensures efficiency, speed, effectiveness, and frugality of digital transformation; fourthly, has sufficient functionality to perform the system-forming role of the core of the digital platform of an industrial enterprise.

Additional advantages for holdings, corporations, and other organizational forms (comprising multiple legally independent entities) compared to single enterprises: new enterprises are quickly integrated into a common supply chain; continuity of planners creates long-term sustainability of planning processes; commonality of planning of holding enterprises ensures rotation of planners between enterprises and horizontal connections at the planning level between holding enterprises; competitive advantages due to the speed of planning processes and discipline of deadlines.

At the same time, at the theoretical level, it is necessary to develop an evolutionary approach to the formation of planning systems applicable to machine-building holdings, including such issues as the impact of digitalization on this process and historically existing planning systems at enterprises included in the holding, and the resulting opportunities to improve the efficiency of planning and business as a whole.

Holding structures are undergoing restructuring, presenting challenges for planning systems. A striking example of this trend is Russian railway engineering, which determines the object of the study: a Russian industrial holding that includes railway engineering enterprises.

Addressing new challenges in the planning system through theoretical and practical approaches defines the objective of this article - justification of the effectiveness of digitalization of intra-company planning in industry. This goal defined the following research objectives: to study existing approaches to intra-company planning and applied industrial specifics using the example of Russian mechanical engineering holdings; to identify the prerequisites for the implementation and problems of building a planning system in Russian railway engineering holdings; to form the stages of implementation of the planning system in holdings; to determine the level of execution of the stages of implementation of the planning system, the results and the effects obtained.

2 Literature Review

Planning is the core of the organization of economic activity of industrial enterprises. Contemporary approaches to intra-company planning have been evolving for over a century. Since then, the development of planning has been ensured by the harmonious interaction of such scientific disciplines as economics, management, mathematics, engineering (including information technology). Contemporary planning trends necessitate refining terminology to accurately represent real economic entities. At the same time, theoretical continuity in the sense of the methodological and methodical apparatus of planning has not yet exhausted its development potential. Practical examples of digitalization of planning, including on platform principles, which have been actively developed in the last decade, pose new challenges in both theoretical and applied areas.

The literature review is organized into four subsections to examine existing approaches to intra-company planning. The unique experience of the USSR in the formation of planning systems is noted. Works with a focus on methodological issues of production planning are studied. Theoretical aspects of digitalization in the field of specialized information technologies and planning algorithms are considered. Recommendations of leading consulting agencies specializing in planning, including as part of comprehensive services for the digitalization of enterprises, are considered. Considering the object of the study, an extended review of the works of Russian authors is carried out.

It should be noted that special attention was paid to planning at the macro- and meso-level during the development of the USSR. Great contributions were made by Bogdanov [11], Kantorovich [1], Kondratiev [12], Nemchinov [13], Strumilin [6]. The advisability of isolating these studies into a separate group is due to: the isolated development of planning in the Soviet period due to the Cold War; significant expenditure of resources and attention for the development of planning at the state level, which, among other things, was the reason for advanced achievements, especially in terms of creating a mathematical apparatus for planning; the desire to create an end-to-end planning system that links all levels of planning with methodological tools - from the state to industries, enterprises and workers. The remarkable accomplishments of the USSR in planning are acknowledged by the global community, for example: Kantorovich [1] was awarded the Nobel Prize for creating the foundations of linear programming, which are actively used in the calculation algorithms of advanced information planning systems to this day. Bogdanov [11] and Strumilin [6] paid considerable attention to such problems of creating a planning system as a balance between: directiveness and forecasting, arithmetic calculation and consensus discussion, closedness and openness of the planning system to achieve long-term stability. These issues are relevant today, especially at the strategic and tactical levels of planning, as well as when creating a heterogeneous planning system for company associations in conditions of instability of external and internal factors.

Many studies have been devoted to the methodological aspects of the implementation of internal corporate planning and the development of planning systems. Forrester [2], Orlicky [3], Wight [4] laid the foundations for the most common approaches to planning, which are implemented in the vast majority of information systems with planning functionality. Wallace and Stahl [14], Goldratt and Cox [15] proposed effective methods for developing internal corporate planning based on their own methods and consolidated experience.

Zhang and Sharifi [16], Gligor, Holcomb and Stank [17], Rahiminezhad Galankashi et al. [18] examine the role of planning system in ensuring flexibility of industrial enterprises. Okongwu et al. [19] explores the possibilities of finding an optimal balance in the planning system between customer focus and costs.

Smirnova [20], Karlik, Belousova and Migunova [5], Giniyatullina et al. [21], Elsukov and Kirillova [22] explore theoretical issues of the evolution of enterprise planning systems, their modifications and the relationship with economic development. Khmelnitskaya [23] and other authors pay attention to the specific features of the practical construction of a planning system in specific industries. Evchenko [24] develops the theory of end-to-end enterprise planning from the point of view of information models. Gavrilov [25], Lukina, Sadykov and Faizullin [26] formulate a comprehensive description of the enterprise planning system based on the standards of the ASCM group (Association for Supply Chain Management is a non-profit international educational organization that implements programs for standardization and certification of specialists in the field of production operations management).

Scientists also pay attention to the development of mathematical and technical tools designed specifically for solving planning problems. Lupeikiene, Dzemyda and Caplinskas [7] propose methodological solutions for creating a digital planning system consisting of multiple planning systems. Solodovnikov [26] studies the specifics and effects of the use of digital solutions in planning for the optimization of industrial ferrous metallurgy enterprises in the Russian Federation and Europe. Bozutti and Esposto [28] analyze the development of planning processes in terms of increasing flexibility and integration of functions, enterprises. Khanuja and Jain [29] study the impact of planning tools on supply chain integration. Bushueva and Afanasyev [8] consider the problems of developing information support for planning at enterprises.

Among consulting agencies, the most interesting approaches are those of planning software manufacturers for applying advanced planning methods in their products. The rating of software providers is published by Gartner [30–32]. Leading companies that conduct methodological research, develop software and consult industrial companies in the field of planning are SAP, Siemens, Dassault Systems, Oracle continue to invest significant efforts in planning competencies. The observed trends in software product changes are characterized by the creation of their own digital platforms, in which planning is a key element. This statement is confirmed by SAP - previously a separate software for SAP planning AP O has become part of the ERP system based on HANA. Industrial companies continue to actively implement planning systems to improve their business performance, as evidenced by the information from the Project of the Year award from the Russian software provider 1C [33].

The above literature review allows us to conclude that planning issues remain relevant for theory and practice, and that industrial enterprises are in demand for planning in theoretical, methodological and technical aspects. In theoretical terms, mathematical methods that form the basis for digitalization of complex calculation and organizational planning tasks deserve special attention. In the methodological aspect, the authors formulate approaches to the implementation of business planning processes, the information flow of which should be implemented in a digital environment. Software manufacturers continue to improve planning information systems and adapt them to the industry and specific industrial specifics of the enterprise. At the same time, the issues of digitalization of the construction of an end-to-end planning system in holding structures and achieving an optimal balance between efficiency and manageability remain insufficiently studied.

3 Methods and Materials

The study spanned an extended period, employing theoretical and empirical methods alongside applied methodological tools at various stages.

To form the author's theoretical provisions, firstly, scientific research on the topic was studied and analyzed and, secondly, an adaptive approach was used, which made it possible to reflect industry specifics, as well as consider the trends in the digitalization of industrial enterprise management systems.

Event-driven process chain method (EPC diagram) was used to model the holding's end-to-end planning system process chain). First, a concept was formulated based on the analysis of existing theoretical approaches to intra-company planning, as well as recommendations from leading global vendors of IT planning solutions. The concept of an end-to-end holding planning system obtained at the theoretical level was decomposed at the technical and process levels, considering the actual IT infrastructure of the holding (more than 10 enterprises with heterogeneous IT infrastructure) and the standard hierarchy of MRP 2 plans adapted to the specifics of the holding (machine-building enterprises of single and small-scale production). An experiment was conducted to confirm the practical adequacy of the proposed end-to-end planning model, clarify data flows and expand functionality.

To establish goals, a survey was administered among top managers at the holding level and key business units: 20 respondents, 33 questions, a 5-point scale, 2 states for assessment (as is and as should be). The baseline interview was conducted in 2019, then updated in 2021 and 2024. The questionnaires and results are located on the internal server of JSC Sinara - Transport Machines. The most valuable for the study are the comments that made it possible to formulate the factors and circumstances in which the enterprise operates.

To evaluate the efficiency of the business process, a set of indicators was used, 5 of which are presented in this article: just-in-time shipment, inventory level, planning speed, planning labor intensity, speed of integrating new assets into the holding structure. Measurements of actual indicators were carried out based on transactions in objects of the information system based on 1C: plan/plan and plan/fact analysis, history of changes to objects, user activity in the system.

Study materials included results from corporate research and consulting projects conducted by the authors in collaboration with the National Research University Higher School of Economics, developers and suppliers of planning software (RiverLogic, DassaultSystems, SAP, Siemens, Rightstep, 1C company), consulting agencies (ABC - consulting, Open School of Business); methodological materials of production systems of ROSATOM and CATERPILLAR companies; analysis of systematized interviews with top managers of industrial companies; regulatory and accounting data of enterprise information systems - inventory levels, design and technological documentation, information on the plan and fact of production. This study was influenced by an internal corporate survey previously carried out by the authors in Russian holdings of various product specializations (in particular, United Machine-Building Plants - heavy engineering of a single type; Rosatom Fuel Company TVEL - medium engineering), which showed that losses in solving individual planning problems amounted to 70% of the total labor intensity of planning.

4 Results

The object of the study are the holdings of the railway engineering of the Russian Federation, namely the holding "Sinara - Transport Machines" (hereinafter - STM) and the holding "TransMashHolding" (hereinafter - TMH). They are leaders in transport engineering in the Russian Federation and compete in the product line. Other participants in this market are limited by a smaller range: Industrial and Engineering Group PTK - a manufacturer of track machines. PC Transport Systems - a manufacturer of urban public transport Ust-Katavsky Carriage Works - a manufacturer of trams. Some enterprises represented in this market segment produce less high-tech products: manufacturers of freight cars - United Carriage Works, RM Rail, Altaivagonzavod, Uralvagonzavod, etc. For some participants, the railway engineering market is not the main one: KAMAZ - a manufacturer of motor vehicles, Yaroslavl Motor Plant - diesel engines and mechanical gearboxes for motor vehicles.

Based on materials from analytical reports of industry information agencies Polikarpov [34, 35], Belov [36], enterprise reports STM [37], Shupletsov [38], Misharin [39], Pozdnyakov [40], reports on disclosure of information on implemented 1C solutions Nesterov [41] some characteristics of the main holdings of railway engineering of the Russian Federation are given in Table 1.

The effects of implementing a planning system in a railway engineering holding consist of two components: eliminating losses and obtaining additional benefits. The planning system ensures synchronization of purchasing, production and shipments. Holdings become less efficient than individual plants when they increase safety stocks to compensate for the lack of synchronization. This is a consequence of the lack of a centralized internal holding planning system.

Gavrilov [25], Karlik, Belousova, and Migunova [5] drew attention to the fact that correct goal setting is necessary for designing appropriate planning stages. It should be agreed with them.

First, it is necessary to collect, systematise and process information for correct setting of goals, to develop a way to achieve the goals. Then proceed to enterprise planning, selection and application in practice of appropriate elements of the planning system [5]. To determine the structure and content of the planning system development stages: significant or not significant changes, contractor or independent. Planning system implementation stages: enterprise survey, hypotheses, scope of planning survey, survey, summary, decision making, implementation.

The team implementing the planning system is recommended to adhere to the following rules.

At the stage of enterprise survey, the team should obtain general information about the enterprise from publicly available materials: the industry in which the enterprise operates; reasons for initiating the construction of a planning system; the organizational outline of the enterprise; names of some enterprise managers in whose hands decision-making power is concentrated; characteristics of industrial capacities. This information helps to move on to the next stage of implementation.

At the stage of formulating hypotheses about the elements of the future system, those responsible for building the planning system must assume about what the elements of the future planning system should be. The main prerequisites for choosing certain elements are the best practices method - using the experience of similar industrial enterprises (the same or similar industry and problems) that have managed to build a planning system. This assumption is not final, but is sufficient for moving on to the next stage.

At the stage of defining the scope of the survey of the planning system, the team of the creation of the planning system must form events that consist of a subject-specific

Table 1. Characteristics of the main holdings of railway engineering in the Russian Federation.

Indicator	STM	TMH	Others
Revenue in 2023, billion rubles	105.85	411.83	Scientific and production corporation "United Wagon Company" and RM - Rail, manufacturers of freight cars, are approaching 100 billion rubles
Number in 2022, thousand people	25	38	-
Quantity factories, no less	24	26	-
Number of service centers, not less than	80	90	-
Basic information system for planning	1C	1C	-
Export	Yes	Yes	Yes
Production			
Electric trains, mainline diesel locomotives and electric locomotives	Yes	Yes	No
High speed trains	Yes	No	No
Diesel trains, subway cars	No	Yes	No
Travel technique	Yes	No	PTC, etc. total share - less than 3% of the market
Trams	Yes	Yes	PC Transport Systems, Ust-Katav Carriage Building Plant, Ural Plant of Transport Engineering
Engines big power	Yes	Yes	Kama Automobile Plant (KAMAZ), Yaroslavl Motor Plant
Diesel locomotives shunting	Yes	Yes	less than 5% of the market
Systems control and signaling	Yes	Yes	Horizon, Flight
Wagons	Yes	Yes	More than 10 large manufacturers
Services: railway infrastructure support	Yes	No	Yes
Technologies: engineering, production, service, operation	Yes	Yes	Yes

familiarization with the elements of the planning system, as well as with interrelated functions. The survey outline includes: existing methods of implementing planning; indicators that the company's management hopes to improve by implementing the planning system; personnel at all levels of the organizational hierarchy - from decision makers to executors; tools used to implement planning; planning data. In the case of a holding structure, a management company and one or two plants are usually involved as typical representatives of the production environment. The prepared plan of activities for the survey is approved by the first person of the holding for implementation.

At the survey stage, the planning system creation participants must implement the approved survey action plan. Execute the survey action plan: interviewing; planning value stream mapping; data analysis; calculation of actual and target indicators; monitoring of planning and material flows. The results are facts about the current planning system and the attitude of all stakeholders towards the planning system. It is important to preserve the original data and present the facts as they were received - quotes, photographs, and so on. Check the accuracy of facts from different sources. Confirm the accuracy of the presentation in the final report. This will avoid the need to prove veracity.

At the summary stage, it is necessary to propose a final solution for building a planning system. This solution contains information on how all elements of the planning system should look in the target form, what needs to be done to achieve the target state and what resources are needed for this. The draft solution is formed on the basis of actual survey data. The draft solution should look in such a way that both the current and target state of the planning system at the top level of indicators are formulated by the enterprise management, this will allow for support for implementation. Based on this top-level statement of the problem and the survey results, the project team proposes how all elements of the planning system should change from the current state to the target state.

At the decision-making stage, the project team should ensure that all stakeholders make a final decision on the implementation of the planning system and the provision of the necessary resources. Typically, a final meeting is held at this stage, where the implementation team presents the results of the survey and proposals for decision-making. Management must approve the decisions. Also, at this stage, a number of formal procedures for resource allocation take place, such as signing orders for the enterprise, concluding contracts, preparing feasibility studies, and drawing up technical specifications.

At the implementation stage, the planning team must implement the approved implementation decision. It is necessary to act in accordance with the decisions made, but keep in mind the changing situation, adapt operational implementation work. Implementation usually occurs through projects in the classical or flexible methodology. During and upon completion of implementation, it is necessary to check the dynamics of achieving the established goals, provide reports on the implementation status to management in order to maintain interest. Immediately after the completion of the implementation project, it is recommended to start a new project to improve the planning system, considering the improvement reserves identified in the process of building the planning system and the emergence of innovative solutions.

In 2018–2020, a business survey of STM was conducted to build a holding planning system. Top managers, functional heads of the holding and one of the STM plants took part in the survey. The survey included a questionnaire and measurement of indicators. In 2020–2022, based on the survey results, changes were made to the holding planning system. In 2022–2024, the holding planning system was monitored to assess the stability and effectiveness of the changes made.

As a result of the survey, eight driving forces of changes in the holding's functioning were identified. The first driving force is a new level of interaction with a key customer (Russian Railways) that requires increased integration between private label and Russian Railways through automation and digitalization of information exchange and management throughout the entire product life cycle, the formation of contracts for the future item and life cycle contracts. The second is the restructuring of the company, the transition to a holding model, as a consequence of the extensive type of economic growth of the company; the need to integrate the acquired private label companies into the general structure of the holding. The third is the overwhelming number of orders for one customer: the state-owned vertically integrated company Russian Railways. The fourth is an insufficient level of quality of private label products, delivery time discipline and long production times. The fifth is unsatisfactory quality of suppliers' products. The sixth is digitalization. The seventh is competition. Within the Russian Federation: TMH. The closest international competitors: Alstom Transport, Hitachi Rail Systems, Siemens Mobility, Hyundai Rotem and others. Eighth – incomplete compliance of regulatory documentation with current processes at the enterprise: some of the regulatory documentation is not relevant in relation to current processes and procedures.

A reserve of 20–60% of economically inexpedient management activity was identified, which can be released by ensuring the completeness and availability of information and reuse of data.

The technical and methodological assessment of the planning system encompassed observing the activities of planners and accountants, interviewing functional and line managers of business units, studying the state of information systems of planning and accounting and the data in them. As a result of the survey, factors, characteristics and prerequisites of the planning system were identified (Table 2).

The decision is based on the survey, all the circumstances and best practices in STM: to develop methods of planning at all levels (from the holding company to the enterprise); set goals and monitor the indicators of the planning system; improve planning role competencies; implement practices and tools, availability accurate planning data. To implement this decision, a special planning unit was created, cross-functional and cross-organizational projects were organized, and the necessary resources were allocated.

The outcome of the initial phase of building a planning system was the implementation of the sales and operations planning (S&OP) process - an integrated planning process, with the help of which synchronization of all functions and organizations is achieved on an ongoing basis. The EPC approach to modeling was applied in the formation of a conceptual model of the end-to-end planning system of the holding with a single information flow in the digital environment for all levels and participants. Analysis of theoretical works on intra-company planning made it possible to formulate a set of methods that ensure the solution of all planning tasks in the holding under consideration, considering industry specifics. The best practices of the world's leading vendors of planning software were considered, which made it possible to create a digital environment covering the entire information flow of planning and fact. The process model is shown in Fig. 1.

The S&OP phases: NPI (New Product Introduction) and sales, master planning, economic and financial planning, control. Segmenting the process into four phases facilitates

Table 2. Factors, characteristics and prerequisites of the planning system in the holding company "Sinara - Transport Machines" based on the results of the survey.

Factors	Characteristic	Prerequisites
Planning systems elements	Differences in structure and maturity level at each enterprise	Systems planning elements standardization
IT infrastructure	Inadequacy and disunity in planning and accounting IT systems	IT systems common requirements based on planning standardization
IT basic	Basic planning practices are supported	Planning tools are available
collaborative planning IT	Capacity limitations, optimization, linking plans across management levels and functions, collaboration are not supported	Reducing the labor and duration of calculation, balancing and approval of plans, analyzing assumptions, considering current restrictions and target indicators
Responsive IT tools	Does not support changes in demand, deviations in supply, production processes, operational rebalancing of production	Minimizing the negative impact on finances due limited economic resources
Plans	Are changing weekly	Fast planning based on data sets with visual display of results
Many production schedules	Each schedule does not satisfy all constraints by organizational methods (without IT)	Purchase and production orders are in target indicators
Fulfilment data	There is no up-to-date data	The situation assessment, agile decision- making
Key production technologies	Design, production preparation, supply, procurement production, machining, welding, assembly, testing, sales, service	Planning of all functions and production technologies due their features
Deadlines production products	Considering the procurement cycle up to 1 year, considering the development of new products - up to 5 years	Product life cycle planning and control

(continued)

Table 2. *(continued)*

Factors	Characteristic	Prerequisites
Production	More than 100 thousand technological operations, more than a dozen levels of nesting of specifications, more than 100 factories and workshops	Coordination plans
Internal and external supply chains	Changes quickly - new production sites are added, changes occur at existing ones	Accounting and management of changes to obtain maximum economic effect through optimization and synchronization of cooperation schedules, loading of competence centers, increasing the efficiency of resource use, completeness of supplies, and alignment of production flows
Market conditions	Determine the need for a client-oriented approach across all chains, horizontal and vertical, based on a single information field and common goals	Achieving competitive advantage in the global market by leading value chains

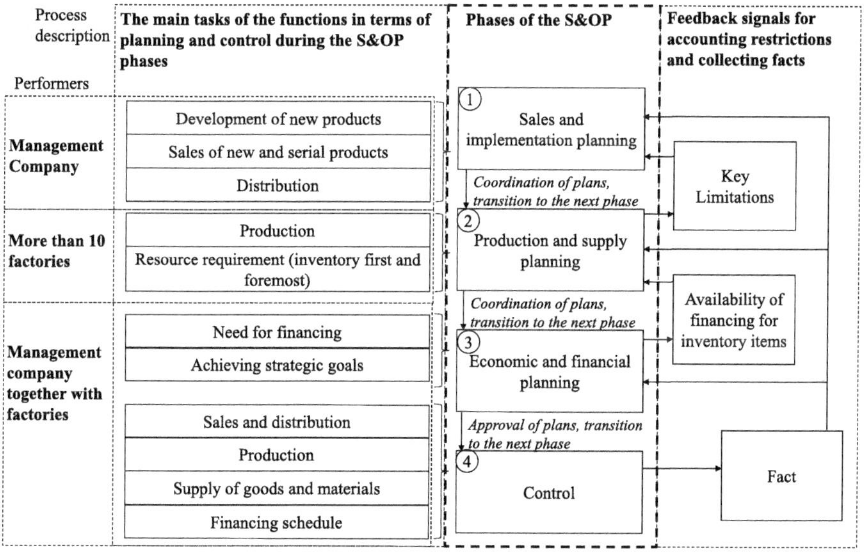

Fig. 1. Model of the sales and operations planning (S&OP) process for the STM holding.

management. The first phase includes planning new products and sales of new and serial products, since product projects and sales were managed at the level of the management company, this phase is attended by the heads of the management company responsible for the relevant areas of activity. The second phase consists of production planning, the plants participating in planning, based on the plans approved in the previous phase, form their production plans, based on which they calculate the need for resources. In the third phase, economic services determine planned economic indicators, the result of this phase is an approved set of plans. In the fourth, control over the execution of plans is carried out. The first, second and fourth phases in terms of finished products are formed in a single centralized end-to-end IT planning system, which allows for parallel and synchronous planning, eliminating losses at planning stages, and tracking the status of execution of the planning process phases. Feedback flows have been designed separately: feedback on the limitations and availability of financing for inventory items (I&M) allows for a reduction in the number of iterations of balancing plans considering the availability of resources; feedback on the fact allows for a single actual result for the entire team.

The second stage included the implementation of a centralized process for all plants to plan the need for purchased inventory items. The need for such implementation is due to the centralization of the supply function. In addition to the tools used in the S&OP process, integration solutions were developed using the 1C data conversion tool, and the plants' information systems were improved to ensure integration. 19 types of data are regulated and fall under centralized management.

The conceptual model of the S&OP planning process for the holding company is decomposed into separate subprocesses and data objects. Detailing to the following level is performed: the existing information infrastructure, technical and methodological descriptions in relation to the information systems of the holding company's plants, user actions. To ensure the unity of the information flow in the digital environment of end-to-end planning, the integration of disparate systems into a centralized system was performed based on clear requirements in both technical and methodological and organizational aspects. As a result, an enlarged model of planning the need for purchased inventory items was formed, which is presented in Fig. 2.

The process of planning the need for purchased goods and materials combines at the methodological and technical level the plant planning and accounting systems and the holding planning system. From more than 10 plant information systems, the centralized system receives data on warehouse balances of inventory items, write-offs of inventory items from the central warehouse, returns of inventory items to the central warehouse, and future receipts on orders to suppliers. In a semi-automatic mode, information about the product is entered from product management systems into a centralized system - the composition of products, acceptable substitutions. The centralized system subsequently establishes requirements for plant systems and oversees their implementation, which allows for the harmonization of systems. Planners and suppliers work directly in the centralized system, which is carried out accordingly by planning and ensuring the need for purchased goods and materials. The centralized planning system has increased overall system of planning systems efficiency due to the functionality of increasing data

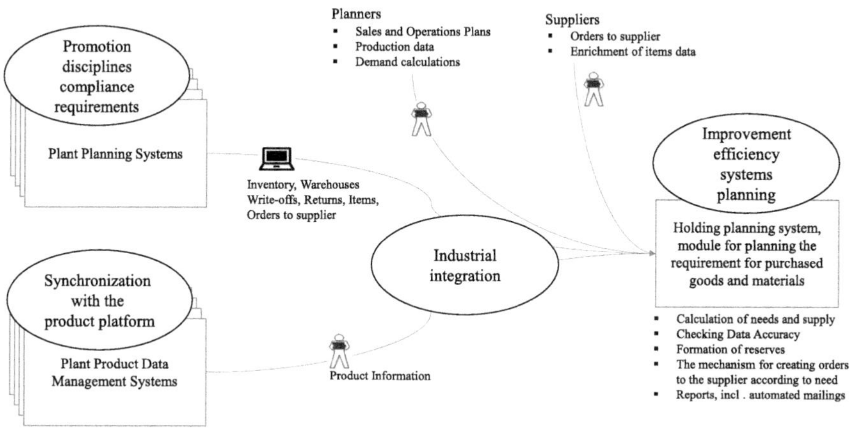

Fig. 2. An enlarged model for planning the need for purchased inventory items for a private label holding.

accuracy, unified automated, more advanced mechanisms for working with demand and reports.

Co-operation planning, operational production planning at the holding company level and at the plant level were included in the subsequent stages of planning system development. Lupeikiene, Dzemyda and Caplinskas [7] proposed approaches for designing and developing a planning system consisting of several systems. These approaches were used to develop the subsequent stages of creating an end-to-end holding planning system.

A developed planning system makes business processes more efficient and increases the speed of solving non-standard tasks (for example, supplying a new type of product to Guinea in a short time), creating competence centers for metalworking and the production of trolleys, quickly reconfiguring the business considering changes in the contract with Russian Railways regarding the depth of contracting.

The resulting effects from creating an end-to-end planning system for the holding included a conscious balance between costs and effectiveness. As noted by Okongwu et al. [19], note, the development of unified planning systems across multiple enterprises coordinates product deliveries to customers and enables informed decision to be made about striking a balance between customer satisfaction and order fulfillment costs, especially in conditions of uncertainty. In practice, in STM such a decision was made due production futures and client expectations. The production of unique products results in the production lead-time being longer than the customer order lead-time. In such a situation, all factors can be processed by the planning system: a production order is created after confirmation of the order from the client, planning of fines and other negative consequences of violation of delivery terms under the contract, while there is no risk of excess stocks in case of non-confirmation of the order; a production order is created before registering a customer order in order to comply with the planned delivery date, while achieving maximum customer satisfaction, but there were risks of the formation of unclaimed orders; various intermediate options for balancing and considering the possibility of reallocating inventory and reassigning orders between customers in the event of instability. It is necessary to compensate not only external instabilities, but also internal ones, based on comparable factors. The planning system made it possible to prepare information for making such decisions.

The efficiency of the planning system in terms of increasing the intensity of interplant cooperation provides the opportunity to obtain advantages from the specialization of individual sections of enterprises in the supply of certain products for many enterprises of the holding. As a result, revenue is increased for some enterprises (suppliers), quality is improved and stocks are reduced for other enterprises (consumers).

5 Discussion

As a result of the conducted research, the following results were obtained: approaches to the formation of a centralized end-to-end planning system in the holding were formulated; a model of the end-to-end planning system in the holding was proposed and the tasks of its modification were identified using the example of the Sinara - Transport Machines holding.

The implementation of an end-to-end planning system in the holding is the most effective option compared to others. This is confirmed by the analysis of possible benefits both at the theoretical level and at the empirical level by the results of work in a single planning system in the STM holding. It is more expedient to implement an end-to-end centralized planning system in the holding using an incremental -iterative approach: starting from planning at the top level and moving on to planning at the operational level, gradually increasing the detail and volume of tasks solved with the help of the planning system. The most "sensitive" for planning were the processes of production, sales, the need for purchased inventory items, interplant cooperation.

The main focus was on: increasing the manageability of planning processes and monitoring of execution; technical and methodological improvement of the planning system, including through the unification of solutions and approaches used for different planning tasks; accuracy of normative and reference information for planning. In theoretical terms, confirmation was obtained of the possibility of creating a unified heterogeneous planning system with the prospect of developing into an end-to-end heterogeneous system in a common digital environment.

The monitoring conducted in the STM holding in 2022–2024 showed the following characteristics of the implemented planning system. Long-term preservation of the effects of planning processes, such as increased speed of planning tasks and integration of new enterprises into a single centralized planning system. Instability of business effects (stock levels, customer satisfaction levels) from the planning system in the context of significant changes in the external and internal environment - trends towards decentralization of management, a decrease in the number of long-term contracts, asynchronous development of functions related to planning. The planning system made it possible to objectively monitor and analyze these processes at the corporate level.

The built system of internal corporate planning in the holding partially bears the features of centralized and end-to-end planning. Centralization is expressed in the presence of the same action of the planning system both at the level of the holding and at the level of each enterprise included in the holding - uniform templates, terms of procedure, standards are used. However, modification of the planning system is required precisely to ensure end-to-end planning from top to bottom - from the holding to the enterprise, structural division, each worker, and back.

In its target form, the end-to-end planning system should ensure, without losses, the consistency and feasibility of the planned task on the one hand, and a unified understanding of the actual execution for everyone, on the other hand. The task of building an end-to-end planning system for a holding company becomes both more complex and potentially brings greater positive effects.

6 Conclusion

The development of planning theory is determined by both scientific achievements in such areas as economics, mathematics, information technology, management, and emerging industrial practices, the best and most common of which become part of the theoretical and methodological apparatus of planning. Consulting agencies and IT companies that consolidate industrial experience make a significant contribution. Changes are characterized by the development of terminology for designating newly emerging phenomena, often as a result of the synergistic effects of scientific and technological progress from several directions. The basis for today's all-consuming digitalization was laid by research in the field of cybernetics, planned economy, and linear programming. The terminological shift from algorithmization, informatization, computerization, automation to digitalization is justified from the point of view of reflecting the new industrial and economic reality.

In the future, based on the findings and identified trends, a study will be conducted in the field of sustainability and development of the planning system and the effects it generates on a holding scale, development of a mechanism for managing the life cycle of the enterprise planning system in the context of changing external and internal factors. Particular attention is expected to be paid to the issues of the relationship of the planning system with external functions in the context of a changing external environment.

The effectiveness of the creation and operation of a planning system is largely determined by the degree of compliance with the industrial environment for which the planning system is being created. As a rule, the creation of a planning system is carried out iteratively - a survey of the production environment is conducted, hypotheses are formulated about the target state of the planning system based on the application of best practices, a model of the planning system is built, this model of the planning system is tested for adequacy through coordination with customers and trial planning cycles. After a decision on the feasibility of the former planning model, it is necessary to carry out rapid implementation so that the decisions taken are relevant during the implementation period. Then the planning system must be updated and developed to consider changes in internal and external environmental factors.

The effectiveness of the internal corporate planning system based on digitalization is no longer in doubt in general. Many scientists and practitioners have paid considerable attention to the various effects resulting from the implementation and digitalization of the planning system. This study has once again confirmed the achievement of positive business results for industrial enterprises from the digitalization of the planning system, in particular: increasing the discipline of production deadlines and shipment of products to customers (just-in-time) to 99% with a simultaneous reduction in inventory by 15%, multiple increase in speed and reduction in labor intensity of planning, a significant reduction in the time for integrating new assets into the holding structure.

Today, digitalization is not only a competitive advantage, but also an urgent need to maintain the viability of an industrial enterprise. At the same time, insufficient attention is still paid to methods that would ensure the effectiveness, efficiency, speed, and frugality of the digital transformation of the planning system itself. This study makes a theoretical and applied contribution to solving these issues.

References

1. Kantorovich, L.V., Nemchinov, V.S., Novozhilov, V.V.: Lenin Prize laureates of 1965. Economics and Mathematical Methods **1**(3), 463–464 (1965)
2. Forrester, J.W.: Urban dynamics. IMR; Industrial Management Review (pre-1986) **11**(3), 67 (1970)
3. Orlicky, J.: Material requirements planning: The new way of life in production and inventory management. McGraw-Hill, New York (1975)
4. Wight, O.: MRP II: Unlocking America's productivity potential. CBI Publishing Co, Boston (1981)
5. Karlik, A.E., Belousova, L.S., Migunova, E.A.: Development of information support for planning at an industrial enterprise. Economic Revival of Russia **4**(38), 120–128 (2013)
6. Strumilin, S.G.: On criteria in optimal planning. Vopr. Ekon. **4**, 114–130 (1968)
7. Lupeikiene, A., Dzemyda, G., Kiss, F., Caplinskas, A.: Advanced planning and scheduling systems: modeling and implementation challenges. Informatica **25**(4), 581–616 (2014). https://doi.org/10.15388/Informatica.2014.31
8. Bushueva, L.I., Afanasyev, V.B.: Managing the digital transformation of the sales and operations planning process in an organization. Corporate Governance and Innovative Development of the Northern Economy: Bulletin of the Research Center for Corporate Law, Management and Venture Investment of Syktyvkar State University **4**(1), 53–64 (2024)
9. ASCM: ASCM's top 10 supply chain trends in 2024 (2024a). Retrieved 16 November 2024. from https://www.ascm.org/ascm-insights/ascms-top-10-supply-chain-trends-in-2024/
10. ASCM: The Association for Supply Chain Management (2024b). Retrieved 16 November 2024, from https://www.ascm.org/
11. Bogdanov, A.A.: Organizational science and economic planning. Proceedings of the 1st All-Russian Initiative Conference on Scientific Organization of Labor and Production (January 20–27, 1921), **1**, 8–12 (1921)
12. Kondratiev, N.D.: Problems of economic dynamics. Ekonomika, Moscow (1989)
13. Nemchinov, V.S.: Theoretical issues of inter-industry and interregional balance of production and distribution of products. Proceedings of the Scientific Conference on the Application of Mathematical Methods in Economic Research in Planning (April 4–8, 1960), Vol. 3, pp. 54–113 (1962)
14. Wallace, T.F., Stahl, R.A.: Sales & operations planning: The how-to handbook, 3rd edn. T. F. Wallace & Co., Cincinnati, OH (2008)
15. Goldratt, E.M., Cox, J.: The goal: a process of ongoing improvement. Routledge (2016). https://doi.org/10.4324/9781315270456

16. Zhang, Z., Sharifi, H.: A methodology for achieving agility in manufacturing organisations. Int. J. Oper. Prod. Manag. **20**(4), 496–513 (2000). https://doi.org/10.1108/01443570010314818
17. Gligor, D.M., Holcomb, M.C., Stank, T.P.: A multidisciplinary approach to supply chain agility: Conceptualization and scale development. J. Bus. Logist. **34**(2), 94–108 (2013). https://doi.org/10.1111/jbl.12012
18. Rahiminezhad Galankashi, M., Helmi, S.A., Abdul Rahim, A.R., Rafiei, F.M.: Agility assessment in manufacturing companies. Benchmarking: An International Journal **26**(7), 2081–2104 (2019). https://doi.org/10.1108/BIJ-10-2018-0328
19. Okongwu, U., Lauras, M., Dupont, L., Humez, V.: A decision support system for optimising the order fulfilment process. Production Planning & Control **23**(8), 581–598 (2011). https://doi.org/10.1080/09537287.2011.566230
20. Smirnova, E.V.: Evolution of enterprise planning systems, their modifications and relationship with economic development. Bulletin of Orenburg State University **8**(127), 111–121 (2011)
21. Giniyatullina, L.R., Korbanova, Ch.S., Yunusova, L.I., Burganov, R.A.: Features of planning at enterprises in the context of using digital technologies. Economics and Management: Problems, Solutions **4**(5), 50–57 (2024). https://doi.org/10.36871/ek.up.p.r.2024.05.04.007
22. Elsukov, M.Yu., Kirillova, N.N.: Formation of planning in Russia in the 1920s and modern realities. Management Consulting **12**(168), 100–112 (2022). https://doi.org/10.22394/1726-1139-2022-12-100-112
23. Khmelnitskaya, S.V.: Formation of an effective system of intra-firm planning in agro-industrial holdings. Business. Education. Law **2**(12), 106–110 (2010)
24. Evchenko, A.V.: Implementation of graphic models of information flows and document flow in systems of end-to-end production planning and operational management at enterprises. Innovative Economy: Prospects for Development and Improvement **2**(44), 95–104 (2020)
25. Gavrilov, D.A.: Production management based on the MRP2 standard, 2nd edn. Piter, St. Petersburg (2005)
26. Lukina, S.G., Sadykov, A.A., Faizullin, R.V.:. Optimization models in the SCM system: Progressive supply chain management. University Bulletin: State University of Management **8**, 116–127 (2023). https://doi.org/10.26425/1816-4277-2023-8-116-127
27. Solodovnikov, V.V.: Methodology of integrated planning of supply chains of industrial enterprises on the example of ferrous metallurgy complexes. OAO ITKOR, Moscow (2017)
28. Bozutti, D.F., Esposto, K.F.: Sales and Operations Planning: a comparison between the demand-driven and traditional approaches. Int. J. Product. Manage. Eng. **7**(1), 23–38 (2019). https://doi.org/10.4995/ijpme.2019.9469
29. Khanuja, A., Jain, R.K.: Supply chain integration: a review of enablers, dimensions and performance. Benchmarking: Int. J. **27**(1), 264–301 (2019). https://doi.org/10.1108/BIJ-07-2018-0217
30. Gartner: Manufacturing execution systems solutions reviews and rating (2024a). Retrieved 16 November 2024, from https://www.gartner.com/reviews/market/manufacturing-execution-systems
31. Gartner: Material requirements planning solutions reviews and rating (2024b). Retrieved 16 November 2024, from https://www.gartner.com/reviews/market/material-requirements-planning-mrp-software
32. Gartner: Supply chain planning solutions reviews and rating (2024c). Retrieved 16 November 2024, from https://www.gartner.com/reviews/market/supply-chain-planning-solutions
33. 1C: Project of the year (2024). Retrieved 16 November 2024, from https://eawards.1c.ru/projects/
34. Polikarpov, A.: Railway engineering of Russia, 2nd ed. (2024a). Retrieved from https://rollingstockworld.ru/wp-content/uploads/2024/06/zheleznodorozhnoe-mashinostroenie-rossii-ver.-2-2024.pdf

35. Polikarpov, A.: The world's largest rolling stock manufacturers by revenue in 2023 (2024b). Retrieved from https://rollingstockworld.ru/ekonomika/krupnejshie-mirovye-proizvoditeli-podvizhnogo-sostava-po-obemu-vyruchki-v-2023-godu/
36. Belov, S.: The world of high speeds: A review of modern trains (2024). Retrieved from https://rollingstockworld.ru/passazhirskij-ps/mir-vysokih-skorostej-obzor-sovremennyh-poezdov/
37. STM: Annual report of Joint Stock Company "Sinara - Transport Machines" on the results of work for 2023 (2024). Retrieved from https://sinaratm.ru/upload/iblock/41b/Godovoy-otchet-AO-STM-za-2023-year-for-revealing.pdf
38. Shupletsov, V.M.: Annual report of the joint-stock company "Transmashholding" for 2023 (2024). Retrieved from https://tmholding.ru/upload/iblock/02a/6uj4qvot5i818tnmo63srbxf3gj0g2nl.pdf
39. Misharin, A.S.: Information for investors of JSCSinara-Transport Machines (2021). Retrieved from https://sinaratm.ru/upload/medialibrary/cf4/prezentatsiya-dlya-investorov.pdf
40. Pozdnyakov, E.G.: Joint Stock Company "Sinara - Transport Machines" consolidated financial statements in accordance with International Financial Reporting Standards and auditor's report of the independent auditor (2023). Retrieved from https://sinaratm.ru/upload/iblock/216/STM-MSFO-2022-Auditorskoe-zaklyuchenie.pdf
41. Nesterov, A.A.: Automation of the largest transport engineering holding in Russia - Transmashholding CJSC (2021). Retrieved from https://v8.1c.ru/holding-solutions/19/

Equilibrium and Inequality: Issues of Economic Justice

Beyond Equilibrium and Disequilibrium Economics

Sara Casagrande(✉) and Bruno Dallago

Department of Economics and Management, University of Trento, Via Inama, 5, 38122 Trento, Italy
{sara.casagrande,bruno.dallago}@unitn.it

Abstract. The economic discipline moves between two opposite approaches: the orthodox economics of equilibrium and the heterodox economics of disequilibrium. While the complexity of economic phenomena reduces the explanatory power of classical mathematical modelling, attempts at realism imply descriptive analysis. An overlooked aspect is that reality is not random, as the discovery of deterministic chaos within natural and social complex systems confirms. The parts of a system do not add up, but they combine through feed-back relationships, so that the system displays an emergent and self-organizing behaviour that cannot be inferred from that of its parts. This complex behaviour is chaotic, it leads to unregular and perpetual patterns which "form" can be studied using geometric-qualitative analysis instead of the classical one, analytic and deductive. This geometric approach allows to identify harmony rather than (dis)equilibrium as the fundamental property of systems. The dynamics of capitalist systems follows a chaotic complex behaviour marked by cyclical growth, but also threatened by a lack of social harmony. Indeed, social groups interact through power relations giving often raise to drift dynamics (e.g., inequality, depletion of resources, consumerism). The article clarifies these concepts and highlights their potential for economic discipline.

Keywords: Capitalism · Chaos · Cycles · Equilibrium · System

JEL Classification: A12 · A13 · B40

1 Introduction

At the dawn of the economic discipline, two opposing conceptions of economic phenomena faced each other: the "positive, abstract and deductive" of Marginalism and the "ethical, realistic, and inductive" one carried out by the German Historical School [1, p. 9]. The contrast is known in the history of economic thought as the "battle over method" and resulted in the overwhelming victory of Marginalism.

Marginalism developed into the orthodox economics of Walrasian general equilibrium, while heterodox approaches did not develop an alternative "ethical, realistic, and inductive" approach, which was considered unscientific. Many heterodox approaches hinge on the concept of disequilibrium of a non-Walrasian economics, a concept that is anyway based on the same scientific assumptions as the Walrasian approach. What both

E. Kuzmin et al. (Eds.): EASET 2024, SPBE, pp. 87–101, 2025.
https://doi.org/10.1007/978-3-031-91159-0_6

approaches are unable to proper understand, model and predict are systemic phenomena, due to their common scientific roots. Both fail to fully understand the role that the discovery of chaos had for Newtonian mechanism, with dramatic repercussions for the understanding of economic phenomena.

The discovery of chaos occurred in an attempt to answer the 3-body problem, thus compromising the deterministic vision of the solar system. Similarly, it jeopardized also the mechanistic vision of the economic system. Order and equilibrium are not synonymous, and chaos is neither disorder nor randomness. Therefore, limiting the economic debate to equilibrium and disequilibrium is misleading, because both lack a real understanding of systemic nature. A true alternative conception must hinge on the concept of harmony. This passage is possible thanks to the systemic conception of socio-economic phenomena. Within a system, the parts combine through feed-back relationships and display a chaotic behaviour, i.e., cyclical oscillations that do not explode or fade, and never repeat themselves in identical forms. The study of systems implies a radical methodological change, because the "form" of these patterns can be studied using geometric-qualitative analysis instead of the classical analytic and deductive analysis. Moreover, a systemic vision of the economy implies also a methodological change in the study of the economic system itself: a network of social groups interacting through power relations and generating institutions.

In the second section, the paper reviews how economic theories developed around the concepts of equilibrium and disequilibrium, leaving aside the legacy of the "battle over method". The third section discusses the importance of the systemic approach and the qualitative method for economics. The fourth section analyses the implications of a systemic view of the economy, social groups and institutions. The fifth section concludes.

2 A Review of Economic Theories Between Equilibrium and Disequilibrium

2.1 The "Debate on the Method" and Its Forgotten Legacy

The Methodenstreit (the "debate on the method") opposed in the 1880s two alternative methodologies used in social sciences: the "positive, abstract and deductive" of the Austrian School founded by Carl Menger and the "ethical, realistic, and inductive" one carried out by the German Historical School (GHS), founded by Wilhelm Roscher and guided also by his fellow Gustav von Schmoller [1, p. 9]. The approach proposed by the Austrian school aimed to apply a pure deductive positivist axiomatic approach to social sciences [2]. It set the path towards methodological individualism and the reliance on supposed exact laws [3] to be identified through marginal analysis. On the contrary, the GHS promoted an inductive multidisciplinary approach that was accused to be grounded on historical empiricism without any theoretical background. The outcome of the debate was predetermined: the GHS approach was considered essentially unscientific [4] and it never became dominant anywhere [5].

The factor that determined the overwhelming victory of the Austrian school was its adherence to scientific positivism, while what led to the GHS oblivion was its presumed, yet unproved unscientific nature. Indeed, the GHS advanced a research agenda for a non-positivist scientific approach that was never adequately developed despite recent developments [6]. Schumpeter summarized Schmoller's approach by identifying some fundamental topics: the historical relativity of theoretical visions, the role of interdependence in social life, the rational and non-rational roots of economic motives, the evolutionary perspective in social dynamics, the role of an anti-mechanistic and organicist approach [7].

As Betz [4, p. 412] explains, the "organicismic metaphor involved treating society and its constituent parts like a living, growing thing [that] can be understood only in terms of this essential unity". The organicist approach, refused by Menger [8], induced Schmoller to disapprove axiomatic methods that "necessarily isolate a fragment of reality, through the ceteris paribus clause implicit in any model (including general economic equilibrium models)" [9]. Schmoller interpreted modern societies as unstable and complex characterized by class struggles and policy conflicts. These features determine the cyclical contours of social development process [7]. Schmoller refused a simplistic application of biological metaphors within human societies as a consequence of the need of "an adequate conceptualisation of human action in terms of psychological will-power, institutionalised habits and rational calculation" [7, pp. 119–120].

2.2 Walrasian and Non-Walrasian Economics

The economic discipline as a social science evolved consistently with the postulates of positivism. It sought parallels between the laws that govern nature and those that should govern society. Consequently, also mainstream economists kept Newtonian mechanics and its vision of reality as points of reference: natural (and thus social) phenomena are predictable, intrinsically stable, made of a chain of decomposable independent events [10, 11].

At the end of the nineteenth century, the Romanian mathematician and astronomer Spiru C. Haret was convinced that the difficulty of modelling social phenomena was due to "our complete ignorance of the laws which undoubtedly govern social phenomena as they do all other natural phenomena" [12, p. 815]. The belief that natural laws could govern social systems in a way similar to how they govern the solar system gave economists confidence in the possibility of identifying a general economic equilibrium. According to Vilfredo Pareto [13, p. 493] the "conception of economic aggregate finds an analogy in the conception which an astronomer has of the solar system when he has apprehended the general equations of mechanics". The same can be said for Walras's market equilibrium and many other economists [14, p. 461].

By applying the methods and metaphors of the hard sciences, economics has been purified from the sociological dimension and ethical aims. This allowed for equating market laws with natural laws, and any attempt to influence market forces has been considered harmful for the natural achievement of the social optimum.

Keynesianism is the main challenge to neoclassical marginalist theory, supported by the evidence, provided by the Great Depression in the 1930s, that no natural mechanism guarantees stability or economic growth. Keynes called into question the markets' ability to restore themself to full employment and the postulate that equilibrium is the normal state of the economy. The strength of Keynesian thought lies in its realism, the ability to show the fallacy of laissez-faire and to propose policies capable of concretely impacting employment and economic growth [15]. To this, Keynes' brilliant intuitions regarding the role of uncertainty, animal spirits, crowd behaviour and complexity (e.g., beauty contest, the fallacy of composition), must be added. These topics continue to interest economists (e.g., Schettkat [16], Chick and Jespersen [17], Morinaga [18]).

An important legacy of Keynesian thought was the development of non-Walrasian models and macroeconomics that allow to investigate allocation within imperfect markets [19]. According to some authors, Keynes's General Theory can be considered a seminal work in disequilibrium economics [20]. However, disequilibrium risks being interpreted as a temporary phenomenon that can be incorporated into a long-term equilibrium dynamic. This is exactly what happened to the dominant Keynesian theory which has been effectively adapted to Walrasian microfoundations (i.e., the new Keynesian economics) through the introduction of price and wage stickiness, imperfect competition and market failures. Garegnani identified the most serious shortfall of Keynesian analysis: "except for brief unsystematic statements we do not find in his work [of Keynes] any alternative to the orthodox long-period theory of the level of aggregate output" (see Garegnani [21, pp. 75–76]). Not even Keynes engaged in the development of a "ethical, realistic, and inductive" economic approach.

2.3 The Challenge of Economic Modelling

Despite Keynesianism, economic models appeared unable to describe the complexity of real economies. In the attempt to incorporate dynamics, heterogeneity and interaction, neoclassical economists developed a wide range of models aimed to simulate the dynamics of the exchange process (e.g., agent-based models, Applied Computable General Equilibrium (ACGE) analysis, Dynamic Stochastic General Equilibrium (DSGE)).

However, it is not clear to what extent this evolution changes the nature of neoclassical economics. According to Arthur [22, pp. 142–143] "complexity economics relaxes the assumptions of neoclassical economics [...] is neither a special case of equilibrium economics nor an addition to it. On the contrary, it is economics done in a more general way. This broadening of principles is not due to a shift in ideology. It is due, I believe, to new tools becoming available to economics".

Complexity seems to imply only the adoption of new methodologies able to make reality compatible with the postulates of optimization, equilibrium and rationality (e.g., Mauersberger and Nagel [23]). Many agent-based models, in the wake of behavioural economics, while admitting cognitive biases, still interpret human decision-making in terms of mathematical utility optimization problems with bounded rationality, instead of satisfiability problems [24] as proposed by Herbert Simon.

Those who do not follow orthodox modelling, however, often fall back on descriptive analyses. This is the case of Hyman Minsky's financial instability hypothesis [25, 26]. The lack of modelling is often interpreted as an absence of scientific rigour, despite many economists do not share this vision (e.g., Sen [27]). James Tobin accused Minsky of not providing a mathematical model which would have allowed economists to establish the endogeneity of crises and therefore the cyclical nature of the economic system. As Watkins [25, p. 158] correctly observes: "lack of a formal model, however, was intentional. [...] Minsky used such models to show that the economic process is inherently unstable".

3 The Systemic Approach and the Qualitative Method

3.1 Who is Afraid of Chaos?

Newton's mathematical modelling had a fundamental symbolic value. In particular, the proof of the stability of the solar system through the solution of a system of equations, the so-called 3-body problem, would have allowed scientists to demonstrate that the Universe is a great and perfect equilibrium governed by immutable mathematical laws. Newton represented the 3-body problem as a system of nine ordinary differential equations of the second-order to be solved. However, Newton did not solve the problem. For decades, a high number of astronomers tried to solved this "long-standing open problem" without success [28]. Henri Poincaré provided a shocking answer: there is no general solution for the 3-body problem. Indeed, a very small change in initial conditions is sufficient to provide a vast number of different possible orbits. Substantially, Poincare's attempts to solve the puzzle resulted in the discovery of chaoticity even in a simple system of equations. This is a discovery which, in addition to establishing that our solar system is a chaotic system with an unpredictable future in the very long run [29], has destroyed involuntarily many certainties of modern science.

Chaos theory seemed to confirm the intrinsic instability and unpredictability of natural complex system. All this induced many scholars to conclude that chance is the real engine of a purposeless and unpredictable nature [30]. Yet if determinism is eliminated at an ontological level, science loses its reason to exist, because determinism is essentially a vision of the world, that induces scientists to believe that phenomena have a meaning [31].

The decline of determinism was also evident within the philosophy of science and coincides with the weakening of positivism and Thomas Kuhn claim that scientific knowledge is no longer a process approaching inexorably the truth but a succession of paradigms defended by the scientific community and strongly dependent on ideologies and human decisions (see Brown [32]).

The economic discipline, with its strong political and social impact, could not admit that no theory is free from ideology. It is therefore not surprising that a waned positivism remained a desirable point of reference, despite the criticism [33], capable of showing apparent methodological rigor and ideological neutrality.

3.2 Defining Systems: the Role of Unity and Order

A system is more than the sum of its parts because it is more than a simple aggregation of units. The parts interact and this interaction is the creative force of the system, at the base of its order, because it induces the parts to become a unity with a purpose. Interactions are impulses, continuous exchanges of energy and information. These can be classified as reinforcing (positive) or balancing (negative) feedback loops. The former induces amplified changes moving the system away from its equilibrium (i.e., the system tends to explode). The latter implies a different direction of variations, dampening changes and bringing the system back to equilibrium (i.e., oscillations fade away). The coexistence of both feedback loops allows the system to survive by fluctuating, without converging towards a stable equilibrium or drifting away.

Interactions can be non-linear when the system does not respond proportionally to impulses. Systems that evolve through non-linear positive and negative loops are called complex systems and display emerging behaviour (i.e., the global behaviour cannot be inferred from the behaviour of the individual parts) and self-organization (i.e., through the spontaneous emergence of new structures and behaviours).

3.3 From Equilibrium to Harmony

Systems made up of positive and negative feedback loops are widespread in nature. Population dynamics is one of the fields of research best suited to understanding how to mathematically model these feedback relationships [34]. Populations growth and interactions dynamics can be approximated by positive and negative feedback loops and these systems can be analysed using differential equations. Population theory has a long tradition which intersects with the economic discipline [35]. According to Thomas Malthus human population grows exponentially (in geometric progression) as a consequence of the presence of only positive feedback loops, while natural resources grow in a slower arithmetic progression. Only exogenous factors (disease, famine and wars) are able to restore a balance. Darwin's evolutionary theory introduces the role of the struggle for scarce resources leading to the survival of the fittest to explain what limits the exponential growth of populations [36]. In 1838, Pierre Verhulst developed a model in which population growth is endogenously limited by competition for scarce resources. It is represented by a differential equation in which both positive and negative feedback loops are present and the dynamic depends on parameter' values (i.e., a combined rate of reproduction and mortality). Verhulst's model was overlooked for decades, until in 1976 Robert May introduced the so-called logistic map. It is a second-degree polynomial, obtained through a discretization of the logistic equation.

Along with the analytical solutions (equilibria) of the logistic equation, it is possible to analyse the "form" of the solutions using the geometric-qualitative method introduced by Poincaré, consisting of the study of the different out-of-equilibrium dynamics associated with different parameter values, through a graphical investigation of the "vector flow" [37]. According to the value of the parameter, which measures the balance between positive and negative loops, the model can diverge or be "attracted" towards particular dynamics.

This analysis demonstrates how the system displays an oscillating sinusoidal behaviour when feedback loops have balancing effects. Under certain conditions, these oscillations give way to the onset of chaos: the system oscillates, cycles do not explode, do not fade, but never repeat themselves. In other words the system generates a deterministic chaos[1], a form of chaos generating order and patterns that are scale-invariant and self-similar, the so-called fractal shapes[2].

[1] Entropic chaos, on the contrary, produce disorder without resolving into stable patterns.

[2] Fractals are geometric object in which the whole can be broken down into smaller parts, each of which echoes the whole, i.e., it is a reduced image of it [38,39]. Typical examples of fractals are the shape of cauliflower, lungs, trees, flowers, coasts, mountains, clouds, galaxies, crystals. Fractal are present also in the human body, art, architecture, music, road networks, cities and socio-economic systems [40].

The logistic equation is often used to describe the population growth dynamics of a single species. However, the case of two antagonistic populations that compete for scarce resources is even more frequent in nature. The equation is able to incapsulate the concept of coevolution: different species survive thanks to a continuous fluctuation in their populations (i.e., both avoid extinction or unlimited growth). Different variants of the prey-predator Lotka-Volterra model (a system of nonlinear differential equations of the first order) are used within social sciences (e.g., Su et al. [41], Zhang et al. [42]) and nature seems dominated by strange attractors and chaotic behaviour [43].

It is clear the difference between the classical analytic-deductive approach, which stops to the analytic solutions, and the qualitative method which studies how the "form" of the solution develops. The qualitative method is an approach of analysis situs (i.e., topology), it studies forms, i.e., morphogenesis. This geometrical approach and its strong connection with mathematics can be traced back to Leibniz [44]: "besides quantity, figure in general includes also quality and form. And as those figures are equal whose magnitude is the same, so those are similar whose form is the same. The theory of similarities or of forms lies beyond mathematics". According to the "theory of similarities", despite their different dimensions, two figures are similar if they have the same proportions. Proportions describe relationships between parts that do not add up but combine in a system. In a system, parts must be coherent and ordered to produce a harmonious unity. The concept of harmony becomes fundamental, because it is what guarantees the survival and coherence of the system. As noted by Leibniz, "harmony is when many things are reduced to some unity. For where there is no variety, there is no harmony. Conversely, where variety is without order, without proportion, there is no harmony" [45]. Harmony is a geometric, systemic and dynamic concept and therefore qualitatively superior to that of equilibrium. Harmony recalls good, well-being and beauty [46].

4 A Systemic Conception of the Economy: from Social Groups to Institutional Development

4.1 The Chaotic Dynamics of Economic Systems

Chaotic dynamics concern natural systems as well as socio-economic ones. The economic literature has made some steps in this direction (see Ribeiro and Morais [47]). Non-linear and chaotic models have been extended to the analysis of arms race and strategic behaviour [48, 49], political parties [50, 51], innovations [52], market dynamics [53], knowledge [54], investment [55] and labour markets [56].

The chaotic nature of social systems is also reflected in the presence of fractal forms. For example, fractal shapes are frequent in stock markets [57, 58]. This is because financial markets are characterized by the presence of two social groups (or populations), the bullish and bearish investors, who co-evolve and interact in a way similar to what is predicted by the Lotka-Volterra model [59].

However, the economy as a whole can also be interpreted as a system of systems within which various social group interact through power relations. Richard Goodwin tried to model the relationship between workers and producers as a prey-predator relationship (see also Dosi et al. [60]). Goodwin affirms: "it has long seemed to me that

Volterra's problem of the symbiosis of two populations – partly complementary, partly hostile – is helpful in understanding of the dynamical contradiction of capitalism" [61, p. 55].

The dynamics of the economic system is therefore the result of a complex network of systems whose interactions generate perpetual non-uniform oscillations, as already understood by Schumpeter in his conceptualization of the so-called inner vibratory system [62], a model able to generate an endogenous cyclical growth that he couldn't develop with the mathematics of his time because it was a chaotic system in which cycles generate non-identical patterns.

All this brings to mind the theories of the economic cycle, to which Schumpeter himself contributed, and which were put aside as they were incompatible with both equilibrium and disequilibrium economics after the Keynesian revolution [63].

However, it is precisely within the theory of economic cycles, and especially long waves, that it is possible to find traces of intuitions consistent with the theory of systems and complexity and that "ethical, realistic, and inductive" vision able to grasp the organic and cyclical nature of socio-economic phenomena as intuited by Schmoller. In particular, Nicolaj Dmitrievivh Kondrat'ev (also known as Kondratieff), hypothesized the endogenously cyclical nature of the capitalist economic system. From a methodological point of view, Kondrat'ev rejected exogenous causality in favour of an "organic, holistic, and non-atomistic epistemology" that "was the necessary counterpart of the reality of social processes, in which the rationality of 'human interventions' implies the creation of a greater diversity than in natural sciences" [64, p. 187]. Perez [65, p. 1] noted how "Kondrat'ev's long waves are not a strictly economic phenomenon, but rather a manifestation, measurable in economic terms, of the harmonious and non-harmonious behavior of the socio-economic and institutional system as a whole". Despite the skepticism towards long waves, various scholars continue to investigate Kondrat'ev's legacy with interesting results (see Hecht [66], Tyulin et al. [67]).

4.2 Social Groups, Power Relations and the Genesis of Institutions

The dynamics of systems are not generated by the interaction between rational and optimizing individuals but between populations of individuals, social groups, who belong to communities (e.g., workers and capitalists as in Goodwin [61]). Adam Smith was among the first to understand the importance of analysing economic phenomena in terms of interaction between social groups: "The workmen desire to get as much, the masters to give as little as possible. [...] In the long-run, the workman may be as necessary to his master as his master is to him; but the necessity is not so immediate" [68, pp. 83–84].

Smith was not interested in the behaviour of an anonymous and ahistorical *homo oeconomicus* but in the components of precise social groups: workmen, farmers, masters and merchants; and the power relationships among them. These are "ideal-typical actors", coherently with Max Weber who defined them as "'average' member[s] of a social stratum [...] not concrete human beings but ideal types" [69, pp. 39–40]. Karl Marx also showed little sympathy for *homo oeconomicus* and his most famous literary metaphor (i.e., Robinson Crusoe economics), he labelled as a "Robinsonade" [70]. Marx believed that "Economic categories are only the theoretical expressions, the abstractions of the social relations of production" [71, p. 109].

These “ideal-typical actors” are distinguished not by their consumption preferences but on the basis of their social role, which depends on the relationship with the product of their working activity and the power relations with other social groups. Economic categories change with the evolution of economic systems. However, what changes is not the relationship with the product of the working activity, but the type of relationship between social groups. In the capitalist system, this unbalanced competition extends to all social groups. It is a dense network of prey-predator relationships with different degrees of imbalance which, not surprisingly, give rise to cyclical economic fluctuations.

The focus on social groups and “ideal-typical actors” assumes that people are influenced by the institutional and cultural context and are often forced to adapt to collective behaviour. Different types of behaviour (conformism, imitation etc.) are not irrational, but make sense within systems (the so-called combinatory systems) that are the basis of an infinite number of social and natural self-organization phenomena: from flocks of birds to applause, from speculative bubbles to bank runs (see Mella [72]).

Some social self-organization phenomena can generate habits and conventions which can become the base of a spontaneous social order [73, 74]. Let’s think about how a path is formed in the woods. By chance one person leaves a trail, but if many other people follow the same trail, it will form a path. If this path, the result of an emergent behaviour, is considered useful, it could be marked on the maps, in a certain sense it is institutionalized: “preserved in the environment with suitable strengthening actions because it is held to be useful” [72, p. 47].

Also agent-based simulations are concerned with investigating the nature of similar emerging phenomena, such as in the case of traffic rules. According to Hodgson and Knudsen [75] drivers’ habit to drive on a particular side of the road is a random phenomenon. However, this habit becomes a self-stabilizing convention that constrains drivers’ behaviour. This result induced Hodgson and Knudsen [75] to recognize that conventions are not uniquely the result of rational calculations, as supposed by mainstream literature.

4.3 Beyond Biological Metaphors: Social Harmony and the Role of Ethics

There is a substantial difference between the self-organizing phenomena that emerge in the animal world and those that emerge in the human context. Animals do not reason while people react to self-emerging phenomena [76]. Only emerging phenomena considered “good” for society are institutionalized. Consequently, emerging social phenomena do not automatically guarantee social harmony (i.e., peaceful coexistence of social groups based on social justice). Adam Smith first addressed this issue. His metaphor of the “invisible hand” clearly demonstrates his awareness of the systemic nature of the economy and its self-organizing properties. Smith was certain not only of the efficiency of the invisible hand but also of its virtue as a consequence of peoples’ “moral sentiments” and “sympathy” [77]. According to Smith, people first search well-being in their socio-economic relations, a personal inner equilibrium. This implies that there is a “bargaining in feelings” that precede and influence the following economic bargaining in prices, so that the baker and the butcher are looking for the “right price” that allows them to preserve dignity [78]. This “moral tuning” [79] leads to social harmony, that Smith describes using a musical metaphor: “[a person] that desires a more complete sympathy [...] must flatten, if I may be allowed to say so, the sharpness of its natural tone, in order to reduce it to harmony and concord with the emotions of those who are about him" [77, p. 22].

Smith changed various times his opinion about what guarantees the domain of sympathy and thus social harmony. First, he thought to Providence, then to natural theology by postulating an inner tendency towards emotional balance, encapsulating "harmony doctrine" [80] into the doctrine of progress [81]. Stating that nature guarantees moral tuning was certainly one of Smith's most ambiguous passages. Indeed, it paves the way for the elimination of the ethical dimension [78] and for the legitimation of selfishness as a promoter of public virtues.

Economic reality is full of examples in which emerging behaviour does not guarantee harmony. Modern capitalism contains various sub-systems dominated by trajectories that tend towards infinity, and which are therefore unsustainable, i.e. not harmonious. Mella [72] reports many examples, including economic ones, in which social systems lead to unsustainable emerging global behaviours which are not the result of irrationality and which are therefore difficult to correct without an ethical approach (see also the "paradox of incentives" [82]). For example, within competitive markets, enterprises are forced to increase productivity and induce people to buy more and more products. Although this behaviour is rational, at an aggregate level it can be harmful in terms of future exhaustion of resources, progressive pollution and consumerism.

5 Conclusions

Neither equilibrium nor disequilibrium economics seem to capture the systemic nature of the economy, with serious consequences both for a correct understanding of economic phenomena and for an adequate modelling of the same. The systemic vision allows to overcome the interpretation of the economic system as a set of (more or less) rational agents to focus on the feedback relationships, power relations, that exist within and between social groups. The economy therefore, is interpreted as a complex system capable of generating chaotic dynamics, i.e., cyclical growth. Although chaos and systems theory are commonly accepted today, it is often ignored that they allow us to grasp order within both natural and social systems.

The order of chaotic natural systems produces harmony, that is, a consonance between the components that generate the unity of the system through proportionate and coherent relationships. Poincaré, on the footstep of Leibniz's thought, introduce a geometric-qualitative method able to grasp the "form" of phenomena in the sense of the internal harmony between the parts (see Stump [83]).

This harmony, this beauty, this good, in economic terms correspond not only to the surprising ability of markets to make millions of economic actors interact, produce and progress but, more importantly, to concepts such as well-being, social justice and sustainability. The capitalist development has demonstrated that the natural tendency towards social harmony has been undermined by individual selfishness and the interests of various social groups poorly suited to a search for rebalancing and reach sustainable trajectories. The harmony of natural systems can be compromised by human choices in the socio-economic field, which makes the need of ethics evident.

This systemic approach to the study of the economic discipline is consistent with that "ethical, realistic, and inductive" approach evoked by Schmoller. It is consistent also with modern science, which has long since overcome that positivistic approach so unsuitable for understanding the complexity of reality, be it astronomical (like the solar system) or socio-economic.

References

1. Keynes, J.N.: The scope and method of political economy. Macmillan and Co, London (1897)
2. Boettke, P.J.: Libertarianism and the Austrian School of Economics. In: Zwolinski, M., Ferguson, B. (eds.) The Routledge Companion to Libertarianism, pp. 502–517. Routledge, New York (2022). https://doi.org/10.4324/9780367814243-41
3. Louzek, M.: The battle of methods in economics: The classical Methodenstreit—Menger vs. Schmoller. American Journal of Economics and Sociology **70**(2), 439–463 (2011). https://doi.org/10.1111/j.1536-7150.2011.00780.x
4. Betz, H.K.: How does the German historical school fit? History of Political Economy **20**(3), 409–430 (1988). https://doi.org/10.1215/00182702-20-3-409
5. Schumpeter, J.A.: History of economic analysis. Routledge, London (1954 [1987])
6. Gioia, V.: Economic growth and social sustainability: How useful can it be to go back to the research programme of the German Historical School? In: Meramveliotakis, G., Manioudis, M. (eds.) Sustainable Economic Development, pp. 53–80. Routledge, London (2024). https://doi.org/10.4324/9781003349402-7
7. Ebner, A.: The institutional analysis of entrepreneurship: Historist aspects of Schumpeter's development theory. In: Backhaus, J. (ed.) Joseph Alois Schumpeter: Entrepreneurship, Style and Vision, pp. 117–139. Kluwer Academic Publishers, Dordrecht (2003). https://doi.org/10.1007/0-306-48082-4_4
8. Matson, E.W.: Ethical economics or economical ethics? Considerations out of Carl Menger. The Review of Austrian Economics **36**, 311–330 (2023). https://doi.org/10.1007/s11138-022-00596-7
9. D'Ippoliti, C.: Schmoller's method as a critique and alternative to marginalist economics: A comment to Louzek. Am. J. Econ. Sociol. **72**(2), 319–328 (2013). https://doi.org/10.1111/ajes.12012
10. Ekeland, I.: The best of all possible worlds: Mathematics and destiny. University of Chicago Press, Chicago (2006)
11. Zhang, W.B.: Chaos, complexity, and nonlinear economic theory. World Scientific, Singapore (2023). https://doi.org/10.1142/13173
12. Ward, L.F.: Review: two books on social mechanics. Am. J. Sociol. **18**(6), 814–819 (1913). https://doi.org/10.1086/212162
13. Pareto, V.: The new theory of economics. J. Polit. Econ. **5**, 485–502 (1897). https://doi.org/10.1086/250454
14. Hollander, S.: On P. Mirowski's 'Physics and the "Marginalist Revolution"'. Cambridge Journal of Economics **13**(3), 459–470 (1989). https://doi.org/10.1093/oxfordjournals.cje.a035104
15. Dillard, D.: The pragmatic basis of Keynes's political economy. J. Econ. Hist. **6**(2), 121–152 (1946). https://doi.org/10.1017/S0022050700056904
16. Schettkat, R.: The behavioral economics of John Maynard Keynes: Microfoundations for the world we live in. Edward Elgar, Cheltenham (2022). https://doi.org/10.4337/9781802204896
17. Chick, V., Jespersen, J.: Holism and the fallacy of composition in macroeconomics. In: Jespersen, J., Chick, V., Tieben, B. (eds.) Routledge Handbook of Macroeconomic Methodology, pp. 54–63. Routledge, New York (2023). https://doi.org/10.4324/9781315745992-7

18. Morinaga, N.: Between probability and animal spirits: Reading Keynes. In: Urai, K., Katsuragi, M., Takeuchi, Y. (eds.) Realism for Social Sciences. Translational Systems Sciences, Vol. 36, pp. 37–66. Springer, Singapore (2023). https://doi.org/10.1007/978-981-99-4153-7_3
19. d'Autume, A.: Non-Walrasian equilibria and macroeconomics. In: Barrère, A. (ed.) The Foundations of Keynesian Analysis. Keynesian Studies, pp. 66–92. London: Palgrave Macmillan (1988). https://doi.org/10.1007/978-1-349-08062-5_4
20. Ogawa, S.: Survey of non-Walrasian disequilibrium economic theory. Munich Personal RePEc Archive, MPRA Paper No. 116798 (2022). https://mpra.ub.uni-muenchen.de/116798/
21. Garegnani, P.: Two routes to effective demand: Comment on Kregel. In: Kregel, J. (ed.) Distribution, Effective Demand and International Economic Relations, pp. 69–80. Macmillan, London (1983)
22. Arthur, W.B.: Foundations of complexity economics. Nature Reviews Physics **3**, 136–145 (2021). https://doi.org/10.1038/s42254-020-00273-3
23. Mauersberger, F., Nagel, R.: Levels of reasoning in Keynesian beauty contests: A generative framework. In: Hommes, C., LeBaron, B. (eds.) Handbook of Computational Economics, Vol. 4, pp. 541–634. North-Holland, Amsterdam (2018). https://doi.org/10.1016/bs.hescom.2018.05.002
24. Kao, Y.F., Velupillai, K.V.: Behavioural economics: Classical and modern. The European J. History of Econ. Thought **22**(2), 236–271 (2013). https://doi.org/10.1080/09672567.2013.792366
25. Watkins, J.P.: The origins and evolution of consumer capitalism: A Veblenian-Keynesian perspective. Routledge, New York (2023). https://doi.org/10.4324/9780429443763
26. Fazzari, S., Ferri, P., Greenberg, E.: Cash flow, investment, and Keynes-Minsky cycles. J. Econ. Behav. Organ. **65**(3–4), 555–572 (2008). https://doi.org/10.1016/j.jebo.2005.11.007
27. Sen, A.: Description as choice. Oxf. Econ. Pap. **32**(3), 353–369 (1980). https://doi.org/10.1093/oxfordjournals.oep.a041484
28. Kol, B.: Natural dynamical reduction of the three-body problem. Celest. Mech. Dyn. Astron. **135**(29), 1–30 (2023). https://doi.org/10.1007/s10569-023-10144-5
29. Cordani, B.: But to what extent is a solar system stable? In: Cordani, B. (ed.) Geography of Order and Chaos in Mechanics: Investigations of Quasi-Integrable Systems with Analytical, Numerical, and Graphical Tools, pp. 329–356. Springer, Cham (2024). https://doi.org/10.1007/978-3-031-72226-4_10
30. Monod, J.: Chance and necessity: Essay on the natural philosophy of modern biology. Random House, New York (1971)
31. Amaldi, U.: Le idee della fisica. Zanichelli, Bologna (2001)
32. Brown, H.I.: Perception, theory, and commitment: The new philosophy of science. University of Chicago Press, Chicago (1979)
33. Drakopoulos, S.A.: Value judgments, positivism and utility comparisons in economics. J. Bus. Ethics **189**(3), 423–437 (2024). https://doi.org/10.1007/s10551-023-05395-z
34. Berryman, A.A.: Principles of population dynamics and their application. Taylor & Francis, New York (2020). https://doi.org/10.1201/9781003062790
35. Rodriguez-Gonzalez, P.T., Rico-Martinez, R., Rico-Ramirez, V.: Effect of feedback loops on the sustainability and resilience of human-ecosystems. Ecol. Model. **426**, 109018 (2020). https://doi.org/10.1016/j.ecolmodel.2020.109018
36. Herbert, S.: Darwin, Malthus, and selection. J. Hist. Biol. **4**(1), 209–217 (1971). https://doi.org/10.1007/BF00356983
37. Cristallini, A.: Ordine, disordine, caos: Determinismo e causalità nella scienza. Tab Edizioni, Roma (2022)
38. Mandelbrot, B.B.: Fractals: Form, chance, and dimension. Freeman, San Francisco (1977)
39. Mandelbrot, B.B., Hudson, R.L.: The (mis)behavior of markets: A fractal view of risk, ruin, and reward. Basic Books, New York (2004)

40. West, G.: Scale: The universal laws of growth, innovation, sustainability, and the pace of life in organisms, cities, economies, and companies. Penguin Press, New York (2017)
41. Su, Y., Yan, Y., Liu, C.: Symbiosis evolution of regional knowledge innovation ecosystem: The relevance of Lotka-Volterra model. Science, Technology and Society **29**(3), 373–396 (2024). https://doi.org/10.1177/09717218241232857
42. Zhang, N., Shi, S., Li, Z.: Constructrons of symbiosis system for rural industry revitalization based on Lotka-Volterra model and stability study. Journal of Grey System **36**(4), 33–55 (2024)
43. Hastings, A., Hom, C.L., Ellner, S., Turchin, P., Godfray, H.C.J.: Chaos in ecology: Is mother nature a strange attractor? Annu. Rev. Ecol. Syst. **24**(1), 1–33 (1993). https://doi.org/10.1146/annurev.es.24.110193.000245
44. Leibniz, G.W.: What is an idea? In: Loemker, L.E. (ed.) Philosophical Papers and Letters. The New Synthese Historical Library, Vol. 2, pp. 207–208. Springer, Dordrecht (1989). https://doi.org/10.1007/978-94-010-1426-7_22
45. Lomas, J.D., Xue, H.: Harmony in design: A synthesis of literature from classical philosophy, the sciences, economics, and design. The Journal of Design, Economics, and Innovation **8**(1), 5–64 (2022). https://doi.org/10.1016/j.sheji.2022.01.001
46. Poincaré, H.: Mathematical creation. Monist **20**(3), 321–335 (1910). https://doi.org/10.5840/monist19102037
47. Ribeiro, S., Morais, H.: The paradigms of complexity and chaos and the economy: Some evidence and clues. In: Erçetin, Ş.Ş., Açıkalın, Ş.N., Tomé, L. (eds.) Chaos, Complexity, and Leadership 2023, pp. 57–67. Springer, Cham (2024). https://doi.org/10.1007/978-3-031-64265-4_4
48. Saperstein, A.M.: Chaos – a model for the outbreak of war. Nature **309**, 303–305 (1984). https://doi.org/10.1038/309303a0
49. Founta, K., Zachilas, L.: Mathematical modeling of strategic behavior: The Battle of Midway, 1942. The Journal of Defense Modeling and Simulation (2023). https://doi.org/10.1177/15485129231160182
50. Brown, C.: Politics and the environment: Nonlinear instabilities dominate. American Political Science Review **88**(2), 292–303 (1994). https://doi.org/10.2307/2944704
51. Guirao, J.L.G., Alsulami, M., Baskonus, H.M., Ilhan, E., Veeresha, P.: Analysis of nonlinear compartmental model using a reliable method. Math. Comput. Simul. **214**, 133–151 (2023). https://doi.org/10.1016/j.matcom.2023.07.001
52. Lian, C., Pei, J., Zheng, S., Li, B.: How does trade policy uncertainty affect green innovation in the USA and China? A nonlinear perspective. Environ. Sci. Pollut. Res. **31**(13), 19615–19634 (2024). https://doi.org/10.1007/s11356-024-31954-6
53. Liu, D., Gao, X., An, H., Jia, N., Wang, A.: Exploring market instability of global lithium resources based on chaotic dynamics analysis. Resour. Policy **88**, 104373 (2024). https://doi.org/10.1016/j.resourpol.2023.104373
54. Shi, Y., Cao, H., Chen, S.: Order and disorder in the evolution of online knowledge community: An investigation of the chaotic behavior in social tagging systems with evidence of Stack Overflow. Aslib J. Inf. Manag. **76**(1), 132–152 (2024). https://doi.org/10.1108/AJIM-08-2022-0353
55. Mourelle, E., Cuestas, J.C.: Investment dynamics in central and eastern Europe: A nonlinear approach. Post-Communist Econ. **35**(5), 496–512 (2023). https://doi.org/10.1080/14631377.2023.2209296
56. Law, C.H., Law, S.H.: The non-linear impacts of innovation on unemployment: Evidence from panel data. Int. J. Financ. Econ. **29**(1), 402–424 (2024). https://doi.org/10.1002/ijfe.2691
57. Mandelbrot, B.B.: A multifractal walk down Wall Street. Sci. Am. **280**(4), 70–73 (1999). https://doi.org/10.1038/scientificamerican0299-70

58. Goyal, R.: Exploring the fractal geometry of financial time series. Modern Dynamics: Mathematical Progressions **1**(1), 1–5 (2024). https://doi.org/10.36676/mdmp.v1.i1.01
59. Plummer, T.: Forecasting financial markets: The psychology of successful investing, 6th edn. Kogan Page, London (2009)
60. Dosi, G., Usula, D., Virgillito, M.E.: Increasing returns and labor markets in a predator–prey model. J. Evol. Econ. **34**, 375–402 (2024). https://doi.org/10.1007/s00191-024-00861-x
61. Goodwin, R.M.: A growth cycle. In: Feinstein, C.H. (ed.) Socialism, Capitalism, and Economic Growth: Essays Presented to Maurice Dobb, pp. 54–58. Cambridge University Press, Cambridge (1967)
62. Louçã, F.: Intriguing pendula: founding metaphors in the analysis of economic fluctuations. Camb. J. Econ. **25**(1), 25–55 (2001). https://doi.org/10.1093/cje/25.1.25
63. Tarascio, V.J.: Kondratieff's theory of long cycles. Atl. Econ. J. **16**(4), 1 (1988). https://doi.org/10.1007/BF02304218
64. Louçã, F.: Nikolai Kondratiev and the early consensus and dissensions about history and statistics. History of Political Economy **31**(1), 169–205 (1999). https://doi.org/10.1215/00182702-31-1-169
65. Perez, C.: Structural change and assimilation of new technologies in the economic and social system. Futures **15**(5), 357–375 (1983). https://doi.org/10.1016/0016-3287(83)90050-2
66. Hecht, J.: Are long waves 50 years? Reexamining economic and financial long wave periodicities in Kondratieff and Schumpeter. Review of Political Economy, 1–35 (2023). https://doi.org/10.1080/09538259.2023.2280803
67. Tyulin, A.E., Chursin, A.A., Ragulina, J.V., Akberdina, V.V., Yudin, A.V.: The development of Kondratieff's theory of long waves: the place of the AI economy humanization in the 'competencies-innovations-markets' model. Humanities and Soc. Sci. Comm. **10**(1), 1–13 (2023). https://doi.org/10.1057/s41599-022-01434-8
68. Smith, A.: An inquiry into the nature and causes of the wealth of nations. Liberty Press, Indianapolis (1776 [1981]). https://doi.org/10.1093/oseo/instance.00043218
69. Rosenberg, M.M.: Generally intended meaning, the 'average' actor, and Max Weber's interpretive sociology. Max Weber Studies **13**(1), 39–63 (2013). https://doi.org/10.1353/max.2013.a808750
70. Karagöz, U.: The neoclassical robinson: antecedents and implications. History of Economic Ideas **22**(2), 75–100 (2014)
71. Marx, K.: The poverty of philosophy. International Publishers, New York (1847 [1979])
72. Mella, P.: The combinatory systems theory: Understanding, modeling and simulating collective phenomena. Springer, Cham, Switzerland (2017). https://doi.org/10.1007/978-3-319-54805-0
73. Ashford, N.: Principles for a free society, 2nd edn. Jarl Hjalmarson Foundation, Institute for Humane Studies, Stockholm, Sweden (2001)
74. Roos, M.: Self-organization. In: Roos, M. (ed.) Principles of Complexity Economics, pp. 339–418. Classroom Companion: Economics. Springer, Cham (2024). https://doi.org/10.1007/978-3-031-51436-4_8
75. Hodgson, G., Knudsen, T.: The complex evolution of a simple traffic convention: The functions and implications of habit. J. Econ. Behav. Organ. **54**(1), 19–47 (2004). https://doi.org/10.1016/j.jebo.2003.04.001
76. Gilbert, N.: Simulation: An emergent perspective. New Technologies in the Social Sciences Conference. Bournemouth, UK (1995)
77. Smith, A.: The theory of moral sentiments. Bohn's Standard Library, London (1759 [1853]). https://doi.org/10.1093/oseo/instance.00042831
78. Bee, M.: Introduzione. In: Smith, A. (ed.) Economia dei sentimenti, pp. 5–37. Donzelli Editore, Rome (2011)

79. Sivertsen, S.S., Halstead, J., Slaattelid, R.T.: Moral tuning. Metaphilosophy **49**(4), 435–458 (2018). https://doi.org/10.1111/meta.12319
80. Lynn, A.: Ethics, economics, and the specter of naturalism: the enduring relevance of the harmony doctrine school of economics. J. Bus. Ethics **178**(3), 661–673 (2022). https://doi.org/10.1007/s10551-021-04819-y
81. Kim, K.: Adam Smith: natural theology and its implications for his method of social inquiry. Rev. Soc. Econ. **55**(3), 312–336 (1997). https://doi.org/10.1080/00346769700000003
82. Tamvada, J.P., Chowdhury, R.: The irrationality of rationality in market economics: a paradox of incentives perspective. Bus. Soc. **62**(3), 482–487 (2023). https://doi.org/10.1177/00076503221101888
83. Stump, D.: Henri Poincaré's philosophy of science. Stud. History and Philosop. Sci. Part A **20**(3), 335–363 (1989). https://doi.org/10.1016/0039-3681(89)90011-3

Justice and Efficiency: Economic Development Criteria

Maria Nosova(✉) and Nikolay Tyukavkin

Samara National Research University, 34 Moskovskoe Shosse, Samara 443086, Russia
maria0301nosova@yandex.ru

Abstract. Striking a balance between justice and efficiency is an urgent problem of modern social and economic policy. Thus, the aim of this research is to determine the interrelation of categories "justice", "efficiency" and economic development government ensuring and to suggest ways of their application in the system of public finance management improvement. The paper analyses the main concepts of justice, their development key trends and reveals various points of view on the "justice-efficiency" correlation in different social systems. The hypothesis of unidirectional positive intercorrelation of these categories and economic development is confirmed with the help of classification methods. Within the framework of the "Value for money" concept, an interpretation of efficiency criteria is suggested. The prospectives of introducing dual "equity" criterion and its indicators in the state program-targeted budget planning are observed. Authors also conclude that fair and productive government spending shares can be a criterion for identifying the type of country's economic development along with financial system efficiency indicators. The article highlights the limitations, such as inflation risk and fiscal dominance long-term negative consequences, which should be taken into account when the efficiency of fair budget policy for sustainable economic development is estimated.

Keywords: Justice · Efficiency · Economic development · Fiscal policy

JEL Classification: D63 · C55 · P43

1 Introduction

Justice is one of the fundamental categories, the views on which determine the key postulates of many social development concepts. The subjectivity of justice determines the plurality of interpretations of this term, which makes it difficult to choose the most appropriate one and, at the same time, increases the importance and necessity of this choice in order to organize public life in all its fields, including economics.

Efficiency can be presented as a category that contradicts the principles of justice. Due to the fact that modern behavioural economics is based on the expectations of economic agents, which are not always rational, and people rely on intellectual simplifications and fall into cognitive traps, the problem of defining the justice and efficiency terms,

E. Kuzmin et al. (Eds.): EASET 2024, SPBE, pp. 102–121, 2025.
https://doi.org/10.1007/978-3-031-91159-0_7

their correlation and role in the process of economic development becomes especially relevant in order to reduce the risk of manipulation and substitution of meanings.

The goals of justice and efficiency may coincide. Government policy fairness increasing helps to achieve its efficiency and vice versa, when the policy goals are fair. However, taking into account resource shortage, striking the right balance between efficient resource allocation and fair access to services can be challenging. Hence, the purpose of this research is to determine the interrelation of categories "justice", "efficiency" and economic development government ensuring and to suggest ways of their application in the system of public finance management improvement. The authors have analyzed the works of scientists in the fields of philosophy and economics, such as I. Kant, A. Smith, F. Dessauer, B. Russell, J. Rawls, R. Nozick, A. Sen, raised the question of equity (justice), efficiency and development intercorrelation.

2 Justice and Efficiency in Philosophy and Economy

2.1 The Problem of Justice Defining

The interpretation of the concept of justice depends on whether it can be applied to a subject or an object and, consequently, which subject can be called the bearer of justice or which object can be characterized as "fair".

Confucianism considers justice ("義") as the main characteristic of the Confucian ideal of a man - a "noble man". Justice is expressed by the unity of true knowledge and due deed [1]. Correlation between "due" and some social role distinguishes the concept of "義" from justice in its general (broadest) sense. "義" accepts and justifies inequality based on a distribution of duties and functions that preserves social order. "義" does not depend on sympathy, respect, morality, being, according to Mencius, the supreme value [2]. At the same time, justice comes from human nature, inherent in it (in contrast to Gaozu theory of the human nature neutrality). In Ancient Chinese philosophy following justice and ritual as an external expression of "義" ensures the state prosperity [3]. Justice can also be a measure of resources allocation, which are a reward for the functions (duties) performed, taking into account provided opportunities (Sun-Tzu) or showed talents (Mencius). "義" is intended to restrain humanity in resource constraints. Allocation in accordance with justice contributes to the social cohesion and development. According to Moists, there is a certain opposition between the "due", predetermined by fate, and justice, requiring a person to make wise decisions, and origins should not be a criterion of the functions and opportunities distribution. In Taoism justice comes from Heaven and is opposed to human nature.

In Antiquity the understanding of "fair" as corresponding to the original order, along with the possibility, necessity and inevitability of justice restoring, also shows the higher order of the "justice" in comparison with social justice in Ancient Chinese Confucian and Moist philosophy. According to Anaximander, justice is considered as recompense, injustice violate natural world order. Avoiding the social context of justice excluded humanity as a justice principle, attributing the natural character to this category. Early pre-Socratics' understanding of justice as recompense presupposes the dichotomy "justice-injustice", which is contrary to the natural character of justice. Injustice is perceived by the pre-Socratics as a violation of some "ideal", not natural state of nature or society, which is considered fair. This contradiction is resolved with the help of giving by Parmenide the status of embodiment of truth to the just social law, with the acceptance of which it is possible to speak of injustice as a temporary phenomenon inevitably followed by the restoration of justice.

According to Pythagoras, justice is equal recompense for equal and comes from the gods, as well as laws. Heraclitus endowed justice with a broader meaning: the struggle of justice in the narrow sense with injustice is the motive power of movement, a necessary natural process, in the harmony of which lies cosmic justice. According to the Sophists, justice is relative and conditional, determined by human [3]. Justice becomes a more social category, loses its natural character. According to Socrates (like Mencius), true knowledge is already contained in a human.

Socrates and his followers recognised the existence of injustice, believing that, like everything in the world, justice arises from its opposite and turns into it when it is destroyed. Plato considered justice in two aspects - as a state of the soul, which is under the reason control and as a universal principle of recompense for deeds in the next rebirths (total justice). In "The State" Plato analyses a third aspect of this category - justice in the polis, where everyone acts in fulfilment of his natural purpose and occupies a corresponding social position depending on his proximity to the "idea of the good" [4]. According to Aristotle, justice and injustice are social categories. Aristotle distinguishes commutative and distributive justice. Like Socrates, Aristotle gives the state law the status of the measure of justice and names a public good justice, which serves the common good. The understanding of justice as utility is found both in the philosophy of Ancient China and in Ancient philosophy.

According to Epicurus, the result of justice is serenity [5], and extrapolating this statement to society and state, the result of social justice is social stability. According to Stoics (Zeno) justice is "reasoning in matters of allocation" [3]. Some philosophers noted the natural character of justice as allocation on merit (Marcus Aurelius), others - the necessity of establishing justice by human [6]. The Stoics' categories of justice and injustice implicate the notion that agents cause each other's benefit or harm [7]. The subjectivity and relativity of justice, its social nature was noted by Pyrrhon, Enesidemus, Plotinus and Origen.

This mindset expanded in the Middle Ages. The idea of "poetic justice" as an inevitable recompense on merit is transformed and replaced by the principle of the interrelation between divine grace and divine predestination (Augustine). The incommensurability of human merit and divine grace, the impossibility of human cognition of divine truth determine the inexplicability of the grace distribution basis and the agnosticism of justice. To overcome this problem, Thomas Aquinas divides four kinds of law: eternal, divine, natural, and human [8]. The idea of total, social and individual justice dividing becomes relevant again.

Scholastics, expanding Aristotle's theory, consider economic relations through the prism of compliance with the principles of equal exchange and fair distribution. Renaissance philosophers emphasised individual justice (achieved through creativity) and social justice (equality of opportunities for creativity) [9]. Justice becomes achievable. The principle of wealth distribution is changing, and More and Campanella raise a question of private property abolishment. Need-based distribution of goods, the absence of class divisions, a democratic political regime and freedom of religion become the new principles of justice.

The transition from the medieval elitist concept of justice to the egalitarian concept of social equity continued in the philosophy of the New Age. In F.Bacon's philosophy justice becomes more primary than law. The basis of justice is individual person's sovereignty [10]. The philosopher considers the concept of "justice" as the combination of the Ancient Chinese "humanity" and the "義", which is not the equivalent reactivity of behaviour, but its compliance with the due. The New Age recognises the subjectivism of justice.

The identification of a human being as a subject leads to the humanisation not only of justice itself, but also of its source. Justice becomes a strictly social phenomenon, and the norms of justice are established by society on the basis of its own ideas about reciprocity and equality of recompense. Bacon's concept of justice presupposes the natural equity of the members of society, which implies taking into account and levelling social inequity. The concept of natural law (Hobbes, Locke) links the institution of the state and the category "justice", which is increasingly used in the legal context. Since the opportunities and basis for property obtaining changes, the law protection of property in the framework of a social contract or agreement (D.Hume) becomes the basis of justice.

Pascal, supported justice and state coercion interrelation, separates justice from the truth and associate it with a certain positive effect. Leibniz distinguishes between universal justice (the principle "to live honestly") and particularistic justice, which includes distributive justice (the principle "to each his own") and commutative justice (the principle "not to harm others") [11].

According to I. Kant, the criterion of justice is the universality and acceptability of an act's principle-justification. Helvetius considered it fair to reduce the disproportion in property distribution by guaranteeing a minimum amount of goods.

A. Smith separates legal justice from fairness. Smith accepts the concept of total divine (sacral) justice and, at the same time, considers justice as an innate human feeling [12]. A. Smith considers the factor of luck, talking about fairness and legal justice, highlights the problem of intentionality of an act and risk assessment.

Modern philosophy has continued some justice concepts of the New Age. Marx, highlighting the social character and source of justice denies justice as a moral category and applies the term "fair price", presupposing the existence of commutative justice [13]. The idea of justice, according to Popper, is generated by the desire for finding something rational in the world and for understanding it [14]. Nowadays justice is connected with the cognisability of the world and is as possible as the world is cognizable. This thesis reveals a divergence between modern philosophy and the nature- and theocentric philosophy of Ancient and Medieval, according to which world's justice is aprioristic, taken on faith, and social justice is idealized, as a reflection of the supreme total justice, and can be established by tradition or law. Formerly Socrates made a thesis that virtue (justice) is based on knowledge and understanding [15]. Dessauer notes, that justice as an ideal value is not a scale, measuring fairness. He talks about the necessity to distinguish individual justice along with total and social justice. Considering Dessauer's thesis of pursuit of justice as one of the imperatives of the human soul, it should be noted that its interpretation depends on the discussing paradigm. In other words, when individual and social justice are not a reflection of some ideal justice, and assessment scales of each type of justice are different, both the goals and the results of the idea of justice realisation should be distinguished. It is a problem not only of philosophy and sociology, but also of economics and politics. Since the same act can be recognised as fair and unfair in different paradigms of justice, it is difficult to find the common essence (the idea) of justice and (according to B. Russell) justice as impartiality in action [16]. According to Keynes, justice is not so much in equality as in impartial evaluation, and fair prices are those which help to evaluate accurately talents and efforts (meritocracy).

In the concept of J. Rawls, justice is understood as fairness, has a restrictive (similar to Hegel's theory) rather than purposeful character, assign "the permissible forms of life" [13]. Justice is ensured by impartiality and rationality of decisions [17]. In order to find a universal idea of good, shared by all citizens and therefore suitable for political purposes, it is necessary to formulate the idea of rational benefit within the political concept [18]. Rawls recognises social equity as a key moral requirement. However, establishing the correlation of the principles of justice as fairness, he defines the following sequence in descending order of priority: liberty equality, equality of opportunities, social equity (Pareto efficiency).

R.Nozick questions Rawls's idea of distributive justice, concerning the redistribution of factor incomes in order to smooth social inequality. If the distribution (appropriation) of production factors is fair, redistribution is a violation of the owners' rights and liberties, or fair distribution (appropriation) of production factors can lead to unfair distribution of factor incomes [19]. Can unfair distribution (appropriation) of production factors result in fair distribution of factor incomes? Does commutative injustice always lead to distributive injustice? Does distributive justice take precedence over commutative justice?

It seems that the contradiction of Rawls's concept is that, being liberal (establishing liberty priority) and at the same time deontological (the goal is compliance with the principles of proper behaviour in the Kantian tradition) rather than teleological (utilitarianism), it accepts the adjustment of the results of commutative justice action (even when it is proper) through redistribution for distributive justice purposes. Commutative justice is prioritised and "a distribution is fair if it legally derives from another fair distribution" [19]. If the historical principle of justice is not respected (commutative justice violation), distributive justice becomes impossible, but if this principle is respected, redistribution is unfair.

Rawls defends the idea of fair opportunity equality along with the natural, social inequality and "inequality of luck" levelling. Human well-being, according to Rawls, should depend only on the results of personal free choice [20]. A. Sen insists on constant discussion, comparison and ranking of the different concepts of justice priorities - utility, equality, procedure observance (legality) [21], versus sole institutional arrangement or universal principle (basis) [22]. Sen avoids justice idealisation, questioning the existence of such a principle or perfectly fair social order possibility. The individualisation and discursiveness of justice, the necessity of taking into account the opinions of individuals, who are not members of the contracting within the social contract group, become key conclusions of Sen.

It is interesting to consider the impact of the artificial intelligence (AI) deployment on ensuring justice. AI is associated with reducing decision-making (including wealth allocation process) subjectivity. According to Sen, universalisation of the fairness degree determining algorithm can lead to justice violation.

2.2 Justice and Efficiency Interrelation

The term "efficiency" in its modern interpretation appeared in the 18th century and has some predecessors. Ancient Chinese philosophy emphasises the concept of "utility". Impartial actions for the greater good represent justice, which is not connected with personal benefit [1]. The late Moists regarded "義" as utility for the state and the world. Justice as utility is not associated with a certain result. Note that justice is prioritised over benefit (Sun-Tzu), being its basis, as the benefit is impossible without justice.

Dessauer's work refers to Socrates' statement: "every good is useful" [15]. Thus, if justice is good ("public good", according to Aristotle), then, everything that is fair is useful, but, at the same time, what is not useful is not fair. Everything that creates and preserves well-being in a state, and everything that constitutes its happiness Aristotle calls justice [23]. Epicurus, despite justice subjectivism, considers the mutual benefit of individuals as a justice criterion. Art in its broader sense is called the ability of being useful.

Scholasticism links distributive justice with a social goal and the individual's contribution to its achievement. The goal-setting aspect appears, but the goal is unified, abstract and not correlated with a particular result. According to Pascal [24], justice is actually equated with usefulness for life. For the social life maintenance, some directly interested in justice implementation people are stood out by the others (state power) [25]. Thus, justice ensuring is the purpose of public authority and its efficiency depends on society fairness. "Public happiness" (Leibniz), "public good" (Helvetius) become society's purpose.

For the first time "efficiency" was considered by W. Petty, F. Kenet as effectiveness - public authorities impact on the economic development [26]. Thus, efficiency means utility, since there is no particular measurable result. A. Smith does not equate utility with justice, because the moral aspect of justice may not coincide with the utility principle or may be not exhausted by them [12]. A fair act has some objective value that is not related to its utility. In the works of Ricardo, then Emerson, Friedman efficiency is connected not only with the particular result of the economic actor's activity, but also with the amount of spent resources, counting as a ratio of these values [27].

Marx considers economic efficiency at the micro-level as result of production maximisation, using minimum of resources [28]. The principles of economy and labour productivity maximisation constitute efficiency in the works of Lenin. According to marginalist Menger, efficiency is the ratio of profit to the labour or production value. Nozick considers this concept [19], noting that since profit is not always determined by labour value, productivity can be high and efficiency – low. The reason, according to Marx, is the social necessity of labour level, established by the market.

B. Pareto defined efficiency as a system's state, making impossible one's advancement without worsening another's position. This concept is reflected in the "Theory of

Justice" [17], although the author notes that fair distribution of benefits (rights, obligations) is always preferable to efficient distribution, he points out that a totally fair system is efficient. J. Rawls establishes the idea of equality effectiveness: equal opportunities should contribute society development. In contrast to utilitarians, believed that justice is efficiency as the best satisfaction balance, Rawls emphasises the importance of procedural justice and equity. However, if there are inequalities that lead to all society members' advancement, the basic structure should allow these inequalities to the extent that they are compatible with liberty and opportunity equality.

In economic science there are the "justice-efficiency" dilemma (Robinson) and the "liberty-efficiency-justice" trilemma (Keynes). Referring to Keynes, Rawls notes that since full implementation of the justice principles is impossible, some social inequalities can be justified if their reducing leads to even greater inequality of opportunities: such inequalities are not unjust and the priority of justice over efficiency is kept. Efficiency is defined through market value, but income allocation according to the contribution to this value is not fair, according to the non-labour theory of value. Rawls calls a market a perfect mechanism, leading to efficiency, while elections and legislatures are always imperfect in justice ensuring.

The distinction between utility and efficiency is that utility or usefulness contains some idea of good, while efficiency contains some idea of purpose or result. Efficiency as a criterion of economic development should be considered at the micro- and macro-level. To determine the amount of each material good to be produced, it is necessary to take into account benefits and costs for each level of output varying. It seems logical to choose the level of output with a maximum excess of total benefits over total costs - the highest net benefits are achieved (utilitarism). However, this is just an allocation or output level efficiency [29]. "Efficiency" can be presented as a simultaneous observance of four principles, arranged in the order of their appearance in philosophy and economics (Fig. 1).

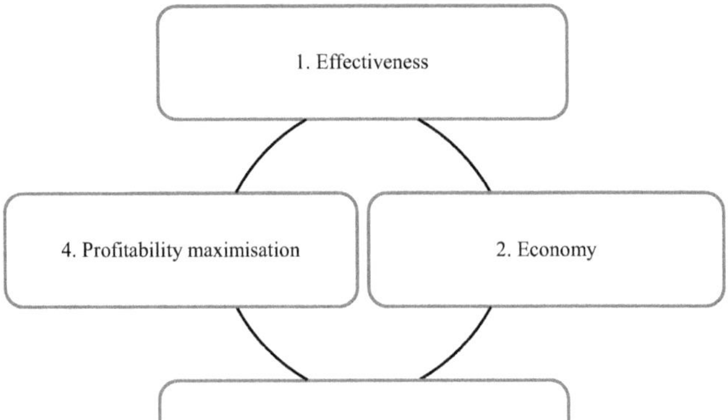

Fig. 1. Efficiency criteria in the history of philosophy and economics.

These categories are measurable and require accurate determining (with some social contract) the following characteristics: target, expected results, available and used resources, social and individual value. These criteria and characteristics quantitative assessment at the macro-level is challenging, because of the assessment integrality, subjectivity, the planning perspective expanding, the non-commercial nature of public activity and non- financial results. Economy criterion despite its subjectivity, is aimed at the economic entities' (including states) profit maximising [30]. Consequently, "economy" through profit maximisation contributes to the added value growth, leading to the gross domestic product (GDP) growth, which is usually understood as economic growth. Since the factors of extensive development are exhausting, labour productivity increasing (through scientific and technological progress (Solow's model)), is the main factor of economic growth.

Game theory was designed to find economic equilibrium. If this equilibrium is necessary for economic development, then utility or efficiency become factors of economic development too. In economic theory, along with Pareto equilibrium, there are: dominant strategy (the intersection of strategies that maximize utility for each participant despite of another's actions); Nash equilibrium (utility maximisation for one participant, depending on another's actions); Stackelberg equilibrium (maximisation utility for participants, making non-simultaneous decisions). Nash equilibrium may not be consistent with justice principles.

Public expenditures as benefits redistribution at the national level instrument, can be divided into productive and unproductive. Public expenditures, aimed at social justice maintainance (social protection, public services, etc.), usually called unproductive, as they do not contribute to economic growth, but affect consumer demand and can cause inflation increasing. Unproductive expenditures also include expenditures on public order and safety, general public services, housing and community amenities, and most part of defence expenditures, that do not accelerate economic growth in the long term [31]. The unproductive expenditures take the largest share of total government expenditures in many European countries in the COVID-19 period [32].

Economists do not confirm that social inequality can be a factor of economic development by stimulating individual effort, private initiative, wealth accumulation [33]. According to A. Weber, allocation equality creates more favourable conditions for economic growth [34]. The approach, considering social expenditures as a burden for the economy, is based on the market equilibrium model and the assumption of perfect competition, which are not observed in reality. Extreme inequality has a negative impact on society development indicators, leading to human capital, key factor of economic growth, reduction. Society equity level is correlated with the economic growth rate.

Governmental social policy should counteract market disfunction. In countries with top-quality social systems, social expenditures dynamics positively correlates with economic growth indicators. However, the factor-result relationship in this case requires additional study in order to avoid the mistake of substituting the cause by the effect. The World Bank experts note the importance of social justice as one of the factors of sustainable development (inequality reducing is one of the sustainable development goals) [35]. Inequality of opportunity leads to human capital inefficient using and resources inefficient allocation. Long-term economic development goals achieving requires alignment with justice principles, positively correlated with economic efficiency in the long run. These findings are consistent with the results of International Monetary Fund research [36], observing the correlation between inequality rising and the economic growth instability. Inequality impedes progress in socially important sectors, creates instability risk and, consequently, decreases investment activity, undermines the social consensus, needed to adapt to shocks, and thus reduces economic growth rate and its duration.

Distinguishing market inequality (before taxes and social transfers) and net inequality (after taxes and transfers) made reliable and robust redistribution impact on economic growth assessment possible [33]. The conclusions are: greater inequality causes greater redistribution; lower net inequality is correlated with accelerated and prolonged growth; in general, redistribution accelerates growth.

3 Methodology

The concept of justice main aspects dynamics is analyzed through interaction with philosophical trends - from Ancient Chinese philosophy to modern philosophy, dating back to the beginning of the 21st century. The term "justice" is used in this paper mostly in its broadest sense, which can be not backed by the law, like fairness. The efficiency criteria research has been conducted within the framework of the "Value for money" concept. However, it should be noted that the criterion "efficiency" in the field of government finance for the purposes of this paper has the same meaning as the term "performance", which is used in ISSAI 300 "Performance Audit Principles". "Efficiency" includes three main criteria: "effectiveness", "economy" and "resource efficiency".

In the article machine learning methods (classification methods) such as logistic regression, nearest neighbors methods, linear discriminant analysis, decision tree, random forest are used for recognizing the intercorrelation of government expenditures structure, economic, financial indicators and country development level. Solving the classification problem allows to identify the features (independent variables) that could most accurately become a criterion for identifying the level of country's development.

All dependent variables are quantitative. The target variable is categorical, but importantly, it is indicated by a numeric value (0, 1, 2). In order to bring the values of the independent variables to a single scale, the data are normalized. Training (70%) and test (30%) samples were prepared for the study. The total sample size was 630 observations.

In order to prove the intercorrelation of the expenditures on maintaining social fairness (spending on education, health, social sphere) share and the level of economic development, we reduced the classification problem to searching in the initial feature space for such pairs of features that provide the best separability for given classifiers (Logistic Regression, Naive Bayes, Nearest Neighbors 3,Nearest Neighbors 5, Nearest Neighbors 7, Linear Discriminant Analysis, Quadratic Discriminant Analysis, Decision Tree 2, Decision Tree Max, Random Forest, SVM linear, SVM RBF kernel, SVM Poly, SVM Sigmoid, LinearSVC). The Random Forest method was chosen as the most accurate one (accuracy 0.96).

Analyzing the dataset of economic and financial indicators (Expenditure on economic affairs [% of total], Expenditure on health [% of total], Expenditure on education [% of total], Expenditure on social protection [% of total], Expenditure on housing & community amenities [% of total], GDP growth [% per annum], Consumer Price Index (CPI) [% per annum], Financial Development Index (FDI) [index value], Unemployment Rate [%]) of 56 countries for the 12 years (2010–2021), applying the methods of machine learning (Random Forest with the accuracy 0,96 was recognized as the best one), helps to solve the problem of classification and identify country indicators that can be criteria for dividing countries into major advanced economies (country group (CG) type 0), advanced economies (CG type 1), emerging and developing economies (CG type 2).

4 Results

4.1 Justice and Efficiency Balancing for Economic Development

The idea of justice evolution (Fig. 2) not only have transformed the idea itself, but also influenced the processes of socio-economic, scientific and technical development, anticipating them (frequently with criticism) and determining their main directions.

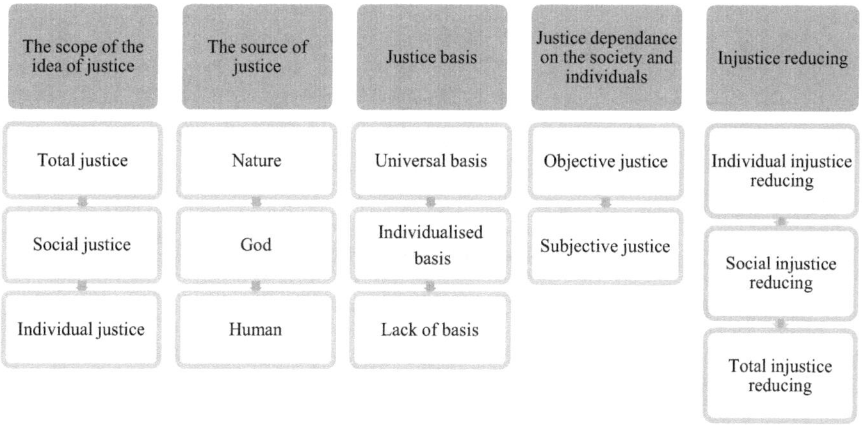

Fig. 2. Main aspects of the concepts of justice evolution.

The main concepts (definitions) of justice are: justice as proper (due, morality), as equivalent recompense, as utility, as humanity, as law, as a social contract and its principles adherence, as equality (natural, social, equality of "luck", equality of liberties, equality of opportunities), as rational impartiality, as Pareto efficiency, as fairness. The priority of distributive or commutative justice is cyclical. Justice, utility and efficiency are intercorrelated in the history of philosophy and economics.

The growth of satisfaction with the public services quality contributes to the related spheres of economy development. Thus, initially unproductive expenditures and subsidised industries become economic growth drivers. This is one of the justice and economic development intercorrelation channels, along with social stability ensuring.

Unproductive expenditures share of total and payments to individuals share of total were larger in more economically developed countries in the period of COVID-19 shock (Fig. 3). Unproductive expenditures are correlated with inflation and geopolitical shocks. Firstly, their increasing can cause consumer demand growth, accelerating inflation. The reduction of, for example, social transfers leads to social tensions with economic and political consequences. Secondly, in response to inflation acceleration and macroeconomic shocks, governments have to increase unproductive expenditures to ensure social sustainability. Despite the economically inefficient nature of some social protection expenditures, the reviewed countries' budgets are socially oriented: this type of expenditure amounts the largest share of total allocations.

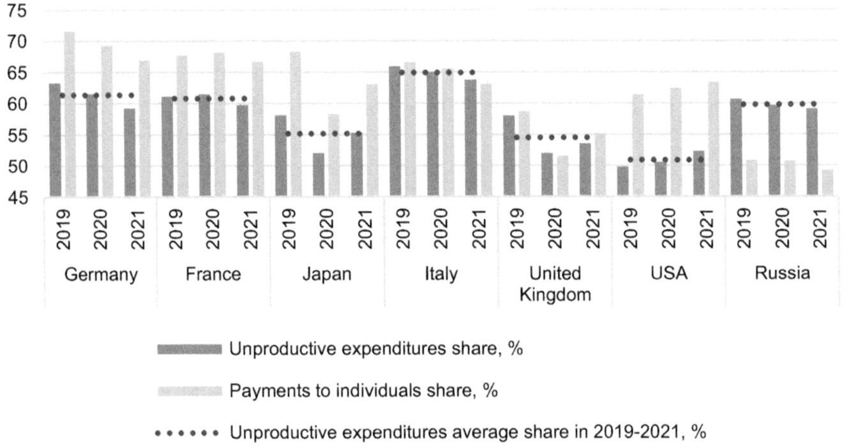

Source: authors' calculations based on the OECD data.

Fig. 3. Unproductive expenditures share dynamics in 2019–2021. Source: authors' calculations based on the OECD data.

According to the results of the classification algorithm realization (Figs. 4, 5, 6, 7 and 8) and research analysis of the data, revealed the relationship of several variables with early mentioned target country groups: FDI and Expenditure on health share (of total expenditures amount); Expenditure on education share and FDI; Expenditure on health share and Expenditure on housing & community amenities share; Expenditure on health share and annual Gross Domestic product (GDP) growth; FDI and Expenditure on social protection share.

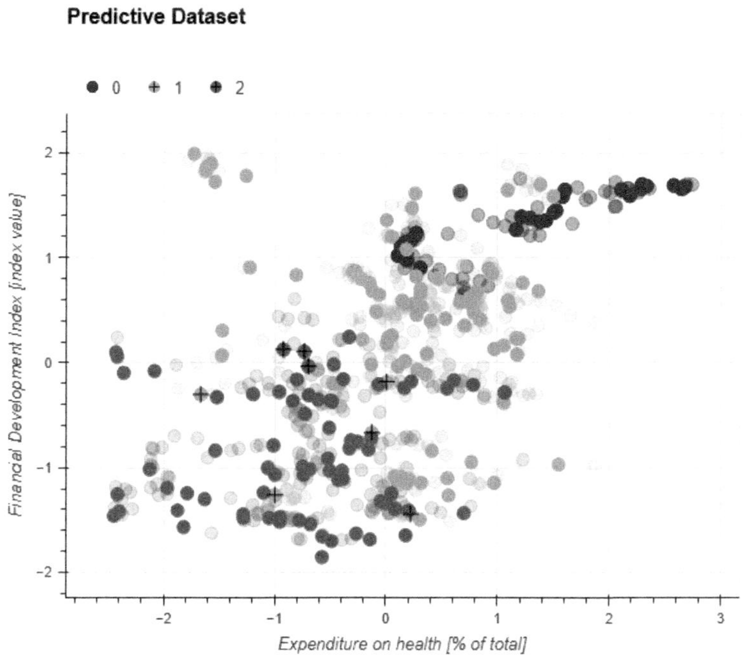

Fig. 4. Country separation by FDI and Expenditures on health share.

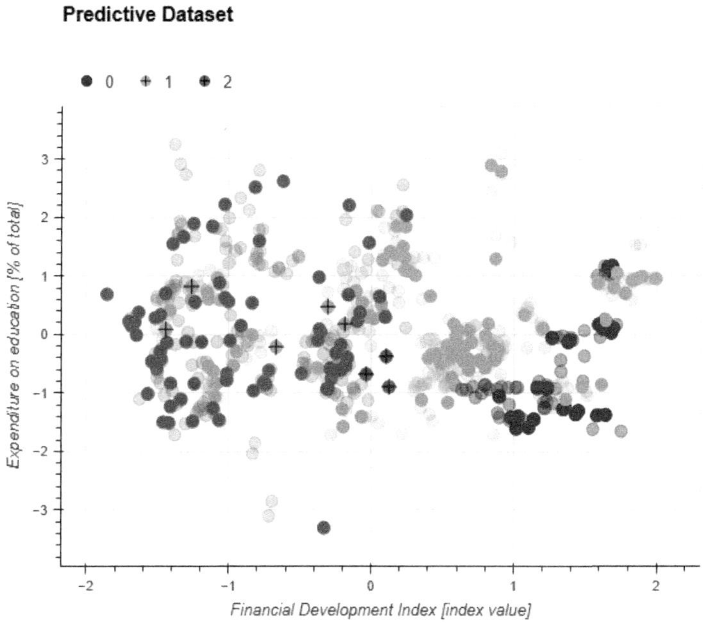

Fig. 5. Country separation by Expenditures on education share and FDI.

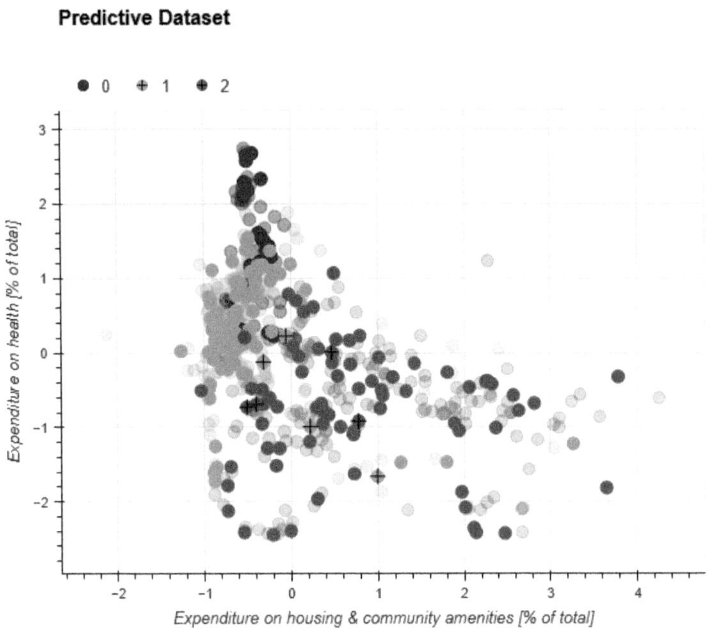

Fig. 6. Country separation by Expenditures on health share and Expenditures on housing and community amenities share.

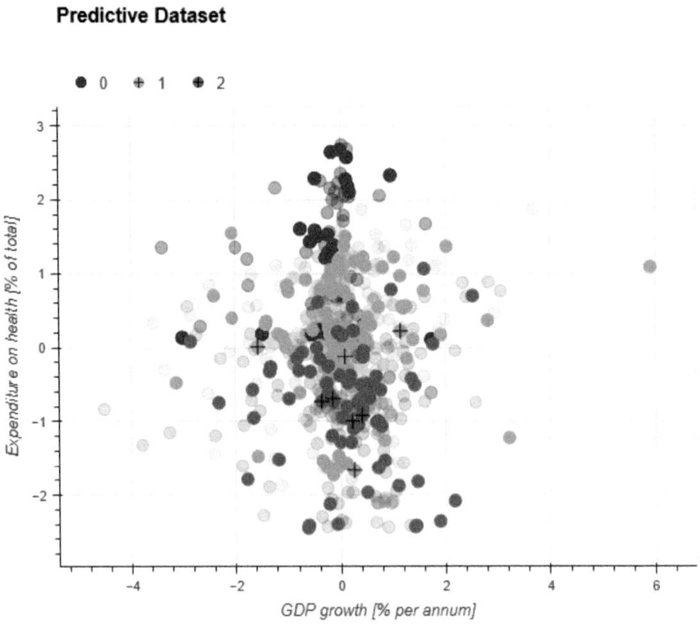

Fig. 7. Country separation by Expenditures on health share and GDP growth.

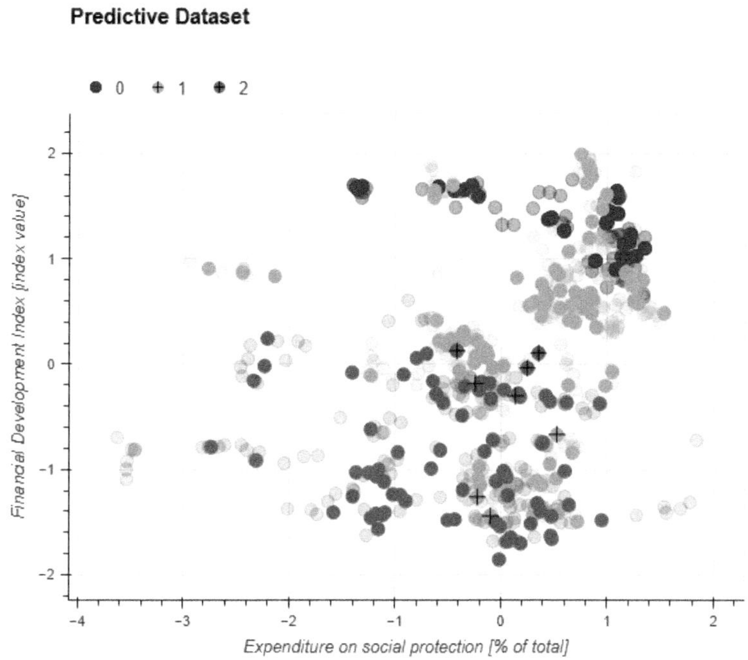

Fig. 8. Country separation by FDI and Expenditures on social protection share.

Government expenditures on health, education, housing & community amenities and social protection include spending on activities, contributing to inequality levelling out. Mentioned indicators in combination with FDI and GDP growth can help to accurately identify the type of country's economic development. The empirical research reveals that share of particular types of expenditures aimed at maintaining social equity (such as expenditures on health) can be one of the main features that make it possible to classify an economy by type of economic development. The primacy of a fair state distribution in relation to the level of economic development may be questioned, but the productive nature of expenditures on health, for example, confirmed by research in this field, suggests that this type of government spending may be a factor in economic development. Noteworthy, that more economically developed countries are characterized not only by a larger share of this group of spending, but also by a higher FDI, which reveals finance system efficiency level. This allows to suppose: an advanced finance system facilitate more efficient allocation and using of government spending. GDP growth indicator, which shows the efficiency of the whole economic system is not recognized as one of the most important features of country classification by economic development level.

Although expenditures on health share is directly interrelated with economic development, unproductive expenditures, aimed at social inequality reducing through direct payments to the population, share expansion is a pro-inflationary factor [32]. Though, spending on socially important industries: fiscal stimulation of public services supply, rather than solvent demand encouraging, can be socially and economically effective. Government spending volume planning is connected with expected budget revenues amounts. Taxation as a fiscal policy instrument influences goods and services affordability, because tax rates changing can be a pro-inflationary factor. Fair taxation system, requires striking a balance between rights and liberties of economic agents respecting within the framework of the social contract and equality of opportunities ensuring, taking into account Rawls's difference principle.

4.2 Equity Criterion for Efficiency Assessment in Public Sector

The result of government spending is usually some non-monetary positive effect, assessment of which is always challenging for public administration, that makes it necessary to define efficiency criteria. In public finance practice the "Value for Money" concept (VFM), assessing the efficiency of resource utilisation, has become widespread. VFM implies striking a balance between three criteria (3E - economy, efficiency, effectiveness) (Table 1).

Table 1. "Value for money" concept criteria.

criterion	Economy	Efficiency	Effectiveness
definition	Cost minimisation	Positive effect of spending maximisation	Defined targets or results complete achievement

These criteria are used for performance audit in public sector organisations [37]. The variety of performance audit criteria, including efficiency and equity analysis (Appendix A) allows to conclude, that there are some differences in their interpretation according to INTOSAI standards and national guidelines, standards and methodological recommendations, concerning the content of such terms as "resources", "efficiency", "effectiveness". That is why, the following interpretation of performance audit criteria can be suggested by the authors:

1)resource efficiency maximisation - getting the maximum result from the resources used (rather than the resources available or budgeted): maximising the result of using a unit of resource.
2)economy - minimising resource costs: resources of appropriate quality should be available in a timely manner, in the required quantity and at the lowest possible price.
3)effectiveness - completeness of targets and results achieving within the planned amount of resources.
4)equity: target equity - setting a result of budget spending, focused on achieving equality of freedoms, rights and opportunities of society members; process equity - using "fair" instruments for main target (results) achievement or increasing equality of freedoms, rights and opportunities level as a consequential effect of budget spending.

Criteria 1) and 3) consider savings as deviations from the plan, needed to be justified. Criteria 1) and 3) may also take into account non-financial government spending results. VFM concept sometimes includes a criterion of equity, which characterises the availability of services (range of consumers) and the principle of benefits from services distribution among consumers. The criterion of justice in the VFM concept implies equity, i.e. the unnecessary, surmountable, unjust and undue differences between individuals and groups elimination. Equity includes:

- equitable (fair) government spending based on identified inequalities to level them out, i.e. allocation that ensure a fair and equitable outcome;
- the promise to "leave no one behind" (sustainable development), i.e. to ensure the availability of high-quality services to a wide range of people (including the most vulnerable social groups);
- equitable outcomes providing for the least advantaged groups not only by ensuring equality of opportunity, but also by removing social structure barriers.

These three principles can be taken into account in determining the expected result of government spending, and the degree of their achievement can be measured by the effectiveness criterion. Thus, justice principles should be used in budget planning, especially in countries, using programme-targeted method.

Equity VFM indicators may include: a share of socially unprotected economic agents, covered by a public service (process equity); cost or accessibility of provided public service for socially unprotected economic agents (process equity); a number or degree of removing barriers for socially vulnerable economic agents (target equity); a number of socially vulnerable agents, provided with a certain public service (target equity). These indicators can be correlated with some social program result, but integrating them into the budgetary planning system in various areas, not only in the social sphere, is preferable. The equity criterion may have priority over other efficiency criteria and determine the strategic goals of long-term budget policy.

5 Conclusion

The main stages of philosophy evolution, cosmocentrism, theocentrism, anthropocentrism, scientocentrism, as well as political (communism, liberalism, libertarianism, meritocracy) and economic (classical economics, Marxism, marginalism, Keynesianism) theories have determined the plurality of views on the interpretation of justice and its relationship with efficiency. The analysis of the justice concepts' key aspects allows to conclude that this category plays a determining role in the process of socio-economic, scientific and technical development along with "efficiency". This hypothesis confirming has led to the necessity of joint integration justice and efficiency criteria into the budgeting process, although, in the history of philosophy, the thesis of the justice priority over efficiency is the most widespread, except of some concepts, equating utility with justice or establishing utility as a necessary and sufficient condition of justice.

Several directions and proposals for introducing performance audit criteria (including "equity") in the public finance system, according to VFM concept, were suggested by the authors. The criterion of equity and suggested indicators of equity assessment is divided into two groups of criteria – target equity and process equity.

A larger share of productive government spending, aimed at maintaining social equity (spending on health), is one of the hallmarks of developed countries along with finance system efficiency. Inflationary risk of unproductive expenditures and the fiscal stimulus caused by the growth of productive expenditures should be taken into account in the budget planning. The positive effect of using the sources of public expenditures increasing financing (such as tax revenues) for social support should not be offset by availability or quality of goods and services decreasing.

Inflation risk monitoring should be implemented at all budget process stages. Introducing equity criterion into the budget management system requires justice principles and equity indicators for taxation and budget allocation establishing by impartial social contract. These indicators should not only be used within the particular government social programmes, but also be introduced in each structural element of other programmes.

Prioritisation of government interventions in the economy should balance the criteria of efficiency and justice. For example, cost-benefit analysis of different decisions can help to strike a better balance between efficiency and justice. Resource allocation should be done through a transparent and inclusive deliberative process, involving key stakeholders, including socially disadvantaged and other economically underserved groups, and impartial entities.

Appendix A

Table A1.

Table A1. VFM concept criteria in national and international performance audit standards.

Standard (methodology)	Efficiency Assessment Criteria	Criteria content
ISSAI 100 Fundamental Principles of Public-Sector Auditing	economy	-
	efficiency	-
	effectiveness	-
ISSAI 300 Performance Audit Principles	economy	resource costs minimization: the resources used should be provided on time, in the right amount, of the right quality and at the best possible price
	efficiency	return on available resources: refers to the relationship between resources deployed and results, in terms of volume, quality and timeliness
	effectiveness	set goals and desired results achievement
ISSAI 3000 Performance Audit Standard	economy	-
	efficiency	-
	effectiveness	-

(*continued*)

Table A1. (*continued*)

Standard (methodology)	Efficiency Assessment Criteria	Criteria content
GUID 3910 Central Concepts for Performance Auditing	economy	resource costs minimization: the resources used must be available at the right time, in the right amount, of the right quality, and at the best possible price
	efficiency	maximization of results with available resources: refers to the correlation between used resources and the outputs in terms of quantity, quality and delivery timing
	effectiveness	set goals and intended results achievement
	equity	equal civil, political and social rights of all society members providing
	cost effectiveness*	combines elements of efficiency and effectiveness: the interrelation of the outcome of an instrument, project, programme and resources used in terms of funds and human capital
GUID 3920 The Performance Auditing Process	economy	-
	efficiency	-
	effectiveness	-
ESAS 104 Efficiency Audit (CIS)	efficiency includes:	relationship between the results achieved and the federal and other resources used to achieve them, reflecting economy and/or efficiency of federal and other resources using
	economy	achievement of certain results using the least amount of federal and other resources
	effectiveness	achieving the best results using a certain amount of federal and other resources
Methodology of indicators/key national indicators selection in Performance audit	efficiency	-
	effectiveness	-
	economy	-
Performance Audit Manual – SAI Brazil, 2010/11	equity	recognizing the difference among individuals and taking it into account in government policy providing

Note:
* Cost effectiveness is not singled out as a separate criterion.

References

1. Rykov, S.Y.: Duty or justice: once again about the term Yi 義 in ancient Chinese philosophy. History of Philosophy **2**, 22–46 (2005)
2. Mengtzu: (V. S. Kolokolov, Trans.). Saint Petersburg: Petersburg Oriental Studies (1999). ISBN: 5-85803-136-6
3. Vasiliev, V.V., Krotov, A.A., Bugai, D.V.: History of philosophy. Academic Project, Moscow (2005). ISBN: 978-5-8291-0921-9
4. Plato: The state. (A. N. Egunov, Trans.). Saint Petersburg: Science (2005). ISBN: 5-02-026877-1
5. Shakiradze, A.S.: Epicurus. Socekgiz, Moscow (1963)
6. Cicero: On the nature of the gods. (M. I. Rizhsky, Trans.). Moscow: Science (1985)
7. Seregin, A.V.: Stoicism and justice. Philosophical Journal **1**, 34–47 (2019). https://doi.org/10.21146/2072-0726-2019-12-1-34-47
8. Chernix, S.N.: Concept justice in medieval philosophy. Bulletin of Voronezh State Technical University **4**, 130–133 (2011)
9. Erdnieva, B.D.: The idea of justice in philosophies of the Renaissance cultural context. Philosophical Thought **12**, 65–74 (2022). https://doi.org/10.25136/2409-8728.2022.12.39237
10. Bulgakov, V.V., Bulgakova, D.V.: The concept of "justice" during the historical stages of the development of society. TSU Journal **5**, 325–328 (2012)
11. Perelman, C.: Three aspects of justice. (E. G. Samohina, Trans.). Jurisprudence **2**(307), 211–225 (2013)
12. Zulfugarzadeh, T.E.: Adam Smith: Law and justice. Russian Law Online **2**, 56–61 (2020)
13. Sushentsova, M.S., Miroshnitchenko, M.A., Lymar, F.A.: Marxism and liberalism on justice and economy: A comparative analysis. Publishing House of the HSE, Moscow (2020)
14. Popper, K.R.: Objective knowledge: An evolutionary approach. (D. G. Lahuti, Trans.). URSS, Moscow (2002). ISBN: 5-8360-0327-0
15. Dessauer, F.: Dispute on technology. (A. Y. Nesterov, Trans.). Samara Humanitarian Academy, Samara (2017). ISBN: 978-5-98996-202-0
16. Russell, B.: Problems of philosophy. Science, Novosibirsk (2001). ISBN: 5-02-030621-5
17. Rawls, J.: A theory of justice. (V. V. Tselischev, V. N. Karpovich, & A. Shevchenko, Trans.). Novosibirsk University Publishing, Novosibirsk (1995). ISBN: 5-7615-0365-4
18. Rawls, J.: The priority of right and ideas of the good. (L. B. Makeeva, Trans.). House of Intellectual Book, Progress-Tradition, Moscow (1998). ISBN: 5-7333-0005-1
19. Nozick, R.: Anarchy, state and utopia. (B. Pinsker, Trans.). IRISEN, Moscow (2008). ISBN: 5-91066-007-0
20. Belkovich, R.Y., Vinogradov, S.V.: Equality of luck: Evolvement of egalitarian theories of justice in the late 20th century. Politiya **4**(111), 51–66 (2023). https://doi.org/10.30570/2078-5089-2023-111-4-51-66
21. Sen, A.: Development as freedom. (R. M. Nureev, Trans.). New Publishing, Moscow (2004). ISBN: 5-98379-009-9
22. Balashov, D.V.: Amartya Sen's idea of justice. Politiya **4**(95), 25–38 (2019). https://doi.org/10.30570/2078-5089-2019-95-4-25-38
23. Aristotle: Ethics of Nicomachus. (I. Kemere & V. Zarins, Trans.). Zvaigzne, Riga (1985)
24. Pascal, B.: Oeuvres completes. Gallimard, Paris (2000). ISBN: 2-07-011407-4
25. Hume, D.: Works: In 2 vols. Thought, Moscow (1996). ISBN: 5-244-00763-7
26. Klyuev, A.V.: The nature, relations and possible joint use of the concepts "effectiveness" and "efficiency." Bulletin of Ural Federal University. Series Economics and Management **4**(16) (2017). https://doi.org/10.15826/vestnik.2017.16.4.026

27. Arkhireev, A.V.: Genesis of the concept of efficiency: Structure, state, evaluation. Context and Reflection: Philosophy of the World and Human Being **12**(10A), 36–49 (2023). https://doi.org/10.34670/AR.2024.43.45.004
28. Marx, K., Engels, F.: Opus (2nd ed., Vol. 46, Pt. II). (V. S. Vygodskij & E. S. Kruglikova, Trans.). Publishing House of Political Literature, Moscow (1969)
29. Le Grand, J., Propper, C., Smith, S.: The economics of social problems. (L. S. Zasimova, Trans.). Moscow: Publishing House of the HSE (2013). ISBN: 978-0-230-55300-2
30. Dessauer, F.: Man and space. Experience. (A. Y. Nesterov, Trans.). Samarama, Samara. ISBN: 978-5-6049241-4-3 (2022)
31. Dunne, J.P.: Economic effects of military expenditure in developing countries: a survey. Contrib. Econom. Anal. **235**, 439–464 (1996). https://doi.org/10.1108/S0573-8555(1996)0000235025
32. Tyukavkin, N.M., Nosova, M.K.: Global trends in budget policy in terms of public spending: structural analysis. Samara Federal Research Centre of the Russian Academy of Sciences, Samara (2023)
33. Weber, A.: Social justice and development. Free Thought **5**(1653), 95–108 (2015)
34. Burdzhalov, F.: The economic role of social activity of the state. IMEMO RAN, Moscow (2009). ISBN: 978-5-9535-0198-9
35. World Bank: World development report 2006: Justice and development. The World Bank, Washington, D.C. (2006). ISBN: 978-0-8213-6412-3
36. Ostry, J.D., Berg, A., Tsangarides, C.G.: Redistribution, inequality, and growth. IMF Staff Discussion Note, 2014(002). International Monetary Fund (2014). https://doi.org/10.5089/9781484352076.006
37. Nosova, M.K., Milova, L.N.: Improving the value for money concept to assess the efficiency of using budget funds in the Russian Federation. Economics and Entrepreneurship **3**(152), 114–118 (2023). https://doi.org/10.34925/EIP.2023.152.3.020

Interdependence of the Level and Structure of Household Income: The Case of Municipalities

Aleksey Pasynkov(✉) and Ekaterina Zakharchuk

Institute of Economics of the Ural Branch of the Russian Academy of Sciences, 29 Moskovskaya Street, 620014 Ekaterinburg, Russia
monografia@mail.ru

Abstract. The global literature extensively addresses the problem of uneven household income across regions, which is particularly evident in countries with vast territories. However, studies at the municipal level are scarce due to a lack of data. This article aims to explore the specifics and interrelations of income inequality and their sources, using the example of municipalities in the Russian Federation. The study focuses on six regions within the Ural Federal District, each exhibiting distinct economic development patterns. Utilizing resources from the Russian statistical agency and the authors' methods for calculating and comparing income from various sources, the key relationships between the level and structure of population income in municipalities of the Ural Federal District were identified. In the northern regions (Yamal and Yugra), high household income is attributed to elevated wages for hired workers, while entrepreneurial income exerts minimal influence. In the southern regions (Sverdlovsk, Chelyabinsk, Kurgan, and Tyumen), mixed dynamics of mutual influence were observed. In large regional cities (Ekaterinburg, Tyumen, Chelyabinsk), high income levels are primarily attributed to a 50% share of entrepreneurial income. Overall, municipalities demonstrate a concentration of labor income ranging from 60% to 80%, with relatively low average per capita income for Russia.

Keywords: Labor income · Entrepreneurial Income · Households

JEL Classification: J31 · D31 · O18

1 Introduction

Inequality of household income across countries, regions, and territories is an essential component of economic theory, as understanding the sources of household wealth has been a relevant topic since the work of Adam Smith. At the same time, the level of population income may depend not only on institutional factors (e.g., freedom of trade or political systems) but also on various resource, natural, and settlement conditions. For instance, the income levels of citizens in the Persian Gulf countries (Kuwait, Saudi Arabia, Qatar) are relatively high by global standards, primarily due to the export of oil and

E. Kuzmin et al. (Eds.): EASET 2024, SPBE, pp. 122–132, 2025.
https://doi.org/10.1007/978-3-031-91159-0_8

gas. A similar situation is observed within certain countries, where household incomes vary based on the specific economic development of regions. This phenomenon is particularly evident in large countries like the Russian Federation, where labor mobility is constrained for various reasons. Moreover, within Russian regions, there is considerable differentiation in household income, as the vast size of regions often exceeds that of many European countries. Therefore, research into the sources of household wealth in the Russian Federation is highly relevant for both regional and municipal levels. Additionally, the methodologies employed may be applicable to other countries with similar settlement structures.

Theoretically, in world science the problem of income inequality of households in different countries and regions has been studied for quite a long time, the starting point is considered to be the work of Lorenz [1]. A large-scale review of the causes of income inequality for different countries is carried out in the works of Harvey et al. [2], Wiese et al. [3]. Thus, using the example of Indonesian regions, the factors of income inequality are studied [4], the authors highlighted the contribution of government programs to stimulating economic growth aimed at reducing interregional inequality. Using the methods of studying median income and expenditure, a study of the inequality of wealth among regions in Malaysia was conducted [5]. The work Ivanovski et al. [6] identifies structural changes in income inequality between states and territories using Australian data, highlighting various factors of such changes. Using the example of seventeen European countries (for the period from 2004 to 2020), the article Balcilar and Namazli [7] studies the impact of inflation on income inequality. At the same time, several control variables are included in the analysis: GDP per capita, unemployment rate, trade openness, and foreign direct investments. The study found that gross domestic product growth and inflation increase economic inequality, while trade openness and foreign direct investment do not have a significant impact.

Research on household income structure also focuses on inequality. The relationship between entrepreneurial income and the cost of starting a business was determined using the example of 50 states and 73 cities in the United States, but such a relationship, according to O'Reilly [8], is not very significant. The ratio of income derived from labor and capital, based on data from thirty European countries between 2003 and 2017, was studied by Petrova and Ranaldi [9]. They argue that the difference depends on the policy preferences of governments. Korean researchers [10] conducted a study on the relationships between economic growth, functional income distribution (labor income share) and household income distribution (Gini coefficient). Using data from 99 countries (1970 to 2014), they concluded that the share of income received from the employer has increased and the income gap has simultaneously widened with economic growth.

Diversity of income sources is often viewed through the issue of poverty reduction. The work of Koiry et al. [11] notes that in theoretical terms there is a debate about the relationship between poverty and diversification of income sources. Using a tea plantation in Bangladesh as an example, the authors conducted a survey of households and found that diversity of income sources reduces poverty, although only slightly. The problem of persistent poverty in metropolitan suburbs is considered in the work of Allen et al. [12] using the example of Canadian agglomerations. An analysis of household income declarations showed that the main factor behind low income in suburban areas of Canada's major cities is habituation to poverty, with immigration and cost-cutting having a lesser influence. Chinese scientists [13] consider the pension system as a factor in reducing poverty. The study notes that pensions have different effects on poverty reduction in China depending on the area (urban/rural, different regions). However, an increase in pension provision by 1% leads to a decrease in the probability of falling into the poor category by approximately 4–5%. A similar topic is addressed in the study by Wang et al. [14], focusing on the nutrition of older adults in China. The authors conclude that income increases are more significant for households with relatively high incomes than for those with low ones. Since in rural areas, the nutrition of older people is based on local agricultural products, and a small increase in income does not affect the quality of life. There are also some rather controversial studies, for example, a scientist from Uganda (Kyagera [15]), using the example of the Kisoro municipality, calculated that the size of household income depends on the number of operating microfinance institutions.

In world literature, research devoted to income inequality between rural and urban areas occupies a special place. Polish scientists [16] conducted research on the sources of inequality between households in rural areas and came to the conclusion that income stratification is higher than the average for all households. The impact of income levels on the risk of illness and mortality from COVID-19 is examined in the study by Amate-Fortes et al. [17], which analyzes data from 2,805 U.S. counties to highlight disparities in health risks.

In Russian scientific research, the relationship between income structure and poverty is also considered from different points of view. Arzhenovskiy [18] estimated the hidden income of households and presented the results of an analysis on its impact on poverty alleviation. It is concluded that the relative indicator of shadow income among the poor segments of the population is higher than among the non-poor group of households. A team of Russian authors [19] assessed the impact of the economic complexity index on regional income inequality in the regions of Russia, and concluded that there is a direct dependence of these indicators, since the remuneration of highly qualified specialists increases the gaps in wages.

Thus, a review of the literature showed that the study of income structure and inter-regional inequality is based on different premises, and their relationship is not obvious. There are very few such studies at the municipal level, since there is a problem with obtaining data worldwide. Therefore, the aim of our study is to determine the relationship between the structure and level of income in municipalities of the Russian Federation; the main task is to correlate the average per capita and labor income of households at the territorial level based on official statistical data.

2 Methods and Data

This study forms part of the authors' System of Territorial Accounts (STA) [20], aimed at constructing financial balances for institutional sectors at regional and municipal levels, methodologically based on the System of National Accounts. In the STA framework, households act as recipients of income from corporate and public sectors while serving as the primary consumers of goods and services (final consumption). Examining the relationship between the level and structure of household income complements the broader construction of the STA.

Using databases from the Russian statistical agency, the study assesses labor and entrepreneurial income for municipalities in several Russian regions. Labor income is derived from municipal databases that include the "Wages fund of all employees of organizations (excluding small business entities)", encompassing data on large and medium-sized enterprises. As a comparative source, we used data from the table "Volume of social payments and taxable cash income of the population by municipalities," which accounts for all household income and social payments. The difference between these indicators represents income from activities unrelated to wage labor, such as small business revenues, property income, dividends, and royalties. The study focused on regions within the Ural Federal District, characterized by diverse economic specializations. To confirm data comparability, calculations of total wage funds for municipalities and income structures derived from regional data were conducted. The results are shown in Table 1.

The results of this comparison showed that, in general, the data are comparable (the difference is due to the inclusion of other income in regional data), except for the Chelyabinsk region. Apparently, the system for collecting information on primary income from labor in this region has systemic failures, and therefore in 2022 the results for total taxable income were not presented in statistics.

Table 1. Correlation of data on labor income in regional/municipal statistics, as a percentage of total taxable income, by region of the Ural Federal District, 2018–2022.

	2018	2019	2020	2021	2022	Region/ municipalities ratio
Kurgan region	54.8/ 56.6	55.3/ 56.8	55.0/ 57.0	55.0/ 49.9	55.7/ 53.1	1.01
Sverdlovsk region	53.9/ 52.1	54.0/ 51.8	57.4/ 48.1	57.6/ 42.8	56.8/ 45.5	1.17
Tyumen region	76.3/ 76.0	74.6/ 70.4	72.8/ 72.8	73.4/ 71.9	74.0/ 75.0	1.01
Khanty-Mansi Autonomous Okrug	83.6/ 77.9	81.5/ 82.7	82.3/ 83.2	82.1/ 78.4	83.1/ 79.8	1.03
Yamalo-Nenets Autonomous Okrug	65.8/ 59.4	63.4/ 58.1	59.8/ 53.0	59.8/ 41.6	60.5/ 47.8	1.21
Chelyabinsk region	62.0/ 46.6	62.7/ 44.5	59.7/ 43.0	58.6/ 37.5	60/ no data	1.42
Year average	1.09	1.09	1.11	1.25	1.12	

To determine the standard of living of the population, we use the estimated data on average per capita income in the municipality, obtained in the article by Pasynkov and Zakharchuk [21]. The values of average per capita income of the population and the share of labor income in the total volume of taxable cash income were compared, using comparative analysis methods.

3 Results and Discussion

The economic diversity across regions and municipalities in the Ural Federal District necessitates an analysis of relationships between labor and business incomes. Table 2 illustrates the share of labor income in household income for urban and rural municipalities of the Ural Federal District during 2020, selected for its high-quality, complete data availability.

Table 2. Share of labor income in total taxable household income by urban/rural municipalities of the Ural Federal District, 2020, %.

	Urban Territories				Rural Territories				Average Urban-Rural
	Average	Max	Min	Max-Min	Average	Max	Min	Max-Min	
Kurgan region	0.59	0.68	0.58	0.10	0.53	0.71	0.14	0.58	0.06
Sverdlovsk region	0.48	0.88	0.36	0.52	0.63	0.73	0.57	0.16	−0.25
Tyumen region	0.52	0.72	0.50	0.22	0.57	0.78	0.43	0.36	−0.05
Yugra	0.65	0.83	0.55	0.28	0.89	0.96	0.73	0.24	−0.24
Yamal	0.77	0.83	0.62	0.21	0.89	0.91	0.85	0.06	−0.12
Chelyabinsk region	0.40	0.77	0.39	0.37	0.60	1.60	0.35	1.25	−0.20

As can be seen from the table presented, the share of wages of hired workers varies significantly between regions of the Ural Federal District. The lowest value overall for regional municipalities was recorded in the Chelyabinsk region (only 43%). Moreover, the share of labor income in rural areas is 60%, while in urban areas it is only 40%. The maximum value of labor income in rural settlements of the Chelyabinsk region is 1.6 (that is, it exceeds all incomes), which confirms our hypothesis about the unreliability of data for this region.

More than half of the income of households in the Sverdlovsk region (about 52%) is generated by entrepreneurial income; such income has a minimal impact in the city of Pelym (88% – labor income), the maximum – in the city of Verkhnyaya Pyshma (only 36%). The specifics of the economic development of these cities confirm the adequacy of the approach we use; in the first municipality, a significant part of highly profitable jobs relate to the maintenance of gas pipelines of the Gazprom company; in the second case, the parent company of the holding, the Ural Mining and Metallurgical Company (UMMC), pays dividends in the territory of Verkhnyaya Pyshma. In the Sverdlovsk region, the capital of the region, the city of Yekaterinburg, has a great influence on the structure of household income. Since the population of the agglomeration makes up more than a third of the region's residents (almost 1.5 out of 4.3 million people), and the share of labor income is quite low – only 42%. The Kurgan region (labor income – 57%) and the Tyumen region (59%) have fairly similar parameters of household income under consideration. These regions also have a similar share of labor income in rural and urban settlements; the indicators do not differ significantly within regions. In the Kurgan region, the share of labor income in urban settlements is slightly higher than in rural settlements (a difference of 0.06 points), in the Tyumen region it is the opposite (−0.05 points).

The difference between the values of the studied indicator within the Kurgan rural and urban areas is greater than that of Tyumen, which is explained by different approaches to the administrative-territorial formation of regions. The lowest share of entrepreneurial income of households is in the Khanty-Mansi Autonomous Okrug (Yugra) and the Yamalo-Nenets Autonomous Okrug (Yamal). In total, the share of labor income of households in Yugra is 73%. At the same time, in the rural areas of the region this indicator is 89%, which is 24 points higher than in the urban areas. In some rural settlements there is practically no income from business activities; for example, in the Nizhnevartovsk region, labor income is 96%. In the cities of Yugra, the contribution of labor income ranges from 55% (the city of Surgut, the largest settlement in the district) to 83% (Pokachi, a small city remote from the main settlement zone). And finally, the last region of the Ural Federal District, the Yamalo-Nenets Autonomous District, is the most dependent region of the Ural Federal District on labor income. On average, in the municipalities of Yamal, household income received in the form of wages from large and medium-sized enterprises is estimated at 83%. In rural areas, this contribution is even higher, amounting to 89%, ranging from 85% (Purovsky municipal district) to 91% (Yamal municipal district). In cities, the influence of entrepreneurial income is more significant, on average 23% of all income. The lowest importance of labor income is observed in the city of Labytnangi (62%), and in the city of Novy Urengoy this share was 83%.

In general, across the regions of the Ural Federal District, there is a clear geographic relationship between the growth of labor income when moving north. The southern parts of the district (Sverdlovsk, Tyumen and Kurgan regions) show approximate parity of labor and business income of households. For the population of Ugra, located to the north, three quarters of their income comes from labor income. Households in Yamal, located in the Arctic zone, are almost entirely dependent on payments from large and medium-sized employers.

The next stage of this study was to find the relationship between the labor income of settlements of different types and their income level (average per capita income). To visually display such dependencies, a graph was constructed, presented in Fig. 1. It shows that there is a fairly strong scatter in the ratio of these indicators, so let's take a closer look at each of the regions.

Kurgan Region. The lowest per capita income values are observed among the regions under consideration, both for rural and urban settlements (since there are only two of them). The figure shows that almost all territories of the region are located in the lower part of the range, and the share of labor income is average (50–70%). The data for the Chastoozersky Municipal District are very different from the series. It has the lowest labor income rate (14%) and the highest per capita income (almost 45,000 rubles per

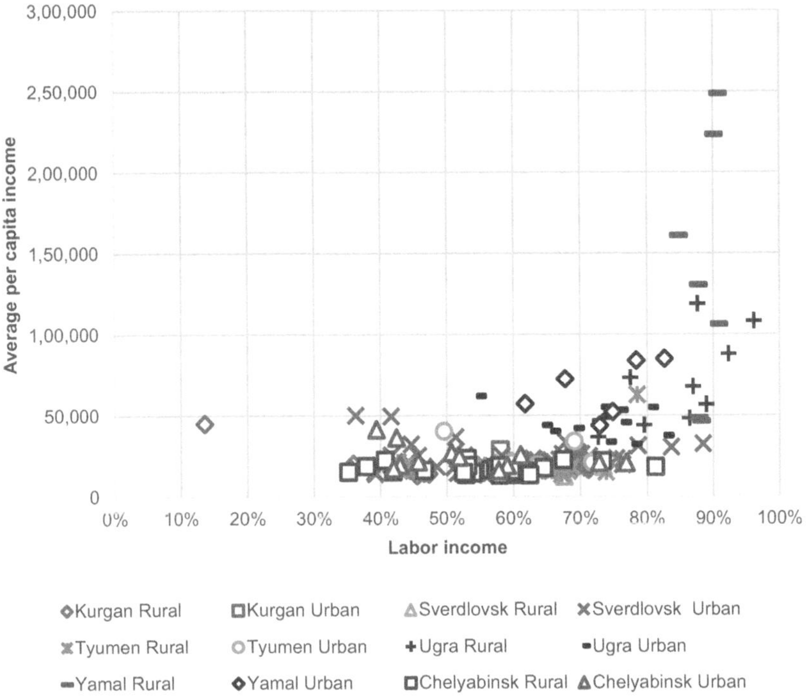

Fig. 1. Correlation of income from labor activities and average per capita income of urban and rural municipalities of the Ural Federal District, 2020, in % and rubles.

month) in the Kurgan Oblast. The population of the municipal district is small (only about 5,000 people). Therefore, we can assume that such a distribution was formed due to significant payments of entrepreneurial income in the territory (a high share of entrepreneurial income occurs in 2018–2022). In general, for the territories of the Kurgan region, no clear dependencies were identified for the studied indicators.

Sverdlovsk Region. A high per capita income in municipalities is observed only in two territories – the cities of Yekaterinburg and Verkhnyaya Pyshma (49,399 and 50,006 rubles, respectively). These cities are leaders in the share of entrepreneurial income in total income (58 and 64%). The next group of cities with relatively high average per capita incomes is about 30,000 rubles (Verkhnesaldinsky District, Zarechny, Pelym, Reftinsky District), here the situation is the opposite, the share of labor income is quite high (from 68 to 88%). The remaining territories of the Sverdlovsk region have mixed dynamics; there are municipalities with low incomes and a high share of labor, and vice versa. For example, the cities of Staroutkinsk and Degtyarsk, which have a high share of entrepreneurial income (almost like the city of Verkhnyaya Pyshma), occupy one of the lowest places in the Sverdlovsk region in terms of average per capita income.

Tyumen Region. The location of the region's territories in the presented figure approximately corresponds to the other municipalities considered. As in the Sverdlovsk region, the administrative center, Tyumen, has a great influence on the formation of average values for this region. It accounts for more than two-thirds of all income in the Tyumen region, and the ratio of business and labor income is exactly 50/50%. However, in terms of average per capita income, the capital is surpassed by the Uvat municipal district, with an indicator 1.5 times higher than in Tyumen (62,504 versus 40,245 rubles). At the same time, the Uvat district is the leader in the share of labor income among the territories of the region, with a value of 78%. One can also note a fairly high dependence of the income of urban settlements in the Tyumen region (excluding Tyumen) on the income of hired workers, which is more typical for rural settlements.

Khanty-Mansiysk Autonomous Okrug. If the regions of the southern part of the Ural Federal District are characterized by a mixed ratio for rural and urban municipalities, then in Yugra there is a clear grouping. The figure shows that the region's urban agglomerations are located in one quadrant, which characterizes the per capita income as being higher than the federal district average, as well as a fairly high dependence on labor income. The only exception here is the city of Surgut, where entrepreneurial income is higher (but less than in large cities in other regions), and the average income per person is the highest among cities. The rural areas of Yugra are located higher and to the right on the graph, which means higher income per person with a higher share of income from hired labor.

Yamalo-Nenets Autonomous Okrug. The income levels of rural and urban settlements in Yamal are very close to those of Yugra. The difference is that the gaps in per capita incomes are more significant. This is especially evident in rural settlements, where the difference in income reaches more than five times, with approximately the same ratio of labor/entrepreneurial income. In the urban settlements of Yamal, such gaps are smaller, the share of entrepreneurial income is higher, but remains at a high level for the region.

Chelyabinsk Region. As we noted earlier, statistical data for municipalities in the region are quite dubious, but a number of conclusions can be drawn. In urban agglomerations, the level of income is higher due to the excess of business income over labor income; in rural settlements there is a low standard of living and an increased share of labor income. Based on the data, the second largest city in the Chelyabinsk region, Magnitogorsk, has an average income higher than in the capital. At the same time, the share of entrepreneurial income is maximum for municipalities. The cities of Chebarkul and Zlatoust, which have approximately the same structure of household income per capita, show low results.

To determine the impact of labor income on the standard of living of the population, calculations of the correlation dependence of these indicators for 2020 were carried out. The greatest impact of labor income on the per capita average was determined in rural settlements of Yugra (correlation coefficient of 0.65), cities (0.50) and rural settlements of Yamal (0.32). A negative dependence was determined in rural settlements of the Kurgan region (−0.60), urban settlements of the Chelyabinsk region (−0.42), Yugra (−0.37). On average, for all territories of the Ural Federal District, the dependence is positive, with a fairly high coefficient of 0.43.

4 Conclusions

A study of the relationship between the level and structure of income at the level of municipalities showed that there are some problems in statistical information characterizing the relationship between entrepreneurial and labor income. At the same time, the data and results obtained made it possible to identify some relationships and trends in this issue.

1. Our study showed that, in general, across the territories of the federal district, the most significant component is income from hired labor. However, if we directly compare regions by the level of per capita income, then the conclusion suggests itself about a direct relationship between the level of income and the share of labor income.
2. However, the specific features of the socio-economic development of the polar regions (Yugra and Yamal), where highly profitable oil and gas production sectors are located, do not allow this conclusion to be used as a standard.
3. In the southern territories of the federal district, large cities (regional capitals) have a great influence on the studied indicators, since a significant proportion of the population lives in them. The specifics of Russia's spatial development, when the business sector (especially in the field of trade and small business) is concentrated mainly in large cities, has a strong impact on the income of the entrepreneurial sector in small towns and rural settlements.
4. An interesting effect was discovered in several urban settlements of different regions, such as the cities of Verkhnyaya Pyshma (Sverdlovsk region), Magnitogorsk (Chelyabinsk region), Chastoozersky municipal district (Kurgan region), where extremely low labor incomes and high per capita income indicators were determined. It is likely that significant payments of business income by large corporations in these municipalities have a strong impact on income statistics. We assume that such payments occur in large cities, but they are dissolved in total household income.
5. Despite all this, we can conclude that the greatest concentration of territories occurs in the range from 60 to 80% of labor income, while average per capita income is low for Russia. It can be stated that the following model has emerged: a high share of entrepreneurial income allows large cities to lead in per capita income; other cities and rural settlements are more focused on hired income, which does not bring a high standard of living (except for the northern regions).

The results of this study can be used to adjust the system of spatial development of Russian territories, based on the ratio of income received in municipalities of different types, and the developed research methodology can be used in other countries with similar statistical reporting.

Acknowledgements. The study was supported by the Russian Science Foundation grant No. 23-28-00431, https://rscf.ru/project/23-28-00431/.

References

1. Lorenz, M.O.: Methods of measuring the concentration of wealth. Publ. Am. Stat. Assoc. **9**(70), 209–219 (1905). https://doi.org/10.1080/15225437.1905.10503443

2. Harvey, L.A., Mierau, J.O., Rockey, J.: Inequality in an equal society. Oxford Bull. Econ. Stat. (2024). https://doi.org/10.1111/obes.12611
3. Wiese, R., Jalles, J.T., de Haan, J.: Structural reforms and income distribution: new evidence for OECD countries. Oxf. Econ. Pap. **76**(4), 1071–1088 (2024). https://doi.org/10.1093/oep/gpae002
4. Rahman, A., Sirojuzilam, S., Lubis, I., Pratomo, W.A.: Income inequality between provinces in Indonesia. Jurnal Ekonomi Malaysia **57**(3), 59–74 (2023). https://doi.org/10.17576/JEM-2023-5703-05
5. Zakaria, S., Sulaiman, N., Abd Malik, S.: Examining the pattern of household monthly income and expenditures by state in Malaysia. Economics (2024). https://doi.org/10.2478/eoik-2024-0042
6. Ivanovski, K., Awaworyi Churchill, S., Inekwe, J.: Convergence in income inequality across Australian states and territories. Soc. Indic. Res. **148**, 127–142 (2020). https://doi.org/10.1007/s11205-019-02201-0
7. Balcilar, K., Namazli, I.: Inflation effect on income inequality: A study on European countries (Version 1). *figshare* (2024). https://doi.org/10.6084/m9.figshare.25889026.v1
8. O'Reilly, C.: Barriers to entry, entrepreneurship, and income inequality within the USA. J. Entrepreneurship Public Policy **11**(4), 332–356 (2022). https://doi.org/10.1108/JEPP-06-2022-0069
9. Petrova, B., Ranaldi, M.: Determinants of income composition inequality. SocArXiv (2021). https://doi.org/10.31235/osf.io/vyrz7
10. Lee, J., Lee, K.: Decoupling of functional and household income distribution by economic growth: New findings from analysing the three-way growth-equity nexus. J. Int. Dev. **36**(5), 2270–2299 (2024). https://doi.org/10.1002/jid.3903
11. Koiry, S., Kairi, B., Pooja, P.: Impact of income diversification on multidimensional poverty: Household-level evidence from tea estates in Bangladesh. Heliyon **10**(5), e26509 (2024). https://doi.org/10.1016/j.heliyon.2024.e26509
12. Allen, J., Farber, S., Tiznado-Aitken, I.: Pathways to suburban poverty in nine Canadian metropolitan areas. Cities **147**, 104848 (2024). https://doi.org/10.1016/j.cities.2024.104848
13. Li, Q., Dong, L., Zhang, L.: Have pensions reduced the relative poverty? Empirical analysis from China CHARLS data. Heliyon **9**(12), e22711 (2023). https://doi.org/10.1016/j.heliyon.2023.e22711
14. Wang, G., Hao, Y., Ma, J.: Family income level, income structure, and dietary imbalance of elderly households in rural China. Foods **13**, 190 (2024). https://doi.org/10.3390/foods13020190
15. Kyagera, Y.: Microfinance institutions and household income of people in Kisoro District: a case study of Kisoro Municipality. Metrop. J. Soc. Educ. Res. **3**(3), 823–832 (2024)
16. Wołoszyn, A., Głowicka-Wołoszyn, R.: Income inequality of rural households in Poland: analysis by source of income. Ann. Polish Assoc. Agric. Agribusiness Economists **26**(1), 324–337 (2024). https://doi.org/10.5604/01.3001.0054.3788
17. Amate-Fortes, I., Guarnido-Rueda, A., Martínez-Navarro, D., Oliver-Márquez, F.J.: Income inequality and COVID-19 in the USA. Crit. Public Health **33**(5), 814–827 (2023). https://doi.org/10.1080/09581596.2023.2287961
18. Arzhenovskiy, S.: Statistical analysis of inequality and poverty with under-reporting incomes of Russian households. Voprosy Statistiki **31**(2), 39–51 (2024). https://doi.org/10.34023/2313-6383-2024-31-2-39-51
19. Ivakhnenko, T., Polbin, A., Sinelnikov-Murylev, S.: Economic complexity and income inequality in Russian regions. Voprosy Ekonomiki **5**, 105–127 (2024). https://doi.org/10.32609/0042-8736-2024-5-105-127

20. Zakharchuk, E., Pasynkov, A.: Regional balance model of financial flows through sectoral approaches system of national accounts. Econ. Reg. **13**(1), 318–330 (2017). https://doi.org/10.17059/2017-1-28
21. Pasynkov, A., Zakharchuk, E.: Inequality of household income in urban and rural territories of Russia. E3S Web Conf. **435**, 04003 (2023). https://doi.org/10.1051/e3sconf/202343504003

Regional Inequality in Household Incomes in China and Russia: Similarities and Differences

Alina Steblyanskaya[1], Aleksey Pasynkov[2(✉)], and Zhang Jiandong[3,4]

[1] School of Economics and Management, Harbin Engineering University, 31 Nantong Street, Nangang District, Harbin, China
alina_steblyanskaya@hrbeu.edu.cn

[2] Institute of Economics of the Ural Branch of the Russian Academy of Sciences, 29 Moskovskaya Street, 620014 Ekaterinburg, Russia
monografia@mail.ru

[3] Yongji Economic Development Zone, Jilin Railway Vocational Technical Institute, No. 1 Jihua East Road, Jilin City, Jilin Province, China

[4] Russian University of Transport (RUT MIIT), 9 Obraztsova Street, 127994 Moscow, Russia

Abstract. The purpose of this study is to compare the interregional differences in household incomes in the territories of China and Russia; in terms of economic development, the countries have both similar and different parameters. The study subjects were 31 provinces of China and 85 regions of Russia. The analysis of income sources across countries showed that in China households are focused on receiving income from business activities, and in Russia from social payments. Calculating the Per Capita Income ratio (further – PCI) for 2015–2022 revealed a gradual convergence of the income levels of China and Russia. At a regional level, PCI analysis determined that from 2015 to 2022 the difference in income between provinces decreased in China, while in Russia it increased. An additional comparison of the Minimum-to-average wage ratio (%) in the territories of Russia and China leads to a conclusion about a more substantial differentiation of economic indicators for the regions of the Russian Federation. As a result, the authors concluded that trends in changing disproportions in household income in China and Russia differ.

Keywords: Regions of Russia · Provinces of China · Interregional inequality · Households

JEL Classification: J31 · R13 · R28

1 Introduction

The expansion of trade, economic and cultural cooperation between the People's Republic of China and the Russian Federation, which has been actively continuing in recent years, is attributed to several factors. The most important ones include a common long border in the east of Eurasia, interest in deepening export and import transactions between

E. Kuzmin et al. (Eds.): EASET 2024, SPBE, pp. 133–145, 2025.
https://doi.org/10.1007/978-3-031-91159-0_9

countries, and integration in various interstate formats. Despite the different weights of economies in the world, there are many similarities between China and Russia: large territories, heterogeneity of economic indicators, the developing nature of the economy, and multiculturalism of the inhabiting peoples. Because China and Russia have approximately the same position in terms of nominal gross domestic product per capita (about 11–12 thousand dollars), the similarity only intensifies. Therefore, the purpose of this study is to compare regional disproportions in the level of income of Russia and China, as the leading indicator reflecting the standard of living of households.

First of all, there are many studies devoted to disparities in regional development. For example, Hindls et al. [1], using the example of 30 developed countries for 2000–2019, showed uneven relationships between the share of wages in total income and final household consumption.

A large study on the impact of structural changes in the Chinese economy on regional income inequality is presented in the publication of Tan & Akita [2] for 2000–2017, highlighting the components of reducing the income gap. Using extensive provincial income data in China from 2002–2018, Zhuang et al. [3] explored the causes of income inequality. The study showed that the main factors in reducing the income gap in the provinces were a reduction in wages between urban and rural areas, the massive movement of labor resources to urbanized areas, and the equalization of average wages between industries. Factors that reduce imbalances are also highlighted: technological progress, government regulation and structural economic transformations in China. In support of these findings, the publication of Liu et al. [4] examined the impact of financial technology on reducing income inequality in China. The authors argue that the widespread penetration of such technologies positively impacts income gaps, especially in low-income areas. The publication of Chen & Xu [5] provides a study of the relationship between the level of minimum wages and the likelihood of poverty in the provinces of China. The impact of international trade on income inequality between urban and rural areas is studied in the article Liang [6], and a conclusion is drawn about the relationship between income growth in the urbanized part of China and the expansion of exports. Chinese scientists are also developing research based on the relationship between the standard of living of the population and consumption of various types of energy [7], introducing innovations to increase incomes in rural areas [8], increasing efficiency land use outside urban areas [9], improving the income of older people in rural areas [10].

The Russian scientific research segment assesses income disparity among regions differently. The tax system's impact on household income is discussed in Pugachev's publication [11]. Through the concept of convergence, income inequality in Russian regions is considered in the publication Polbin & Ivakhnenko [12]. It is concluded that income inequality across Russian regions decreased in 2000–2010 (due to general economic growth and social transfers); this process slowed down in subsequent years. A resonably popular direction in Russian science is the study of income inequality through the study of spatial development. The article [13] examines spatial heterogeneity through the investment in fixed capital indicators and concludes that significant gaps exist. Other aspects of the uneven development of Russian regions are also studied: spatial imbalances in the context of strategic development [14], regional factors of production activity [15], economic indicators of regional development [16], gaps in the leading indicators of Russian regions [17], heterogeneity of innovative development [18], forecasting household income in the Arctic [19, 20].

However, there are practically no studies comparing the levels and dynamics of incomes of the Chinese and Russian populations. Therefore, this study will try to fill this research gap.

2 Methods and Data

. The object of study is the territorial-administrative subnational level. China has 34 provincial-level administrative units, however, three of them have limited data in the required volume for this study (Hong Kong, Macau, and Taiwan are not within the scope of the study). Thus, the authors use data from China's 31 territories (22 provinces, five autonomous regions and four directly administrated cities), hereinafter referred to as provinces. In Russia, even though the population is 10 times smaller, there are 85 regions (a total of 89 regions since 2022, but no data for Donetsk and Lugansk People's Republic, Zaporizhia and Kherson regions), they are different in size.

We use the following approaches to identify the features of disproportions in household income. First, we analyze some households' macroeconomic indicators, reflecting the sources of the population's well-being (labor and entrepreneurial income, social payments). A comparative analysis of the overall household income level in Russia and China in comparable units allows us to supplement the general idea of income dynamics. Secondly, we study the interregional income differences between China and Russia. First of all, this is regions and provinces PCI, which is a recognized indicator of the population's monetary well-being level. The available research period is from 2015 to 2022, the data source is the National Bureau of Statistics of China (https://data.stats.gov.cn/english/easyquery.htm?cn=E0103) and the Russian Statistical Service (https://rosstat.gov.ru/folder/210/document/13205). Another important indicator analyzed is the ratio of average wages in every region of Russia and every provinces of China, with the minimum wage established in each territory. In the PRC, the minimum wage was introduced in 1994. The establishment of its size was delegated to the provincial level. Also, the minimum level of income from labor activity is divided into monthly (full working day) and hourly levels, there are also established allowances for overtime and work in unfavorable working conditions. As of 2022, the lowest value of the indicator is set in Anhui (1,650 yuan per month), the highest in Shanghai (2,590 yuan), and the average value for all provinces is 1,980.6 yuan. In the Russian Federation, the minimum wage long existed since the Soviet Union. However, after 1991, it was more formal, reflecting the limit of physical survival. Currently, his indicator reflects the actual economic requirements, in Russia it is set by order throughout the country, as of 2022 it is equal to 15,279 rubles. Regions have the right to adjust the minimum amount upwards, depending on economic development conditions. However, as shown by the study of data tables, only 20 regions took advantage of this opportunity, slightly increasing the amount. Therefore, several researchers [21] rightly criticize the use of this indicator as an assessment of the income gap, preferring analogs of the indicator "The amount of the subsistence minimum in the regions of the Russian Federation". However, this indicator has a different economic nature in statistics, and there is no analog in China. Therefore, using the official minimum wage in this study allows to compare the income levels of households in Russia and China.

3 Results

A study of the relationship between sources of income and the standard of living of households in relation to the regions of China and Russia would make it possible to identify the primary sources of well-being of the population. Thus, in the People's Republic of China statistics, we found data concerning wages of hired workers based on the type of economic activity. Russian regional tables contain data concerning sources of income comparable to the SNA, but their adequacy (in terms of adjustments made) raises doubts among the authors. To display the sources of income of households in Russia and China, we use general data on the national economy, since comparable data on territories is not available in statistical databases. Analysis of such data showed that statistics on sources of income at the national level are grouped comparable in China and Russia, the difference lies in the lack of allocation of social payments. Apparently, in China such payments are insignificant, since the main item of expenditure in Russia is pensions from state funds; in China there is a mixed pension system. Therefore, the indicators of Income from Wages and Salaries, Net Business Income and from Properties are comparable without changes. The fourth component of income in Chinese statistics, Net Income from Transfer, in the Russian system includes social payments and other cash receipts. Data on the structure of household income in Russia and China are presented in Fig. 1.

It shows that income from Wages and Salaries in both countries is approximately the same, in China with a downward trend, in Russia this share is growing significantly. There is a big difference between countries in income from business activities; in China it fluctuates around 17–19% for 2015–2022, and in Russia the peak of such income occurred in 2020 (5.8%), on average it takes just over 5%. A similar situation arises in another source of household income, from property. Chinese households have received 8–9% property income over the years, with a rising trend as a share of total income. In Russia, such income fluctuates around 5%, and the share gradually decreases. The most important in Russia is other income from transfers, accounting for about a third of all household income. At the same time, the share of social payments is constantly increasing (from 18.2% in 2015 to 20.2% in 2022), while other revenues are decreasing (from 17.4 to 11.4%). In the Russian statistical system, the latter indicator broadly shows shadow (unofficial) income, calculated by balancing it with final consumption. In the People's Republic of China, transfers fluctuate around 18% and reflect households' income from abroad. Thus, a comparison of the sources of income of Russian and Chinese households showed that in China a more significant share belongs to entrepreneurial activity, while in Russia the population receives more social payments from the state.

The structure of household income better reflects the sources of well-being of the population, and various indicators are used to determine the population's standard of living. One of the popular indicators is the comparison of income at purchasing power parity (PPP), which shows the population's ability to purchase certain goods on average

Fig. 1. Structure of household income in Russia and China in %, 2015–2022.

income. However, like any assessment technique, this indicator also has disadvantages. Using a limited set of comparable price weights, which often do not reflect the specifics of the economic and social development of territories, the use of PPP does not fully ensure the comparability of the living standards of households. Therefore, in this study we use the traditional approach to measure the income level of the population (in US dollars). Average per capita income is used as a basis for comparison, as it is more fair for assessing the overall well-being of households. Using the yuan' average annual exchange rate (over the years under review it changes slightly) and the ruble (the range of fluctuations is more than 20%), as well as official information from statistical departments on national data on per capita income, Fig. 2 was constructed.

As can be seen from the figure, the PCI level in Russia for 2015–2022 remained higher than in China. However, the difference in income is rapidly narrowing; if in 2015 income in Russia was 1.82 times higher than China, then in 2022 this gap decreased to 1.32 times. At the same time, in the last year there was a sharp increase in Russian income, due to the ruble's depreciation caused by record exports and low import values. In 2021, the gap between household incomes in Russia and China was minimal for the entire period, amounting to only 1.24 times. It is also evident from the graph that despite the constant growth of nominal wages in Russia (from 30,254 rubles in 2015 to 44,937 in 2022), in dollar terms the fluctuations are not so significant, that is, they are approximately at the same level. In the People's Republic of China, with comparable

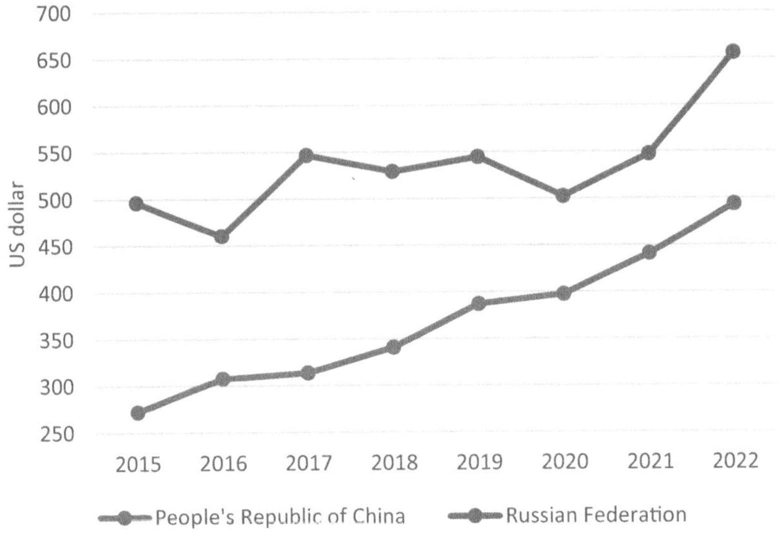

Fig. 2. Russia and China households PCI, US dollars, 2015–2022.

growth rates of per capita income in yuan (from 21,966 to 36,883), due to a stable exchange rate, income measured in dollars is growing steadily. For example, the growth in income of Russian households in 2015/2022 was 32%, and in 2015/2021 it was only 10%. At the same time, the Chinese population became 81% richer in eight years.

In general, this indicator in the Russian Federation shows a slight increase and actually stagnates around the level of 550 dollars per capita. The reasons for this are different, such as a slowdown in economic development, unstable exchange rates, decline in export earnings, etc. At the same time, China maintained a trend of constantly increasing income in dollar terms, despite severe restrictions on economic activity during the pandemic.

As noted earlier, determining income averages across countries is essential to calculating overall household wealth. However, the specificity of the territorial development of both countries, consisting of large territories with different economic potential, makes it necessary to consider living standard' regional characteristics. First of all, using available data for the regions of Russia and provinces of China, we determine the differences and dynamics in per capita income. We compiled a database concerning two countries' territories from 2015 to 2022 and compared the data with the average values for countries (see Figs. 3 and 4).

From the presented figures, it can be seen that China provinces' PCI are pretty evenly distributed. Thus, three regions can be called "rich", exceeding the average value by more than 1.5 times (Beijing, Shanghai, Zhejiang). Minimum per capita incomes are recorded in Tibet (2015) and Gansu (2022), most regions are in the range of 0.75 to 1 of the national average. Over the eight years studied, the greatest increase in living standards was recorded in the Tibet region (income increased from 0.56 to 0.72 of the average) and Guizhou (from 0.62 to 0.69). A significant decrease in per capita income

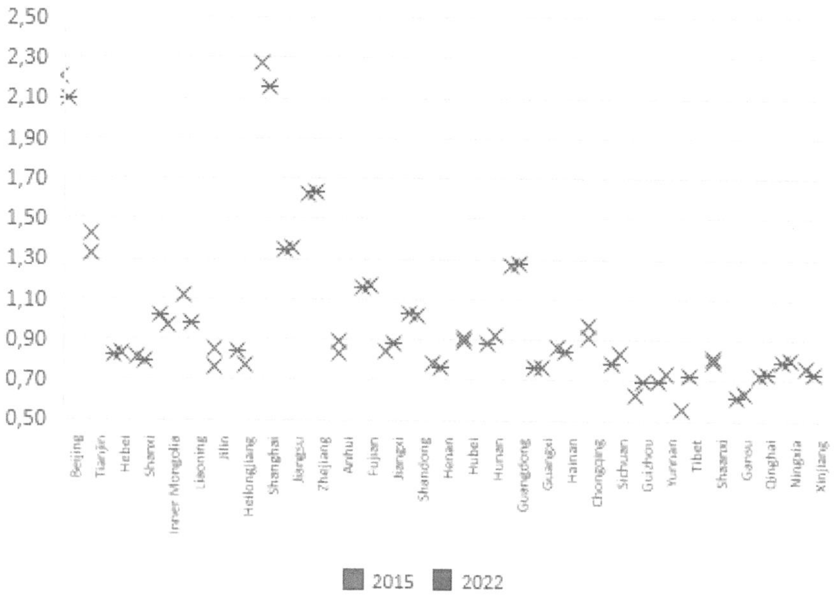

Fig. 3. PCI dynamics in the China' provinces, 2015 and 2022.

was observed in four regions: Liaoning (from 1.12 to 0.98), Shanghai (from 2.27 to 2.16), Beijing (from 2.21 to 2.10) and Tianjin (from 1.42 to 1.30). Other provinces of China show insignificant fluctuations relative to the national average in the range of 10%. In approximately half of the territories, PCI growth occurs synchronously with the average value, deviating by several percent in one direction or another. The minimum value of average per capita income among the provinces of China was 0.56 in 2015, and in 2022 it increased to 0.63. At the same time, the maximum average per capita income level was 2.27 at the beginning of the period, and in 2022 it decreased to 2.16. Thus, the gap between the highest and lowest values decreased from 1.71 to 1.53 times over this period. In our opinion, this indicates an equalization of living standards in the People's Republic of China between regions, when the gap between the richest and poorest areas is narrowing.

The regions of the Russian Federation demonstrate more uneven development in terms of PCI. High values (over 1.5 to the average) are found in 8 regions out of 85. The maximum indicator of excess was in the Nenets autonomous district (2.38) in 2015. In 2020 the leader changed to the Yamalo-Nenets autonomous area (2.60). Also, PCI doubled in the City of Moscow, Magadan region, and Chukotka autonomous district. It is worth noting that almost all of these regions (except Moscow) are remote northern territories with difficult living conditions compensated by high household incomes. The poorest regions of Russia are the Republic of Kalmykia (0.50 of average per capita income) in 2015 and the Republic of Ingushetia (0.46) in 2020. On the contrary, these are the southern regions of Russia, with traditionally low incomes of the population,

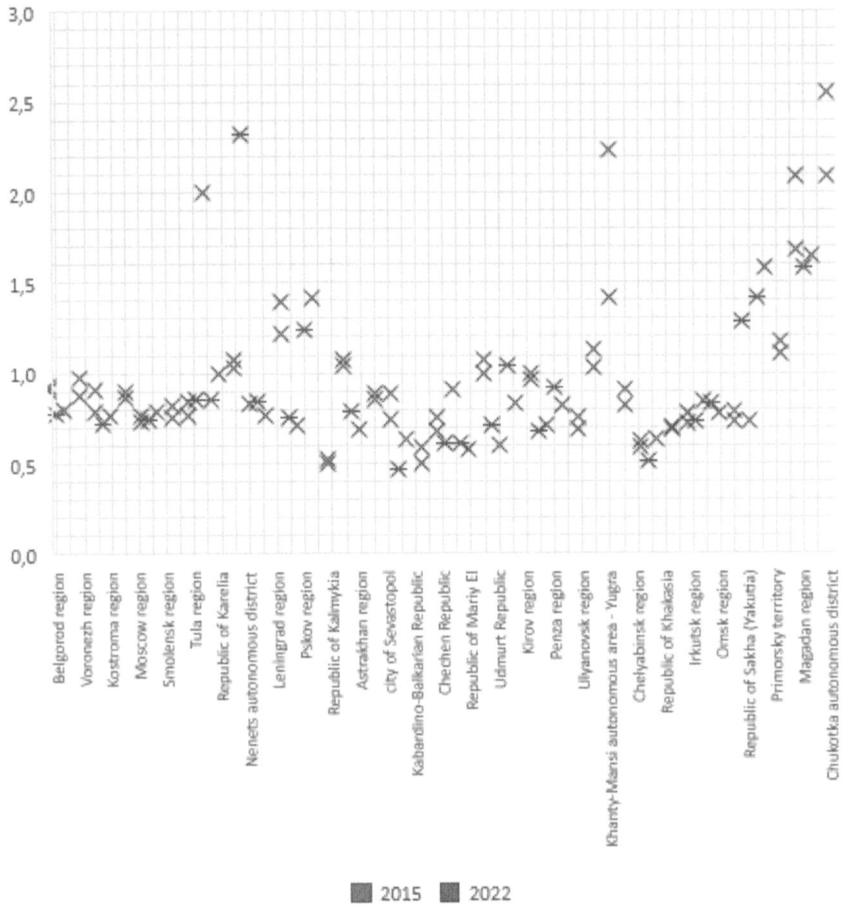

Fig. 4. PCI dynamics in the Russian Federation' regions, 2015 and 2022 (no data for Donetsk and Lugansk People's Republic, Zaporizhia and Kherson regions).

the basis of which constitutes traditional types of economy. The figure shows that most Russian regions are located on the border from 0.5 to 0.75 of the country's average income. In contrast to the Chinese provinces, the difference between the 2015 and 2022 indicators is more noticeable in Russian regions. The leader in household welfare growth was the Chukotka autonomous district (from 2.09 to 2.55, that is, immediately by 0.45 points), as well as the Magadan region (from 1.68 to 2.09). Also, seven more regions (that is, only 9 out of 85) improved their household income indicators: Yamalo-Nenets autonomous area (+0.36 points), city of Sevastopol (+0.20), Murmansk region and The City of Sankt-Petersburg (+0.18), Kamchatka territory (+0.16), Republic of Karelia (+0.14), The City of Moscow (+0.12). On the other hand, seven regions showed more than a 10% drop in household income relative to the Russian average, with the Perm region being the anti-leader (from 1.04 in 2015 to 0.83 in 2022). Other territories showed a smaller decrease in population income: Republic of Dagestan (−0.14), Republic of Bashkortastan and Khanty-Mansi autonomous area – Yugra, as well as Kaluga region (−0.12), Samara region (−0.10). This group has no patterns; there was a decline in oil-producing territories, industrial regions and poor southern territories.

An interesting aspect of the study conducted on Russian regions is the trend in changing the gap between rich and poor areas. If in 2015 the PCI minimum value was 0.5 among Russian regions, then in 2022 this figure became 0.46. The maximum income level in 2015 was estimated at 2.38, in 2022 it was 2.60. Thus, the discrepancy between the minimum and maximum indicators increased from 1.88 to 2.13 over eight years. Taking into account the previously noted changes in the incomes of individual Russian regions, it can be stated that income inequality is increasing.

At the same time, the economic and geographical features of the development of such large countries as China and Russia must consider the specifics of various regions and provinces, due to higher (for example, Arctic regions) and lower (rural areas) cost of living. Therefore, we tried to compare the average wages of regions with a minimum wage. This approach based on the available statistics concerning average wages by region in both countries. Because of China and Russia have almost the same share of labor income in total household cash receipts, it is possible to assess the working population's well-being level using Minimum-to-average wage ratio (%).

The results of comparing of average wages and the minimum wage in the territories of China and Russia are presented in Figs. 5 and 6.

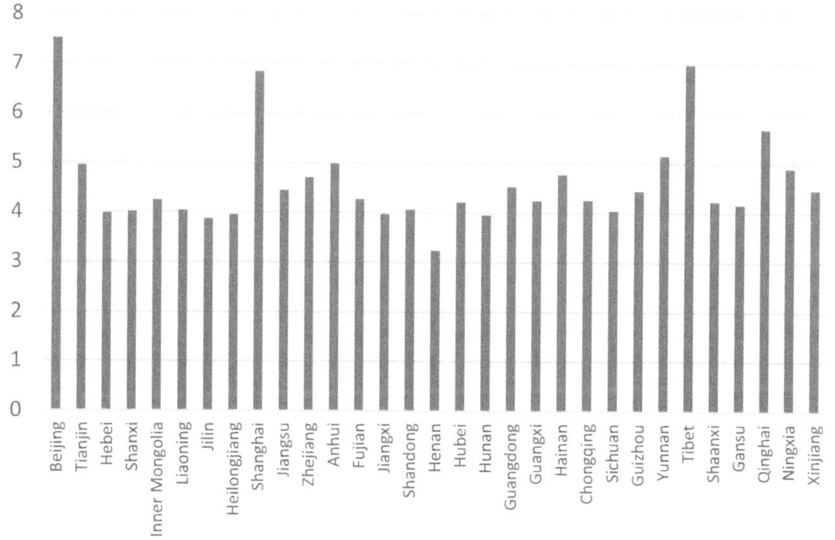

Fig. 5. Minimum-to-average wage ratio (%), Chinese provinces, 2022.

In general, across the regions of China, the average wage exceeds the minimum value by 4.61 times. The maximum gap is observed in Beijing (7.51), followed by Tibet (6.98)

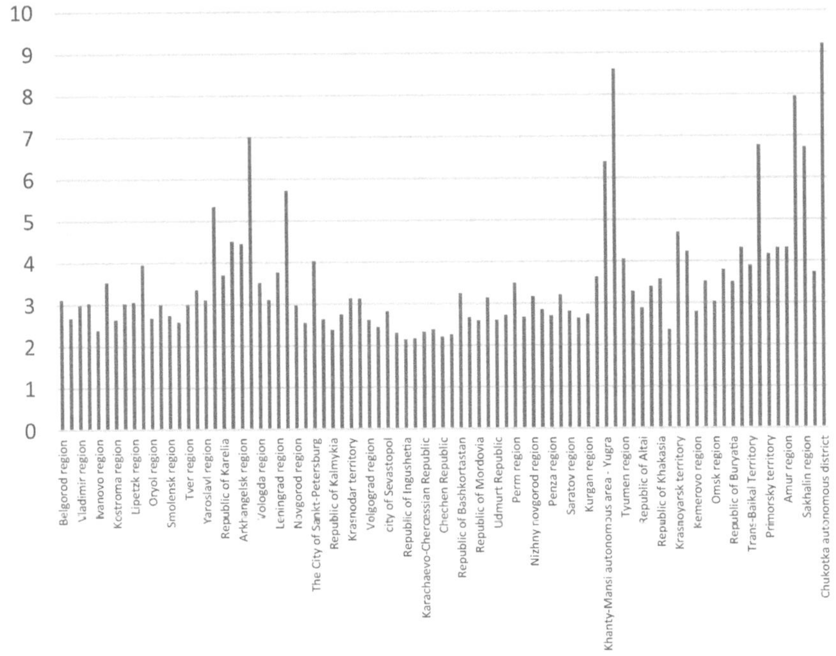

Fig. 6. Minimum-to-average wage ratio (%), Russian regions, 2022 (no data for Donetsk and Lugansk People's Republic, Zaporizhia and Kherson regions).

and Shanghai (6.84). Only six provinces have a minimum-to-average wage ratio (%) of less than four, with the lowest in Henan (3.23). Like the average per capita value, the analysis of average wages in Chinese regions showed a synchronicity of their growth among territories relative to 2015/2022, with slight deviations in some cases. The regions of Russia are more heterogeneous in this regard. Minimum-to-average wage ratio (%) for all Russian regions is 3.5. However, the number of regions with an indicator above 4 is nineteen; the maximum values are in the Chukotka autonomous district (9.20), Yamalo-Nenets autonomous area (8.61) and Magadan region (7.95). Therefore, a significant part of Russian regions are below the average value for the indicator. As the figure shows, wages fluctuate around three minimum payments in most territories. The Republic of Ingushetia (2.15), Kabardino-Balkarian Republic (2.17) and Republic of North Ossetia–Alania (2.21) have the minimum ratio. The gap between the richest and poorest regions in this context is 7.06 points in Russia (in China – 4.27).

4 Conclusions

A study of the relationship between living standards and sources of income of households in the Russian Federation and the People's Republic of China, based on available statistical material, showed sufficient comparability of the available information on regional development. The proposed approaches for the comparative assessment of population welfare indicators for both countries allowed the authors to highlight several main conclusions.

1. An analysis of the sources of income of households in Russia and China showed that the share of income from hired labor is approximately the same in these countries; a significant difference is observed in the structure from other incomes. In China, the population is more focused on receiving income from entrepreneurial activities (from business and property), while Russian households receive a relatively high share of income from government social payments (pensions, benefits). At the same time, during the period under review, the trends of increasing this income share in China and Russia are becoming more pronounced.
2. The different income structures of the countries' populations may have become one of the main reasons for the multidirectional changes in the PCI dynamics in US dollars. In Russian household incomes stagnate from 2015 to 2022. In contrast, there is a systematic and continuous increase in the well-being for the Chinese population. If we continue with the existing trend, then the convergence of average per capita income in US dollars in the near future will be obvious. At the same time, this indicator is significantly influenced by the national currency's exchange rate, which may accelerate or delay income parity between China and Russia.
3. Regional measurements of per capita incomes in Russia and China showed that income gaps are significant in both countries. In China, the highest rates are observed in the major cities of Shanghai and Beijing. There has also been some income polarization between the rich southern and the poorer northern provinces. In Russia, everything is precisely the opposite: the highest values of the ratio of average income to regional ones are recorded in the northern and Arctic territories (where natural resources are extracted for export) and the city of Moscow, and low values are found in the regions of the south.
4. An analysis of the dynamics of the PCI disparity by region revealed that in China there is a tendency for the income gap between territories to decrease. The data shows that income growth across provinces is synchronous, which, given the diversity and vastness of China, indicates an effective policy to reduce interregional differences. In the Russian Federation, the disparity between regions is only increasing, and there are also high fluctuations in the average income of citizens among regions. The reason for this phenomenon can be identified as low population density in most territories, in which a slight change in economic activity significantly changes the local population's income.
5. The presented analysis of average wages in the territories of Russia and China, relative to the minimum wage, revealed its dependence on per capita income. In both countries the wages of hired workers take up more than half, and other incomes most likely have a similar distribution across territories. However, the gaps in the minimum wage in Russian regions are significantly higher than in China, which once again confirms the thesis about the high polarization of incomes in Russian regions.
6. At the same time, different policies for establishing the minimum wage could also impact the comparison of average wages. Since the minimum wage is set for the entire country in Russia, practically without taking into account the cost of living

of individual territories, this had a significant impact on the presented calculation results.

China's regional policy of equalizing living standards generally looks more effective than Russia's. This is due to objective factors (population of territories, closer ties between regions, model of economic development) and subjective ones (different levels of minimum wages by region, minimum level of social security, etc.). When forming a spatial development policy, Russia needs to use the PRC's positive experience in equalizing household's incomes and reducing disparities in the economic development of regions.

Acknowledgements. The study was supported by the Russian Science Foundation grant No. 23-28-00431, https://rscf.ru/project/23-28-00431/.

References

1. Hindls, R., Marek, L., Hronová, S.: Changes in the structure of household disposable income in selected countries as a reflection of crises after 2000. Stat. Transit. New Ser. **23**(4), 1–19 (2022). https://doi.org/10.2478/stattrans-2022-0039
2. Tan, L., Akita, T.: Structural changes and income inequality in China, 2000–2017: a bi-dimensional inequality decomposition analysis. Sustainability **15**(1), 401 (2023). https://doi.org/10.3390/su15010401
3. Zhang, M., Liu, J., Liu, L., Zhou, D.: Inequality in urban household energy consumption for 30 Chinese provinces. Energy Policy **172**, 113326 (2023). https://doi.org/10.1016/j.enpol.2022.113326
4. Liu, K., Hao, Y., Ge, Y., Mu, W.: Can FinTech curb income inequality in China? J. Bus. Econ. Manag. **24**(6), 960–975 (2023). https://doi.org/10.3846/jbem.2023.20653
5. Chen, J., Xu, Z.: Minimum wages and household income distribution: evidence from China. Rev. Dev. Econ. **28**(4), 1572–1601 (2024). https://doi.org/10.1111/rode.13109
6. Liang, S.: International trade and urban-rural income inequality in China. Appl. Econ. Lett. **31**(13), 1243–1246 (2023). https://doi.org/10.1080/13504851.2023.2178622
7. Hu, W., Ho, M.S., Cao, J.: Energy consumption of urban households in China. China Econ. Rev. **58**, 101343 (2019). https://doi.org/10.1016/j.chieco.2019.101343
8. Zhou, Y., Guo, Y., Liu, Y., Wu, W., Li, Y.: Targeted poverty alleviation and land policy innovation: some practice and policy implications from China. Land Use Policy **74**, 53–65 (2018). https://doi.org/10.1016/j.landusepol.2017.04.037
9. Liu, Y.: Introduction to land use and rural sustainability in China. Land Use Policy **74**, 1–4 (2018). https://doi.org/10.1016/j.landusepol.2018.01.032
10. Lu, H., Gao, M., Li, G., Li, T., Luo, Q.: Has the household old-age burden affected farm household incomes? Evidence from a survey of Chinese farm households. Agriculture **14**, 687 (2024). https://doi.org/10.3390/agriculture14050687
11. Pugachev, A.: Impact of the level and structure of the tax burden on citizens' inequality. Financ. J. **15**(3), 59–77 (2023). https://doi.org/10.31107/2075-1990-2023-3-59-77
12. Polbin, A., Ivakhnenko, T.: Convergence of income inequality in Russia's regions. Spatial Econ. **18**(4), 68–92 (2022). https://doi.org/10.14530/se.2022.4.068-092
13. Vyakina, I.V.: Spatial differentiation of regions' investment appeal in the context of economic security. Econ. Anal.: Theory Pract. **16**(8), 1455–1472 (2017). https://doi.org/10.24891/ea.16.8.1455

14. Antipin, I., Vlasova, N., Ivanova, O.: Strategic priorities for managing spatial inequalities in the socio-economic development of Russian regions. Upravlenets **11**(6), 28–43 (2020). https://doi.org/10.29141/2218-5003-2020-11-6-3
15. Drapkin, I.M., Mariev, O.S., Semyonova, Y.O, Kolyagina, A.I.: Determinants of spatial location in the Russian economy: Regional aspect. Bull. Ural Federal Univ. Series Econ. Manage. **15**(5), 717–733 (2016). https://doi.org/10.15826/vestnik.2016.15.5.36
16. Kugan, S.F.: Spatial development of territories in the context of economic development of the region. Корпоративное управление и инновационное развитие экономики Севера (2020). https://doi.org/10.34130/2070-4992-2020-1-95-100
17. Suvorova, A.: Features of spatial development management of the regional economy in the modern Russian conditions. Fundam. Res. **9**, 53–58 (2021). https://doi.org/10.17513/fr.43093
18. Naumov, I., Nikulina, N.: Scenario modeling and forecasting of the spatial heterogeneity of innovation development in Russia. Econ. Soc. Changes: Facts, Trends, Forecast **16**(4), 71–87 (2023). https://doi.org/10.15838/esc.2023.4.88.4
19. Zakharchuk, E.A.: Spatial structure of the formation of value added in the Arctic territories. Econ. Reg. **15**(2), 391–408 (2019). https://doi.org/10.17059/201-2-7
20. Zakharchuk, E.A.: Sanctions and scenarios of economic development of the Russian Arctic territories (the case of the Yamalo-Nenets Autonomous District). R-Economy **8**(3), 281–294 (2022). https://doi.org/10.15826/recon.2022.8.3.022
21. Gluschenko, K.: Costs of living and real incomes in the Russian regions. Reg. Res. Russ. **12**, 365–377 (2022). https://doi.org/10.1134/S2079970522700022

Clustering of Russian Regions: Transformation Factors and Economic Behavior Patterns

Natalia A. Kosolapova, Anastasia Y. Nikitaeva, Olga I. Dolgova, Danil S. Gridnev, and Anna A. Fedorova(✉)

Southern Federal University, 105/42 Bolshaya Sadovaya Street, 344006 Rostov-on-Don, Russia
{nakosolapova,aunikitaeva,oldolgova,dgridnev,afed}@sfedu.ru

Abstract. Currently, Russian regions are developing under challenging conditions shaped by new internal and external factors. In this regard, in order to understand the logic of development, it is important to identify groups of regions that are similar or different in a number of key indicators. Such indicators are highlighted in the study from the perspective of system economic theory and an endogenous approach to economic development. The identification of groups of regions in the study was carried out using cluster analysis performed by affinity propogation method. This, in turn, allowed searching for factors of regional transformations that are adequate to the new realities. The behavioral patterns of Russian regions were identified and analyzed. The analysis of industry specialization and non-economic factors of regional development was carried out on the basis of official statistics and mass media data. As a result of the study, six clusters were identified, and their characteristics are given. The analysis of the dynamics of regional transitions between clusters made it possible to determine the appropriate behaviors. For each region, the number of its transitions from one cluster to another was calculated. The analysis of industry specialization for regions with different models showed the indirect influence of specialization on the stability of the behavior of the subject of Russia. Based on the analysis of non-economic activities, it is concluded that it is important to utilize the potential of regional value chains for the technological and social development of regional economies. Based on the studying news reports, economic, political, scientific, and technical events that can affect the development of regions have been discovered.

Keywords: Regional development · Economic growth · Regional clusters · Industry structure · Economic specialization

JEL Classification: R11 · R13 · O14

1 Introduction

The contemporary development of Russian regions is occurring within a context of considerable complexity and ambiguity. On the one hand, the experience of implementing the regional policy has been accumulated, the importance of the role of meso-level governance entities and the necessity of considering territorial specifics in the establishment

E. Kuzmin et al. (Eds.): EASET 2024, SPBE, pp. 146–160, 2025.
https://doi.org/10.1007/978-3-031-91159-0_10

of economic strategies and programmes has been acknowledged, the Strategy for Spatial Development of the country has been adopted, certain types and specialisations of Russia subjects have been formed, and projects to ensure technological sovereignty are being implemented [1]. On the other hand, the regions of the country have been subjected to a multitude of shocks in recent years, both as a consequence of the global pandemic and the destruction of numerous traditional supply chains, as well as the imposition of sanctions against Russia for geopolitical reasons. Russian regions are required to construct their activities and formulate long-term development plans that take into account the global digital transformation and the Fourth Industrial Revolution (Industry 4.0), the actualising climate and environmental agenda, and the ever-increasing complexity, riskiness, and uncertainty of the environment. The significant changes in the conditions of socio-economic development give rise to questions regarding the practical effectiveness of the key provisions of meso-level economic growth theories and prompt a search for appropriate drivers and constraints of regional transformations that are aligned with the new realities.

In this regard, a series of research questions emerge pertaining to the current delineation of socio-economic development indicators among the constituent territories of Russia, the patterns of regional development observed over the past decade, the causal relationships that underpin the formation and evolution of these patterns, and the extent to which the established economic specialisation or sectoral structure influences the behaviour of meso-economic systems. In accordance with this, the purpose of the study is to identify clusters of Russian regions, determine the factors of their development, and analyze patterns of behavior in modern conditions.

2 Literature Review

The study of regional economic development, both in the context of the establishment and implementation of economic policy and in terms of the search for the most effective approaches, models and factors of regional development, has remained a highly relevant field of study over the past decades.

Kleiner examines the evolution of regions as meso-level economic systems from the vantage point of the system approach and system economics [2, 3]. The meso-economic worldview is concerned with the internal forces of development of the system under consideration. This allows for a significant improvement in the quality of strategic planning, thereby enabling the realisation of the potential of the relevant subject. According to Kleiner's position, the main constituent parts of the region are regional regulatory bodies, regional society, regional economy, and regional business [4].

In the context of the same scientific paradigm, researchers have demonstrated that innovation is a significant driver of technological advancement, which simultaneously addresses the challenges associated with population protection [4].

Furthermore, significant research is conducted on multilevel economic processes and causal mechanisms within the context of the synergetic (self-organisation) paradigm and complexity economics [5]. Other studies look at economic development taking into account the influence of media events and industrial coordination of economic agents under digital transformation [6].

Concurrently, the specifics of the current stage of economic development and the corresponding set of risks, opportunities and mechanisms of transformation of economic systems, including at the regional level and within value chains, are investigated within the framework of the Industry 4.0 concept. In turn, some scholars have examined the impact of Industry 4.0 itself on the organisational coherence of economic ecosystems [7]. In recent years, scholars have increasingly focused their attention on the relationship between technological transformations and their regional dimensions and territorial contexts [8–10]. The spatial patterns of Industry 4.0 technological transformations have been largely unexplored by researchers, and there is a lack of understanding regarding the local drivers of such transformations. Consequently, it is unclear which types of regions are most likely to be affected by them [11–13].

The bilateral relationship between the digital space formed in the Russian Federation (RF) subjects and the socio-economic indicators of their development has been the subject of study by Akberdina, Naumov, and Krasnykh [14].

The endogenous approach also considers modern economic development in the territorial-sectoral context, with a particular emphasis on intra-regional ties and relations. In its application, development is considered a territorial process, rather than a functional one. Internal interests are given priority, and the balance of territorial-localised industrial systems is achieved through the development of partnerships and the formation of ecosystems of various types, thereby increasing the connectivity of the environment [15, 16]. Some researchers have identified the importance of the spatial distribution of regional resources as an environment that affects the cohesiveness of economic structures in industry [17]. Territorial characteristics also influenced the processes of transition of regional industrial ecosystems to circular and sustainable patterns [18–20].

A comprehensive assessment of the existing regional specialisation and an economic profile of Russian regions, were conducted by the team of Higher School of Economics [21].

A significant challenge in the field of regional economic development is the multitude of studies that adopt a perspective aligned with the concept of sustainable development [22–25]. Concurrently, the sustainable development of regions is examined from a comprehensive perspective, encompassing numerous dimensions in alignment with the United Nations Sustainable Development Goals. Additionally, the implementation of this concept is scrutinized, with a particular focus on circular economy models [26]. In contrast, Novoseltseva, Palatkin and Rasskazova examine the sustainability of territorial systems, specifically the tendency towards positive macroeconomic dynamics, in the context of economic indicators [27].

The research conducted by the Institute of Economics of the Ural Branch of the Russian Academy of Sciences has made significant contributions to the understanding of Russian regional development, with a particular focus on its risks and opportunities [28].

It is similarly important to emphasise a block of interdisciplinary studies that considers non-economic factors of regional economic development. Thus, in the case of German regions, researchers have demonstrated that trust constitutes an essential resource for territorial development, exerting an influence on the innovative activities of economic entities [17]. Furthermore, studies conducted in China corroborate the significant role of trust in the socio-economic development of regions [29, 30].

Despite the extensive body of research on regional development, there is a scarcity of studies that adopt a comprehensive, structural and dynamic approach to analysing groups of regions. Instead, studies tend to focus on individual aspects or specific characteristics of the corresponding meso-economic systems. There is a need to identify and investigate the behavioural patterns of Russian regions and the factors that influence them in greater depth.

3 Material and Methods

The presented research is methodologically based on a combination of quantitative and qualitative methods. At the first step, in accordance with the theory of system economics and the endogenous approach to regional development, a set of indicators characterizing Russian regions was selected. The data source was official statistical data, characterising various subsystems of the regional economy. The selected indicators included: per capita energy consumption, gross regional product, fixed assets investment, average per capita income, depreciation of fixed assets, innovation activity level, share of loss-making firms and manufacturing index.

An unsupervised learning algorithm was employed for the analysing the dataset. This is due to the absence of data regarding the true classes of the regions. Such classes cannot be objectively established by a scoring method. Consequently, the structure of the data had to be learned directly from the data themselves, relying on metrics of similarity between sample units. This necessitated the application of clustering algorithms. Cluster analysis is an effective exploratory data analysis technique that can reveal internal patterns and regularities in a data set. Among the clustering algorithms, the Affinity Propagation algorithm was selected because it best aligned with the nature of the objectives [32].

In contrast to other algorithms, such as k-means or hierarchical algorithms, this algorithm does not require the number of clusters to be known in advance. In the absence of prior knowledge regarding the classification of Russian regions, it is essential to employ algorithms that do not necessitate the specification of the number of clusters. Secondly, some common algorithms (such as k-means) produce even clusters. However, in regional studies, this is an inadequate approach, as the actual distribution of regions into classes is likely to be uneven due to current economic and demographic trends. Affinity Propagation, on the other hand, produces clusters of varying sizes. Thirdly, Affinity Propagation is one of the few algorithms capable of exploring non-linear relationships in a dataset. However, this algorithm also has some disadvantages, the most significant of which is its computational complexity.

The Affinity Propagation algorithm is founded upon an initial search for exemplary sample units around which the final clusters are formed [33]. The exemplary cluster points are identified through an iterative process of message exchange between sampling units, continuing until the algorithm converges or the maximum number of iterations is reached. The messages exchanged between points contain information regarding the similarity of the sampling units to each other, as well as the suitability of the sampling unit as a representative sample for the cluster. Upon completion of the algorithm, the most suitable sample units are selected as sample units (centroids), and the final clusters are formed around them.

A single data panel was generated using the Pandas module, consisting of 1,058 sample units spanning the period from 2010 to 2022 across eight features. Before clustering, the data were standardized and normalized using the preprocessing module from scikit-learn, as the dataset's traits exhibited varying scales and units [34, 35].

The Silhouette coefficient was selected as the metric that controls the training of the model [36]. As the true values of the classes (targets) in the data are unknown, the model performance must be estimated from the model itself. The Silhouette coefficient serves this purpose, with higher values corresponding to denser and better-separated clusters, and vice versa. The coefficient itself varies between −1 and 1 [37]:

$$S = \frac{(b - a)}{max(a, b)}, \tag{1}$$

where, a is the average distance between the sample and all other points in the same class; b is the average distance between the sample and all other points in the next closest cluster.

In order to implement the algorithm, the sklearn.cluster module was used, which contains the majority of state-of-the-art clustering algorithms [38]. The AffinityPropagation class is responsible for the implementation of the Affinity Propagation algorithm within this module. The 'preference' parameter was set to -50, and the 'damping' parameter was set to 0.90. The maximum number of iterations of the algorithm was set to one thousand rounds. These hyperparameter values were identified as the optimal set through a brute-force search, with the exception of the 'preference' parameter, for which the search was conducted in increments of 25. It was necessary to conduct a manual search of values due to the algorithm's inability to converge on all points within the hyperparameter space.

This allowed us to analyse the typology and structure of the clusters. Based on this, patterns of regional behaviour in terms of maintaining or altering their affiliation with a specific cluster were determined. For a number of regions exhibiting particularly extreme behaviours, an in-depth analysis was conducted to examine the sectoral structure, economic specialisation, and event-news agenda.

4 Results

4.1 Clustering of Russian Regions

The model identified six clusters, the average values of the features of which are presented in Table 1. The Silhouette coefficient for the developed model was 0.332, which corresponds to an adequate level of clustering, particularly in light of the essential heterogeneity of the available regional data.

The resulting clusters have unique characteristics of the economy, on the basis of which their conditional ranking can be carried out. The cluster that showed the worst values of economic indicators can be noted as "cluster 2". The cluster regions are characterized by a low level of production and innovation activity, income of the population,

Table 1. Identified clusters and their average feature values.

Cluster label	0	1	2	3	4	5
Per capita energy consumption, million kilowatt-hours	4.95	6.02	4.75	18.66	6.62	11.26
Gross regional product, Rub	429328.11	646912.93	277055.1	1221274.43	2006971.41	2082664.54
Fixed assets investment, Rub	64947.04	71540.77	66240.96	132218.89	100272.15	302778.54
Average per capita income, Rub	19728.74	24914.19	22082.9	25464.09	31938.48	48009.64
Depreciation of fixed assets	40.09	57.17	45.35	44.89	47.89	44.58
Innovation activity level, percent	7.98	10.18	6.86	7.85	17.93	9.02
Share of loss-making firms, percent	29.63	29.14	40.18	31.96	29.36	36.41
Manufacturing index	111.71	103.61	102.26	102.72	105.07	102.58

Note: calculated by the authors according to data [39]

GRP, a high proportion of unprofitable enterprises, low values of investment in fixed assets, and electricity consumption per capita. Cluster 1 also reflects a rather weak state of the economy due to high depreciation of fixed assets, a low level of investment in fixed assets, and the value of GRP. However, it has indicators higher than cluster 2 in terms of the per capita income of the population and the level of innovation activity and is characterized by a relatively small number of unprofitable enterprises. Cluster 0 demonstrates a high level of production combined with the lowest depreciation of fixed assets and a small number of unprofitable enterprises. The indicators of investment in fixed assets and the level of per capita income are at a low level. Cluster 3 is characterized by positive values of household income, GRP, and the level of investment in fixed assets. The indicator of electricity consumption per capita is also of the highest importance. Cluster 5 has the highest values of investment in fixed assets, GRP, and average per capita income. At the same time, the cluster can be characterized by a low production index and a high proportion of unprofitable organizations. Cluster 4 is characterized by the best values of the following attributes: GRP, the proportion of unprofitable organizations, and the level of innovation activity. The absence of low values of indicators and the average values of investments in fixed assets, depreciation of fixed assets, and the index of production and consumption of electricity together allow us to give a positive assessment of the cluster. During the period 2010–2022, clusters changed the composition of the constituent regions. Figure 1 shows the composition of clusters as of 2022.

Fig. 1. The composition of clusters of 2022.

The number of transitions from one cluster to another was calculated for each region, with the range spanning from 0 to 8 times.

The use of clusters as target variables enables the identification of the importance of certain features for the clustering algorithm. To this end, the XGBoost extreme gradient boosting model was employed, which also incorporates an automated calculation of feature importance [40]. The results of the feature importance calculations using the XGBClassifier are presented in Fig. 2 for lagged one-year data in Fig. 3.

The highest accuracy of the model was achieved by employing the following hyperparameters: colsample_bytree = 0.75; gamma = 0.18; learning_rate = 0.09; max_depth = 5; min_child_weight = 7.0; n_estimators = 34; subsample = 0.65.

Fig. 2. The importance of features in the aspect of clustering by the Affinity Propagation algorithm.

Fig. 3. The importance of features in the aspect of clustering by the Affinity Propagation algorithm with a one-year lag.

Excel's conditional formatting tool was applied to visualise the characteristics and differences of the clusters (Table 2).

To conduct a more detailed analysis, a group of regions was selected based on two characteristics: firstly, a high degree of behavioural stability over the period under consideration (i.e. a number of transitions between clusters equal to zero), and secondly, an instability in terms of the behavioural model under consideration (with the number of transitions between clusters equal to six, seven or eight). The sample comprises 17 regions, 10 of which exhibit a total of zero transitions between clusters, while the remaining seven demonstrate a minimum of six transitions between clusters over the 2010–2022 period (Table 3).

In light of this evidence, the regions displaying erratic behaviour with regard to cluster participation over the course of the decade under examination were identified. The resulting summary of transitions enables the identification of the years in which transitions were observed (Fig. 4).

Table 2. Characteristics of clusters according to the average values of indicators in the period 2010–2022.

Cluster	0	1	2	3	4	5
Per capita energy consumption, million kilowatt-hours	4.95	6.02	4.75	18.66	6.62	11.26
Gross regional product, Rub.	429328.11	646912.93	277055.1	1221274.43	2006971.41	2082664.54
Fixed Assets Investment, Rub.	64947.04	71540.77	66240.96	132218.89	100272.15	302778.54
Average per capita income, Rub.	19728.74	24914.19	22082.9	25464.09	31938.48	48009.64
Depreciation of fixed assets	40.09	57.17	45.35	44.89	47.89	44.58
Innovation activity level, percent	7.98	10.18	6.86	7.85	17.93	9.02
Share of loss-making firms, percent	29.63	29.14	40.18	31.96	29.36	36.41
Manufacturing index	111.71	103.61	102.26	102.72	105.07	102.58

Table 3. List of regions with a low degree of behavior stability.

Region	Cluster label of the region in a particular period													Transitions count
	2010	2011	2012	2013	2014	2015	2016	2017	2018	2019	2020	2021	2022	
Kaluga Oblast	0	0	0	0	0	2	0	4	4	4	5	4	5	6
Kamchatka Krai	0	4	4	5	2	5	4	4	5	5	5	5	5	6
Penza Oblast	2	2	1	4	2	2	4	4	4	1	4	4	4	6
Novosibirsk Oblast	0	0	0	0	0	2	1	4	1	1	2	1	4	7
Republic of Dagestan	0	0	2	0	2	0	0	1	1	2	1	1	0	8
Republic of Ingushetia	2	2	2	0	4	2	2	1	1	2	0	2	0	8
Tomsk Oblast	4	4	1	4	1	1	1	4	1	1	4	1	4	8

0–5 – cluster's label

The clustering that was performed can be visualised using the t-SNE method (Fig. 5, upper right subgraph). A number of informative features are also visualised in Fig. 5 (the other three subgraphs).

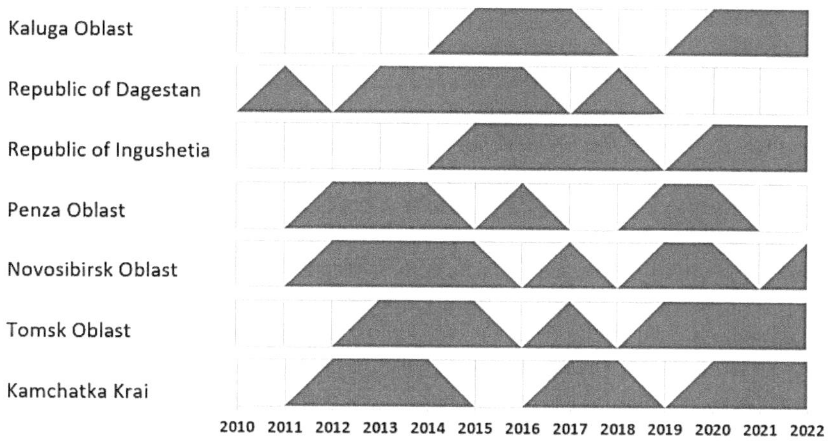

Fig. 4. Regional transitions by years 2010–2022.

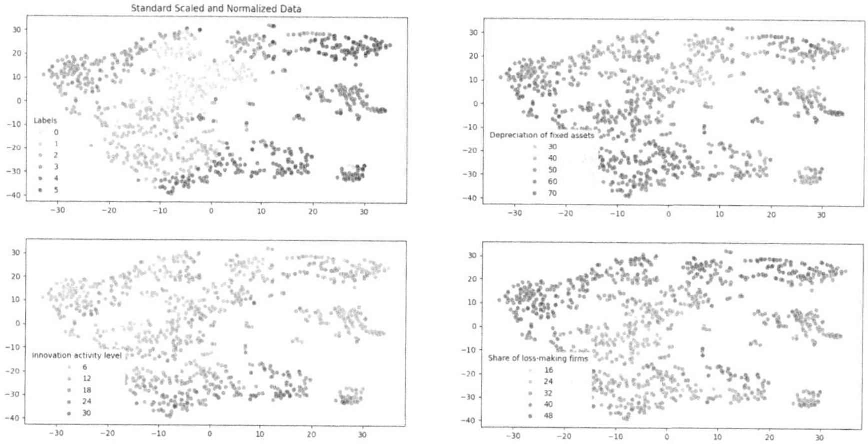

Fig. 5. Visualisation of clusters (upper right subplot) by the t-SNE method.

In order to ascertain the factors influencing the formation of economic clusters, an analysis was conducted to examine the economic specialisation of subjects within the Russia.

4.2 Industrial Structure and Regional Dynamics

The value of this analysis lies in its ability to confirm or refute the hypothesis regarding the relationship between a region's behavioural pattern and its economic specialisation.

The Atlas of Economic Specialisation of Russian Regions by the Higher School of Economics was used as the source of data on regional specialisation [21]. For each region in the sample, the main branches of specialisation were considered, as well as the type of specialisation by national and local significance. The Strategy of Spatial Development of Russia until 2025 was also used as a source of data [1].

A comparison of economic specialisations enables us to conclude that some regions exhibit a high degree of heterogeneity in their profiles. The initial assessment indicates the absence of a distinctive sectoral structure among the regions, which is a hallmark of a resilient model of regional behaviour. The sectoral structures of the regions included in the sample are heterogeneous in nature. However, among the most stable regions, with no transitions between clusters during the decade under study, the majority have a significant presence of heavy industry sectors within their structure. The specialisation sectors of Astrakhan Oblast, Irkutsk Oblast, Krasnoyarsk Krai, Orenburg Oblast, and the Republic of Khakassia, as well as Sakhalin Oblast, include production and transportation of oil and gas, extraction of metallic and non-metallic ores, and metal processing. In contrast, the list of the least stable regions more frequently comprises specialisation in agricultural and light industry, science, education and culture.

With regard to the type of specialisation, it was observed that the majority of unstable regions exhibited a strongly specialised profile. Conversely, no regions belonging to the strongly specialised category were identified among those displaying a stable behavioural model. This suggests that the economies of strongly specialised regions are more susceptible to change, with transitions between clusters potentially driven by global and regional factors at the national level.

4.3 Events as a Factor Influencing Regional Development: News Analysis

A search and analysis of news events on the Internet was carried out in order to identify economic and non-economic factors that can influence the behaviour of regions in terms of the stability of belonging to a particular cluster. The analysis of news summaries included: identification of regional objects of research by the criterion of the number of transitions between clusters during the period under study; identification of the time period related to the transition of the object between clusters; study of open news sources for the selected period for the presence of large-scale events in the region that could trigger the transition to another cluster. As a result, economic, political, scientific and technical events capable of influencing the activities of the regions were found.

The regions with the highest number of transitions between clusters were: the Novosibirsk region, the Republic of Dagestan, the Republic of Ingushetia and the Tomsk region.

Kamchatka Krai made a transition from cluster 0 to cluster 4 (which was a cluster improvement) in 2011. At that time, news sources published data on the resignation of the incumbent governor and the appointment of Ilyukhin as head of the region [40]. In 2015, the region moved from cluster 2 to cluster 5 (which was a cluster improvement again). In 2014 the regional authorities were active in promoting investment projects [41]. Also in 2014, the Far East 2014 investment forum was held, where promising investment projects were considered [42]. In 2015, the decree "On the creation of the territory of advanced socio-economic development "Kamchatka" was signed, which implies the creation of a special regime of entrepreneurial activity, opens prospects for the development of the port industry and tourism [43].

Tomsk Oblast had the first transition from cluster 4 to cluster 1 in 2011–2012 (which was a cluster deterioration) and returned to cluster 4 in 2013 (a cluster improvement). In this period the news of the region was studied. In 2012 the governor of Tomsk Oblast Kress left office. Election of the new governor resulted in a new structure of the regional administration and a new strategy of regional development [44]. In 2017 the region moved from cluster 1 to cluster 4 (cluster improvement). In 2016 the special economic zone "Tomsk" was created, which allowed improving the region's infrastructure [45]. The year 2016 is also significant for the implementation of innovative projects in Tomsk Oblast: unification of medical centres into the National Research Medical Centre and creation of the Siberian Robotics Centre [46].

5 Conclusion

From the standpoint of a system economy and an endogenous approach, focusing on the internal reserves of regional development makes it possible to improve the quality of management due to the possibility of promptly taking into account changes in development indicators. This, in turn, facilitates the timely identification of emerging trends and the realignment of development vectors.

From the perspective of the synergetic paradigm and complexity economics, it is crucial to consider the potential risks associated with regional development and technological transformation, including the digitalisation of the region. This is defined as a significant factor influencing the region's socio-economic situation. Based on the sustainable development imperatives, the system of indicators delineating the factors of regional development needs to take into consideration balance in the development of specific social spheres. It is also noteworthy that a number of studies, in addition to economic indicators (such as gross regional product and investments), underscore the significance of non-economic factors, which are subjectively measured and for which a set of indicators is formulated on the basis of expert opinions.

The analysis of a number of concepts enabled the formation of a set of indicators due to the correlation between these concepts and the characteristics traditionally used to assess the socio-economic development of the region. The study of regional development dynamics and features was conducted using an original methodology that employs a comprehensive approach, combining quantitative and qualitative methods. By means of clustering procedures, we were able to identify stable groups of regions that exhibited similarities in their economic development patterns. The resulting classes cannot be unambiguously characterised as the best or the worst; rather, they are distinguished by the uniqueness of the combination of characteristics that allow us to identify positive or negative trends in socio-economic development and to trace the improvement or deterioration of the subject's position based on the directions of transition between clusters. Of particular interest are the regions that regularly transitioned between classes and could not maintain stable positions in one or another cluster for a long time.

In order to analyse the reasons for the transition between clusters, it is necessary to consider not only quantitative indicators, but also to analyse the conditions of regional development, determined by a number of factors including administrative resources, interaction of regional executive authorities with regional elites, information support of regional authorities' activities, and public trust. This allows us to talk about the potential of this study from the perspective of analysing not only economic factors, but also such subjective factors as public trust in regional authorities.

Thus, the research contributes to the understanding of regional development of Russian territories from the perspective of system economic theory and endogenous approach. The study made it possible to identify different patterns of behavior of regions regarding the stability of their belonging to certain clusters, as well as to assess the importance of various factors in meso-economic dynamics

References

1. Government of the Russian Federation: Strategy of spatial development of the Russian Federation for the period until 2025 (Order No. 207-r) (2019). https://economy.gov.ru/material/dokumenty/rasporyazhenie_ot_13_fevralya_2019_g_207_r.html
2. Klejner, G.B.: Systemic Economics: Steps of Development. Nauchnaya Biblioteka Publishing House, Moscow (2021). (in Russian)
3. Kleiner, G.B.: System paradigm as a theoretical basis for strategic economic management in modern conditions. Manage. Sci. **13**(1), 6–19 (2023). https://doi.org/10.26794/2304-022X-2023-13-1-6-19
4. Kleiner, G.B.: Mesoeconomics of Russia: The strategy of the run-up. Central Economics and Mathematics Institute of the Russian Academy of Sciences. Nauchnaya Biblioteka Publishing House, Moscow (2022). (in Russian)
5. Maevsky, V.I., Kirdina-Chandler, S.G. (eds.): Mesoeconomics: Elements of a New Paradigm. Institute of Economics of the Russian Academy of Sciences, Moscow (2020). (in Russian)
6. Jiang, Y., Lyu, B.: Relationship between official visits, industry chain coordination, and digital transformation in China. Heliyon **10**(24), e40028 (2024). https://doi.org/10.1016/j.heliyon.2024.e40028
7. Strazzullo, S.: Fostering digital trust in manufacturing companies: Exploring the impact of Industry 4.0 technologies. J. Innov. Knowl. **9**(4), 100621 (2024). https://doi.org/10.1016/j.jik.2024.100621
8. Ash, J., Kitchin, R., Leszczynski, A.: Digital turn, digital geographies? Prog. Hum. Geogr. **42**(1), 25–43 (2018). https://doi.org/10.1177/0309132516664800
9. Fraske, T.: Industry 4.0 and its geographies: A systematic literature review and the identification of new research avenues. Digit. Geogr. Soc. **3**, 100031 (2022). https://doi.org/10.1016/j.diggeo.2022.100031
10. Haefner, L., Sternberg, R.: Spatial implications of digitization: state of the field and research agenda. Geogr. Compass **14**(2), e12544 (2020). https://doi.org/10.1111/gec3.12544
11. Capello, R., Lenzi, C.: Industry 4.0 and servitisation: Regional patterns of 4.0 technological transformations in Europe. Technol. Forecast. Soc. Change **173**, 121164 (2021). https://doi.org/10.1016/j.techfore.2021.121164
12. De Propris, L., Bailey, D.: Pathways of regional transformation and Industry 4.0. Reg. Stud. **55**(10–11), 1617–1629 (2021). https://doi.org/10.1080/00343404.2021.1960962
13. Hervas-Oliver, J.-L., Gonzalez-Alcaide, G., Rojas-Alvarado, R., Monto-Mompo, S.: Emerging regional innovation policies for Industry 4.0: analyzing the digital innovation hub program in European regions. Competitiveness Rev.: An Int. Bus. J. **31**(1), 106–129 (2020). https://doi.org/10.1108/CR-12-2019-0159
14. Akberdina, V.V., Naumov, I.V., Krasnykh, S.S.: Digital space of regions: assessment of development factors and influence on socio-economic growth. J. Appl. Econ. Res. **22**(2), 294–322 (2023). https://doi.org/10.15826/vestnik.2023.22.2.013

15. Tochenaya, T.I.: The development of the economy of Russian regions and federal priorities. Problem. Reg. Econ. **4**, 47–59 (2008)
16. Matveeva, L., Nikitaeva, A.: Mechanisms of Endogenous Industrial Development. Southern Federal University (2023). https://doi.org/10.18522/801300075
17. Bischoff, T.S., Hipp, A., Runst, P.: Firm innovation and generalized trust as a regional resource. Res. Policy **52**(8), 104813 (2023). https://doi.org/10.1016/j.respol.2023.104813
18. Manolchev, C., Cherrington, R., Crabolu, G.: Untangling circularity: transitioning to a regional circular economy in the clothing and textile sector in England. J. Clean. Prod. **482**, 144188 (2024). https://doi.org/10.1016/j.jclepro.2024.144188
19. Zhou, J., Xu, W., Yan, D.: Breaking the resource curse: the impact of the digital economy on the sustainable transformation of resource-based cities. Sustain. Cities Soc. **113**, 105707 (2024). https://doi.org/10.1016/j.scs.2024.105707
20. Chen, Y., Yu, Z.: Digitalization, trust, and sustainability transitions: insights from two blockchain-based green experiments in China's electricity sector. Environ. Innov. Soc. Trans. **50**, 100801 (2024). https://doi.org/10.1016/j.eist.2023.100801
21. Abashkin, V.L., et al.: Atlas of economic specialization of Russian regions. In: Gokhberg, L.M., Kutsenko, E.S. (eds.), National Research University Higher School of Economics, Moscow (2021). (in Russian)
22. Shen, C., Zhang, X., Li, X.: Revisiting regional sustainable development from the perspective of multi-system factor flows: evidence in the Yangtze River Delta of China. Heliyon **9**(8), e18893 (2023). https://doi.org/10.1016/j.heliyon.2023.e18893
23. Brodny, J., Tutak, M.: Assessing regional implementation of sustainable development goal 9: "Build resilient infrastructure, promote sustainable industrialization and foster innovation. Technol. Forecast. Soc. Chang. **195**, 122773 (2023). https://doi.org/10.1016/j.techfore.2023.122773. in Poland
24. Lyu, X., Li, X., Wang, K., Dang, D., Cao, W., Lou, A.: Using a pattern-process-service-sustainability framework to clarify the relationship between regional ecosystem quality and sustainable development. Ecol. Ind. **165**, 112174 (2024). https://doi.org/10.1016/j.ecolind.2024.112174
25. Jiang, Y., Shi, C.: Estimating sustainability and regional inequalities using an enhanced sustainable development index. Sustain. Cities Soc. **99**, 104555 (2023). https://doi.org/10.1016/j.scs.2023.104555. in China
26. Kosolapova, N.A., Matveeva, L.G., Nikitaeva, A.Y., Chernova, O.A.: The drivers of the circular economy: theory vs practice. Terra Economicus **21**(2), 68–83 (2023). https://doi.org/10.18522/2073-6606-2023-21-2-68-83
27. Novoseltseva, G.B., Palatkin, I.V., Rasskazova, N.V.: Sustainability of territorial systems in the context of economic indicators. Mod. innov. razvit. **14**(3), 467–483 (2023). https://doi.org/10.18184/2079-4665.2023.14.3.467-483
28. Lavrikova, Y.G. (ed.), Risks and opportunities for the development of Russia's regions under sanctions pressure. Ekaterinburg: Institute of Economics of the Ural Branch of Russian Academy of Sciences (2022) (in Russian). ISBN 978-5-94646-669-1
29. Chen, N., Yang, H.: From rural to urban: clan, urbanization, and trust. China Econ. Rev. **85**, 102172 (2024). https://doi.org/10.1016/j.chieco.2024.102172
30. Ding, C., Ma, Q.: Does social trust promote the size of enterprises? evidence from China. J. Asian Econ. **91**, 101705 (2024). https://doi.org/10.1016/j.asieco.2023.101705
31. Scikit-learn Developers: Overview of clustering methods. https://scikit-learn.org/stable/modules/clustering.html#overview-of-clustering-methods (n.d.). Retrieved 1 July 2024
32. Brendan, F., Delbert, D.: Clustering by passing messages between data points. Science **315**(5814), 972–976 (2007). https://doi.org/10.1126/science.1136800
33. Pandas Development Team:. Pandas: Python Data Analysis Library. https://pandas.pydata.org (n.d.). Retrieved 1 July 2024

34. Scikit-learn Developers: sklearn.preprocessing module. https://scikit-learn.org/stable/api/sklearn.preprocessing.html (n.d.). Retrieved 1 July 2024
35. Rousseeuw, P.J.: Silhouettes: A graphical aid to the interpretation and validation of cluster analysis. Comput. Appl. Math. **20**, 53–65 (1987). https://doi.org/10.1016/0377-0427(87)90125-7
36. Scikit-learn Developers: Clustering performance evaluation. https://scikit-learn.ru/clustering/#clustering-performance-evaluation (n.d.). Retrieved 1 July 2024
37. Scikit-learn Developers. sklearn.cluster module. https://scikit-learn.org/stable/api/sklearn.cluster.html#module-sklearn.cluster (n.d.). Retrieved 1 July 2024
38. Federal State Statistics Service: Official website of Rosstat. https://rosstat.gov.ru/ (n.d.). Retrieved 1 July 2024
39. XGBoost Developers: XGBoost Python API Reference. (n.d.). https://xgboost.readthedocs.io/en/stable/python/python_api.html. Retrieved 1 July 2024
40. TASS: News about the change of governor in Kamchatka Krai. https://tass.ru/info/9428635 (2011). Retrieved 10 May 2024
41. EastRussia: Kamchatka Krai: Results of the year. https://www.eastrussia.ru/material/kamchatskiy_kray_itogi_goda/ (2014). Retrieved 10 May 2024
42. Logistika-Prim: Investment forum "Far East – 2014". http://www.logistika-prim.ru/press-releases/investitsionnyi-forum-%C2%ABdalnii-vostok-%E2%80%93-2014%C2%BB (2014). Retrieved 10 May 2024
43. Government of Kamchatka Krai:. Yury Trutnev identifies the first 18 investors for the Kamchatka advanced development territory. https://www.kamgov.ru/news/urij-trutnev-opredeleny-pervye-18-investorov-tor-kamcatka-1592 (2015). Retrieved 10 May 2024
44. RIA Novosti: Change of governor in Tomsk Oblast. https://ria.ru/20121230/498718669.html (2012). Retrieved 10 May 2024
45. RIA Tomsk: Tomsk: Results of 2016. https://www.riatomsk.ru/article/20161231/tomsk-itogi-2016-goda/ (2016). Retrieved 10 May 2024
46. RIA Tomsk: Tomsk science 2016: Risky ideas, smart machines, and many robots. https://www.riatomsk.ru/article/20161227/tomskaya-nauka-2016-riskovie-idei-umnie-mashini-i-mnogo-robotov/ (2016). Retrieved 10 May 2024

Exploring Environmental Justice and Climate Awareness in Italy: Citizen Perspectives on Sustainability and Policy

Federica Murmura, Giada Pierli, and Laura Bravi(✉)

Department of Economics, Society, Politics, Carlo Bo University of Urbino, 61029 Urbino, Italy
{federica.murmura,laura.bravi}@uniurb.it,
g.pierli@campus.uniurb.it

Abstract. Understanding the extent of community awareness and engagement regarding government efforts concerning the development, implementation, and enforcement of environmental laws, regulations, and policies is vital for identifying areas where effective interventions can be applied. This study aimed to achieve this by conducting an online quantitative survey among Italian citizens over three months in 2023. 231 Italian respondents participated in the survey. The results of the study show that despite the growing urgency of environmental challenges, there persists a significant gap between European citizens' knowledge and their participation in shaping these crucial policies. There is a notable disparity between citizen awareness of climate change and their limited understanding of European initiatives designed to tackle these issues. While public awareness of climate change has increased in recent years, many individuals remain unaware of the specific plans and policies that the European Union (EU) has implemented or proposed to address this global challenge. This gap in knowledge highlights a crucial communication and education challenge. Effective communication strategies are needed to bridge this gap and ensure that citizens are informed about EU climate action initiatives, such as the European Green Deal and related policies.

Keywords: Environmental Justice · European Green Deal · Climate Change · Environmental Policy Awareness

1 Introduction

The development of sustainable practices has significantly reshaped human perception of ecological responsibilities and transformed the global economy's approach to environmental resources [1]. Previously, economic models followed a linear path – extracting resources, processing, and producing goods, ultimately ending with the disposal of waste [2]. However, the circular economy has recently gained traction due to escalating environmental challenges and resource constraints. Unlike traditional linear approaches, a circular economy emphasizes resource conservation, longevity of products, and regeneration of materials, aligning closely with sustainability objectives [3].

E. Kuzmin et al. (Eds.): EASET 2024, SPBE, pp. 161–172, 2025.
https://doi.org/10.1007/978-3-031-91159-0_11

The call for a shift to a circular economy has intensified with the growing awareness of climate change, biodiversity loss, and the depletion of finite resources [4]. In place of an "end-of-life" concept, circular models advocate for reduction, reuse, recycling, and recovery across all levels of production and consumption. Operating at multiple levels—from micro (products, companies, respondents) to macro (cities, regions, nations)—the circular economy aims to foster sustainable development, achieving environmental quality, economic stability, and social equity for both current and future generations [5]. Experts interpret the benefits of a circular economy in various ways, from economic gains to environmental protections; however, it is increasingly evident that principles of social equity and responsibility towards vulnerable communities must be prioritized alongside these goals [6].

In March 2020, the European Commission incorporated the circular economy into the European Green Deal, an initiative that includes proposals for more sustainable product designs, waste reduction, and citizen empowerment. This action plan, updated in February 2021, aims to achieve a fully circular, zero-carbon, and toxic-free economy by 2050 [7].

A circular economy aligned with environmental justice requires comprehensive government initiatives and active public engagement. Environmental justice, as defined by the United States Environmental Protection Agency, involves fair treatment and meaningful participation of all people—irrespective of race, color, nationality, or income level—in the development and enforcement of environmental policies [8]. Addressing climate change impacts equitably requires a focus on human rights and social justice, ensuring that vulnerable communities are protected from disproportionate environmental burdens [9]. In practice, environmental justice seeks an equitable distribution of environmental benefits and responsibilities, specifically addressing disparities that marginalized communities often face [10]. When environmental justice is integrated with circular economy principles, such as resource regeneration and waste minimization, it becomes a powerful mechanism for addressing both environmental and social inequities [11, 12].

Governments play a central role in promoting environmental justice through policies that ensure equitable resource allocation and conservation benefits, including regulatory standards to mitigate extraction and waste impacts on vulnerable communities, support for green job creation, and broad education initiatives to increase public awareness [13]. Effective environmental policies hinge on an informed citizenry that understands and participates in the sustainable governance process. This study, therefore, aims to assess the extent of community awareness and engagement with government initiatives regarding the development and enforcement of environmental regulations and policies. To this end, a quantitative survey was conducted among the Italian population, providing insights into areas where impactful interventions can be introduced.

2 Theoretical Background

2.1 Progress and Challenges in Italy's Environmental Justice and Sustainability Efforts

Italy has emerged as a leader in European recycling efforts, with a recycling start-up rate exceeding 83%, notably higher than the European average of less than 40%, as reported by Assoambiente [14]. In particular, Italy ranks just below France in terms of recycled materials returned to the market, though it leads in recycled metal use with a substantial 47.2% share compared to France's 39.3% and Germany's 27.3%. Lombardy stands out for its efficient processing, managing over 31 million tons of waste per year, followed by Veneto (12 million) and Emilia-Romagna (10 million). However, Italy continues to face challenges with the export of approximately 4.2 million tons of industrial and urban waste annually, underscoring the need to expand domestic recycling capacity to support economic growth and job creation [14, 15].

In 2018, the Circular Economy Network (CEN) was established through a partnership between the Foundation for Sustainable Development and various industry sectors [16]. Nevertheless, the CEN report indicates that Italy has not fully decoupled economic growth from raw material consumption, suggesting further integration of environmental and social justice into these initiatives [17]. While Italy ranks among the top EU nations alongside France for its circular economy practices, targeted policies are essential to address social inequities and ensure sustainable economic development. Italy has recently introduced policies aligned with the European Green Deal, such as the National Recovery and Resilience Plan (PNRR) and the National Ecological Transition Plan (PTE), with an emphasis on environmental equity in sustainable development [18].

The PNRR, launched in 2021, allocates around €235 billion to 134 investments and 63 reforms focused on ecological transition, digitalization, and social cohesion, with a reporting deadline of 2026. Within this framework, the PNRR promotes a National Strategy for the Circular Economy, incorporating eco-design, regenerative bioeconomy, and the sustainable use of critical raw materials [19]. By placing an emphasis on both environmental and social equity, these policies reflect a commitment to participatory justice principles, addressing systemic environmental disparities as advocated in works by [12].

The PTE, presented in October 2021, further aligns Italy with European Green Deal goals, aiming to increase circularity to 30% by 2030 and reduce waste production by 50% by 2040. Through administrative and fiscal measures, the PTE promotes equitable access to environmental benefits, shared responsibility in sustainable practices, and an expanded market for secondary raw materials [18]. Finally, the 4th report on Italy's circular economy identifies digital platforms as pivotal in spreading best practices, making environmental data accessible to industries and respondents and enhancing transparency around national sustainability efforts [20].

2.2 Green Deal Policy and Areas of Application

The European Green Deal stands as one of the European Union's most ambitious and transformative initiatives, specifically focused on advancing environmental sustainability and tackling climate change. Announced by the European Commission in December

2019, this strategic initiative aspires to make Europe the world's first climate-neutral continent by the year 2050. As a cornerstone of EU policy, the Green Deal addresses an extensive range of environmental, social, and economic issues, with objectives that include fostering sustainable economic growth, advancing social justice, and safeguarding the environment [6].

This comprehensive plan spans multiple intervention areas, such as cutting greenhouse gas emissions, enhancing energy efficiency, advancing the shift toward a circular economy, protecting biodiversity, boosting renewable energy adoption, promoting sustainable mobility, and fostering the creation of green jobs. Through a combination of innovative policies, strategic investments, and robust regulatory frameworks, the Green Deal seeks to drive a transformative shift across Europe's economic landscape [21].

Beyond its environmental ambitions, the Green Deal is also designed to stimulate sustainable job growth, drive technological advancement, and promote social fairness. In line with these goals, the initiative emphasizes active involvement from economic sectors, social groups, and local communities to support a just and inclusive transition toward a more sustainable future [22].

As for the Green Deal policy, this aims to protect, conserve, and improve the natural capital of the European Union and to protect the health and well-being of citizens from environmental risks and their consequences. The active participation of all citizens, therefore, is of fundamental importance for this policy to be accepted and functional: a new pact is needed such that citizens, with their diversity, are put in close collaboration with the institutional bodies of the European Union [6, 21]. The Green Deal initiative sets out numerous key objectives, including the ambitious reduction of harmful emissions, establishing a zero-emission economy, achieving a complete transition to renewable and clean energy sources, conserving and revitalizing Europe's natural and shared resources, driving a transformative shift in business and industrial practices toward circular economy models, and accelerating the move to sustainable and efficient transportation systems [23].

When the Green Deal program was developed in 2019, the onset of the Covid-19 pandemic was unforeseen. The pandemic had a profound impact on Europe and globally, straining health and social systems to their limits [24].

In response to these challenges, the European Commission proposed maximizing the economic resources of the EU budget, combined with a new post-pandemic recovery fund, NextGenerationEU. This fund is set to boost the EU budget's capacity by €750 billion (based on 2018 prices) to support recovery across all sectors and lay the groundwork for sustained growth and stability [25].

Of these, a part has been allocated to a just transition fund, for an amount of around 40 billion, which will be used to help all member states achieve the objectives set by the Green Deal policy [26].

Italy, like the rest of the member states, cannot achieve the objectives of the Green Deal alone, but needs help from the European Union.

Of the resources allocated by the NextGenerationEU fund for post-pandemic recovery, Italy is entitled to the largest portion, i.e. 209 billion and of these approximately 37% will be allocated to achieving the objectives of the Green Deal and therefore to the ecological transition [25]. European Union member countries have to propose to the European Commission their detailed programs to address economic recovery and improve the resilience of their economies. These programs have to include policy changes and planned investments that will be implemented by 2026. The main objective is to obtain funding from the European Union up to the previously agreed sum. The plan aims to mitigate the negative effects of the pandemic, strengthen economic and ecological resilience, accelerate the transition towards a digital and clean energy-based economy and promote job creation and prosperity in the European Union.

3 Methodology

3.1 Data Collection

At a time when our planet is witnessing unprecedented climate transformations, it is critical to understand our community's perceptions, concerns, and actions regarding this global challenge. Climate change, caused primarily by human activities, has significant impacts on our society, the environment, and global economies. Knowing the level of awareness and involvement of our community in relation to this issue is crucial to identifying areas where effective actions can be implemented.

Therefore, a questionnaire survey has been developed to evaluate the level of community awareness and involvement in relation to government initiatives related to the development, implementation, and enforcement of environmental laws, regulations, and policies. Data were collected using a questionnaire survey distributed online via computer-assisted web interviewing (CAWI) methodology. This method was selected for several advantages, such as quickness and low cost, anonymity of respondents, automated database creation, geographic spread of respondents, and completeness of data collection [27, 28]. The online questionnaire was distributed through social networks over three months in 2023. 231 Italian respondents participated in the survey.

The questionnaire was divided into three sections: the first section collects the participants' sociodemographic data, including age, gender, area of origin, educational qualification, employment and monthly income range; the second section focuses on the central topic of the questionnaire, i.e. Citizens' perception of the phenomenon of climate change; the third section goes more specifically as it concerns the areas the participants belong to and how the phenomenon manifests itself in these areas.

3.2 Data Analysis

The data collected were analyzed using basic statistical methods through SPSS software (version 23.0) to provide an accurate interpretation of participants' responses. Descriptive statistics, including frequencies, means, and standard deviations, were used to summarize key findings and present an overview of sociodemographic characteristics and response trends.

Likert scales with 5-point options were employed to define value scales, allowing participants to express levels of agreement or importance on various statements related to environmental justice and climate awareness. The resulting data was used to calculate mean scores, providing insights into general trends and participant attitudes toward EU climate policies and sustainable practices.

4 Results

4.1 Socio Demographic Feature of the Respondents

The sample of respondents analyzed is made up of 57% of people aged between 18 and 25 (Gen. Z), 28% belongs to the Millennial generation, who are aged between 26 and 41 years, while those who are part of Generation X, aged between 42 and 57, make up only 9% of the sample. In terms of gender, female respondents represent 65.4% of the total, while male respondents constitute 33.8%. A small 0.9% of people chose not to declare their gender. Regarding the education of the participants, the majority, equal to 56.3%, obtained a high school diploma, 19.5% obtained a three-year degree, 15.2% completed a master's or single-cycle degree while only 3% obtained an advanced degree after graduation. Furthermore, 4.8% of the sample had a middle school diploma and 1.3% had only an elementary school diploma. As regards the work occupation of the participants, the majority declared that they were male or female students, i.e. 38.5%. 31.2% of the sample are public or private employees, 15.2% are student – workers, 4.8% are unemployed, 4.3% are freelancers or self-employed workers, 1.3% say they are housewives, 0.9% are pensioners and 0.4% are managers. The remaining 3.4% of the sample declared having a different occupation from those indicated above. Finally, with respect to monthly income, most participants, i.e. 39.8%, say they earn less than €500 per month, as expected from the fact that they are aged between 18 and 25 and are mostly students; 24.7% of the sample has a monthly income between €1001 and €1500, 15.2% of participants have a monthly income ranging from €501 to €1000, while 11.3% have a monthly income between €1501 and €2000. Higher income brackets are less frequent in the sample: 3.5% earn between 2001 and 2500 € per month, 1.7% between 2501 and 3000 € and 3.9% say they earn more than 3000 € per month.

4.2 Citizen Perception of Climate Change

Climate change is a complex issue that spans a wide range of dimensions, from causes to consequences, from proposed solutions to impacts on local communities. Respondents were asked about their perception in terms of temperature increases over the last 100 years. The results showed that only 19% of those interviewed chose the correct option, i.e. "about 1 °C". Most participants (43.3%) thought it was "about 2 °C", showing awareness of the large increase in temperatures over the last century, even overestimating it. Using information from ancient climate data, advanced climate prediction models, and satellite observations by James Hansen and his team of researchers [29], it has been concluded that our planet is extremely susceptible to the impacts of global warming. If we do not adequately address the causes of rising temperatures, there is a risk that we will exceed the critical limit of 1.5 °C by 2030. At the current rate of pollution, it seems likely that we will reach an increase of 2 °C well before 2050. In short, our climate is changing more rapidly than many imagine, with significant consequences for the environment and life on Earth.

Global warming is accelerating at a faster rate than expected, and current climate mitigation and control measures are far from solving the problem. Extraordinary actions are needed to reduce human-induced net radiative forcing; global warming must be reduced and highly undesirable consequences for humanity and nature must be avoided.

Subsequently it has been tried to investigate how worried people perceive urgency and responsibility and evaluate the effectiveness of actions against climate change. The results indicate that there is broad consensus among participants regarding concern and awareness of the importance of acting quickly. The data obtained from our results confirm what was previously identified in the scientific literature; respondents are developing a growing awareness of sustainability issues. This awareness translates into greater concern and attention towards ethical, social, and environmental aspects [30]. On average, participants strongly agree with the proposed statements (see Table 1), and among these they agree the most with the fact that we need to intervene to counteract the effects of the current climate crisis both on a social and environmental level.

Table 1. Sample agreement on current climate crisis.

	Mean	St. Dev (SD)
The current global climate crisis is a direct consequence of past and present human activities	4.18	0.992
The current climate crisis generates disasters on a global level (hurricanes, floods, fires, etc.)	4.24	0.919
The current climate crisis impacts the various production sectors (agriculture, livestock, fishing, etc.)	4.37	0.855
It is necessary to intervene to counteract both the social and environmental effects of the current climate crisis	4.43	0.873

Participants were then asked to indicate, in their opinion, how important the intervention of institutional bodies is, to address the problems related to climate change. The sample considers the intervention of all the bodies listed to be quite important: first of all it considers the role of citizens and civil society to be fundamental (Mean: 4.31; SD: 0.973), followed by the European Union (Mean: 4.26; SD: 1.025), national governments (Mean: 4.25; SD: 1.016), international organizations (e.g. UN) (Mean: 4.14; SD: 1.025), regional and/or provincial governments (Mean: 4.00; SD: 1.103) and finally municipalities (Mean: 3.92; SD: 1.137).

The important task of the institutions is to raise people's awareness of this issue in such a way as to make them understand the true importance of every single individual gesture. To do this, a wide range of global initiatives have been proposed in recent years that seek to bring institutions into contact with citizens. The last of these was "All4Youth" and "Youth4Climate" which are, in fact, awareness campaigns, aimed especially at younger people, which include a series of initiatives by institutional entities and the private sector aimed at underlining the essential role of young people, or in general of citizenship, in the fight against climate change [31].

After understanding how citizens perceive climate change and how informed they are about definitions and statements related to this phenomenon, it is important to examine the means and sources they use to obtain information about the climate change phenomenon and the strategies adopted to address it. This is essential because environmental communication and information channels significantly influence how people perceive the problem of climate change [32]. The research shows that the tool most used by the sample to obtain information are websites and/or social media (83.5%), followed by television (65.4%) and schools/universities (30.3%). At the lowest levels of the ranking there are sources such as radio and podcasts (25.1%), newspapers and magazines (23.8%), word of mouth through family or friends (22.5%). Finally, academic journals (6.5%) and books (12.1%) seem to be the least used tools.

Subsequently, we also wanted to analyze the degree of reliability that the participants attribute to the sources they use and, in general, also to the other sources they do not use. Among those considered most reliable there are academic journals (Mean: 3.84; SD: 1.117) and school/university (Mean: 3.84; SD: 1.100). Those considered less reliable are word of mouth through family or friends (Mean: 2.40; SD: 1.045). Among the sources considered most reliable there aren't internet and social media (Mean: 3.24; SD: 0.964) or television (Mean: 3.05; SD: 1.160), being instead among the most used for information. This means that people receive information from communication/information tools that they do not consider very reliable, and despite this, they prefer them over other sources considered more reliable.

Instead, analyzing the sample's degree of knowledge regarding the main national and European programs that Italy and the European Union are carrying out to aim to achieve the objective of climate neutrality by 2050, it emerges that the sample who participated in the questionnaire has very little knowledge of the main programs in force such as: European Green Deal Policy (Mean: 2.18; SD: 1.209), NextGenerationEU Fund (Mean: 2.14; SD: 1.223), Sustainable and Smart Mobility (Mean: 2.52; SD: 1.301), REPowerEU (Mean: 1.88; SD: 1.070), Just Transition Fund (Mean: 1.93; SD: 1.121), LIFE Program (Mean: 1.77; SD: 1.010), Horizon Europe (Mean: 1.92; SD: 1.128), "Fit for 55" regulation (Mean: 1.80; SD: 1.074).

4.3 Climate Change Impact in the Territory of Belonging

In the last section of the questionnaire, attention was paid to the manifestation of the phenomenon of climate change in the territory to which the individual participants belong. The sample fairly agrees that the effects of this phenomenon are quite significant in their territory. The areas most influenced by the phenomenon of climate change appear to be that which concerns "natural hazards and land management" (Mean: 4.00; SD: 1.093), followed by "vegetation and forestry" (Mean: 3.90; SD: 1.157), "agriculture and livestock" (Mean: 3.84; SD: 1.098) and "water and resource management" (Mean: 3.82; SD: 1.135). On the contrary, the sector least affected by the effects of the phenomenon in the perception of the sample appears to be that of "transport and infrastructure" (Mean: 3.06; SD: 1.227). Lastly, it has been investigated how worried citizens are about the possible effects that could occur in their territory. As can be seen from Table 2, all the negative effects of the phenomenon worry the sample quite a bit. What is most worrying is the possibility of an increase in phenomena such as floods, inundations, landslides, debris flows, followed by an increase in drought phenomena and scarcity of water resources and the impacts on vegetation. While it is not believed that climate change could have large effects in terms of negative impacts on local tourism.

Table 2. Degree of concern about the possible negative effects of the climate change phenomenon in local areas.

	Mean	St. Dev (SD)
Increased phenomena such as flooding, landslides, debris flows, etc	4.42	0.933
Negative impacts on tourism	3.26	1.095
Degradation of ecosystems and loss of biodiversity	4.07	1.032
Increased drought phenomena and water resource scarcity	4.35	0.974
Increased restrictions on the use of drinking water	4.16	1.065
Negative impacts on human health	4.27	1.045
Negative impacts on agriculture and food production	4.28	0.962
Negative impacts on vegetatio	4.32	0.906

5 Conclusion and Limitations

In the evolving framework of European environmental policy, citizen participation is essential not only for democratic integrity but also for achieving effective and equitable policy outcomes. Environmental justice—focusing on the fair distribution of environmental benefits and burdens—depends heavily on the active involvement of citizens. This study demonstrates that, despite increasing global awareness of environmental issues, a significant knowledge gap persists among European citizens, limiting their engagement in shaping critical environmental policies. This gap is particularly concerning given the economic implications of environmental justice, where equitable access to resources and fair policy implementation can drive both social well-being and sustainable economic growth.

A central issue revealed by this research is the intersection of accessible information, institutional barriers, and the need for stronger civic empowerment. Limited knowledge about environmental policies, especially regarding their economic and social impacts, often leads to disengagement, reducing the potential for active public participation. Addressing this issue is crucial for achieving the Green Deal's sustainability targets, which have substantial economic stakes both for the EU and internationally. Key strategies for bridging this gap include:

- Education and Training: Providing targeted education on the economic aspects of environmental justice and the circular economy enables citizens to make informed decisions and advocate for economically sustainable practices.
- Promoting Sustainable Economic Practices: Encouraging actions such as recycling and energy conservation not only benefits the environment but also contributes to economic resilience by reducing waste and resource dependency.
- Advocacy and Activism: Supporting grassroots efforts focused on environmental justice can amplify public influence, fostering accountability in policymaking and ensuring economic resources are used equitably.

- Partnerships and Collaboration: Strengthening collaborations among governments, businesses, nonprofits, and communities is key to leveraging resources and aligning economic incentives with sustainable and just practices.
- Access to Information: Ensuring transparency in environmental and economic decision-making equips citizens to engage more meaningfully, supporting policies that reflect both ecological and economic priorities.

This study's findings hold significant implications beyond Europe, as citizen engagement and informed advocacy can influence policy developments globally. As economic impacts of environmental policies increasingly cross borders, fostering informed and active citizen participation in sustainability issues can drive international cooperation and economic growth.

Ultimately, the path toward environmental justice in Europe and beyond requires dismantling barriers to citizen engagement. Empowering individuals with the knowledge and means to participate in environmental policy co-creation will strengthen democratic governance and foster a more sustainable, equitable, and economically viable future.

The main limitations of the study derive from the fact that the sample interviewed was relatively small and only considered Italian citizens. It would be relevant for future research to consider a wider sample in different European countries to have a broader vision of the awareness of citizens on the European environmental policy, compare the practices implemented by individual nations to involve the population and make them more aware to create best practices to be developed throughout the European Union.

References

1. Ruggerio, C.A.: Sustainability and sustainable development: a review of principles and definitions. Sci. Total Environ. **786**, 147481 (2021). https://doi.org/10.1016/j.scitotenv.2021.147481
2. Virlanuta, F.O., David, S., Manea, L.D.: The transition from linear economy to circular economy: a behavioral change. FORCE: Focus Res. Contemp. Econ. **1**(1), 4–18 (2020)
3. Merli, R., Preziosi, M., Acampora, A.: How do scholars approach the circular economy? A systematic literature review. J. Clean. Prod. **178**, 703–722 (2018). https://doi.org/10.1016/j.jclepro.2017.12.112
4. Kirchherr, J.: Circular economy and growth: a critical review of "post-growth" circularity and a plea for a circular economy that grows. Resour. Conserv. Recycl. **179**, 106033 (2022). https://doi.org/10.1016/j.resconrec.2021.106033
5. Kumar, V., Sezersan, I., Garza-Reyes, J.A., Gonzalez, E.D., Al-Shboul, M.D.A.: Circular economy in the manufacturing sector: benefits, opportunities, and barriers. Manag. Decis. **57**(4), 1067–1086 (2019). https://doi.org/10.1108/MD-09-2018-1070
6. Filipović, S., Lior, N., Radovanović, M.: The green deal–just transition and sustainable development goals nexus. Renew. Sustain. Energy Rev. **168**, 112759 (2022). https://doi.org/10.1016/j.rser.2022.112759
7. Environmental Protection Agency (EPA): The concept of environmental justice (2024). https://www.epa.gov/ Accessed 31 Mar 2024
8. Figueroa, R.M.: Environmental justice. In: Hale, B., Light, A., Lawhon, L. (eds.) The Routledge Companion to Environmental Ethics, pp. 767–782. Routledge, New York (2022). https://doi.org/10.4324/9781315768090-75

9. Levy, B.S., Patz, J.A.: Climate change, human rights, and social justice. Ann. Glob. Health **81**(3), 310–322 (2015). https://doi.org/10.1016/j.aogh.2015.08.008
10. Amorim de Oliveira, Í.: Environmental justice and circular economy: Analyzing justice for waste pickers in upcoming circular economy in Fortaleza, Brazil. Circ. Econ. Sust. **1**(3), 815–834 (2021). https://doi.org/10.1007/s43615-021-00045-w
11. Mohai, P., Pellow, D., Roberts, J.T.: Environmental justice. Annu. Rev. Environ. Resour. **34**(1), 405–430 (2009). https://doi.org/10.1146/annurev-environ-082508-094348
12. Málovics, G., Creţan, R., Méreine-Berki, B., Tóth, J.: Socio-environmental justice, participatory development, and empowerment of segregated urban Roma: Lessons from Szeged, Hungary. Cities **91**, 137–145 (2019). https://doi.org/10.1016/j.cities.2018.11.013
13. Harrison, J.L.: From the inside out: the fight for environmental justice within government agencies. MIT Press (2019). https://doi.org/10.7551/mitpress/12063.001.0001
14. Assoambiente: L'Italia che ricicla [The Italy that recycles]. http://www.assoambiente.org/ (2022). (accessed April 17, 2024)
15. Repp, L., Hekkert, M., Kirchherr, J.: Circular economy-induced global employment shifts in apparel value chains: Job reduction in apparel production activities, job growth in reuse and recycling activities. Resour. Conserv. Recycl. **171**, 105621 (2021). https://doi.org/10.1016/j.resconrec.2021.105621
16. Circular Economy Network. https://circulareconomynetwork.it (n.d.). Accessed 1 April 2024
17. Barker, T., Scrieciu, Ş, Taylor, D.: Climate change, social justice and development. Development **51**(3), 317–324 (2008). https://doi.org/10.1057/dev.2008.33
18. Laimer, S., Pagliarini, C., Perathoner, C.: Next generation EU e i piani nazionali di ripresa e resilienza [Next generation EU and national recovery and resilience plans]. Giuffrè Francis Lefebvre Editore (2023)
19. D'Arrigo, G., David, P.: Next generation EU e PNRR italiano. Analisi, governance e politiche per la ripresa [Next generation EU and Italian PNRR. Analysis, governance and policies for recovery]. Rubbettino Editore (2022)
20. Frittella, M.: Italia green. La mappa delle eccellenze italiane nell'economia verde [Green Italy: The map of Italian excellence in the green economy]. Rai Libri Editore (2020)
21. Pianta, M., Lucchese, M.: Rethinking the european green deal: an industrial policy for a just transition in Europe. Rev. Radical Politic. Econ. **52**(4), 633–641 (2020). https://doi.org/10.1177/0486613420938207
22. Rifkin, J.: Un Green new deal globale. Il crollo della civiltà dei combustibili fossili entro il 2028 e l'audace piano economico per salvare la terra [A global green new deal: The collapse of fossil fuel civilization by 2028 and the bold economic plan to save the earth]. Mondadori Editore (2019)
23. Igliński, B., et al.: How to meet the Green Deal objectives—Is it possible to obtain 100% RES at the regional level in the EU? Energies **15**(6), 2296 (2022). https://doi.org/10.3390/en15062296
24. Troiani, L.: Neutralità climatica e decarbonizzazione. Interessi in gioco e salvaguardia del creato [Climate neutrality and decarbonisation: Interests at stake and safeguarding creation]. Biblion Edizioni (2023)
25. Bartolomei, G., Marcozzi, A.: Fondi europei 2021–2027 e Next Generation EU [European funds 2021–2027 and Next Generation EU]. EPC Editore (2022)
26. Next Generation EU Funds. https://www.europarl.europa.eu/ (n.d.). Accessed 23 Mar 2024
27. Kraut, R., Olson, J., Banaji, M., Bruckman, A., Cohen, J., Couper, M.: Psychological research online: report of board of scientific affairs' advisory group on the conduct of research on the internet. Am. Psychol. **59**(2), 105–117 (2004). https://doi.org/10.1037/0003-066X.59.2.105
28. Thompson, L.F., Surface, E.A., Martin, D.L., Sanders, M.G.: From paper to pixels: moving personnel surveys to the web. Pers. Psychol. **56**(1), 197–227 (2003). https://doi.org/10.1111/j.1744-6570.2003.tb00149.x

29. Hansen, J.E., et al.: Global warming in the pipeline. Oxford Open Clim. Change (2023). https://doi.org/10.1093/oxfclm/kgad008
30. Fraschini, F., Hunt, A., Zoboli, R.: Decision tools for adaptation to climate change: Portfolio analysis of tea plantation investments in Rwanda. Ecol. Econ. **200**, 107528 (2022). https://doi.org/10.1016/j.ecolecon.2022.107528
31. Karhu, M., Häkkilä, J., Timonen, E.: Collaborative media as a platform for community powered ecological sustainability transformations: a case study. In: Proceedings of the 18th International Conference on Mobile and Ubiquitous Multimedia, pp. 1–5 (2019). https://doi.org/10.1145/3365610.3368413
32. Iovino, R., Testa, F., Iraldo, F.: Do consumers understand what different green claims actually mean? An experimental approach in Italy. J. Advert. **53**(2), 200–214 (2023). https://doi.org/10.1080/00913367.2023.2175279

Influence of the Mutual Trade of the CIS Countries on Their Economic Convergence: Methodical Approach and Empirical Analysis

Elena Andreeva and Artem Ratner(✉)

Institute of Economics of the Ural Branch of the Russian Academy of Sciences, 29, Moskovskaya Street, 620014 Ekaterinburg, Russia
{andreeva.el,ratner.av}@uiec.ru

Abstract. The relevance of the study is determined by the commitment of integration associations of countries to the economic convergence of their members. The goal is to substantiate the methodical provision assessing the influence of mutual trade of such countries on their convergence and to test it through the example of the Commonwealth of Independent States (CIS) as a part of the Big Eurasian partnership. The hypothesis is that this influence is stronger for production and accumulation and weaker for human development. The research methods included selecting the relevant indicators from existing indicators of mutual trade and macroeconomic development. The authors selected 8 indicators on trade, including on certain commodity groups, and 14 indicators on macroeconomic development – production volume, investments, financial sustainability, and social aspects. An equation was proposed to calculate the average degree of convergence of participants in the integration association on each macroeconomic indicator. Between indicators of trade and convergence, for each pair of indicators, the correlation coefficient was calculated using the method of least squares. As a result, an assessing methodical provision was formed. Its testing on the CIS showed that the correlation was high in the case of governmental debt, industrial value added, and international reserves, and low in the cases of inflation, employment, investments, and science expenses. The results can be used to analyze the effectiveness of strategies for developing intercountry integration.

Keywords: Free trade zone · Countries' mutual trade · Economic convergence · Macroeconomic development

JEL Classification: F13 · F15 · F43

1 Introduction

The relevance of the study is determined by the fact that regional integration associations of countries strive, among other things, for economic convergence, because creating a common market of goods, capital, labor, and currency protects the participants against

E. Kuzmin et al. (Eds.): EASET 2024, SPBE, pp. 173–187, 2025.
https://doi.org/10.1007/978-3-031-91159-0_12

excessive overflow of goods and production factors between countries. The scientific problem that arises from this is how to assess the influence of an association's intra-trade on the economic convergence of its members. The research object, consequently, is the trade and economic development of the integration association, and the research subject is the influence of countries' mutual trade of some association on their economic convergence. To solve the scientific problem indicated, it is necessary not simply to work out the toolkit for assessing this influence but also to test it on the example of an association with long-term experience of existence. One such example is the Commonwealth of Independent States (CIS). According to the methodology of the UNCTAD (the United Nations Conference on Trade and Development), it includes Armenia, Azerbaijan, Belarus, Kazakhstan, Kyrgyzstan, Moldova, Russia, Tajikistan, and Uzbekistan. Within it, attempts were made to develop integration interaction, and April 15, 2024 marked the 30th anniversary of the first agreement of the CIS countries on the free trade zone (FTZ).

Thus, the research goal is to reveal the methodical possibility to assess the influence of mutual trade of countries of the interstate association on their economic convergence and to illustrate it using the example of the CIS countries.

Logically, countries' mutual trade has to influence what they produce (that is, what is not provided through import and what is needed for export) and what income they earn from export (and consequently, accumulate), but it does not directly influence the indicators of human potential development (employment, inflation, healthcare and research and development (R&D) expenses, Internet use). Therefore, the hypothesis is that the intensification of mutual trade positively influences the convergence of the trade association's countries in the gross indicators of production and accumulation and to a lesser extent – convergence in the indicators of human potential development.

Based on this hypothesis, the objectives of the study are as follows: to analyze the nomenclature of the published statistics of countries' mutual trade; to analyze the nomenclature of the published statistics of countries' internal socio-economic development; to substantiate the technique of calculating the extent of countries' economic convergence; to substantiate, which indicators and how should be compared, in order to reveal the narrowness of the relationship between mutual trade indicators and indicators of countries' economic convergence; to test this assessing toolkit on the CIS. Thus, the chapter is empirical in nature and is devoted to: first, developing the methodological toolkit based on an analysis of the nomenclature of indicators; and second, testing this toolkit using statistical data from a specific integration association.

The chapter begins with an introduction that highlights the relevance of the study, formulates the research problem, and sets the objectives and hypotheses. It then provides a review of the literature and theoretical background, discussing existing approaches to the relationship between mutual trade and economic convergence and identifying research gaps. The objectives and hypotheses are further detailed, emphasizing the distinction between production and accumulation indicators versus human development indicators. The methodology section explains the selection of indicators, data sources, and statistical methods used, including the proposal of 13 mathematical operations (outlined in Subsects. 3.1 and 3.2 of this chapter) through which 1,076 intermediate and 205 resulting values are calculated. This is followed by an empirical analysis where the proposed toolkit is applied to the data of the integration association, yielding key findings. The discussion contextualizes these results, comparing them with existing literature and exploring their implications. The chapter concludes by summarizing the main findings, addressing the study's limitations, and offering recommendations for future research and policy applications.

2 Dilemma in the Theoretical Basis of the Studied Problem

From the existing studies, two approaches can be logically drawn:

2.1 The First Approach: Mutual Trade Promotes Convergence

Indeed, the growth of inequality between economies is the challenge that has arisen during globalization [1, p. 11]. In order to protect themselves from the challenges of globalization, economies strive for trade regionalization. Accordingly, one of its goals is the economic convergence of participants. This is also fair for developing countries, as the examples of the ASEAN [2, p. 209], the East African Community, and the West African Economic and Monetary Union [3] show. This is seen from agreements on FTZs: they intend not only to eliminate customs duties but also to unify the competition policy (the example of the African Continental Free Trade Area [4, p. 306]). It follows from [5, pp. 7–8] that economic convergence is a necessary condition for deepening trade integration, and consequently, is also its target. As proof of this, the intensity of integration is quite often assessed through indicators of economies-participants' similarity: for example, the presence of knots of single production chains in countries-participants [6, p. 237], the unity of requirements for production (for instance, in part of carbon footprint [7, p. 75]).

Using data for 43 countries of the North and South for 1995–2014, it is shown that trade in intermediary goods leads to structural convergence of partner countries [8, p. 602]. At that, the success of convergence requires sufficient financing and time [9, pp. 25, 31]. Thus, it makes sense to assess convergence only when the FTZ has already existed for many years; and the CIS FTZ is exactly a suitable case. Gorbunova and co-authors come to the conclusion that the CIS by countries' convergence corresponds to the EU [10, p. 40]. However, the analysis is carried out only using one indicator – GDP per capita [10, p. 38], although literature also uses the human development index and its components [9, p. 26].

2.2 The Second Approach: Mutual Trade Does not Certainly Promote Convergence

On the other hand, the conclusion can be drawn from the literature that the task of mutual trade is to develop countries economically, to develop their production cooperation, to integrate participants into international value creation chains [11, p. 2038], but not convergence – it is not always a goal in itself but can take place as an additional bonus. This is testified by the fact that the influence of the openness of economies in literature is studied more often not on their convergence, but on their growth (for example, [12]).

Convergence in industrial policy is, most likely, a means [13, pp. 95–96]. It is even shown by the example of seven African FTZs that a similar structure of the economies of countries-participants does not give an incentive to develop trade within FTZs [14, p. 250]. Branches with high productivity are aimed more not at integration into FTZs but at trade within their own global value creation chains [15, p. 25]. Convergence does not always take place. For instance, although the new (since 2004) EU members show convergence in inflation, this does not occur automatically [16, p. 232–234]. After 2008, divergence was also observed [17, p. 15]. Since the new millennium, international trade has led to the divergence of economies in the carbon footprint of production [8, p. 602].

In any case, the influence of FTZs on the members' convergence depends on the institutional environment [18, p. 16]. To achieve convergence in any economic institution (for example, in developing small and medium businesses), it is necessary to carry out additional strategies of the single for all members regulation for these institutions [19]. The assessment of convergence also depends on what assessing technique is used [20, pp. 45–46].

The revealed dilemma induces to study the nomenclature of the published indicators – both in trade and in economic development – and to compare mutually as many pairs of indicators as possible, in order to reveal particular cases of influence of mutual trade of countries on their economic convergence.

3 Materials and Methods

The data and methods used correspond to the above-stated tasks (Sect. 1 of the chapter). Methods of logical and statistical analysis are used, including calculation of shares and relations, averages, differences, and modules, as well as methods of econometric analysis. At that, the 4th task requires taking as long time series as possible. As for the time interval (1995–2019), it should be noted that the analysis was thought up by the authors at the end of 2021 – and all necessary data were downloaded then. However, the development of the assessment technique was finished just now. However, now it was not possible to search for the CIS data in the UNCTAD database. Therefore, the authors were forced to test the technique on the interval finishing not later than 2020. At that: 1) statistics of Russian foreign trade in any case have not been published by its customs service since 2022; 2) the time series is taken long – 25 years; 3) the practice of analyzing the dynamic series without taking current years is popular in international research space (for example, [12] studies the influence of the trade of 15 countries on their economies in 1990–2012, [8, p. 587] studies 43 countries of the North and the South for 1995–2014); 4) and more important – that in 2020 a shock has occurred, caused by the pandemic. When studying the convergence dynamics, it may be useful to avoid taking into account similar exogenous shocks. That is what was done, for instance, in [2, p. 188]. Therefore, the interval of 1995–2019 was taken.

3.1 On the First Task: Mutual Trade Indicators

Thus, the statistics of the mutual trade of the CIS countries for a long time series (since 1995 – just since the moment of the formation of the first CIS FTZ) have been published in open access by the UNCTAD. The UNCTAD included nine countries in the CIS: Armenia, Azerbaijan, Belarus, Kazakhstan, Kyrgyzstan, Moldova, Russia, Tajikistan, and Uzbekistan (here and further, the source is Table 1). The analysis in this chapter by solving all tasks comes from this composition.

Since export in mutual trade is equal to import, it is enough to take data on export. It is expedient to take:

- mutual trade in all commodities in total. Its dynamics are considered to be the most important measure of integration [5, pp. 4–5].

Trade in intermediary goods also serves as a convergence factor [8, p. 602]. This induces to take also trade in certain groups of commodities, of those, which are statistically presented by the UNCTAD:

- primary (i.e. raw) commodities (groups (0 + 1 + 2 + 3 + 4 + 68) of the SITC (Standard International Trade Classification of the UNCTAD));
- non-primary (i.e. non-raw) commodities (Eq. 1). It is expedient to consider them, because their purchase and sale stimulate the development of technologies;

$$\varphi\left(EX_{m(nr)}\right) = 1 - \frac{EX_{m(r)}}{EX_m}, \tag{1}$$

  where $\varphi\left(EX_{m(nr)}\right)$ is a share of non-primary (i.e. non-raw) commodities in the CIS intra-export, $EX_{m(r)}$ is the CIS intra-export of primary (i.e. raw) commodities, EX_m is the CIS intra-export of all commodities.
- food (SITC groups (0 + 22 + 4) – basic food). This group of commodities is the most important for life; consequently, the influence of its trade can be the highest one.

It is necessary to note the following. To assess the economic convergence of the CIS countries, relative indicators should be calculated (i.e., as a percentage of GDP or other indicators). Therefore, the indicators of mutual trade must also be relative, so that the expression of their dynamics is comparable to the expression of dynamics of convergence indexes. It is necessary to carry out correlation analysis correctly. For example, in works on analyzing the influence of the openness of the economy on convergence, the export [2, p. 193] and foreign investments [17, p. 3] as integration indicators are taken as a ratio to GDP. Thus, indicators of the association's total intra-trade should be taken:

- as a ratio to the association's GDP;
- in addition – as a ratio to the "above staying" trade indicator. So, in the case of intra-trade in all commodities – as a ratio to the total foreign trade of the association (i.e., to trade with all countries of the world); in the case of intra-trade in commodities of a certain group – as a ratio to intra-trade in all commodities.

3.2 On the 2nd and 3rd Tasks: Convergence Indexes

It is expedient to analyze the published indicators and choose the most suitable ones. Statistics on countries' macroeconomic indicators are published by the World Bank (World Development Indicators), the International Monetary Fund (World Economic Outlook), and the UNCTAD. It is expedient to select the indicators, which clearly illustrate economic development. At that, in literature, GDP per capita [2, p. 193; 10, p. 38], productivity [17, p. 3], the human development index and its components [9, p. 26], and inflation [16, p. 222] are used to analyze convergence. Consequently, it is required to take into account not only the indicators of production and accumulation (the volume of manufactured products, including in non-raw branches; investments; the country's international reserves) but also indicators of the social sphere (education and healthcare expenses; employment; inflation).

Since statistics on mutual trade were published by the UNCTAD only for the CIS as a whole, it is also necessary to calculate the values of the convergence indexes of CIS countries for the CIS as a whole – on the basis of convergence indexes for certain countries:

1. To calculate the average value of the macroeconomic indicator for countries for the 1st year of the dynamic series. Since the scale of the CIS economies is various, relative macroeconomic indicators should be taken: GDP per capita, governmental debt in relation to GDP, international reserves in relation to the monthly volume of imports, etc.
2. To calculate for each country the module of deviation from the average (i.e., to calculate the value of convergence of this country with the value that is average on all countries).
3. To calculate the average (on countries-participants) degree of correspondence of an indicator's value to the average (for countries' association) value of this indicator, i.e., the average (on countries) degree of convergence on this indicator (Eq. 2). The dimensionality of this index (Eq. 2) is the number of times. The meaning of values of the index (Eq. 2): the higher they are, the closer to each other the development levels of the association's countries.

$$\overline{C(y)} = \frac{\overline{y}}{\overline{|y_i - \overline{y}|}}, \tag{2}$$

   where $\overline{C(y)}$ is the average (on countries) degree of convergence of the association's countries on a certain macroeconomic indicator y, y_i is the value of this indicator by country i, $\overline{y}$ is the average (on countries) value of this indicator, $\overline{|y_i - \overline{y}|}$ is mean linear deviation, i.e. is the average (on countries) module of deviation of the value of the indicator from the average (on countries) value of the indicator y.
4. To carry out these calculations for each year of the taken time series.
5. To implement actions 1–4 for each indicator.

3.3 On the 4th and 5th Tasks: Correlating the Indicators and Testing the Toolkit

In literature, when analyzing the influence of international trade on structural convergence, the correlation degree is searched [8]. In particular, it is possible to solve the 4th (and, correspondingly, the 5th) task by calculating the correlation degree using the least squares method. For this, it is necessary to assess the degree of the link between each indicator of mutual trade (x) and each convergence indicator (y). It is possible through correlation-regression analysis (calculation of paired linear regression) in the "Data Analysis" package of the "Microsoft Excel" program. It gives the correlation coefficient reflecting the relation degree. According to the Chaddock scale, its value from 0.3 to 0.5 reflects a moderate degree of link, from 0.5 to 0.7 – noticeable, from 0.7 to 0.9 – high, and from 0.9 to 0.99 – very high. For the present study, only the link not lower than high is of interest.

Forecasting (i.e. search for a regression equation, reflecting the link between the indicator *x* and indicator *y*) is not a goal of this study. Therefore, not only those cases of correlation may be considered, where both the correlation coefficient (multiple *R*) and coefficients of the regression equation (i.e., both Fisher's *F*-criterion (significance of $F \leq 0.05$) and Student's *t*-criterion (*P*-values of *t*-statistics of equation coefficients ≤ 0.05) are fulfilled) are statistically significant, but also those cases, where only the correlation coefficient is statistically significant (i.e., only Fisher's *F*-criterion is fulfilled). In the case of a low correlation coefficient (including the case, when it is not statistically significant), and when the length of the time series allows (i.e., by long dynamic series), it makes sense to carry out experiments: to cut down the length of the time series and to measure the correlation degree again.

Thus, the analysis of the mutual trade dynamics of the association's countries, including in the section of goods, the use of these indicators' relation to GDP, considering the production and social convergence indicators, and search for the correlation degree of trade to convergence indicators are already present in previous studies. Also, the equation already exists in the statistical analysis of mean linear deviation. However, the wide complexes of indicators of mutual trade and convergence and their econometric comparison proposed in this chapter, as well as the method of calculating the average (on countries) convergence extent, are the authors' novelty.

4 Results

According to the criteria from Subsect. 3.1 of this chapter, eight indicators of mutual trade illustrating intra-CIS trade were taken, and their relative expression was calculated (Table 1). The calculations showed that the indicators remained stable, excluding the intra-trade in raw commodities: its share in the intra-trade in all commodities in 2019 amounted to 40.5%, compared to 33.0% in 1995. In 1995–2011, the share only in one of the years exceeded 37% (in 1997–45.5%) and on average was 30.7%. At the same time, in 2012–2019 it did not fall lower than 40.5%, on average amounting to 46.5%. A similar share of non-raw commodities in these periods was 69.3% and 53.5%, respectively. This shows that the mutual trade interests of the CIS countries are increasingly determined by raw materials. If one interprets this in the context of the conclusion of the work [8, p. 602], the significance of raw materials as intermediary goods in intra-CIS trade has increased. However, the growth of the share was also observed in the case of intra-trade in food: from an average of 9.5% in 1995–2011 to 15.6% in 2012–2019. Since it is a paramount group of commodities, this trend testifies to the increasing significance of the CIS countries for each other.

According to the criteria from Subsect. 3.2 of this chapter, 14 macroeconomic indicators of countries were selected. At that, statistics for the whole period of 1995–2019 for all of the CIS countries (which will be included in the CIS by the UNCTAD) were simultaneously presented only in the case of several indicators. In the rest of the cases, the dynamic series was shorter. The values of the average degree of convergence of

Table 1. Values of indicators of intra-CIS trade.

Year	Indicators of intra-CIS trade (x)							
	x_1	x_2	x_3	x_4	x_5	x_6	x_7	x_8
	Total intra-trade (% of GDP of the CIS)	Share of intra-trade in total foreign trade, %	Intra-trade in raw commodities (% of GDP)	Share of raw commodities in total intra-trade, %	Intra-trade in non-raw commodities (% of GDP)	Share of non-raw commodities in total intra-trade, %	Intra-trade in food (% of GDP)	Share of food in total intra-trade, %
1995	3.2	15.6	1.1	33.0	2.1	67.0	0.3	9.3
1996	3.8	16.3	1.4	36.9	2.4	63.1	0.5	12.2
1997	3.8	17.0	1.7	45.5	2.1	54.5	0.5	12.1
1998	5.1	19.3	1.7	33.3	3.4	66.7	0.4	8.6
1999	5.0	14.3	1.7	33.9	3.3	66.1	0.5	9.5
2000	5.3	13.5	1.4	25.5	4.0	74.5	0.3	6.5
2001	4.8	14.2	1.4	30.2	3.3	69.8	0.4	7.7
2002	4.3	13.4	1.2	27.8	3.1	72.2	0.3	7.1
2003	4.3	13.3	1.1	25.7	3.2	74.3	0.4	8.5
2004	4.5	13.8	1.2	27.5	3.3	72.5	0.4	9.2
2005	3.7	11.0	1.1	30.2	2.6	69.8	0.4	9.6
2006	3.6	11.2	1.1	29.4	2.6	70.6	0.3	9.2
2007	3.6	12.3	1.1	29.9	2.6	70.1	0.4	9.7
2008	3.6	11.5	1.1	30.2	2.5	69.8	0.3	9.3
2009	3.4	12.7	1.1	31.9	2.3	68.1	0.4	12.3
2010	3.1	11.0	0.8	25.2	2.3	74.8	0.4	11.5
2011	3.3	11.6	0.9	26.1	2.4	73.9	0.3	9.8
2012	3.0	11.2	1.6	52.9	1.4	47.1	0.4	12.7
2013	2.8	11.1	1.4	49.4	1.4	50.6	0.4	14.9
2014	2.8	10.8	1.4	49.4	1.4	50.6	0.5	16.5
2015	2.9	11.6	1.5	50.7	1.4	49.3	0.5	17.9
2016	3.4	14.1	1.5	43.3	1.9	56.7	0.6	16.9
2017	3.6	14.3	1.5	42.5	2.1	57.5	0.5	15.2
2018	3.7	12.8	1.6	43.2	2.1	56.8	0.5	14.9
2019	3.8	14.1	1.5	40.5	2.3	59.5	0.6	16.0

Source: calculated by the authors on: Data center // UNCTAD. URL: https://unctadstat.unctad.org/wds/ReportFolders/reportFolders.aspx (date of access: November 23, 2021).

the CIS countries on these macroeconomic indicators were calculated (Table 2). The calculations showed that for part of the indicators (from y_1 to y_6; from y_9 to y_{11}; y_{14}), convergence increased, and for the rest, it reduced or did not change. In particular, the degree of countries' convergence (Eq. 2) is increased by inflation rate (y_6) (from 2.1 to 39.5 units) (which is a success even in comparison with the Eurozone [16, p. 234]), by governmental debt (y_3) (from 1.59 to 2.64 in 2004–2019) and by international reserves (within 2013–2019 from 1.22 to 1.53 units in relation of reserves to external debt (y_4)

and from 1.73 to 1.99 in relation to the import (y_5)), by the scale of value added in industry (y_{10}) (from 3.45 to 7.06 units within 2012–2019) (for comparison, in the EU, the convergence by productivity, i.e. by the indicator reflecting the value creation in industry, has demonstrated unambiguous results already since the 1990s, especially after 2008–2009 [17, p. 2], but convergence in the industry share in GDP is observed in ASEAN [9, p. 27]), by the inflow of foreign direct investments (y_9) (from 1.09 to 2.91 units), of Internet use by physical persons (y_{14}) (from 2.73 to 3.64). Convergence reduced for expenses on healthcare (y_7) (from 7.86 to 3.90 units within 2000–2018) and R&D (y_{13}) (from 1.70 to 1.33 within 2003–2018) (it is notable that significant differentiation in R&D expenses is also observed in ASEAN [9, p. 26]) and by gross capital formation (y_8) (from 12.0 to 4.29). The convergence degree for employment (y_2) fluctuated (33.0 in 1995, 35.1 in 2019), however, if in 1995–2008 it averaged 51.90, in 2009–2019 – 34.15 units (Table 2).

Then, according to the technique from Subsect. 3.3 of this chapter, the coefficients of the correlation of the indicators of mutual trade (x) with the indexes of countries' convergence on macroeconomic indicators (y) were calculated (Table 3). The authors analyzed 112 cases of correlating the influencing and dependent indicators. In the case when the correlation coefficient was statistically not significant and if the length of the dynamic series allowed, experiments were additionally carried out on reducing the length of the time series. In particular, for y_2 by correlating with x_1, x_2, x_7 as an experiment, the time series was additionally taken without observations number 1–4 (the years of observations are given in Table 2); for y_1 by correlating with x_2, x_4 – the time series without observations 1–4, with x_5 and x_7 – without observations 1–4 and 1–6, with x_8 – without 1–6; for y_6 by correlating with x_1 and x_3 – without observation 1, with x_6, x_7, x_8 – without observations 1–9.

5 Discussion

Of the 112 cases of correlating the trade indicators with the indexes of economic convergence, in 26 cases, both Fisher's criterion and Student's criterion are fulfilled; in 12 cases, a high or very high correlation degree is observed (here and further – Table 3). At the same time, only 2 of these 12 cases fall on those "y", for which the long series (16 years and longer) are presented. The rest of the cases refer to those "y", for which the short time series (7–8 years) are presented. This testifies not in favor of the statistical significance of the total picture of the correlation of mutual trade with economic convergence.

Nevertheless, in 12 cases of correlating x with y, a high correlation degree is observed (by fulfilling the F- and the t-statistics). In particular, it is observed between the dynamic series of the following pairs of indicators: between mutual trade in all commodities (x_1) and the degree of countries' closeness by international reserves (y_4) (the correlation coefficient is 0.98), as well as closeness by healthcare expenses (% of GDP) (y_7) (0.92); between the share of mutual trade in the total foreign trade of countries (x_2) and closeness by value added in manufacturing (y_{11}) (0.77); between mutual trade in raw commodities (x_3) and value added in medium- and high-tech manufacturing (y_{12}) (0.72); between the share of raw commodities in mutual trade (x_4) and value added in industry (y_{10}) (0.75)

Table 2. Values of the average degree of convergence of the CIS countries on economic indicators, number of relative units*.

Year	Economic indicator (y), the convergence index for which is presented													
	y_1	y_2	y_3	y_4	Y_5	y_6	y_7	y_8	y_9	y_{10}	y_{11}	y_{12}	y_{13}	y_{14}
	GDP per capita (current prices), USD	Employment (% of the total labor force)	General government gross debt, % of GDP	Total reserves (% of total external debt)	Total reserves (in months of imports)	Consumer price indices (taken as a chain growth rate)	Current healthcare expenditure (% of GDP)	Gross capital formation (% of GDP)	Foreign direct investment, net inflows (% of GDP)	Industry (including construction), value added (% of GDP)	Manufacturing, value added (% of GDP)	Medium- and high-tech manufacturing value added (% of GDP)	R&D expenses (% of GDP)	Individuals using the Internet (% of the population)
1995	1.44	33.0	n/a	n/a	n/a	2.1	n/a	12.00	1.09	n/a	n/a	n/a	n/a	n/a
1996	1.48	24.6	n/a	n/a	n/a	2.4	n/a	10.40	0.97	n/a	n/a	n/a	n/a	n/a
1997	1.53	38.1	n/a	n/a	n/a	5.0	n/a	1.32	1.18	n/a	n/a	n/a	n/a	n/a
1998	1.74	39.9	n/a	n/a	n/a	6.8	n/a	1.34	1.25	n/a	n/a	n/a	n/a	n/a
1999	1.97	55.7	n/a	n/a	n/a	2.7	n/a	6.24	1.49	n/a	n/a	n/a	n/a	n/a
2000	1.89	54.4	n/a	n/a	n/a	4.5	7.86	6.75	1.19	n/a	n/a	n/a	n/a	n/a
2001	1.64	58.5	n/a	n/a	n/a	7.8	6.24	9.30	1.01	n/a	n/a	n/a	n/a	n/a
2002	1.59	55.6	n/a	n/a	n/a	10.8	4.62	4.77	1.00	n/a	n/a	n/a	n/a	n/a
2003	1.51	73.0	n/a	n/a	n/a	18.0	5.38	3.09	0.86	n/a	n/a	n/a	1.70	n/a
2004	1.42	69.9	1.59	n/a	n/a	32.9	4.81	3.36	1.17	n/a	n/a	n/a	1.72	n/a
2005	1.42	65.5	1.43	n/a	n/a	36.2	4.07	3.68	1.08	n/a	n/a	n/a	1.72	n/a
2006	1.42	65.2	1.38	n/a	n/a	45.8	3.48	5.04	1.79	n/a	n/a	n/a	1.64	n/a
2007	1.48	54.7	1.43	n/a	n/a	47.1	3.43	4.80	2.31	n/a	n/a	n/a	1.35	n/a
2008	1.48	38.6	1.63	n/a	n/a	29.6	3.55	4.64	2.74	n/a	n/a	n/a	1.42	n/a
2009	1.53	31.8	1.65	n/a	n/a	29.2	3.20	4.81	2.12	n/a	n/a	n/a	1.52	n/a
2010	1.44	31.5	1.66	n/a	n/a	95.0	3.07	5.03	2.46	n/a	n/a	n/a	1.45	n/a
2011	1.39	31.7	1.57	n/a	n/a	12.9	3.00	6.85	2.46	n/a	n/a	n/a	1.54	n/a
2012	1.38	32.9	1.77	n/a	n/a	10.1	3.17	7.17	2.32	3.45	3.81	1.15	1.55	2.73
2013	1.37	35.7	1.84	1.22	1.73	32.0	3.14	6.57	2.95	3.86	3.60	1.38	1.49	2.61
2014	1.43	33.6	1.93	1.16	1.55	35.1	3.15	7.49	2.80	4.05	3.75	1.37	1.56	3.09
2015	1.61	31.9	2.08	1.24	1.53	34.0	3.63	5.63	1.36	6.36	4.25	1.33	1.56	3.35
2016	1.83	38.3	2.08	1.38	1.67	26.3	4.08	5.81	1.39	6.00	4.35	1.44	1.48	3.60
2017	1.62	38.7	2.30	1.46	1.85	34.4	3.92	7.54	1.93	6.03	4.37	1.33	1.35	3.64
2018	1.63	34.6	2.31	1.43	1.97	34.6	3.90	4.86	2.20	5.81	4.28	1.28	1.33	n/a
2019	1.67	35.1	2.64	1.53	1.99	39.5	n/a	4.29	2.91	7.06	4.05	1.23	n/a	n/a

Note:

"n/a": the data at least for one country of the CIS on an indicator are not available.

*The higher is value, the stronger is convergence (subsection 3.2 of this chapter).

Source: calculated by the authors according to Eq. 2 on: 1) y_2, y_4, y_5, from y_7 to y_{14} – on: World Development Indicators // World Bank. URL: databank.worldbank.org/source/world-development-indicators; 2) y_1, y_6, y_{11}, y_{12} – on: Data Center // UNCTAD. URL: https://unctadstat.unctad.org/wds/ReportFolders/reportFolders.aspx; 3) y_3 – on: World Economic Outlook Database, October 2021 // International Monetary Fund. URL: https://www.imf.org/en/Publications/WEO/weo-database/2021/October (date of access: November 23, 2021).

Table 3. Values of the correlation coefficient (multiple R) for cases, where it is statistically significant (Fisher's F-criterion is fulfilled).

		Influencing variables (x) – indicators of mutual trade of the CIS countries							
		x_1	x_2	x_3	x_4	x_5	x_6	x_7	x_8
Dependent variables (y) – indexes of convergence of countries of the CIS on various economic indicators	y_1[1]	0.65*	**0.72**[9]	0.54*	–	–	–	0.66*[10]	**0.79**
	y_2[1]	0.67[9]	–	–	0.55*	0.65	0.55	–	0.61*
	y_3[2]	–	0.58	**0.75**	0.60*	–	0.60*	**0.93**	**0.82***
	y_4[3]	**0.98***	**0.92**	**0.83**	**0.96***	**0.98***	**0.96**	**0.85**	–
	y_5[3]	**0.84**	–	–	**0.83***	**0.85***	**0.83**	–	–
	y_6[1]	0.52*[11]	0.56*	0.54*[11]	–	–	–	–	–
	y_7[4]	**0.92***	0.63	–	–	**0.80**	–	–	0.54*
	y_8[1]	–	–	–	–	–	–	–	–
	y_9[1]	0.57*	0.54*	–	–	0.54*	–	–	0.46
	y_{10}[5]	**0.75**	**0.79**	–	**0.75***	**0.77**	**0.75**	**0.96***	–
	y_{11}[6]	–	**0.77***	–	–	–	–	**0.78***	–
	y_{12}[6]	–	–	**0.72***	–	–	–	–	–
	y_{13}[7]	–	–	–	–	–	–	–	–
	y_{14}[8]	–	**0.83**	–	–	**0.81**	–	**0.96**	–

Note:
* Apart from Fisher's F-criterion, Student's t-criterion is fulfilled.
"–": the correlation coefficient is not statistically significant.
Intervals: [1]1995–2019, if otherwise not mentioned; [2]2004–2019; [3]2013–2019; [4]2000–2018; [5]2012–2019; [6]2012–2019; [7]2003–2018; [8]2012–2017; [9]1999–2019; [10]2001–2019; [11]1996–2019.
Italics print: high and very high correlation degree.
Source: calculated by the authors in the "Data Analysis" package of the "Microsoft Excel" program on the basis of the data from Tables 1 and 2, according to Subsect. 3.3 of this chapter.

and international reserves of countries (0.96 and 0.83, depending on whether the reserves were expressed through governmental debt (y_4) or through import (y_5)); between mutual trade in non-raw commodities (x_5) and international reserves (y_4, y_5) (0.98 and 0.85); between mutual trade in food (x_7) and value added in industry (y_{10}) (0.96), including in manufacturing (y_{11}) (0.78) (Table 3).

Apart from this, 18 cases of high correlation are observed with a statistically significant correlation coefficient, but not significant coefficients of the regression equation (explained in Subsect. 3.3). For example: between the scale of mutual trade and convergence on value added in industry (y_{10}) (0.75 – for the ratio of mutual trade to GDP (x_1), 0.79 – for the ratio to total foreign trade (x_2)); between GDP per capita (y_1) and mutual trade share in total foreign trade (x_2) – 0.72 (for comparison, in the work on ASEAN [2, p. 204], the result is obtained showing that mutual trade is not the basic convergence factor; in [10, p. 39], it is shown that in the case of the EAEU (5 countries), convergence on GDP per capita is high, but when broadening the cooperation contour, it reduces, which corresponds to the results of the present research); etc.

It can be noted that the following cases of a high correlation degree possess an outstanding economic meaning:

- between mutual trade and countries' convergence on international reserves and on governmental debt, because expenses on import and export incomes essentially influence international reserves and governmental debt. So, for international reserves as a ratio to external debt (y_4) in all cases, except x_8, the degree of correlation is high; also, the degree of correlation is high in 4 cases of the ratio of reserves to import (y_5). The correlation coefficient for governmental debt (y_3) is high, for example, in the case of mutual trade in food: 0.93 (if trade is expressed in % of GDP (x_7)) and 0.82 (if trade is expressed in % of total mutual trade (x_8)). Countries' convergence on governmental debt (y_3) is also influenced by mutual trade in raw commodities (x_3) (0.75) (Table 3);
- between mutual trade in non-raw commodities (x_5) and the share of the population using the Internet (y_{14}) (0.81; only R is significant, but not the equation coefficients (explained in Subsect. 3.3)). Purchase (as well as sale) of non-raw commodities by countries stimulates their technological development, including digitalization;
- between mutual trade and convergence on value added in industry (y_{10}). In the majority of cases, the degree of correlation is high. I.e., mutual trade positively influences the convergence of the CIS countries in terms of the industrial result.

In general, each of the mutual trade indicators (except the share of food in mutual trade (x_8)) possesses a high degree of correlation with at least three indexes of macroeconomic convergence. At that, each of the three indicators of mutual trade (the share of mutual trade in total foreign trade (x_2), the ratio of mutual trade in non-raw commodities (x_5) and food (x_7) to GDP) gives five cases of high correlation.

At the same time, in part of some indexes of socio-economic convergence of the CIS countries (investments (y_8), R&D expenses (y_{13}), employment (y_2), and inflation (y_6)), correlation with mutual trade is not observed (in any case, if the high degree is meant).

The scientific novelty and relevance of the received results consist in working out the methodical provision for assessing the relation of the mutual trade of countries of some integration association to their economic convergence. This methodical provision: 1) considers in part of trade both raw and non-raw trade, in part of countries' convergence – both indicators of production and indicators of investments, financial sustainability, and social aspects; 2) with the aim of comparability compares relative indicators with relative; 3) proposes a comparison of all possible combinations of indicator pair of; 4) uses the econometric method for comparison.

The practical relevance of the results consists in the assessment of the effectiveness of developing trade integration within a certain association of countries, where an FTZ exists – within the CIS. In particular, the results demonstrate the cases of a high (i.e., more direct) relation of indexes of macroeconomic convergence of the association's countries to their mutual trade, and the cases of low relation (i.e., of the influencing mechanism that is lengthier in time). The experience of this study can be applied also in the case of any other group of countries, if they de jure and/or de facto cooperate in trade and economics, not depending on the achieved extent of the orientation of their foreign trade to each other and on the achieved socio-economic convergence and not depending on the mutual geographical location.

6 Conclusion

Thus, the analysis of the nomenclature of published statistics made it possible to propose the following composition of indicators for assessing the influence of the mutual trade of countries of the interstate association on their economic convergence: 1) indicators of mutual trade – the relation of the total mutual trade and the mutual trade separately in raw and non-raw commodities and in food to GDP and to the total foreign trade of the association; 2) macroeconomic indicators, concerning the production volume (GDP per capita; value added in industry, including in manufacturing, including in the medium- and high-tech one (% of GDP)), investments (including foreign direct investments; R&D expenses (% of GDP)), financial sustainability (governmental debt (% of GDP), international reserves (relation to external debt and to the month import)), social aspects (employment, inflation, healthcare expenses, Internet use (% of the population)). The equation is proposed to calculate the average degree of convergence for countries of the integration association in terms of each macroeconomic indicator. To assess the influence of mutual trade on convergence, it is proposed to take each of the trade indicators and correlate it with each of the convergence indexes in pairs, by calculating the coefficient of the correlation of the dynamic series of values using the method of least squares.

The testing has shown that the influence of the mutual trade of the CIS countries on their economic convergence has a various nature in the case of various macroeconomic indicators. If in the case of indicators of governmental debt, value added in industry, and international reserves (the 1st group of macroeconomic indicators), the correlation is high, in the case of inflation, employment, investments, and R&D expenses (the 2nd group), influence is not observed by means of correlation-regression analysis on the taken time intervals. It can be logically remarked concerning these two groups of macroeconomic indicators that the causal link with foreign trade is more direct for the 1st group, while for the 2nd group it is more indirect (the influencing mechanism is lengthier in time). This for the most part confirms the hypothesis put forward: the 1st group includes total indicators of production and accumulation and the 2nd group – indicators of human potential development (perhaps, also includes total investments).

It can be also remarked that the share of intra-trade in the total foreign trade of the CIS countries is very low – on average, in 1995–2019 it was 13.3%. Its relation to the CIS GDP was on average 3.8%. This also explains the impossibility for mutual trade to essentially influence the economic convergence of countries. However, the importance of the mutual trade of the CIS countries for their economic development, apart from correlation analysis, is confirmed through the fact that during the whole considered interval (1995–2019), the ratio of intra-trade to the total foreign trade of the CIS and to the CIS GDP remained relatively stable (15.6% and 3.2% in 1995; 14.1% and 3.8% in 2019, respectively), despite the growth of the total foreign trade of the Commonwealth (from 95 to 561 billion USD) and of its GDP (from 463 to 2086 billion USD).

The limitations of the conducted study are related to the fact that the published relevant statistics on a number of indicators are presented only for a short time interval.

Besides, it is difficult to summarize a multitude of resulting assessing indicators into a single conclusion. This grants the potential for further investigations.

The results of the study can be used by the authorities of integration associations of the Big Eurasian partnership and of certain countries when analyzing the effectiveness of strategies and plans of integration development taking into account the extent to which they have succeeded in achieving the desired degree of convergence on various indicators and the influence of the mutual trade of countries, including in the commodities section.

Acknowledgements. The study was conducted at the cost of the grant of the Russian Science Foundation Number 25-28-01505, https://rscf.ru/project/25-28-01505.

References

1. Zagashvili, V.: Economic globalization and regional integration in the post-COVID era. World Econ. Int. Relat. **66**(4), 5–13 (2022). https://doi.org/10.20542/0131-2227-2022-66-4-5-13
2. Verico, K.: Indonesia's International Economic Strategies. Palgrave Macmillan, Singapore (2023). https://doi.org/10.1007/978-981-99-8458-9
3. Ibrahim, A., Abdulmalik, M.R.: Do trade openness and governance matter for economic growth in Africa? A case of EAC and WAEMU countries. IEEP **20**(3), 389–412 (2023). https://doi.org/10.1007/s10368-023-00565-w
4. Fox, E.M.: Integrating Africa by competition and market policy. Rev. Ind. Organ. **60**(3), 305–326 (2022). https://doi.org/10.1007/s11151-022-09854-1
5. Vorona, A.A., Borisova, E.M.: Mutual trade of the member states of the Eurasian Economic Union: Impact of the pandemic and development prospects. Eurasian Sci. J. **12**(4), 30 (2020). https://esj.today/PDF/16ECVN420.pdf. (In Russ.)
6. González, G.H., Sapir, E.V., Vasilchenko, A.D.: Global production networks in the regional analysis framework: Case of the EU peripheral automotive manufacturing. Econ. Reg. **19**(1), 230–243 (2023). https://doi.org/10.17059/ekon.reg.2023-1-18
7. Andreeva, E., Ratner, A., Sobolev, A.: Impact of renewable energy development in Germany on Russian energy export. Contemp. Europe **104**(4), 71–82 (2021). https://doi.org/10.15211/soveurope420217182
8. Hübler, M., Bukin, E., Xi, Y.: The effects of international trade on structural convergence and CO2 emissions. Environ. Resource Econ. **83**(3), 579–604 (2022). https://doi.org/10.1007/s10640-022-00698-7
9. Chupina, D., Vyalykh, M.: Inequality in ASEAN through regional integration. Asia Africa Today (2019). https://doi.org/10.31857/S032150750003340-6
10. Gorbunova, M.L., Komarov, I.D., Maslova, T.E.: Study of convergence and divergence of EAEU integration processes based on the Gini index. Eurasian Integr.: Econ. Law Polit. **17**(2), 34–45 (2023). https://doi.org/10.22394/2073-2929-2023-02-34-45
11. Mamba, E., Balaki, A.: Deep regional trade agreement as a driver for global value chains in Africa: the case of ECOWAS region. Econ. Chang. Restruct. **56**(3), 2037–2068 (2023). https://doi.org/10.1007/s10644-023-09503-x
12. Ben Abdallah, A.: The relationship between trade openness, foreign direct investment inflows, and economic growth in Middle East and North of Africa Region: autoregressive distributed lag model vs. vector error correction model. J. Knowl. Econ. **15**, 1118–1141 (2023). https://doi.org/10.1007/s13132-023-01099-x
13. Pak, E.V.: The role of international intra-industry trade in deepening integration in the Eurasian Economic Union. Russ. Foreign Econ. J. **2**, 95–104 (2018). (In Russ.)

14. Diabaté, V., Kholina, V.N., Frolova, E.D.: The change of foreign trade structure of African countries in the context of increasing regionalization in the world economy. Econ. Reg. **16**(1), 242–256 (2020). https://doi.org/10.17059/2020-1-18
15. Kügler, A., Reinstaller, A., Friesenbichler, K.S.: Can value chain integration explain the diverging economic performance within the EU? J. Ind. Bus. Econ. **50**(1), 25–47 (2023). https://doi.org/10.1007/s40812-022-00236-y
16. Hegerty, S.W.: Structural breaks and regional inflation convergence for five new Euro members. Econ. Chang. Restruct. **53**(2), 219–239 (2020). https://doi.org/10.1007/s10644-018-9241-x
17. Lecat, R., Pasquier de Franclieu, D.: Convergence and capital flows in Europe: the role of financial intermediation and investor quality. De Economist **172**, 101–119 (2024). https://doi.org/10.1007/s10645-024-09434-6
18. Alhassan, A., Payaslioğlu, C.: Trade diversion and creation effect of free trade agreements in ASEAN: do institutions matter? J. Knowl. Econ. **15**, 917–935 (2023). https://doi.org/10.1007/s13132-023-01108-z
19. Shkvarya, L., Karabulatova, I., Rusakovich, V., Rapiev, A.: The impact of the Customs Union and the EAEU on the small and medium business in Kazakhstan. Central Asia Caucasus **18**(1), 93–100 (2017)
20. Kosarev, A.E.: Stratification of the EU/OECD and CIS economies based on 2017 purchasing power parities. Stud. Russ. Econ. Dev. **32**(1), 44–51 (2021). https://doi.org/10.1134/S1075700721010081

Human Capital as a Source of Economic Progress

Strategic Human Capital Management: Developing a Conceptual Framework

Evgeny Kuzmin[1](✉) and Bekzod Ummatov[2]

[1] Institute of Economics of the Ural Branch of the Russian Academy of Sciences, 29 Moskovskaya Street, Ekaterinburg 620014, Russia
kuzmin.ea@uiec.ru

[2] Director of Financial Affairs, Diplomat University, 1 Sayilgoh Street, Tashkent 100047, Uzbekistan

Abstract. Human capital has become a key asset that ensures firms' competitiveness and sustainability. The study focuses on developing strategic approaches to human capital management, integrating them with companies' business strategies, and identifying factors influencing the choice of strategies. The study is a theoretical discussion and is presented as an opinion without empirical verification. The article highlights the distinctions between human resource management and human capital management that view employees as a strategic asset creating long-term value and benefits for the organization rather than as a cost driver. To that end, a comparative analysis of the existing approaches to human resource management and human capital management is conducted, highlighting their differences and commonalities. Special emphasis is placed on the typology of human capital management strategies and their scope of application. On this basis, various combinations of the accents of human capital management strategies are proposed. The article also presents an approach to structuring human capital management, which emphasizes the importance of establishing corporate horizontal and vertical links for the successful implementation of strategic management; clarifies the principles and stages of developing a human capital management strategy; and reveals the construct of management. The results of the study may be of use for researchers and practitioners investigating human capital management issues. The findings add to the theoretical understanding of strategic human capital management and allow devising more effective tools for personnel management in a changing business environment. Empirical testing of the expressed opinions and theoretical assumptions may be the subject of future research.

Keywords: Human capital · Strategic management · Adaptability · Business strategy

JEL Classification: E24 · J24 · O15 · L20

E. Kuzmin et al. (Eds.): EASET 2024, SPBE, pp. 191–212, 2025.
https://doi.org/10.1007/978-3-031-91159-0_13

1 Introduction

Human capital has become a key factor that determines competitiveness and sustainable development in the modern socio-economic landscape. Technological advances, demographic shifts, structural changes in the labor market – all these and other challenges have altered the opportunities for effective transformation, where the creation of value within the company has come to the fore. It is the combination of skills, knowledge, experience and abilities of employees that underlie the innovative potential of an organization and its prospects in the market. The significance of human capital is more than obvious: employees act as the main driver of innovation and operational success of the company, thus creating its competitive advantages [1–4]. In this context, human capital is perceived not merely as a resource for performing operational tasks, but as an asset that affects the long-term development strategy.

Modern companies face the need to integrate human capital into their strategic priorities. Recognizing personnel as a strategic asset made it necessary to rethink work processes and management approaches [5–9]. Employees are no longer viewed solely through the prism of costs. Increasing attention is being paid to continuous learning and soft skills development, which makes the company more agile and enhances its flexibility in building processes. The transition from rigid hierarchical structures to network-based ones made human capital management more adaptable to dynamic changes both within and outside the organization.

The use of strategic approaches to human capital management enables both increased labor productivity and creating conditions that facilitate adaptation to a changing environment [10–13]. It advocates the relevance of studies on human capital and the need for its in-depth investigation in the context of strategic management. Thus, the purpose of the given paper is to establish a conceptual framework of strategic human capital management, classify the applied strategies and formulate system approaches to management structuring. To attain the set purpose, the following objectives are to be achieved: to conduct a comparative analysis of approaches to human resource management and human capital management; to compile a typology of human capital management strategies; to identify the strategic directions related to unlocking employee potential; to reveal the factors influencing the choice of human capital management strategies; and to produce recommendations for formulating effective human capital management strategies in a changing business environment.

The study has the following structure. Introduction substantiates the relevance of the study and formulates its purpose and objectives. Section 2 compares approaches to human resource management and human capital management and analyzes their key differences and similarities. Section 3 delves into the existing human capital management strategies and provides their typology and core characteristics. On this basis, various combinations of the accents of human capital management strategies are worked out. Section 4 presents an approach to developing a human capital management strategy, including the stages of this process. By consolidating strategic areas, a way of structuring of human capital management is proposed. Conclusion summarizes the findings of the study and gives recommendations and possible directions for further research in the field of strategic human capital management.

This study is a theoretical discussion presented in the format of an opinion, without empirical verification. Verification of the judgments and theoretical assumptions put forward in the article may become the subject of further research. Implementation of empirical analysis in the future will verify the validity of the proposed ideas, will contribute to a deeper understanding of the issues under consideration, will clarify and strengthen the argumentation.

2 Human Capital Management vs. Human Resource Management

Personnel management, human resource (HR) management and human capital management in a company are closely interwoven, but conceptually different from each other (although they are somewhat similar in focus). While personnel management has traditionally focused on the administrative and operational aspects of working with employees, HR management and human capital management implement broader strategic approaches, in which people management implies shaping policies that make it easier for the company to achieve its long-term goals, including workforce planning, staff development and training, career management, designing motivational and involvement programs, unleashing employees' creative potential, talent retention, etc. [14–21]. The role of employees as a key asset is highlighted by viewing human capital through its basic and secondary manifestation.

Research works address the overlapping areas between personnel management, HR management and human capital management. These areas touch on many aspects and often point to different perceptions of these spheres, as with "human resource" or the "human asset". In personnel management, the focus is on the personnel management systems that are applied to select, develop and effectively use employees' knowledge and skills ("human resource") [22–24]. However, in contrast to the first approach, the accent of the second, resource-based, one is on the employee's personality, that is his/her motivation, relationships, and efforts. HR practices are considered in their entirety, i.e., the extent to which they contribute to employee development and motivation [25–27], which has an impact on organizational performance [28–30]. Strategic human capital management, on the contrary, concentrates on the characteristics of the capital itself, such as its uniqueness and specificity, while human capital attributes are considered as a unit of analysis to understand how exactly individual and collective human capital affects the company's performance ("human asset"). HR effectiveness is traced through the financial and operational performance of companies [31]; it is reflected at the individual level through job satisfaction, engagement and commitment, employee well-being, productivity and organizational behavior [32–36] and represented at the corporate level through sustainability and social responsibility [37–39]. Given these differences in approaches, it seems expedient to clarify the possibilities of their integration in order to expand the understanding of human capital management.

The integration points are located at the intersection of the approaches. Organizational climate and culture theory [40–42], social exchange and trust theory [43–45], person-environment fit approach [46, 47], and signaling theories [48] have been integrated into strategic HR management research to explain how initial HR management systems affect employee perceptions and reactions [49]. Many studies prove that factors such as employee commitment, work effort, job satisfaction, trust and psychological climate play a proxy (mediating) role in the relationship between HR management and performance [50–54]. These factors strengthen the role of cultural adaptability and flexibility of HR management systems in response to changing market demands, including shifts in the workforce structure [55–57]. Expanding the theoretical framework provides a better understanding of how HR management practices can contribute to the creation of an inclusive and productive work environment.

Research adds a “human dimension” to the resource-based approach to strategy development by focusing on dynamics and flexibility, while the very management strategy is of an integrated nature [14–16, 19, 21]. It implies a workforce that is easily adaptable, can effectively use and consolidate the existing organizational knowledge and, as a result, create innovations. It is emphasized that people are the key driver of the company’s success in the market, and people become the main and primary resource, the most valuable asset and, ultimately, the capital of any organization. Awareness of that encourages investment in human capital development, i.e., creating a culture of continuous learning, strengthening employees’ professional skills and experience, promoting their personal growth, etc. [58, 59]. The logical evolution of the idea of integration defined the company’s human capital management as a system of interrelated practices that represent a strategic competence that is difficult for competitors to imitate [60]. These competencies reflect companies’ certain characteristics in terms of human capital and its efficiency (return from its use), which together can be conditionally called ‘strategies’.

Due to the overlapping of these interconnected spheres, there are a number of research questions emerging: how to interpret human capital and an individual in it; what management and dynamics analysis mechanisms to choose; what research methods are better to use. Although an extensive discussion of all potential aspects is beyond the scope of this study, we believe that the integration of various management approaches allows proposing new theoretical models, elucidating the interaction between different practices and their impact on organizational performance, identifying the source of innovation and the specificity of adaptation to changes in the business environment. The distinctive features of the approaches are presented in Table 1.

Conceptual clarification of approaches to human capital management and human resource management has allowed highlighting a number of distinctive features. Being aware of the differences is critical to making theoretical advances in this area that will lead to practical improvements in business strategies.

3 An Overview of Some Human Capital Management Strategies

Human capital management strategies have not yet been strictly formalized in the literature. Classifications and types of strategies are diverse, but in one way or another they are all associated with human capital assessment.

3.1 Combination Selection Strategies

McKinsey experts [61] classify companies based on two key parameters – financial indicators and indicators of human capital development. The indicators were selected based

Table 1. Strategic human capital management vs. strategic human resource management.

Criteria	Strategic human capital management	Strategic human resource management
Interpretation of human	Human as an asset	Human as a resource
Key value driver	Human capital as a value-creating asset	Human resources as costs to be reduced
Focus	Using employees as an asset that can bring long-term value to the organization, which involves investing in the development and training of employees, as well as creating an environment for their more productive work	Operational aspects of personnel management (recruitment, training, performance evaluation, labor relations and exit from the organization)
Preceding concept (continuity of management approach)	Human resource management	Personnel management
Object and purpose of management	Strategic HR planning to achieve long-term business goals	Effective personnel management within established policies and procedures
Level of management	Predominantly, human capital at the macro level. At the same time, human capital is a resource of an individual and/or unit level that is associated with the ability of a firm to create economic value; the total resource of human capital is seen as a combination of individual personal qualities	Predominantly, human resources at the micro level. HR management at micro level focuses on individual employees and their interactions within the organization. The main goal is to maximize the efficiency of each employee and, as a result, increase the overall performance of the company
Management practices	Focus on complementarities that influence human capital at the individual and unit levels	Focus on complementarities between specific HR practices
Methods	Using proxy-based indicators of human capital. Integrated approaches including needs analysis, career path planning, talent management, leadership development, etc	Standard procedures and practices such as recruiting, training, evaluation and compensation. Using psychological measurements
Tools	Econometric models	Cross-sectional surveys, longitudinal studies

(continued)

Table 1. (*continued*)

Criteria	Strategic human capital management	Strategic human resource management
Scope of analysis	Most studies focus on macro-levels of analysis, with limited use of multi-level approaches	Significant increase in the number of multi-level models
Results measurement	Assessing the employees' contribution to the performance of the organization, including such aspects as innovation, quality of work and contribution to strategic sustainability goals	Evaluation of results in terms of HR processes effectiveness

Note: compiled by the author based on the results of a literature review

on correlation with the upward mobility of employees [62]. Financial performance is measured through return on sales. There are three criteria used to assess human capital development: the share of internal transfers (filling vacant positions with internal resources [63]) in the total number of transfers, the average number of training hours per employee, and the overall score of the McKinsey Organizational Health Index (OHI) [64, 65]. Studies have also found a strong correlation between these indicators: high values in one of them are usually accompanied by equally high values in the other two. Thus, McKinsey classify companies into four categories: Performance + People Winners (top positions in both financial indicators and human capital development); Performance-Driven Companies focused on results (top positions in financial indicators and bottom positions in human capital development); People-Focused Companies (bottom positions in financial indicators and top positions in human capital development); Typical Performers (bottom positions in both financial performance and human capital development).

Performance + People Winners concentrate on talent development through internal career moves and intensive training. People-Focused Companies also pay attention to talent, but they are unable to translate it into strong financial performance on a constant basis. Typical Performers, as classified by McKinsey, do not excel in any of these areas. At the same time, companies that invest in human capital demonstrate greater resilience than typical performers.

Developing human capital helps companies retain talent and guarantee higher wages to their employees. Performance + People Winners become talent magnets: attrition rates almost five percentage points lower than those of Performance-Driven Companies. In addition, employees express higher job satisfaction. Interestingly, People-Focused Companies have the same high levels of employee satisfaction and even lower turnover rate than P + P Winners. Although some companies focus on economic results, maintaining talent through effective organizational approaches does not compromise performance.

Performance + People Winners achieve higher returns on investments in human and organizational capital. According to McKinsey estimates, these investments average up to a third of the organization's total income. P + P Winners achieve roughly 30 percent higher revenue growth than both Performance-Driven and People-Focused Companies [66]. By contrast, Performance-Driven Companies generate higher return on investment in R&D and marketing (usually about 10 percent of all firms' revenue). Performance + People Winners achieve higher returns through consultative and challenging leadership. These companies employ bottom-up collaboration, a positive and inclusive work environment, career growth opportunities, a strong motivational policy, and innovation-oriented solutions. Performance-Driven Companies have similar leadership styles but are more oriented to the external environment (customers and competitors), with less emphasis on company-wide innovation, motivation, favorable work environment, and on-the-job coaching. While People-Focused Companies have much in common with P + P Winners (for example, in terms of motivating employees or creating a positive work environment), they do not focus on innovation and building bottom-up communication.

Certain combinations of organizational practices utilized by P + P Winners and People-Focused Companies may be effective in activating human capital potential. Here, it is worth noting the participation of the so-called 'organizational capital'. Organizational capital is the fabric that surrounds employees, and its pattern matters [66]. It includes intangible assets related to organizational learning, procedures and technologies, management system, organizational structure, corporate culture, relationships with stakeholders, etc., which can be a source of competitive advantage [67, 68]. It is widely believed that organizational capital is specific, difficult to copy, and unique to each organization [67, 69–72]. Companies can transform their organizational capital to achieve sustainability goals. Companies that make their mechanisms, systems, processes and procedures more people-oriented not only strive to enhance their long-term performance, but also provide benefits to their employees. Employees are a company's greatest asset, and the organizational principles that govern their work are critical to realizing their potential.

According to McKinsey research, this classification of companies allows identifying appropriate management human capital strategies [73]. First, organizational capital is seen as a key component of success. To stay effective in managing human capital, companies use organizational capital, which includes various practices, systems, and corporate culture. Second, investing in employees creates a solid foundation for unlocking their potential. This implies training and development, career opportunities within the company (internal moves), employee health and well-being programs, etc. The company's decision to invest resources in staff is reflected in many aspects, of which productivity growth is the crucial one [74]. Third, a consultative leadership style is of high importance. For P + P Winners, management is based on a consultative model, in which a special role is attributed to bottom-up communication. It means that, when making a decision, the company takes into account its employees' opinions at all levels. In such a management system, each employee is free to speak out and make suggestions, which contributes to the development of an innovative culture and increases employee involvement. Effective communication between different levels of the organization also helps quickly and accurately pinpoint problems and formulate a corporate strategy that meets real business needs.

Combining different practices enables firms to develop unique human capital management strategies that are adaptable and flexible. This involves a balance of accents in areas such as HR management, knowledge management, talent management, inclusive management, change management, etc. The choice of accents, as well as the choice of combinations in a company's human capital management strategy, must comply with its unique needs and goals [75]. Some combinations of accents that can be attributed to specific human capital management strategies are presented in Table 2.

Table 2. Possible combinations of accents in human capital management strategies.

Strategy's accents	Description
People & Talent	The combination focuses on integrating HR management with overall business strategy and places an emphasis on identifying, developing and retaining key talent. It may cover formulating career paths, training programs, and motivation and reward strategies. This approach helps employees see their future with the company and promotes their long-term motivation
Expertise & Knowledge	The combination is aimed at developing key competencies of employees and creating a knowledge management system in the organization. It may include methods of training, skills development and knowledge sharing, as well as stimulating innovation and work creativity. The combination may also suggest identifying, storing and transferring key knowledge among employees, as well as forming organizational knowledge used to achieve the company's strategic goals
People & Technology	The combination unites traditional employee development programs with cutting-edge technologies such as artificial intelligence and virtual reality training. It helps employees acquire relevant skills and adapt to the changing business reality. The combination aims to prepare both employees and the organization for technological and market changes
Innovation & Environment	The combination strengthens corporate and organizational culture and simultaneously encourages innovation and creativity among employees. It creates a comfortable and supportive environment for new ideas, which contributes to the company's growth. The combination includes assessing the impact of human resources on business and analyzing performance. It can create an inclusive work environment and develop the incentives for inclusion
People & Well-being	This is a combination of flexible work arrangements, remote work opportunities and health and well-being support programs. This approach improves the work-life balance, which increases employee satisfaction and productivity

(*continued*)

Table 2. *(continued)*

Strategy's accents	Description
Environment & People	This is a combination of social responsibility and sustainability practices with strengthening corporate and organizational culture that supports diversity and inclusion, improves the company's reputation and increases employee loyalty. A positive company image attracts talented employees interested in working for a socially responsible company
People & Production	The variant combines regular performance monitoring with offers for career advancement and personal development. This allows employees to pursue their career path within the company and motivates them to achieve better results. Performance feedback helps employees understand their strengths and weaknesses and promotes their professional growth. At the same time, the use of advanced technologies and data analytics in HR management allows for more accurate forecasting of skill needs, efficient resource allocation and optimization of recruitment processes

Effective human capital management requires a flexible approach that combines various strategic priorities. The combinations of accents in human capital management strategies given in Table 2 are not exhaustive and can be extended. Each of these combinations helps organizations formulate a multi-layered strategy that is tailored to the firm's specific needs, goals, and environment.

3.2 Strategies for Choosing Between Extremes

Another set of strategic alternatives is the choice between two parallels, that is internal human resource development vs. external hiring (in other words, developing or buying talent), and process orientation vs. results orientation. Based on that, four dominant types of HR management strategies are distinguished [76]. The first, *Paternalistic,* strategy combines internal employee development with a focus on processes (establishing strong long-term relationships with employees, an accent is on corporate culture and stability of work processes). The second one is *Commitment strategy* that concentrates on long-term development and retention of employees. It involves investing in education and training, creating mechanisms that promote employee loyalty and engagement. The third one is *Free Agent strategy* aimed at attracting highly qualified specialists from outside the company. Companies employing this strategy are often short-term focused and tend to offer high salaries and other incentives to attract the best talent in the market. And the last, *Secondary,* strategy is mostly followed by companies, for which human capital is not a key factor of competitive advantage. Organizations focus on minimizing personnel costs and may use temporary labor or hire part-time workers.

A similar classification of HR management strategies was proposed by Stewart and Brown [77]. It is based on the parameters of the company's strategic orientation (the choice between cost minimization or differentiation) and the approach to talent management (the choice between internal talent development and attracting it from outside the firm). Thus, four strategies are mapped out. The first one is the so-called *'Loyal Soldier'*. It is designed to develop and retain employees within the organization while keeping the focus on cost reduction. It suggests long-term investments in employees, encouraging their loyalty and devotion to the company. The second strategy, *Bargain Laborer,* combines cost leadership with external hiring. The emphasis here is on minimizing personnel costs and using external, often temporary or part-time workers to perform production tasks. This approach is often utilized in industries with intense competition for talent and low profitability, where personnel costs are a critical factor. The third strategy, *Committed Expert,* is based on differentiation and internal development of talent. The idea of the strategy is to invest in employees to develop unique skills and competencies, which should ultimately generate a competitive advantage for the company. The fourth strategy, *Free Agent,* combines differentiation with external hiring. The approach involves bringing in highly qualified specialists to perform specific tasks or projects. This strategy is typical of dynamic industries where specialists are needed for short periods of time. This implies flexibility and the ability to quickly adapt to changes in the labor market.

The visual representation of the two classifications of HR management strategies is given in Fig. 1.

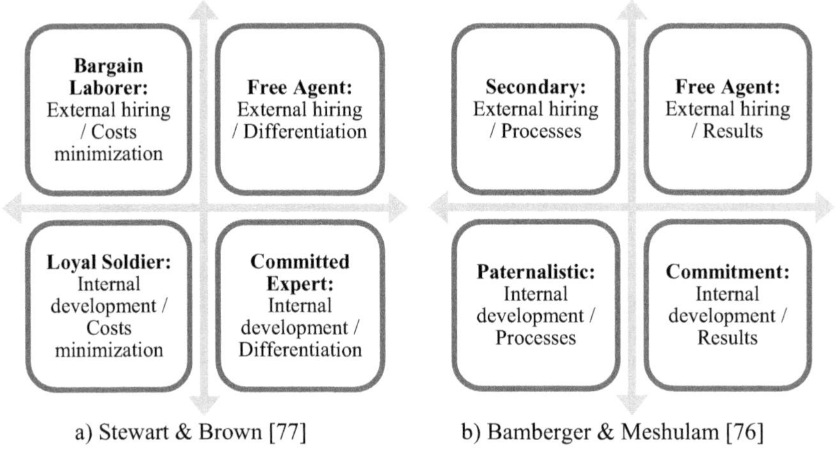

Fig. 1. Classification of HR management strategies.

4 Designing a Human Capital Management Strategy

4.1 The Construct of Management

Strategy is about directional choices made by the company as to how to run the business and what areas and directions of activity to choose [78]. This implies considering not only current priorities but also a long-term perspective.

Strategic guidelines for human capital management can be delineated on an element-by-element basis in accordance with the proposed classification of its elements (see [79]). In it, human capital includes the basis (health, education, professionalism) and the superstructure (adaptability, social skills, leadership qualities and management skills, creativity, corporate and organizational culture, freedom and cultural development, motivation, consumer activity).

Moreover, each component or their combination is part of a theoretical construct, which provides a number of typical management tools and practices. Here, we can note HR management [5, 15, 17, 80], which builds a connection between attracting, developing and retaining employees with the overall strategy of the organization; the competency approach [81–85], which focuses on identifying and increasing key competencies needed to attain the firm's strategic goals; talent management [7, 86, 87], which centers around identifying, promoting, engaging and retaining valuable employees; knowledge management [88–91], which focuses on the creation, storage, transfer, dissemination and use of knowledge; human capital analysis [92–95], which evaluates the contribution of human resources to the organization's performance; corporate and organizational culture management [96, 97], which covers creating a harmonious environment and its connecting ability in the company; and change management [98, 99], which is aimed at adapting to changes through the creation and strengthening of organizational capabilities. These concepts are only a part of a wide range of management aspects. They include various models, methods and tools, which together provide a multifaceted understanding of human capital management.

4.2 Vertical and Horizontal Management Links, Decision-Making Levels

Strategic human resource management emphasizes the importance of establishing *vertical links* that connect key aspects of HR management with overall corporate strategy. This implies that decisions and actions in the HR field (HR practices) must be adjusted to the organization's long-term goals and plans. However, *horizontal links* are also important; they ensure that various HR functions (such as recruitment, training, performance evaluation and promotion) are aligned and integrated to create a coherent system. This approach promotes harmonious interaction within the company, which allows it to gain a sustainable competitive advantage. It is noteworthy that most models typically focus on either vertical or horizontal relationships [100], creating gaps in strategic human resource management. The HR Triad proposed by Jackson and Schuler will help to close the emerging gap [101]. Its participants are line managers, HR management specialists and the employees themselves. Each of them plays an important role in management processes and is responsible for their successful implementation. Line managers are involved in direct personnel management and development, HR specialists are responsible for formulating personnel management policies, systems and tools, and employees are actively engaged in work- and career-related processes. This approach ensures joint and coordinated HR management; its application allows for stronger interaction between all stakeholders and contributes to more effective implementation of corporate strategies.

The structure of management distinguishes three key levels of strategic decision-making: *corporate, business* and *functional* [102–104]. In small and medium-sized enterprises, corporate and business strategies often coincide, whereas in large, multi-industry companies this division is more obvious. At the same time, changes occurring at higher levels exert a significant impact on lower levels. This interaction can be explained through the concept of strategic decisions. And here, consistency is important [105]. Decisions at the top level determine the organization's primary goals, while decisions at lower levels are more often associated with short-term operational tasks. Strategic decisions that establish the firm's long-term goals and activities are first-order strategies. Within the normative model, these decisions have a direct impact on the organization's structure, which is a second-order strategy. First- and second-order strategies provide the basic framework and context in which functional strategies are devised. Strategic decisions in HR management are viewed as dependent on top-order decisions and external factors. Thus, the choice within personnel management becomes a strategic decision of the third level [106]. At the same time, due to its comprehensive coverage, strategic human capital management moves to the top level of the management construct, thus joining corporate and business-level strategies.

4.3 Designing a Human Capital Management Strategy: Principles and Stages

As with any other strategy, a human capital management strategy should uphold systemic principles of construction [107, 108]. In addition to integrity, balance, complementarity and consistency, strategies stick to the principles of flexibility and adaptability. It is also important to ensure continuous analysis and control, commitment to innovation, and keep all stakeholders involved in the strategic planning process. The general rules that a human capital management strategy should adhere to are the following: assessing applicability (ability to meet the need for labor resources of the appropriate quality by the appointed time); assessing the desirability of the strategy (the consequences of the strategy implemented within the framework of the company's policy); formulating the goal(s), which arises from the business strategy and indicates the problems to be solved; determining the means to achieve the goals (identifying how compliant the strategy is with the needs of the business when adapting to changes in the external environment, as well as with the internal situation in the company) [109, 110].

These rules and principles are combined to illustrate the *development stages of a human capital management strategy* (Fig. 2).

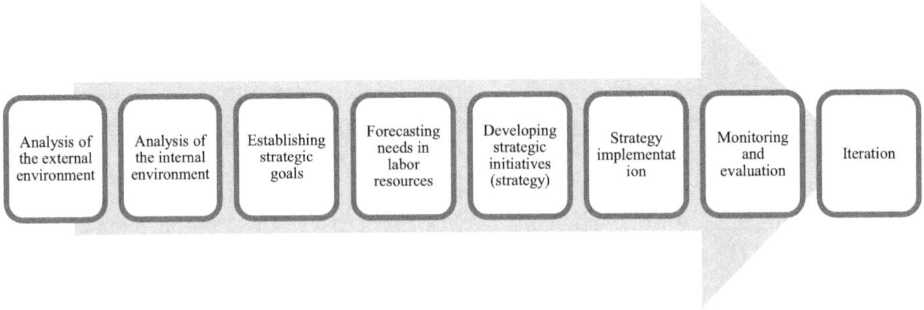

Fig. 2. Development stages of a human capital management strategy.

A human capital management strategy is devised in eight steps:

1. Analysis of the external environment, i.e., assessing market trends and competition, macroeconomic and institutional conditions, technological innovations, etc. This step allows identifying risks and threats, opportunities and prospects for development.
2. Analysis of the internal environment, i.e., assessing the company's resources and organizational capabilities, including its culture, structure, current HR practices and the level of employee competencies. It helps to reveal strengths and weaknesses in the context of HR management.
3. Establishing strategic goals, i.e., setting long-term goals that must be aligned with corporate strategy (human capital management), business strategy (HR management) and functional strategy (personnel management). The human capital management strategy should be closely linked to the overall strategic directions of the company.
4. Forecasting needs in labor resources, i.e., assessing the organization's recruitment needs based on its strategic plans both in quantitative and qualitative terms. The company's strategic goals specify the demand for employees' skills, abilities and expertise and plans their development, reproduction or acquisition.
5. Developing strategic initiatives (strategy), i.e., preparing specific plans and initiatives aimed at achieving set goals. This step may include recruitment, training and development programs, motivation and retention plans, etc. The strategy must consider the state of the external and internal environment and rely on available resources to meet recruitment needs. This stage also involves analysis of various alternatives (strategy variations).
6. Strategy implementation, i.e., integration of the developed human capital management strategy with business processes; implementation and application of the strategy through specific HR programs, policies and practices.
7. Monitoring and evaluation, i.e., regular monitoring of strategy implementation and control over the achievement of set strategic goals. The step implies analyzing the effectiveness of various HR initiatives, both in terms of their impact on the financial and economic activities of the organization and developing human capital potential.
8. Iteration, i.e., making adjustments to the strategy in the event of deviations during implementation, changes in external and/or internal conditions.

These stages of developing a human capital management strategy correspond to general rules and principles and represent a well-structured approach. However, like any other technique, it has its limitations and weaknesses. First, the analysis of the external and internal environment is a rather resource- and time-consuming process. There is a risk that data collected may be out of date by the time it is used in the strategy. Second, the key problem in formulating strategic goals is their connection with the actual operational capabilities of the company. There is a danger of setting unattainable or inappropriate goals. Third, projecting labor requirements may be inaccurate due to both fast changing conditions and errors in the forecasting model. Fourth, it is important to ensure that strategic initiatives (strategy) are not only consistent with goals and aligned with strategies at other levels [77, 111], but are also practically-implementable within the organization. At this stage, employees may become resistant to change, which requires effective change management. Fifth, continuous monitoring requires additional resources and can lead to excessive control. Optimality is of high importance here. It can also be difficult to identify appropriate metrics for evaluation. And sixth, constant revision of the strategy can lead to loss of sustainability. Lack of stability and predictability can be fatal for both the organization and its employees. It is important here to avoid getting stuck in a loop.

The development of human capital management strategies can follow different trajectories. Each variation may be effective in different contexts, as there is no universal solution. The variety of trajectories reflects different methods of change management and behavioral responses to these changes, and points to unique ways of aligning the role of human capital with business goals. It is important to understand that the strategy development process is often as important as its content [112]. Analyzing strategic issues and identifying critical points generate new initiatives, which helps achieve consensus between goals and the practical implementation of the strategy.

4.4 Management Structuring: Consolidating Strategic Areas

The transition from developing a human capital strategy to its implementation involves management structuring. This process includes adopting clear procedures and systems that translate strategic plans into a set of practical activities and actions. Human capital management structuring requires defining roles and responsibilities for each individual in recruiting, training, engaging, evaluating, motivating and retaining employees (and other HR practices); establishing appropriate organizational structures and mechanisms; and ensuring the linkage between HR processes and the overall strategy of the organization to ensure that all activities are aligned and focused on achieving strategic goals. Setting specific, structured management systems and processes is aimed at increasing the efficiency and productivity of the organization. What is important here is understanding the context, that is perceiving human capital as part of a broader organizational system.

Human capital management structuring also includes establishing strategic areas, which can be organized as follows:

- Developing policies and procedures: establishing clear rules, policies and standards in areas such as hiring, training, performance evaluation, compensation, career development and termination of employees;
- Determining roles and responsibilities: strict distribution of tasks, functions, duties and areas of responsibility among stakeholders. This step also suggests establishing a hierarchy in the organization's structure. It is important to involve internal stakeholders in the process of planning and implementing HR strategies. This will help distribute roles and responsibilities effectively;
- Iterative problem-solving process: using agile and iterative methods to manage human capital allows for continuous improvement and adaptation of approaches and processes. At this stage, HR policies and practices are adjusted to the feedback established within the organization and changes in the external environment.

These steps create a structured system approach to human capital management. In Fig. 3, they are represented as a coherent and holistic management system. The steps influence each other, thus forming the overlapping areas that mark points of interaction and integration. This highlights the need for coherence and flexibility in approaches to human capital management.

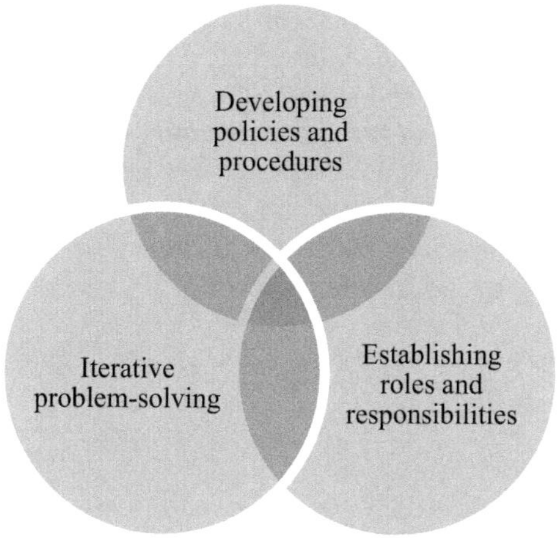

Fig. 3. Human capital management structuring: delineating strategic areas.

Thus, human capital management structuring begins with setting strategic guidelines and accents, which, when established, influence all future aspects of management. Next is the selection of strategic templates that help in shaping the overall direction of activity. An important point is to follow the development stages of a human capital management strategy, which take into account both vertical and horizontal links at the corporate, business and functional levels. This allows delineating and anchoring strategic areas in the organization.

5 Conclusion

Research into human capital confirms its significance as a key asset for companies helping to ensure their competitiveness and sustainable development in a dynamic business environment. The results of the study highlight the role of human capital in attaining strategic goals of the organization, as well as the importance of employees in creating innovations and enhancing operational efficiency. The study has identified some key human capital management strategies and combinations of their accents, which allows companies to flexibly adapt to changing conditions. We have also clarified the process for developing human capital management strategies. The paper substantiates the necessity of establishing vertical and horizontal links in strategic human capital management to achieve consistency. The importance of human capital management structuring is emphasized, where a key role is attributed to clear policies and procedures, distribution of roles and responsibilities, as well as flexibility and adaptability of the management system.

The avenues for further research include expanding the existing management approaches. One of the promising areas is developing and testing multi-level models of human capital management, including analysis of the interactions between individual, team-based, and organizational human capital. Examining multi-level models involves focusing on both the direct influence of each level on overall performance and their interactions. For example, how a team's collective skills and competencies contribute to the development of an individual employee, and how organizational practices affect the formation of team dynamics and individual results. Studying these interactions will allow one to more accurately assess the contribution of human capital at each level to the overall success of the company, identifying key drivers of increased productivity and efficiency. Thus, strategic human capital management remains a relevant and multifaceted area of research that requires further theoretical and practical comprehension in the context of a changing global economy.

Funding. The study was supported by the Russian Science Foundation, grant No. 23-28-01768. https://rscf.ru/project/23-28-01768/.

Conflict of Interest. The authors declare that the research was conducted in the absence of any commercial or financial relationships that could be construed as a potential conflict of interest.

Credit Author Statement. E.K.: Conceptualization, Formal Analysis, Methodology, Project administration, Validation, Visualization, Writing – original draft, Writing – review & editing. B. U.: Formal Analysis, Visualization, Writing – review & editing.

References

1. Barney, J.: Firm resources and sustained competitive advantage. J. Manag. **17**(1), 99–120 (1991). https://doi.org/10.1177/014920639101700108
2. Barney, J.B., Clark, D.N.: Resource-based theory: creating and sustaining competitive advantage. OUP Oxford (2007). https://doi.org/10.1093/oso/9780199277681.001.0001
3. Ulrich, D.: Human resource champions: the next agenda for adding value and delivering results. Harvard Business Press (1996)
4. Campbell, B.A., Coff, R., Kryscynski, D.: Rethinking sustained competitive advantage from human capital. Acad. Manag. Rev. **37**(3), 376–395 (2012). https://doi.org/10.5465/amr.2010.0276
5. Armstrong, M.: Strategic human resource management: a guide to action, 4th ed., Kogan Page Limited (2006)
6. Chambers, E.G., Foulon, M., Handfield-Jones, H., Hankin, S.M., Michaels III, E.G.: The war for talent. The McKinsey Quarterly **3**(44) (1998)
7. Cappelli, P.: Talent on demand: managing talent in an uncertain age. Harvard Business School Press (2008). https://doi.org/10.1108/ict.2008.03740gae.002
8. Wright, P.M.: Rediscovering the "human" in strategic human capital. Hum. Resour. Manag. Rev. **31**(4), 100781 (2021). https://doi.org/10.1016/j.hrmr.2020.100781
9. Samimi, E., Sydow, J.: Human resource management in project-based organizations: revisiting the permanency assumption. The Int. J. Human Resour. Manage. **32**(1), 49–83 (2021). https://doi.org/10.1080/09585192.2020.1783346
10. Hassan, M., Hagen, A., Daigs, I.: Strategic human resources as a strategic weapon for enhancing labor productivity: empirical evidence. Academy of Strategic Management Journal **5**(75) (2006)
11. Shela, V., Ramayah, T., Noor Hazlina, A.: Human capital and organisational resilience in the context of manufacturing: a systematic literature review. J. Intellect. Cap. **24**(2), 535–559 (2023). https://doi.org/10.1108/JIC-09-2021-0234

12. Lengnick-Hall, C.A., Beck, T.E., Lengnick-Hall, M.L.: Developing a capacity for organizational resilience through strategic human resource management. Hum. Resour. Manag. Rev. **21**(3), 243–255 (2011). https://doi.org/10.1016/j.hrmr.2010.07.001
13. Youndt, M.A., Snell, S.A., Dean, J.W., Jr., Lepak, D.P.: Human resource management, manufacturing strategy, and firm performance. Acad. Manag. J. **39**(4), 836–866 (1996). https://doi.org/10.2307/256714
14. Tichy, N.M.: Strategic human resource management. University of Michigan (1981)
15. Hendry, C., Pettigrew, A.: The practice of strategic human resource management. Pers. Rev. **15**(5), 3–8 (1986). https://doi.org/10.1108/eb055547
16. Truss, C., Gratton, L.: Strategic human resource management: a conceptual approach. Int. J. Hum. Resour. Manag. **5**(3), 663–686 (1994). https://doi.org/10.1080/09585199400000053
17. Boxall, P., Purcell, J.: Strategic human resource management: where have we come from and where should we be going? Int. J. Manag. Rev. **2**(2), 183–203 (2000). https://doi.org/10.1111/1468-2370.00037
18. Lengnick-Hall, M.L., Lengnick-Hall, C.A., Andrade, L.S., Drake, B.: Strategic human resource management: the evolution of the field. Hum. Resour. Manag. Rev. **19**(2), 64–85 (2009). https://doi.org/10.1016/j.hrmr.2009.01.002
19. Mello, J.A.: Strategic human resource management. Cengage Learning (2015)
20. Boon, C., Eckardt, R., Lepak, D.P., Boselie, P.: Integrating strategic human capital and strategic human resource management. The Int. J. Human Resour. Manage. **29**(1), 34–67 (2017). https://doi.org/10.1080/09585192.2017.1380063
21. Greer, C.R.: Strategic human resource management. Pearson Custom Publishing (2021)
22. Nyberg, A.J., Moliterno, T.P., Hale, D., Jr., Lepak, D.P.: Resource-based perspectives on unit-level human capital: a review and integration. J. Manag. **40**(1), 316–346 (2014). https://doi.org/10.1177/0149206312458703
23. Wright, P.M., Coff, R., Moliterno, T.P.: Strategic human capital: crossing the great divide. J. Manag. **40**(2), 353–370 (2014). https://doi.org/10.1177/0149206313518437
24. Crook, T.R., Todd, S.Y., Combs, J.G., Woehr, D.J., Ketchen Jr., D.J.: Does human capital matter? A meta-analysis of the relationship between human capital and firm performance. Journal of Applied Psychology **96**(3) (2011). https://doi.org/10.1037/a0022147
25. Appelbaum, E.: Manufacturing advantage: why high-performance work systems pay off. Cornell University Press (2000)
26. Delery, J.E., Roumpi, D.: Strategic human resource management, human capital, and competitive advantage: is the field going in circles? Hum. Resour. Manag. J. **27**(1), 1–21 (2017). https://doi.org/10.1111/1748-8583.12137
27. Lepak, D.P., Liao, H., Chung, Y., Harden, E.E.: A conceptual review of human resource management systems in strategic human resource management research. In: Research in Personnel and Human Resources Management, vol. 25, pp. 217–271. Emerald Group Publishing Limited (2006). https://doi.org/10.1016/S0742-7301(06)25006-0
28. Delery, J.E.: Issues of fit in strategic human resource management: implications for research. Hum. Resour. Manag. Rev. **8**(3), 289–309 (1998). https://doi.org/10.1016/S1053-4822(98)90006-7
29. Wright, P.M., Boswell, W.R.: Desegregating HRM: a review and synthesis of micro and macro human resource management research. J. Manag. **28**(3), 247–276 (2002). https://doi.org/10.1177/014920630202800302
30. Wright, P.M., Snell, S.A.: Toward an integrative view of strategic human resource management. Hum. Resour. Manag. Rev. **1**(3), 203–225 (1991). https://doi.org/10.1016/1053-4822(91)90015-5
31. Huselid, M.A., Becker, B.E.: The impact high-performance work systems, implementation effectiveness, and alignment with strategy on shareholder wealth. Acad. Manag. Proc. **1**, 144–148 (1997). https://doi.org/10.5465/ambpp.1997.4981101

32. Alfes, K., Shantz, A.D., Truss, C., Soane, E.C.: The link between perceived human resource management practices, engagement, and employee behaviour: a moderated mediation model. The Int. J. Human Resour. Manage. **24**(2), 330–351 (2013). https://doi.org/10.1080/09585192.2012.679950
33. Kehoe, R.R., Wright, P.M.: The impact of high-performance human resource practices on employees' attitudes and behaviors. J. Manag. **39**(2), 366–391 (2013). https://doi.org/10.1177/0149206310365901
34. Sun, L.Y., Aryee, S., Law, K.S.: High-performance human resource practices, citizenship behavior, and organizational performance: a relational perspective. Acad. Manag. J. **50**(3), 558–577 (2007). https://doi.org/10.5465/amj.2007.25525821
35. Takeuchi, R., Chen, G., Lepak, D.P.: Through the looking glass of a social system: cross-level effects of high-performance work systems on employees' attitudes. Pers. Psychol. **62**(1), 1–29 (2009). https://doi.org/10.1111/j.1744-6570.2008.01127.x
36. Wu, P.C., Chaturvedi, S.: The role of procedural justice and power distance in the relationship between high-performance work systems and employee attitudes: a multilevel perspective. J. Manag. **35**(5), 1228–1247 (2009). https://doi.org/10.1177/0149206308331097
37. Kramar, R.: Beyond strategic human resource management: is sustainable human resource management the next approach? The Int. J. Human Resour. Manage. **25**(8), 1069–1089 (2013). https://doi.org/10.1080/09585192.2013.816863
38. Taylor, S., Osland, J., Egri, C.P.: Guest editors' introduction: introduction to HRM's role in sustainability: systems, strategies, and practices. Hum. Resour. Manage. **51**(6), 789–798 (2012). https://doi.org/10.1002/hrm.21509
39. Voegtlin, C., Greenwood, M.: Corporate social responsibility and human resource management: a systematic review and conceptual analysis. Hum. Resour. Manag. Rev. **26**(3), 181–197 (2016). https://doi.org/10.1016/j.hrmr.2015.12.003
40. James, L.R., Jones, A.P.: Organizational climate: a review of theory and research. Psychol. Bull. **81**(12), 1096 (1974). https://doi.org/10.1037/h0037511
41. Schneider, B., Ehrhart, M.G., Macey, W.H.: Organizational climate and culture. Annu. Rev. Psychol. **64**, 361–388 (2013). https://doi.org/10.1146/annurev-psych-113011-143809
42. Schneider, B., Ehrhart, M.G., Macey, W.H.: Organizational climate and culture. Sage Publications (2016)
43. Blau, P.M.: Social exchange. Int. Encyclopedia Soc. Sci. **7**(4), 452–457 (1968)
44. Cook, K.S., Cheshire, C., Rice, E.R., Nakagawa, S.: Social exchange theory. In: Handbook of Social Psychology, pp. 61–88 (2013). https://doi.org/10.1007/978-94-007-6772-0_3
45. Nunkoo, R., Ramkissoon, H.: Power, trust, social exchange, and community support. Ann. Tour. Res. **39**(2), 997–1023 (2012). https://doi.org/10.1016/j.annals.2011.11.017
46. Edwards, J.R., Cable, D.M., Williamson, I.O., Lambert, L.S., Shipp, A.J.: The phenomenology of fit: linking the person and environment to the subjective experience of person-environment fit. J. Appl. Psychol. **91**(4), 802–827 (2006). https://doi.org/10.1037/0021-9010.91.4.802
47. Hesketh, B., Gardner, D.: Person-environment fit models: a reconceptualization and empirical test. J. Vocat. Behav. **42**(3), 315–332 (1993). https://doi.org/10.1006/jvbe.1993.1022
48. Connelly, B.L., Certo, S.T., Ireland, R.D., Reutzel, C.R.: Signaling theory: a review and assessment. J. Manag. **37**(1), 39–67 (2011). https://doi.org/10.1177/0149206310388419
49. Jiang, K., Takeuchi, R., Lepak, D.P.: Where do we go from here? New perspectives on the black box in strategic human resource management research. J. Manage. Stud. **50**(8), 1448–1480 (2013). https://doi.org/10.1111/joms.12057
50. Ehrnrooth, M., Björkman, I.: An integrative HRM process theorization: beyond signalling effects and mutual gains. J. Manage. Stud. **49**(6), 1109–1135 (2012). https://doi.org/10.1111/j.1467-6486.2012.01055.x

51. Evans, W.R., Davis, W.D.: High-performance work systems and organizational performance: the mediating role of internal social structure. J. Manag. **31**(5), 758–775 (2005). https://doi.org/10.1177/0149206305279370
52. Bird, A., Beechler, S.: Links between business strategy and human resource management strategy in US-based Japanese subsidiaries: an empirical investigation. J. Int. Bus. Stud. **26**, 23–46 (1995). https://doi.org/10.1057/palgrave.jibs.8490164
53. Whitener, E.M.: Do "high commitment" human resource practices affect employee commitment? a cross-level analysis using hierarchical linear modeling. J. Manag. **27**(5), 515–535 (2001). https://doi.org/10.1016/S0149-2063(01)00106-4
54. Zacharatos, A., Barling, J., Iverson, R.D.: High-performance work systems and occupational safety. J. Appl. Psychol. **90**(1), 77–93 (2005). https://doi.org/10.1037/0021-9010.90.1.77
55. Do, B.R., Yeh, P.W., Madsen, J.: Exploring the relationship among human resource flexibility, organizational innovation, and adaptability culture. Chin. Manag. Stud. **10**(4), 657–674 (2016). https://doi.org/10.1108/CMS-01-2016-0022
56. Ngo, H.Y., Loi, R.: Human resource flexibility, organizational culture, and firm performance: an investigation of multinational firms in Hong Kong. The Int. J. Human Resour. Manage. **19**(9), 1654–1666 (2008). https://doi.org/10.1080/09585190802295082
57. Sabuhari, R.: The role of organizational culture adaptation and job satisfaction in mediating effects of human resource flexibility on employee performance. JDM (Jurnal Dinamika Manajemen **12**(1), 132–145 (2021). https://doi.org/10.15294/jdm.v12i1.27026
58. Zinevich, A.V., Sarilova, O.A.: Features of human capital management as an asset of a modern enterprise. Social and Economic Development of the Asia-Pacific Region: experience, Problems, Prospects **1**, 89–96 (2017). (In Russian) https://www.elibrary.ru/item.asp?id=29677632
59. Nikishina, A.L.: Human resource as a key factor in increasing the competitive advantages. Bulletin of the Volga University named after V. N. Tatishchev **2**(28), 70–77 (2013). (In Russian) https://www.elibrary.ru/item.asp?id=20404241
60. Bamberger, P.A., Biron, M., Boon, C.: Human resource strategy: formulation, implementation, and impact. Routledge (2014). https://doi.org/10.4324/9780203075838
61. Technical Appendix: Performance through people: Transforming human capital into competitive advantage. McKinsey Global Institute (2023). Retrieved from https://www.mckinsey.com/~/media/mckinsey/mckinsey%20global%20institute/our%20research/performance%20through%20people%20transforming%20human%20capital%20into%20competitive%20advantage/appendix-performance-through-people.pdf
62. Madgavkar, A., et al.: Human capital at work: the value of experience. McKinsey Global Institute (2022). Retrieved from https://www.mckinsey.com/capabilities/people-and-organizational-performance/our-insights/human-capital-at-work-the-value-of-experience
63. Huitfeldt, I., Kostøl, A.R., Nimczik, J., Weber, A.: Internal labor markets: a worker flow approach. Journal of Econometrics **233**(2), 661–688 (2023). https://doi.org/10.1016/j.jeconom.2021.12.016
64. Organizational Health Index: McKinsey & Company. Retrieved from https://www.mckinsey.com/solutions/orgsolutions/overview/organizational-health-index
65. Gagnon, C., John, E., Theunissen, R.: Organizational health: a fast track to performance improvement. McKinsey Quarterly (2017). Retrieved from https://www.mckinsey.com/capabilities/people-and-organizational-performance/our-insights/organizational-health-a-fast-track-to-performance-improvement/

66. People & Organizational Performance Practice: Performance through people: Transforming human capital into competitive advantage. McKinsey Global Institute (2023). Retrieved from https://www.mckinsey.com/~/media/mckinsey/mckinsey%20global%20institute/our%20research/performance%20through%20people%20transforming%20human%20capital%20into%20competitive%20advantage/mgi-performance-through-people-full-report-vf.pdf
67. Martín-de-Castro, G., Emilio Navas-López, J., López-Sáez, P., Alama-Salazar, E.: Organizational capital as competitive advantage of the firm. J. Intellect. Cap. **7**(3), 324–337 (2006). https://doi.org/10.1108/14691930610681438
68. Black, S.E., Lynch, L.M.: Measuring organizational capital in the new economy. In: Measuring Capital in the New Economy, pp. 205–236. University of Chicago Press (2005). https://doi.org/10.7208/chicago/9780226116174.003.0007
69. Roos, G., Bainbridge, A., Jacobsen, K.: Intellectual capital analysis as a strategic tool. Strategy & Leadership **29**(4), 21–26 (2001). https://doi.org/10.1108/10878570110400116
70. Gibbons, R., Henderson, R.: Relational contracts and organizational capabilities. Organ. Sci. **23**(5), 1350–1364 (2012). https://doi.org/10.1287/orsc.1110.0715
71. Serrat, O.: Knowledge solutions: tools, methods, and approaches to drive organizational performance. Springer Nature (2017). https://doi.org/10.1007/978-981-10-0983-9
72. Teece, D.J.: Managing intellectual capital: organizational, strategic, and policy dimensions. OUP Oxford (2002)
73. Madgavkar, A., et al.: Performance through people: transforming human capital into competitive advantage. McKinsey Global Institute (2023). Retrieved from https://www.mckinsey.com/mgi/our-research/performance-through-people-transforming-human-capital-into-competitive-advantage
74. Huselid, M.A.: The impact of human resource management practices on turnover, productivity, and corporate financial performance. Acad. Manag. J. **38**(3), 635–672 (1995). https://doi.org/10.2307/256741
75. Gunnigle, P., Moore, S.: Linking business strategy and human resource management: issues and implications. Pers. Rev. **23**(1), 63–84 (1994). https://doi.org/10.1108/00483489410053038
76. Bamberger, P., Meshulam, I.: Human resource strategy: formulation, implementation and impact. Sage, Thousand Oaks, CA (2000). https://doi.org/10.4135/9781452204680
77. Stewart, G.L., Brown, K.G.: Human resource management. John Wiley & Sons (2019)
78. Christensen, R.: Roadmap to strategic HR: turning a great idea into a business reality. Amacom Books (2006)
79. Kuzmin, E.A.: Architecture of human capital: methodological refinement of structure-forming elements. AlterEconomics **20**(4), 822–856 (2023). https://doi.org/10.31063/AlterEconomics/2023.20-4.5
80. Becker, B.E., Huselid, M.A.: Strategic human resources management: where do we go from here? J. Manag. **32**(6), 898–925 (2006). https://doi.org/10.1177/0149206306293668
81. Prahalad, C.K., Hamel, G.:. The core competence of the corporation. In: Knowledge and Strategy, pp. 41–59. Routledge (1999). https://doi.org/10.1016/B978-0-7506-7088-3.50006-1
82. Dubois, D.D., Rothwell, W.J.: Competency-based human resource management: discover a new system for unleashing the productive power of exemplary performers. Nicholas Brealey (2004)
83. Gangani, N., McLean, G.N., Braden, R.A.: A competency-based human resource development strategy. Perform. Improv. Q. **19**(1), 127–139 (2006). https://doi.org/10.1111/j.1937-8327.2006.tb00361.x
84. Boyatzis, R.E.: The competent manager: a model for effective performance. John Wiley & Sons (1991)

85. Butler, M.R., Felts, J.: Tool kit for the staff mentor: strategies for improving retention. The J. Contin. Educ. Nurs. **37**(5), 210–213 (2006). https://doi.org/10.3928/00220124-20060901-10
86. Cappelli, P.: Talent management for the twenty-first century. Harv. Bus. Rev. **86**(3), 74–81 (2008)
87. Blass, E.: Talent management: cases and commentary. Springer (2009). https://doi.org/10.1057/9780230233522
88. Nonaka, I.: The knowledge-creating company. In: The Economic Impact of Knowledge, pp. 175–187. Routledge (1998). https://doi.org/10.1016/B978-0-7506-7009-8.50016-1
89. Sanchez, R.: Knowledge management and organizational competence, Vol. 21. Oxford University Press (2001)
90. Alavi, M., Leidner, D.E.: Knowledge management and knowledge management systems: conceptual foundations and research issues. MIS Q. **25**(1), 107–136 (2001). https://doi.org/10.2307/3250961
91. Bhatt, G.D.: Knowledge management in organizations: examining the interaction between technologies, techniques, and people. J. Knowl. Manag. **5**(1), 68–75 (2001). https://doi.org/10.1108/13673270110384419
92. Fitz-Enz, J.: The ROI of human capital: measuring the economic value of employee performance. AMACOM Div American Mgmt Assn (2000)
93. Cascio, W., Boudreau, J.: Investing in people: financial impact of human resource initiatives. Ft Press (2010)
94. Phillips, J.J.: Investing in your company's human capital: strategies to avoid spending too little – or too much. Amacom Books (2005)
95. Huselid, M.A., Becker, B.E., Beatty, R.W.: The workforce scorecard: managing human capital to execute strategy. Harvard Business Press (2005)
96. Schein, E.H.: Organizational culture and leadership, Vol. 2. John Wiley & Sons (2010)
97. Aycan, Z., Kanungo, R.N., Sinha, J.B.: Organizational culture and human resource management practices: the model of culture fit. J. Cross Cult. Psychol. **30**(4), 501–526 (1999). https://doi.org/10.1177/0022022199030004006
98. Judge, W.Q.: Building organizational capacity for change: the leader's new mandate. Business Expert Press (2011). https://doi.org/10.4128/9781606491256
99. Kotter, J.P.: Leading change: why transformation efforts fail. In: Museum management and marketing, pp. 20–29. Routledge (2007)
100. Werbel, J.D., DeMarie, S.M.: Aligning strategic human resource management and person–environment fit. Hum. Resour. Manag. Rev. **15**(4), 247–262 (2005). https://doi.org/10.1016/j.hrmr.2005.10.001
101. Jackson, S.E., Schuler, R.S.: Managing human resources: a partnership perspective. South Western College Publishing (2000)
102. Wadström, P.: Aligning corporate and business strategy: managing the balance. J. Bus. Strateg. **40**(4), 44–52 (2019). https://doi.org/10.1108/JBS-06-2018-0099
103. Grünig, R., Kühn, R.: Developing the functional strategies. In: The strategy planning process, pp. 279–295. Springer (2018). https://doi.org/10.1007/978-3-662-56221-5_21
104. Moore, J.I.: Writers on strategy and strategic management: theory and practice at enterprise, corporate, business and functional levels. Penguin UK (2001)
105. Wang, D.S., Shyu, C.L.: Will the strategic fit between business and HRM strategy influence HRM effectiveness and organizational performance? Int. J. Manpow. **29**(2), 92–110 (2008). https://doi.org/10.1108/01437720810872677
106. Purcell, J.: The impact of corporate strategy on human resource management. In: New perspectives on human resource management, pp. 67–91. Routledge (2014)
107. Morden, T.: Principles of strategic management. Routledge (2016). https://doi.org/10.4324/9781315602172

108. Fuertes, G., Alfaro, M., Vargas, M., Gutierrez, S., Ternero, R., Sabattin, J.: Conceptual framework for the strategic management: a literature review – descriptive. Journal of Engineering **2020**, 1–21 (2020). https://doi.org/10.1155/2020/6253013
109. Dyer, L., Holder, G.W.: Toward a strategic perspective of human resource management. Cornell University (1987)
110. Dyer, L., Shafer, R.A.: From human resource strategy to organizational effectiveness: lessons from research on organizational agility. Cornell University (1998)
111. Shih, H.A., Chiang, Y.H.: Strategy alignment between HRM, KM, and corporate development. Int. J. Manpow. **26**(6), 582–603 (2005). https://doi.org/10.1108/01437720510625476
112. Armstrong, M., Taylor, S.: Handbook of human resource management practice, Russian Piter, Saint Petersburg (2018)

Reserves for the Mobilization of Human Capital: Classification and Assessment Method

Evgeny Kuzmin[1](✉) and Umida Yakubova[2]

[1] Institute of Economics of the Ural Branch of the Russian Academy of Sciences, 29 Moskovskaya Street, Ekaterinburg 620014, Russian Federation
kuzmin.ea@uiec.ru

[2] Termez State Pedagogical Institute, 1A At-Termizi Street, Yangiabad MFY, Termiz District, Termez, Uzbekistan 190111

Abstract. Human capital is a key strategic asset that drives a company's competitiveness. To use it effectively, it is essential to identify available reserves and evaluate their readiness for quick deployment to meet both immediate and long-term objectives. This study proposes an approach for assessing and classifying Reserves for the Mobilization of Human Capital (RMHC). The article offers a new perspective on evaluating human capital by emphasizing its mobilization potential and laying the groundwork for further development of management strategies that enhance organizational resilience in dynamic environments. The assessment methodology includes parameters such as personnel qualifications, readiness to take on new tasks, replaceability, and training time. To validate the proposed approach, preliminary simulation modeling was conducted using the grid search method to explore all possible parameter combinations. This simulation underpinned sensitivity analysis and facilitated the clustering of human capital mobilization patterns, leading to the identification of various levels of mobilization reserves. At a practical level, RMHC serves as a valuable tool for monitoring the readiness of human capital reserves, forecasting workforce needs, and optimizing resource utilization across different organizational and industrial contexts. This approach, introduced for academic discussion, contributes to the theoretical advancement of human capital management by expanding the understanding of its evaluation potential. The research findings can be applied to strategic planning, the development of human resource management programs, and the refinement of personnel policies.

Keywords: Human capital · Mobilization reserves · Simulation modeling · Human resource potential

JEL Classification: E24 · J24 · O15 · L20

E. Kuzmin et al. (Eds.): EASET 2024, SPBE, pp. 213–233, 2025.
https://doi.org/10.1007/978-3-031-91159-0_14

1 Introduction

The study of human capital has become increasingly vital in addressing the challenges of the modern era. Over recent decades, the concept of human capital has evolved significantly, shifting focus from traditional workforce management to the strategic development of employee competencies and potential [1]. Particular emphasis is placed on identifying internal and external resources to mobilize human capital more effectively, which, in turn, requires comprehensive approach that includes assessing competencies, identifying high-potential employees, and developing growth strategies.

One of the key tasks in the study of human capital is refining assessment criteria to better understand employees' contributions to value creation. As the economy evolves, the importance of soft skills—such as leadership, teamwork, and creativity—has grown alongside traditional professional competencies [2–4]. This shift necessitates the development of more flexible assessment systems that account for both professional expertise and personal qualities. The analysis of employee competencies is critical to the human capital management system. Its primary objective is to identify areas for improvement, enabling organizations to enhance their overall performance and adapt to the demands of a rapidly changing environment.

A crucial aspect of management is identifying the sources of human capital that can be mobilized. The mobilization reserves of human capital represent untapped potential that an organization can activate to tackle both immediate and long-term challenges. To assess this potential, it is important to evaluate employees' readiness to take on new tasks, embrace modern technologies, and the organization's general ability to effectively leverage its workforce to achieve strategic goals.

The above-described considerations have determined the focus of this study: to develop a practical approach for classifying and evaluating human capital mobilization reserves, integrating diverse criteria to ensure real-world applicability. This approach is based on the premise that mobilization reserves are a critical indicator of an organization's capacity to effectively and quickly deploy its human capital. The proposed approach has a wide range of applications, including monitoring changes in mobilization reserves over time, conducting comparative assessments across departments or organizations to identify strengths and weaknesses, and planning initiatives to improve the effective use of human capital. Additionally, the proposed tool aims to not only measure current reserves but also provide strategies for improvement, thereby enhancing organizational resilience and adaptability in addressing modern challenges. The ultimate goal of this research is to establish a robust theoretical foundation for the proposed approach to human capital mobilization reserves.

The article is structured as follows: The first section introduces the topic, emphasizing the relevance of human capital management, the study's objectives, and its theoretical and practical significance. The second section reviews literature on human capital evaluation, focusing on contemporary approaches to mobilization reserves. The third section develops a framework for defining and classifying mobilization reserves, identifying key categories and proposing a classification based on various attributes. The fourth section presents the methodology for assessing reserves for the mobilization of human capital (RMHC), including a simulation model and a discussion of limitations and assumptions. Finally, the conclusion summarizes the findings, highlights key results, and suggests directions for further research.

2 Literature Review: Human Capital Assessment

The literature review in this section clarifies contemporary views on human capital, including its key characteristics, measurement methods, and evaluation models. It also enhances understanding of the factors influencing human capital mobilization while exposing limitations in classifying and evaluating RMHC.

The evaluation of human capital draws on a variety of theoretical approaches that have evolved over decades, reflecting diverse perspectives on its nature and role within organizations. Rather than being mutually exclusive, these approaches complement one another, enabling a more comprehensive and nuanced assessment of human capital. Each approach contributes a unique set of criteria, enriching the overall evaluation framework (see Table 1).

The *economic approach* is based on the concept of investment in human capital proposed by Theodore Schultz [5, 6] and Gary Becker [7, 8]. From this perspective, human capital is viewed as an investment that generates returns in the form of labor productivity [9–11]. The main evaluation criteria, such as training and development costs, productivity, and returns on investments in employees, are easily measurable quantitatively. However, this approach is limited by quantitative indicators and does not account for the impact of soft skills on performance. Additionally, it overlooks motivation, cultural, and social factors, which also play a crucial role in the sustainable development of an organization.

The *sociological approach* emphasizes the social component of human capital, including social connections, norms and values, teamwork, and the level of trust among employees [12–18]. The evaluation criteria in this approach focus on the quality of social interactions, the level of organizational culture, and the degree of employee engagement in company activities. However, this approach has clear drawbacks, including the challenges of quantifying social criteria and measuring the impact of improvements in corporate culture and teamwork.

The *psychological approach* views human capital through the lens of employees' personal characteristics, motivations, and aspirations [19–24]. Human capital is seen as a combination of not only professional skills but also internal drives for active and productive engagement. Key evaluation criteria include motivation levels, job satisfaction, personal and professional ambitions, as well as the ability for self-actualization and self-development. One of the main advantages of this approach is its ability to provide a deeper understanding of the internal factors that influence labor productivity and employee behavior. However, there are also several limitations. First, the subjectivity of criteria such as motivation and satisfaction may impede their accurate measurement and quantitative assessment. Second, there are difficulties in predicting the long-term impact of these factors on employee performance and organizational effectiveness. Motivation can be unstable and fluctuate due to internal and external factors, complicating its long-term analysis. Nevertheless, this approach can be useful when developing personalized motivation programs, improving working conditions, and shaping a corporate culture focused on meeting the personal and professional needs of employees.

Table 1. Criteria for human capital evaluation.

Approach	Description	Criteria
Economic	Human capital is viewed as an investment that generates returns in the form of labor productivity and investment profitability	Training costs, labor productivity, investment returns
Sociological	Human capital is viewed from the perspective of human interactions, organizational culture, and the level of trust in the team	Level of social interaction, trust, and engagement in corporate culture
Psychological	The focus is made on personal characteristics of employees, their motivation and pursuit of career development	Level of motivation, job satisfaction, drive for personal growth
Emotional-intellectual	Human capital is linked to the emotional intelligence of employees, their ability to control emotions and interact effectively with colleagues	Emotional resilience, empathy, teamwork, conflict management skills
Cognitive	The focus is made on the intellectual abilities of employees, their cognitive and problem-solving skills	Cognitive abilities, self-learning ability, creativity, analytical thinking
Competency-based	Human capital is associated with the key professional skills of employees necessary to complete the ongoing and future tasks	Professional competencies, flexibility, ability to learn, productivity
Resource-competency-based	The focus is made on the uniqueness and irreplaceability of employees' skills that can create a competitive advantage	The uniqueness of skills, the difficulty of replacing them, and their intellectual contribution
Cultural	Employees' personal values are aligned with the corporate and organizational culture, the focus is on their ability to adhere to cultural norms	Compliance with corporate and organizational culture, engagement in its development, and team spirit

Note: compiled by the author based on the results of a literature review

The *emotional-intellectual approach* focuses on key soft skills necessary for successful communication, people management, and creating a positive work environment

[25–31]. Within this approach, human capital is assessed not only from the perspective of professional competencies but also through employees' ability to interact with colleagues. The emotional-intellectual approach is particularly useful for evaluating leadership qualities, since successful leadership often requires a developed emotional intelligence. The main criteria for assessing human capital in this approach include emotional and stress management, empathy, relationship-building, conflict resolution, and teamwork skills. This approach is especially relevant for modern organizational structures where interpersonal skills and emotional resilience are playing an increasingly important role.

The *cognitive approach* focuses on employees' cognitive abilities and intellectual potential [32–34]. Human capital is understood as a combination of knowledge, mental skills, and the ability to learn, which together provide intellectual flexibility and creativity. In the cognitive approach, both accumulated knowledge and experience are important, as well as employees' ability to generate new ideas, think analytically, and propose innovative solutions. Thus, the criteria for assessing human capital in this approach include the level of professional knowledge and intellectual abilities, the capacity for self-learning, creativity and innovative thinking, analytical skills, and responsiveness to change. This approach is particularly valuable for companies focused on innovation and research, where intellectual resources, learning ability, and readiness for innovation are key factors for competitive advantage.

The *competency-based* approach views employee competencies as key elements of their professional performance and ability to handle assigned work tasks [35–37]. Competencies are interpreted as a combination of skills, knowledge, personal qualities, and professional attitudes required for an employee to achieve the company's goals. Organizations can leverage this approach to create competency models that identify critical skills and attributes essential for success at various levels of the organization. The competency-based approach also plays a significant role in developing training and employee development programs. Based on competency assessments, personalized training plans can be designed to enhance employees' professional skills. The main criteria for evaluating human capital include the alignment of professional skills with job requirements, the level of development of key competencies, the ability to learn and develop new competencies, projected performance based on competency models, and the evaluation of competencies in the context of future tasks and company objectives.

A variation of this approach is the *resource-competency-based approach*, which views human capital as a unique resource that can be used to ensure long-term competitive advantages [38–40]. Human capital evaluation focuses on unique and valuable competencies that are difficult to replicate or replace. The evaluation criteria include the uniqueness and rarity of skills, the non-replicability or difficulty of replacing competencies in the labor market, the ability to create intellectual and innovative products, restricted access to knowledge and skills (protection against copying), flexibility, and the ability to self-regulate in changing conditions.

In addition to the approaches described above, there are several others proposing unique criteria for evaluating human capital. These approaches focus on specific aspects of human resource management and are sufficiently universal. These include approaches oriented toward corporate and organizational culture values, strategic goals, and more.

The so-called *cultural approach* emphasizes the alignment of employees' personal values with corporate and organizational culture, as well as their ability to adhere to established cultural norms, customs, and traditions [41–45]. This approach highlights the compatibility of employees' personal values with those of the company. The evaluation criteria for human capital include the degree of integration into corporate culture, the alignment of personal and professional values with corporate values, the ability to preserve the company's cultural traditions, maintain and enhance team spirit and corporate identity, and contribute to creating a positive work environment.

The above review leads us to several conclusions applicable to the study of reserves for the mobilization of human capital. First, such diversity of approaches reflects the complex and multifaceted nature of human capital. Mobilization reserves can be linked to both quantitative characteristics and qualitative aspects. Second, the above-described approaches to assessing human capital emphasize various aspects, including social interactions, intellectual potential, and professional competencies. To analyze the reserves for the mobilization of human capital, we need to consider their contribution to workforce readiness and adaptability, especially in different organizational contexts. Third, criteria such as learning ability, flexibility, and adaptability to change—highlighted in cognitive and competency-based approaches—could well be the key to evaluating human capital mobilization reserves, which underscores the need to consider not only the current level of workforce readiness but also their potential for rapid adaptation in changing conditions.

3 Classification Framework for Human Capital Mobilization Reserves

As outlined in the introduction, reserves for the mobilization of human capital refer to unused workforce potential that can be rapidly leveraged to strengthen a company's capabilities and competitive advantage. These reserves consist of employees who can step in to cover temporary staff absences or boost productivity in periods of high demand. They play a critical role in ensuring organizational flexibility, especially in the face of external uncertainties, technological changes, and evolving market dynamics.

Companies must identify key employees to pinpoint their most valuable workforce assets and address potential vulnerabilities that may require action. This process lays the groundwork for succession planning by spotting high-potential employees whose development is vital to the organization's long-term stability and adaptability.

This study examines the factors influencing a company's ability to effectively harness its potential. Key elements include workforce policies, human capital management strategies, employee skills and adaptability, organizational structure and flexibility, a culture of learning and development, employee support and psychological climate, labor market dynamics, regulatory requirements, macroeconomic and industry trends, demographic shifts, and technological advancements. These interconnected factors collectively define mobilization reserves, enabling companies to assess opportunities and challenges in optimizing their workforce potential.

Depending on their origin and usage, we can distinguish between internal and external mobilization reserves. Internal reserves consist of resources and potential already available in the organization but not fully used. These reserves have greater operational flexibility, as they allow for quick redistribution of resources within the company. However, they are limited by the number and qualifications of the available personnel. For their effective use, it is important to maintain a high level of internal flexibility.

Internal reserves include the following:

- *The company's talent pool.* Employees are included in a talent pool and can be quickly assigned to more responsible positions or given temporary assignments, which enables the company to fill vacancies fast and replace key specialists.
- *Cross-functional employee roles.* Employees can take on the duties of other positions or temporarily work in different roles. This enhances flexibility and allows for redistribution of workloads in accordance with the company's current needs.
- *Temporary transfers and staff rotation.* Moving employees between departments or temporarily transferring them to other positions helps enhance the efficiency of personnel use and increases their readiness for different tasks.
- *Work schedule adjustments (shifts).* Changing work schedules allows the company to manage its labor resources flexibly, increasing their availability and productivity depending on current needs. This can be achieved by increasing or reducing the number of shifts, using flexible or fixed schedules, or offering part-time employment.
- *Internal training and development programs.* Training and development programs that help employees quickly acquire new skills and improve their qualifications prepare them to take on more complex roles and handle new tasks.

External reserves refer to the possibility of attracting additional resources from outside the organization. External reserves provide additional options for a rapid increase in workforce capacity but require extra costs for recruitment and adaptation. They can also be limited by external factors, such as labor market conditions or economic instability.

External reserves include the following:

- *Labor market and temporary staff.* Temporary employees or specialists for project work are hired by the company from the external labor market, enabling the company to quickly increase its workforce in response to changes in demand.
- *Outsourcing and subcontracting.* Delegating certain functions to external contractors or using outsourcing services allows the company to relieve internal staff and focus efforts on core tasks. Crowdsourcing, which involves gathering external resources to collaboratively solve specific problems, is gaining popularity in the digital economy.
- *Former employees and retirees.* Hiring former employees who have retired or left the company but are willing to work on a temporary basis provides an opportunity to leverage their experience and knowledge to address urgent tasks.
- *Collaboration with educational institutions and professional associations.* Internship programs, practical training, and involvement in educational projects allow companies to attract young professionals, interns, and graduates for temporary work or inclusion in the talent pool.

The most effective mobilization of human capital is achieved by integrating both internal and external reserves. Internal sources can be supplemented by external ones, creating a synergistic effect that allows organizations to not only optimize the use of existing resources but also respond faster to external challenges. The combined use of both types of reserves enhances the company's resilience and competitiveness.

Depending on which aspects of the company's workforce potential are considered, reserves for the mobilization of human capital can also be divided into quantitative and qualitative. Quantitative reserves are related to numerical indicators that reflect a company's ability to quickly increase or mobilize labor resources to address production tasks. These include the following: the number of employees in the talent pool, the number of employees who have undergone retraining or upskilling, the number of employees who can temporarily replace other specialists, additional working hours, and the proportion of employees with cross-functional roles, among others. Qualitative reserves refer to employee characteristics and competencies that impact work productivity. These include the following: the level of employee qualifications and skills, readiness to learn and quickly acquire new skills, role flexibility (replaceability of employees), diversity of competencies and skills, and employees' readiness for change, among others.

Quantitative and qualitative reserves for mobilizing human capital complement each other and provide companies with the necessary adaptability. Managing these reserves enables enterprises to respond effectively to changes, mitigate risks, and improve productivity, particularly in periods of crisis or uncertainty.

The sources of human capital reserves play a vital role in ensuring an enterprise's sustainable development. To mobilize these reserves effectively, a company can draw on financial, technological, informational, and material resources to enhance human capital management. The following discussion examines the key sources that support the mobilization of human capital reserves (see Table 2).

The sources supporting quantitative reserves focus on organizational and infrastructural measures to enhance flexibility in workforce size and distribution management. Those supporting qualitative reserves aim to foster skill development, boost motivation, and improve the overall quality of human capital. Together, these resources establish the conditions necessary for mobilizing human capital, which is especially important in a dynamically changing external environment.

The relationship between the sources supporting quantitative and qualitative human capital reserves is visualized in Fig. 1. The sources themselves can be divided into direct and indirect. *Direct* sources directly impact the quality and quantity of human capital reserves, while *indirect* sources create favorable conditions for supporting reserves without direct influence.

The given typology classifies RMHC based on several criteria (see Table 3) and can be used to help companies take a more comprehensive approach to human resource management.The criterion "Source of origin" groups reserves by their location—within the company or outside it. "Nature of reserves" indicates the quantitative and qualitative indicators that can be applied. "Readiness for use" determines how quickly reserves can be activated to meet specific tasks. The criterion "Type of competencies" focuses on the skills and knowledge needed to perform specific tasks. "Time horizon for use" refers to planning for short-, medium-, and long-term needs. The criterion "Mobilization costs" helps assess the financial aspect of engaging reserves.

The proposed typology can be used for more detailed planning of human capital mobilization and resource allocation. The classification table facilitates the organization

Table 2. Sources of support for the mobilization of human capital reserves.

Resource type	Source	Description
Financial resources	Funding for employee training and development	Funding for professional development programs, courses, and training to prepare employees for new tasks
	Overtime pay and flexible schedule	Financial compensation for additional working hours
	Bonuses and rewards for participation in the talent pool	Additional incentives for employees in the talent pool to increase their motivation and readiness for new tasks
Technological resources	Automation and digital platforms for human capital management	Implementation of HRM systems and platforms for planning functions, enabling efficient workload management
	Use of technologies for remote work	Technological solutions that expand access to employees and flexible scheduling options
	Performance monitoring and analysis tools	Employee performance evaluation and optimization of workforce resource use through data
Information resources	Databases on employee qualifications and skills	Up-to-date information on competencies, experience, and qualifications for workforce mobilization planning
	Labor market analytics and industry reports	Data on labor market trends, availability of specialists, and competition levels
	Information systems for resource planning and allocation	Optimization of work schedules and rotation planning for more efficient use of personnel
Material resources	Flexible use of production capacities	Rapid adjustment of equipment operation modes to meet current needs
	Creating conditions for employee mobility	Providing necessary equipment and workspaces for remote or mobile work

(*continued*)

Table 2. (*continued*)

Resource type	Source	Description
	Investments in educational infrastructure	Training classrooms, simulators, and simulators for on-the-job training
Organizational resources	Flexible organizational structure and decentralization of management	The ability to quickly reallocate resources between departments for more flexible workforce management
	Internal rotation and career growth processes	Rotation and development programs to enhance employees' readiness to perform various tasks
	Corporate culture that supports change and development	A culture that motivates employees to engage in continuous learning and enhances their readiness for change

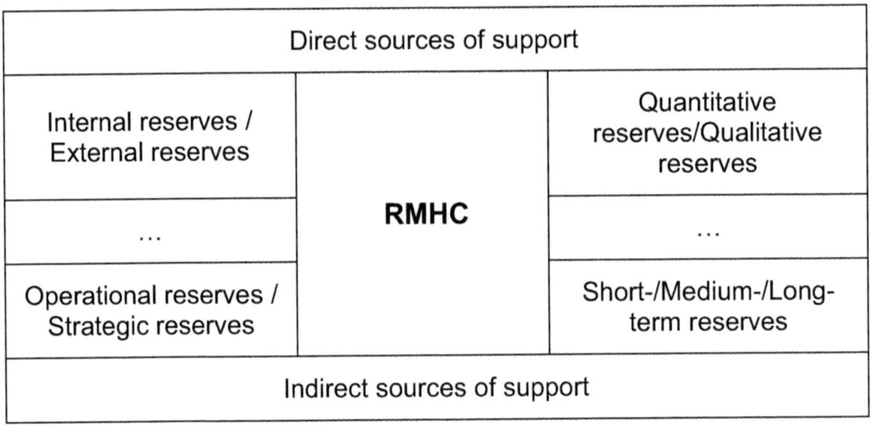

Fig. 1. Structure of the main types of RMHC.

of different types of reserves and helps create a clear, focused management strategy. It also helps identify priorities in human capital development, recognize the most important reserves and their sources of support, and evaluate the actions needed to strengthen both internal and external reserves.

Table 3. Classification of RMHC.

Criterion	Type of reserve	Description and examples
Source of origin	Internal	Human resources in the company: personnel reserve, cross-functional responsibilities, flexible schedule
	External	External resources: labor market, outsourcing, collaboration with educational institutions
Nature of reserves	Quantitative	Numerical indicators: number of employees available for work, number of working hours
	Qualitative	Qualifications, skills, stress resistance, and other competencies important for task execution
Readiness for use	Operational	Resources that can be mobilized quickly: additional shifts, cross-functional duties
	Strategic	Resources requiring prior preparation: talent pool for key position replacements, long-term training
Type of competencies	Technical	Specialists with technical knowledge and skills: engineers, safety and equipment experts
	Managerial	Employees with management competencies: project managers, middle managers
	Social and behavioural	Interaction and collaboration skills: communication, stress resilience, teamwork
Time horizon for use	Short-term	Resources available within days or weeks: temporary assignments, additional shifts
	Medium-term	Require preparation over several months: short-term courses, staff rotation
	Long-term	Long preparation period: career development programs, building a talent pool
Mobilization costs	Low-cost	Resources that can be mobilized with minimal costs: cross-functional responsibilities, flexible schedule
	High-cost	Mobilizing resources requires significant investments: outsourcing, external specialists, long-term training programs

4 Approach to the Assessment of Human Capital Reserves

4.1 Calculation of RMHC

To develop an approach for assessing RMHC, a proposed formula will be used to quantify the size of the reserve. This formula incorporates key factors, including the number of employees, their skill levels, readiness for mobilization, and the time required for training:

$$RMHC = \left[\frac{\sum_{i=1}^{N} K_{skill}}{N} \times \frac{\sum_{i=1}^{N} K_{ready}}{N} \times \frac{\sum_{i=1}^{N} K_{substitution}}{N} \right] \div \frac{\sum_{i=1}^{N} T_{preparation}}{N} \tag{1}$$

where *RMHC* is the size of the human capital mobilization reserve; *N* is the total number of employees available for mobilization; K_{skill} is the qualification coefficient (assesses the level of skill and competency match to job requirements; value from 0 to 1); K_{ready} is the readiness coefficient (assesses how prepared employees are to perform tasks; value from 0 to 1); $K_{substitution}$ is the substitution coefficient (assesses the ability of employees to temporarily or partially replace other employees/ key specialists; value from 0 to 1); $T_{preparation}$ is the preparation time (the time required for employees to adjust to new tasks; measured in days, weeks, or months).

Let's take a closer look at the components of the formula.

The *number of employees available for mobilization (N)* considers the number of workers who can be quickly mobilized to perform specific tasks (within the scope of relevant activities). The more prepared employees in reserve, the higher the likelihood of rapid mobilization of the necessary resources. The calculation of the number of employees available for mobilization takes into account several factors, such as staff availability, their qualification level, and the possibility of redistributing work tasks, and is performed using the following formula:

$$N = N_{general} \times F \times Q, \tag{2}$$

where $N_{general}$ is the total number of employees in the company or department; *F* is the availability coefficient, reflecting the share of employees actually available for mobilization, considering their current workload, vacations, sick leave, and other limitations, %; *Q* is the qualification coefficient, reflecting the level of employees' match to the requirements of the tasks to be performed (value from 0 to 1, where 1 is complete match).

It is evident that the number of employees available for mobilization is influenced by their current workload and schedule (if they are already overloaded at their main job, this can reduce their availability); their skill level and need for additional training (the lower the employees' competencies, the fewer can be mobilized); and their motivation and readiness for mobilization (high motivation can increase the availability factor).

The *qualification coefficient* (K_{skill}) reflects employees' professional skills and required competencies. Several factors are considered when calculating this coefficient:

education, professional skills, work experience, specialized certifications, and other qualifications. A value closer to 1 indicates a high level of qualification, while a value closer to 0 indicates a lack of skills. The coefficient is calculated using the following formula:

$$K_{skill} = \frac{\sum_{i=1}^{n} W_i \times Q_i}{\sum_{i=1}^{n} W_i}, \tag{3}$$

where Q_i is the assessment of the qualification or competency level for a specific criterion (e.g., education, work experience, specialized skills), with a value from 0 to 1; W_i is the weight coefficient of each criterion, reflecting its importance (the weight coefficient should be normalized so that the sum of all criteria weights equals 1); n is the number of assessment criteria.

The *readiness coefficient* (K_{ready}) measures how well employees are prepared to take on new tasks, handle increased workload, or switch to different roles, considering their education, experience, and current knowledge. The higher the value of the coefficient, the better the employees' preparedness. This coefficient is key to planning and managing human capital mobilization and assessing the company's ability to use its workforce reserves. The coefficient K_{ready} can be calculated according to the following formula:

$$K_{ready} = \frac{\sum_{i=1}^{n} W_i \times G_i}{\sum_{i=1}^{n} W_i}, \tag{4}$$

where G_i is the assessment of readiness level for a specific criterion (e.g., having the required education, experience in performing similar tasks, etc.), ranging from 0 to 1; W_i is the weight coefficient for each criterion, reflecting its importance (the weight coefficient must be normalized so that the sum of all weights equals 1); and n is the number of assessment criteria.

The *substitution coefficient* ($K_{substitution}$) indicates the efficiency with which employees can temporarily or partially substitute other specialists or, if necessary, perform additional tasks. This metric reflects the flexibility and multifunctionality of the workforce. The substitution coefficient ranges from 0 to 1, where 1 represents full readiness for substitution and 0 indicates no readiness. A high value, close to 1, suggests the possibility of substitution without significant loss of efficiency. Understanding the dynamics of this coefficient helps companies better plan their HR policies and respond promptly to changes in personnel composition. The calculation is based on the following formula:

$$K_{substitution} = \frac{\sum_{i=1}^{n} W_i \times S_i}{\sum_{i=1}^{n} W_i} \tag{5}$$

where S_i is the assessment of the level of substitutability for a specific criterion (e.g., possessing the skills to perform other tasks, experience in fulfilling similar responsibilities, relevant training), expressed as a value from 0 to 1; W_i is the weight coefficient for each criterion, reflecting its significance (the weight coefficients must be normalized so that their sum equals 1); and n is the number of evaluation criteria.

Examples of substitutability evaluation criteria may include the following: possession of the necessary skills and knowledge (readiness to perform tasks at the level of the substituted specialist); experience in performing similar responsibilities (work on comparable projects or in analogous positions); completion of specialized training or courses (preparation for fulfilling the tasks of the substituted specialist); and willingness to take on additional workload and redistribute responsibilities (motivation to perform tasks in case of substitution).

Preparation time (T) corresponds to the amount of time required to make employees completely ready for performing new tasks, substituting key specialists, or transitioning to other roles. This coefficient includes the time spent on training, adaptation, gaining practical experience, and other activities for preparing personnel. The less time required for preparation, the higher the value of RMHC and, consequently, the more effective the mobilization system. In this context, preparation time can be calculated by considering three fundamental factors: the time needed for training (O), adaptation (A), and gaining practical experience (E):

$$T = O + A + E, \tag{6}$$

where O is the time spent on educational programs, courses, seminars, or training sessions (including core, specialized, and supplementary training); A is the time required for an employee to adapt to new responsibilities or working conditions; and E is the time needed to acquire practical experience that enables the employee to confidently perform new tasks.

Preparation time is influenced by several factors: the initial qualification level of employees (the higher it is, the less time required for preparation); the complexity of new tasks and job requirements (the more demanding the functions, the more time needed for preparation); the availability of mentors or mentorship programs (such support can reduce the time needed to gain practical experience); and the intensity of training (high-intensity courses or educational programs can shorten preparation time).

4.2 Testing RMHC Using a Simulation Model

Simulation modeling was used to analyze the influence of key factors on RMHC and to perform sensitivity analysis. This process identified distinct value gradations for RMHC, allowing the classification of reserves into specific ranges. These classifications make it possible to interpret results across various scenarios and to design targeted human capital management strategies adapted to different socio-economic conditions.

The modeling was conducted using a grid-based exhaustive search method, exploring all possible combinations of parameters within the given ranges. This approach ensured a comprehensive study of the variation space.

The modeling process was implemented using software based on the Python language. The following libraries were used: NumPy for numerical calculations, including data array generation and operations with multidimensional arrays; Pandas for data structuring and analysis; Matplotlib for visualizing simulation results, including sensitivity graph construction.

At the first stage of simulation modeling, parameter initialization was performed, which involved defining the range of variation for the variables (K_{skill}, K_{ready}, $K_{substitution}$, and preparation time T) used in the calculation of the RMHC. The proposed formula (1) was used to model RMHC values, with the parameters combined in various configurations.

The parameters varied within the following ranges: $K_{skill} \in [0,1]$, step 0.04 (discretization of 25 points); $K_{ready} \in [0,1]$, step 0.04 (discretization of 25 points);$K_{substitution} \in [0,1]$, step 0.04 (discretization of 25 points); $T_{preparation} \in [1,10]$, step 0.36 (discretization of 25 points). All coefficients varied within the range of 0 to 1, while preparation time T varied from 1 to 10 (in arbitrary time units). For all parameters, 25 uniformly distributed points were used. As a result, 390,625 parameter combinations were generated.

At the second stage, an exhaustive iteration of all possible combinations of the specified parameters was conducted to calculate the RMHC. The calculations considered all constructed parameter combinations, ensuring comprehensive coverage of the solution space. All computed RMHC values were stored in a database structure to facilitate further analysis.

In the final stage, the results were analyzed and graphs were created to show how RMHC depends on each parameter. Using the calculated data, clustering was applied to group the RMHC dynamics into distinct categories (clusters) representing different levels of mobilization. Additionally, the relationships between RMHC and individual parameters were plotted, with all other parameters held constant (Fig. 2).

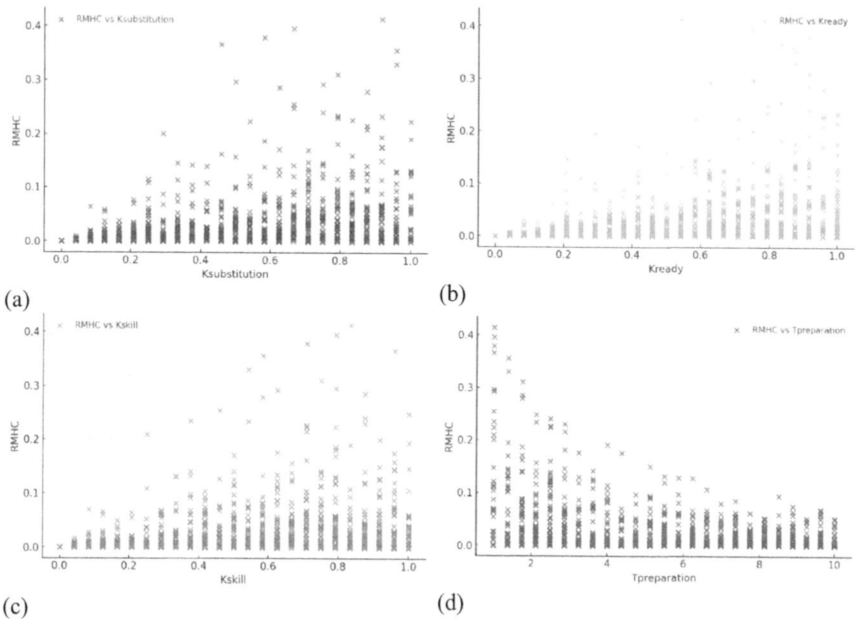

Fig. 2. Analysis of the impact of parameter variations on RMHC values: (a) $K_{substitution}$ vs. RMHC; (b) K_{ready} vs. RMHC; (c) K_{skill} vs. RMHC; (d) $T_{preparation}$ vs. RMHC.

Based on the RMHC calculation formula and the graphical visualization in Fig. 2, it can be concluded that an increase in K_{skill} leads to a linear growth in RMHC, as employee qualifications directly affect their efficiency, which highlights the importance of qualifications in the mobilization of human capital. Similarly, an increase in K_{ready} causes a linear rise in RMHC, emphasizing the need to enhance employee readiness levels to maximize mobilization reserves. In turn, an increase in $K_{substitution}$ also linearly increases RMHC, underscoring the significance of workforce flexibility and the ability to substitute employees effectively to optimize personnel potential. Unlike the other parameters, $T_{preparation}$ has an inverse effect on RMHC. The more time is necessary for preparation, the lower is the RMHC value, which points to the importance of minimizing adaptation and training time.

4.3 RMHC Value Gradation

Based on the results of simulation modeling, RMHC values were categorized into different levels. This gradation helps interpret the company's readiness level for human resource mobilization and the effectiveness of reserve management.

Quantile boundaries were calculated to distribute the RMHC values. The values were divided into five categories: the low mobilization level (20% of the sample with the lowest RMHC values, $Q_{0–20}$); medium mobilization level (20–40% of the sample, $Q_{20–40}$); adequate mobilization level (40–60% of the sample, $Q_{40–60}$); high mobilization level (60–80% of the sample, $Q_{60–80}$); and maximum mobilization level (20% of the sample with the highest RMHC values, $Q_{80–100}$). The analysis was conducted using Python (Pandas and NumPy libraries).

Based on the processed simulation data, RMHC values can be divided into several ranges (Table 4). These defined levels provide a foundation for interpreting the current state and developing strategies to improve the efficiency of human capital utilization. However, it should be noted that the quantitative boundaries may be adjusted if necessary.

Table 4. RMHC value gradation.

RMHC ranges	Level of mobilization readiness	Interpretation
$0.0000 \leq \text{RMHC} < 0.0018$	Low readiness	The level of human capital reserves is insufficient. The number of employees, their qualifications, or readiness in the reserve hinder prompt task resolution. Additional preparation, training, and improvement in substitution capacity are required
$0.0018 \leq \text{RMHC} < 0.0079$	Medium readiness	The company has certain reserves, but they are insufficient for effective management in critical situations. Employees partially meet the requirements, but their skills or training need to be improved
$0.0079 \leq \text{RMHC} < 0.0203$	Adequate readiness	The company has sufficient human capital reserves to respond quickly to changes and solve tasks. Employees possess the necessary competencies and are ready to substitute key specialists, though additional professional development might still be necessary

(continued)

Table 4. (*continued*)

RMHC ranges	Level of mobilization readiness	Interpretation
$0.0203 \leq RMHC < 0.0486$	High readiness	Human capital reserves ensure the company's flexibility and responsiveness in personnel management. Most employees in reserve are highly qualified and prepared to perform complex tasks
$0.0486 \leq RMHC \leq 1.000$	Maximum readiness	The company has very high human capital mobilization reserves, ensuring maximum responsiveness and stability in crisis conditions. Employees in reserve have excellent qualifications, high substitutability, and are ready for mobilization in the shortest time

This *RMHC* value scale enables the company to assess its current readiness level for mobilizing human capital and identify necessary actions to improve its personnel management systems.

Low readiness indicates that the reserves for mobilizing human capital are extremely limited. The company faces staffing shortages, insufficient qualifications, or low replacement capacity. In a crisis situation, the company would face major challenges in maintaining uninterrupted production operations. It is recommended to improve training programs, increase the number of reserve staff, and enhance both qualification levels and replacement capacity.

Medium readiness implies that the company has certain reserves, but their level of professional preparation may not be sufficient to meet all production needs. Reserve staff need to improve their qualifications (competency development) and enhance their readiness for mobilization.

Adequate readiness suggests that the company's reserves are substantial enough to ensure the prompt replacement of workers and the completion of labor tasks in critical situations. Employees possess the required competencies and are prepared to substitute key specialists. However, there is still room for further improvement in employee training, replacement capacity, and adaptability. It is recommended to continue developing employee competencies and to take measures to reduce preparation time.

High readiness indicates that the company has robust reserves and can respond swiftly to changes and effectively handle new challenges. Reserve employees possess the necessary qualifications and are ready to replace key specialists at any time, with most employees prepared to handle complex tasks. At this level, the focus should be made on maintaining the current preparation level, periodically updating employees' skills, and attracting additional reserves to increase resilience.

Maximum readiness signifies that the RMHC have reached their highest level. The company is prepared for any crisis situations and can adapt instantly to changes. Reserve staff are highly qualified, ready to replace key specialists, and capable of promptly taking on new tasks. At this level, it is recommended to maintain and enhance the personnel management system, while fostering additional skills and training programs.

The proposed formula for calculating the RMHC can be used for a more precise evaluation of the company's ability to effectively deploy its human resources. This facilitates the development of management strategies focused on enhancing flexibility, resilience, and readiness to adapt to change.

Additionally, simulation modeling has proven valuable in assessing how RMHC responds to changes in key factors. The resulting classification of readiness levels provides a solid foundation for further analysis and practical use of these insights in human resource management.

4.4 Research Limitations and Assumptions

Considering the applicability of the proposed approach, we also need to account for its limitations and underlying assumptions, as these can affect the accuracy of the results. This section focuses on the key aspects that restrict the overall applicability of the method, as well as the assumptions made to simplify or adapt the approach for practical use.

The RMHC concept is designed to reflect a company's or organization's ability to quickly mobilize human capital. Its application context encompasses a wide range of management tasks, including monitoring changes in mobilization reserves over time, conducting comparative evaluations of different departments or companies to identify competitive advantages and weaknesses, and planning initiatives to enhance the efficiency of human capital utilization. This study assumes that the RMHC tool can capture changes in the readiness and adaptability of personnel to perform tasks under various scenarios. However, for the successful application of this approach, it is crucial to recognize that RMHC is based on a set of parameters that may not fully account for the complexity and diversity of real-world conditions.

Certain simplifications are introduced within the framework of simulation modeling, such as the uniform distribution of resources, to improve computational efficiency. The parameter ranges (K_{skill}, K_{ready}, $K_{substitution}$, and $T_{preparation}$) are uniformly discretized, which may not reflect the actual distribution of parameter values in practical conditions. It is also assumed that the parameters are independent of each other. However, in reality, these parameters may be interrelated, for example, higher employee qualifications may correlate with their readiness levels.

The coefficients K_{skill}, K_{ready}, and $K_{substitution}$ are theoretical in nature, and measuring them in practice may be challenging due to data collection difficulties or subjective evaluationIn the simulation model, the maximum preparation time value, T, is capped at 10 units. While this simplifies the analysis by offering a general perspective on potential RMHC dynamics under the given combinations, it does not account for the complexities of long-term training or employee development processes. Including extreme values (e.g., $K_{skill} = 0$) may not be applicable to real situations, and the ranges used (from 0 to 1 for coefficients and from 1 to 10 for preparation time) may not reflect the actual limits of these parameters in specific conditions. For example, preparation time may vary, being longer in the manufacturing sector than in services. The contribution of individual coefficients can be adjusted depending on the specifics of the applied tasks. Furthermore, only four parameters are used in the calculations. Potential influences from other factors (such as employee turnover, availability of training, or the level of automation in production processes) are not considered. The impact of macroeconomic conditions, technological changes, or competitive environments is also excluded from the analysis.

Neglecting the assumptions and limitations of the model can result in underestimating the complexity of human capital mobilization processes. While these simplifications are essential for making the model practical, they may fall short in capturing the full intricacies of real-world scenarios. Nevertheless, RMHC serves as a valuable analytical tool, providing a foundational framework that can be refined and expanded into more sophisticated, adaptive models. Such models would better accommodate a broader range of factors and interactions, offering greater applicability in real-world conditions.

5 Conclusion

The study contributes to human capital management theory by developing a methodology for assessing RMHC. The proposed methodology considers both quantitative and qualitative aspects of human capital, providing a more accurate assessment of a company's ability to mobilize its workforce. It improves on current methods and allows for a clear evaluation of a company's readiness to deploy human capital, helping to adjust personnel strategies for both current and future needs. The application of these methods not only simplifies the process of adapting companies to external challenges but also enables them to proactively manage their human resource potential.

Avenues for future research include several key areas, which can be divided into theoretical and applied ones. The first area could be to enhance the RMHC assessment model by incorporating additional factors, such as employee turnover, the impact of organizational structure, and the degree of digitalization of processes. The second area could involve adaptation of the RMHC model to specific industries or other characteristics that could impact the RMHC value gradations. The third area could be focused on developing dynamic forecasting models based on RMHC that account for real-time changes in the external environment. Finally, a promising direction would be to create frameworks and recommendations for using RMHC in strategic planning at the company or industry level. These and other future research areas will not only improve the existing RMHC model but also create new tools for human capital management, contributing to sustainable development and increasing organizational competitiveness.

Funding. The study was supported by the Russian Science Foundation, grant No. 23-28-01768. https://rscf.ru/project/23-28-01768/.

Conflict of Interest. The authors declare that the research was conducted in the absence of any commercial or financial relationships that could be construed as a potential conflict of interest.

Credit Author Statement. E.K.: Conceptualization, Data Curation, Formal Analysis, Methodology, Project administration, Validation, Visualization, Writing – original draft, Writing – review & editing. U.Y.: Formal Analysis, Visualization, Writing – review & editing.

References

1. Delery, J.E., Roumpi, D.: Strategic human resource management, human capital and competitive advantage: Is the field going in circles? Hum. Resour. Manag. J. **27**(1), 1–21 (2017). https://doi.org/10.1111/1748-8583.12137
2. Semenova, V.V., Zelenyuk, A.N., Savinov, Y.A.: Human capital development: development of professional competencies through soft skills. Revista Tempos E Espaços Em Educação **14**(33), e15253 (2021). https://doi.org/10.20952/revtee.v14i33.15253
3. Deming, D.J.: The value of soft skills in the labor market. NBER Report. **4**, 7–11 (2017). https://doi.org/10.3386/w23306
4. Lyu, W., Liu, J.: Soft skills, hard skills: What matters most? Evidence from job postings. Applied Energy **300**, 117307 (2021). https://doi.org/10.1016/j.apenergy.2021.117307
5. Schultz, T.W.: Investment in human capital. Am. Econ. Rev. **51**(1), 1–17 (1961)
6. Schultz, T.W.: Reflections on investment in man. Journal of Political Economy **70**(5, Part 2), 1–8 (1962). https://doi.org/10.1086/258770
7. Becker, G.S.: Investment in human capital: A theoretical analysis. Journal of Political Economy **70**(5, Part 2), 9–49 (1962). https://doi.org/10.1086/258724
8. Becker, G.S.: Investment in human capital: Effects on earnings. In: Human capital: A theoretical and empirical analysis, with special reference to education, 2nd ed., pp. 13–44. National Bureau of Economic Research (1975)
9. Mincer, J.: Studies in human capital, Vol. 1. Edward Elgar Publishing (1993). https://doi.org/10.4337/9781782541554
10. Welch, F.: Education in production. J. Polit. Econ. **78**(1), 35–59 (1970). https://doi.org/10.1086/259599
11. Card, D.: The causal effect of education on earnings. In: Ashenfelter, O., Card, D. (eds.). Handbook of labor economics, Vol. 3, pp. 1801–1863. Elsevier (1999). https://doi.org/10.1016/S1573-4463(99)03011-4
12. Bourdieu, P.: The forms of capital. In: Durham, M.G., Kellner, D.M. (eds.) Cultural theory: An anthology, Vol. 1, pp. 81–93. Wiley-Blackwell (1986)
13. Coleman, J.S.: Social capital in the creation of human capital. Am. J. Sociol. **94**(Supplement), S95–S120 (1988). https://doi.org/10.1086/228943
14. Davidsson, P., Honig, B.: The role of social and human capital among nascent entrepreneurs. J. Bus. Ventur. **18**(3), 301–331 (2003). https://doi.org/10.1016/S0883-9026(02)00097-6
15. Fukuyama, F.: Trust: The social virtues and the creation of prosperity. Simon and Schuster (1996)
16. Glaeser, E.L., Laibson, D., Sacerdote, B.: An economic approach to social capital. Econ. J. **112**(483), F437–F458 (2002). https://doi.org/10.1111/1468-0297.00078
17. Granovetter, M.S.: The strength of weak ties. Am. J. Sociol. **78**(6), 1360–1380 (1973). https://doi.org/10.1086/225469
18. Portes, A.: Social capital: Its origins and applications in modern sociology. In: Caplan, L.R. (ed.) Knowledge and social capital, pp. 43–67. Elsevier (2009). https://doi.org/10.1016/B978-0-7506-7222-1.50006-4
19. Argyle, M.: The psychology of interpersonal behaviour. Penguin UK (1994)
20. Deci, E.L., Ryan, R.M.: Intrinsic motivation and self-determination in human behavior. Springer Science & Business Media (2013)
21. Gardner, H.E.: Frames of mind: The theory of multiple intelligences. Basic Books (2011)
22. Goleman, D.: Emotional intelligence: why it can matter more than IQ. Learning **24**(6), 49–50 (1996)
23. Goleman, D.: Working with emotional intelligence. Bantam Books (1998). https://doi.org/10.1002/ltl.40619981008

24. Ryan, R.M., Deci, E.L.: Self-determination theory and the facilitation of intrinsic motivation, social development, and well-being. Am. Psychol. **55**(1), 68 (2000). https://doi.org/10.1037/0003-066X.55.1.68
25. Boyatzis, R.E.: The competent manager: A model for effective performance. John Wiley & Sons (1991)
26. Boyatzis, R.E., Goleman, D.: Emotional and social competency inventory. Hay Group (2007)
27. Boyatzis, R.E.: Competencies as a behavioral approach to emotional intelligence. J. Manage. Develop. **28**(9), 749–770 (2009). https://doi.org/10.1108/02621710910987647
28. Caruso, D.R., Salovey, P.: The emotionally intelligent manager: How to develop and use the four key emotional skills of leadership. John Wiley & Sons (2004)
29. Druskat, V.U., Wolff, S.B.: Building the emotional intelligence of groups. Harv. Bus. Rev. **79**(3), 80–91 (2001). https://doi.org/10.1037/t05468-000
30. Salovey, P., Mayer, J.D.: Emotional intelligence. Imagin. Cogn. Pers. **9**(3), 185–211 (1990). https://doi.org/10.2190/DUGG-P24E-52WK-6CDG
31. Zeidner, M., Matthews, G., Roberts, R.D.: Emotional intelligence in the workplace: a critical review. Appl. Psychol. **53**(3), 371–399 (2004). https://doi.org/10.1111/j.1464-0597.2004.00176.x
32. Sternberg, R.J.: Beyond IQ: A triarchic theory of human intelligence. Cambridge University Press (1985)
33. Carroll, J.B.: Human cognitive abilities: A survey of factor-analytic studies (No. 1). Cambridge University Press (1993). https://doi.org/10.1017/CBO9780511571312
34. Kang, S.C., Snell, S.A.: Intellectual capital architectures and ambidextrous learning: a framework for human resource management. J. Manage. Stud. **46**(1), 65–92 (2009). https://doi.org/10.1111/j.1467-6486.2008.00776.x
35. Spencer, L.M., Spencer, P.S.M.: Competence at work: Models for superior performance. John Wiley & Sons (2008)
36. Gilbert, T.F.: Human competence: Engineering worthy performance. John Wiley & Sons (2013)
37. Hoffmann, T.: The meanings of competency. J. Eur. Ind. Train. **23**(6), 275–286 (1999). https://doi.org/10.1108/03090599910284650
38. Barney, J.: Firm resources and sustained competitive advantage. J. Manag. **17**(1), 99–120 (1991). https://doi.org/10.1177/014920639101700108
39. Barney, J.B.: Is the resource-based "view" a useful perspective for strategic management research? Yes. Academy of Management Review **26**(1), 41–56 (2001). https://doi.org/10.5465/amr.2001.4011938
40. Prahalad, C.K., Hamel, G.: The core competence of the corporation. In: Knowledge and strategy, pp. 41–59. Routledge (2009). https://doi.org/10.1016/B978-0-7506-7088-3.50006-1
41. Handy, C.: Understanding organizations. Penguin UK (1993)
42. Hofstede, G.: Culture's consequences: International differences in work-related values, Vol. 5. SAGE (1984)
43. Nonaka, I., Toyama, R., Konno, N.: SECI, ba and leadership: a unified model of dynamic knowledge creation. Long Range Plan. **33**(1), 5–34 (2000). https://doi.org/10.1016/S0024-6301(99)00115-6
44. Schein, E.H.: Organizational culture and leadership, Vol. 2. John Wiley & Sons (2010)
45. Trompenaars, F., Hampden-Turner, C.: Riding the waves of culture: Understanding diversity in global business. Nicholas Brealey International (2011)

Technological Development and Its Impact on the Family Institution

Evgeniya Tukhtarova(✉) and Natalia Neklyudova

Institute of Economics of the Ural Branch of the Russian Academy of Sciences, 29 Moskovskaya Street, Ekaterinburg 620014, Russia
{tukhtarova.eh,neklyudova.np}@uiec.ru

Abstract. The article analyzes the transformation of the family institution caused by the technological development on the example of the Greater Urals region. The authors have studied the periodization of the change of technological modes with the phases of demographic transition on the example of the Greater Urals. Then the authors studied how the revealed regularities influenced the changes in the demographic characteristics of the family institute not only in the conditions of the change of technological patterns for 250 years, but also in the conditions of the change of the world economic pattern. The results of the analysis led to the conclusion that a strong connection exists between the world economic structure and changes in the institution of the family, as well as the development of human capital and the importance of its transfer in the intergenerational gap. The authors identify contradictions between the need for technological development and changes in the institution of the family. On the one hand, technological development does not involve large numbers of people, while on the other it destroys the traditional model of a family with children. The complication of the socio-economic sphere in the new technological mode implies the formation of a new economic model, which should correspond to the new world economic mode. Scientific and technological progress or new industrialization always contributes to the formation of a new structure of division of labor, in which there will be practically no place for obsolete skills of people specialized in old technological patterns. Consequently, these people and areas will be outside the new economic model.

Keywords: Demographic transition · Family institution · Technological paradigm

JEL Classification: B15 · O14 · O3

1 Introduction

The current period is characterized by a unique situation, namely a change not only in the technological mode but also in the world economic mode. However, there is no consensus among scholars regarding the nature of a post-capitalist society. Consequently, numerous researchers, analysts and scientists are seeking to ascertain the nature of the

E. Kuzmin et al. (Eds.): EASET 2024, SPBE, pp. 234–245, 2025.
https://doi.org/10.1007/978-3-031-91159-0_15

prospective economic model and the underlying principles that will inform the system of relations between productive forces and production relations. According to scholars, the change of technological paradigm occurs approximately every 50–70 years and is the material and technical basis for the transition to the next long Kondratiev cycle [1–3]. Technological paradigm always forms a new organizational mechanism of economic functioning, which has a clearly expressed structure, determining the composition of basic technologies and subsequent innovations. In the future, the formed mechanism becomes the scientific and technical basis for the three levels of development of the new economic model:

1) the basic sectors of the economy, which are not just the basis of the technological wave, but also the link between them and the rest of the economy (households, public sector, services, etc.);
2) innovative technologies that become a new generation of production techniques and are the basis for the competitiveness of means of production and energy sources for the real sector of the economy;
3) dissemination of a new generation of machinery for consumption by households in order to stimulate demand in the economy [4].

The obtained results of the study allowed us to formulate a scientific novelty, which consists in identifying the contradictory situation that began to develop during the first industrialization in the USSR. Today, this situation has not only worsened, but also reached another qualitative level.

Firstly, the new technological mode based on digital technologies implies reformatting of existing professions and less involvement of people in the country's economic activity. In other words, fewer people are needed in the new technological mode. This has an impact on the intergenerational gap in the transfer of knowledge and on the change of the classical family model [5]. In addition, the functional importance of the family in the new technological mode for the economic development of the country is changing [6]. There is no need for people to be born and enter the labor market.

Secondly, technological development has had a serious impact on the institution of the family, making it small, consisting of one or two family members. At the same time, the image of the classical family is preserved in rural areas, which are excluded from technological development because it can be destructive for them.

Among other things, the change of technological patterns completely reformats institutional, social, cultural, educational, etc. institutions and the relations between them. In this context, it is important to answer the question: what is the role of the family institution in the new economic model? Therefore, this research is aimed at studying the transformation of the family institution and identifying its role in the economic development of Russia on the example of the Urals.

2 Theoretical Frameworks

The interconnection between the technological paradigm and the family institution represents a pivotal element within the framework of the national economy. This interconnection exerts a profound influence on a multitude of economic processes, including the global economic order, which is predicated upon the evolutionary principle of family modernization and its adaptation to new realities. The demographic characteristics of the family institution serve as the foundation for the formation of new economic relations. The evolution of the family institution is a fundamental factor in the dynamics of socio-economic and technological development at the societal, national, and macro-regional levels.

This is explained by the fundamental link between technological paradigms and the phases of demographic transition. Furthermore, there is a connection between the shift in the world economic order and the demographic transition, which has lasted for over two centuries. Consequently, if the pre-industrial development of society was characterized by an extended type of patriarchal or rural family (including relatives of different degrees of closeness), then with the change of the world economic system and the transition from feudal relations to capitalist relations, there is a change in the type of family towards a gradual nuclearisation of relations between relatives. In other words, the evolution of modern civilization inevitably leads to the evolution of the family institution.

It is essential to comprehend what is the cause and what is the effect. The English researcher Harold Perkin, who studied the socio-economic development of Great Britain from the Victorian period to the end of the XX century, answered this question. His research demonstrated that the industrial revolution in Great Britain became feasible only after the alteration of social structures within society [7]. The wars that took place in the Middle Ages resulted in the destruction of the majority of the English aristocracy, which in turn necessitated the opening up of the social hierarchy in the country. This in turn led to the emergence of a unique class of gentry.

The shift from traditional open land ownership to a more modernized approach in the context of a warming climate led to a significant transformation in the social structure of society. This, in turn, resulted in the release of a vast number of people from rural areas and the subsequent influx of these individuals into urban centers. This phenomenon played a pivotal role in the development of the bourgeois revolution in Great Britain. Furthermore, the expansion of the urban population had an effect on the evolving structure of the family. New forms of interaction between people emerged, and the institution of the family began to lose its importance with the advent of the capitalist world economy.

Subsequent technological development combined with social engineering tools contributed to tectonic shifts in demographic processes [8]. Furthermore, the phenomenon of large-scale migration has further complicated an already complex social environment, not just in terms of the diversity of peoples and cultures, but also in the emergence of different types of families. Some of these developments corresponded to the new realities of the modern world, while others became archaic and were pushed out of society [9, 10]. This resulted in the formation of not only ethnic enclaves, but also new network forms of relationships. This, in turn, led to the growth of the shadow economy and its non-compliance with the current technological paradigm.

The acceleration of technological development was a prerequisite for a change in the causal relationship between technology and the institution of the family. Now technological development predetermined the modernization of the family institution in most developed Western countries. This process then proceeded to spread throughout the rest of the world [11, 12].

While in Western countries, social structures initially facilitated economic and technological development during the early stages of the capitalist system, in Russia, the situation was the opposite, reflecting a catching-up type of development. Western technologies were introduced first, and only then did the transformation of demographic processes in Russia begin, which influenced the evolution of the family institution.

Russian scholars note that the initial phase of the demographic transition in Russia occurred at a slower pace than in developed countries. Consequently, the extended family type in Russia was delayed for a longer period than in Western European countries. This can be attributed to the later process of industrialization in Russia [13].

Nevertheless, by the mid-1950s, the processes associated with technological paradigms and phases of demographic transition in Russia began to align with those observed in developed countries around the globe.

3 Method and Data

The study used official statistical data from Rosstat, as well as data collected by the Ural demographer Kuz'min [14] (1993) for the period 1845–1942 in his paper "*Family in the Urals. Demographic Aspects of the Life Choice*".

In the study, the territory of the Urals is understood as the "Greater Urals", which includes the following modern subjects of the Russian Federation: Komi Republic, Republic of Bashkortostan, Perm Territory, Orenburg, Kurgan, Sverdlovsk and Chelyabinsk Oblasts.

The division into technological waves is based on the methodology proposed by Glazyev [15]. The first technological wave (1785–1835), based on new technologies in textile industry and the use of water energy. The second technological wave (1830–1890) is associated with the development of railway transport and mechanical production based on the steam engine. The third technological wave (1880–1940) was based on electric energy, development of heavy engineering and electrical industry. The fourth technological wave (1930–1990) was based on hydrocarbon energy, telecommunications, new synthetic materials. The fifth technological wave (1985–2035) is based on achievements in microelectronics, informatics, biotechnology, genetic engineering, new types of energy, materials, space exploration, satellite communications, etc. The new technological paradigm is based on digital technologies, knowledge economy, etc.

We also used statistical methods of data analysis processing in the study, which were imposed on the periodization of technological patterns.

4 Technological Waves and Evolution of the Family Institution in the Urals

The Urals were characterised by a high birthrate during their pre-industrial stage. This was not solely due to religious and moral considerations surrounding family and marriage, but was also influenced by the economic model of the era. The necessity of survival in challenging circumstances and the established tribal traditions within the rural community collectively shaped this phenomenon [14].

The Ural territory is notable for its extended or traditional family structures, in which all generations reside within the same parental home. The patriarchal family was based on the principle of shared family values, with the man as the head of the family [16]. Powers and family roles in the extended type of family had clear-cut functions and delimitations.

The institutionalisation of the Ural family was based on the agrarian type of economy, where all movable and immovable property was in public or collective ownership, and this was an obligatory condition for people's existence. The first changes that affected the family institution are connected with the history of development of metallurgical plants in the Urals. They were located almost all over the Urals. Between the 18th and mid-19th centuries, over 200 water-powered factories were constructed during the second technological wave, which was based on the steam engine. The rapidly developing "mining and metallurgical Ural district" constituted the prerequisites for the transition from a large family to a family with few children, simultaneously engendering the emergence of a novel family type, initially "bourgeois" and subsequently "proletarian" one (Table 1).

Table 1. The evolution of the family in the Urals in the context of changing technological waves.

Period	Family type	Characteristics	Phase of demographic transition	Technological wave / World economic order
Pre-industrial era (16th-17th centuries)	Patriarchal	Strict hierarchy, common property, common interests, large families	Phase I (high mortality and fertility rates)	I wave / early capitalist
18th - first half of the 19th century	Bourgeois	Women's involvement in production, division of labor, medium-sized families (4–5 children), emergence of rented housing and bringing in-laws	Phase I (high mortality and fertility rates)	II wave / capitalist
Late 19th - early 20th century	Proletarian	Children's involvement in production, small families (2–3 children), late marriage period	Phase II (high birth rate, declining mortality rate)	III wave / capitalist
The period between the 1930s and the 1970s	Labor	Industrialization of villages, equalization of women's rights, establishment of small family (2 children), high education, appearance of divorces	Phase III (declining birth rate, declining mortality rate)	IV wave / capitalist

(*continued*)

Table 1. (*continued*)

Period	Family type	Characteristics	Phase of demographic transition	Technological wave / World economic order
The period between the 1980s and the early 21st century	Child-centered and democratic	Small family (1–2 children), emotional attachment between spouses and children, career orientation among women, increased divorce rate	Phase IV (completion of the demographic revolution, birth rates equalized with death rates)	V wave / capitalist
20s-70s of the 21st century	Postindustrial	Growth of "child free" families, delayed marriage and childbirth, delegation of procreation	Declining birth rate, ageing of population	VI wave / postcapitalist

At the same time, Kuz'min notes that in the pre-revolutionary period the development of the Urals was noticeably different from the European part of Russia. This difference lies, first of all, in the stronger institutionalization and role of the family both in society and in economic development [14]. For example, the proportion of unmarried women in both urban and rural areas was much lower than in the rest of Russia. The rate of children born out of wedlock was also low.

The same is evidenced by the analysis of the total birth rate and marriage rate per 1,000 people. Consequently, over the course of approximately two centuries, the birth rate in the Urals has declined significantly; while the marriage rate has remained relatively stable (Fig. 1). It can be posited that the family institution in the Urals serves as the foundation for the economic development of the territory.

In the period of the II and III technological waves in the Urals, as well as all over the world, there were migration processes from rural to urban areas due to the beginning of the industrial era and the growing popularity of large cities. This can be attributed to the fact that in urban areas, employment opportunities were available, and the necessity to have large families for survival diminished. Consequently, the birth rate growth decreased significantly, especially in the beginning of the XX century (Fig. 1).

The industrialisation that took place throughout the country, as well as the implementation of the SCER project (State Commission for Electrification of Russia), formed not only a technological cluster in the Urals, but for the first time there was a large-scale demand for highly qualified personnel of working specialties, specialists of various levels. This demand led to the establishment of scientific school.

Indeed, it is from this period that we can consider the initial point of the report on the accumulation of qualitative characteristics of human capital in the Urals. This was accompanied by not only the mastering of new skills, universal level of education, but also by a wide access to quality medicine, which affected the reduction of mortality, including infant mortality.

Thus, if at the end of the 19th century an average of 500 children under the age of 5 died for every 1000 children born in the Urals [14], in the 50s of the last century this

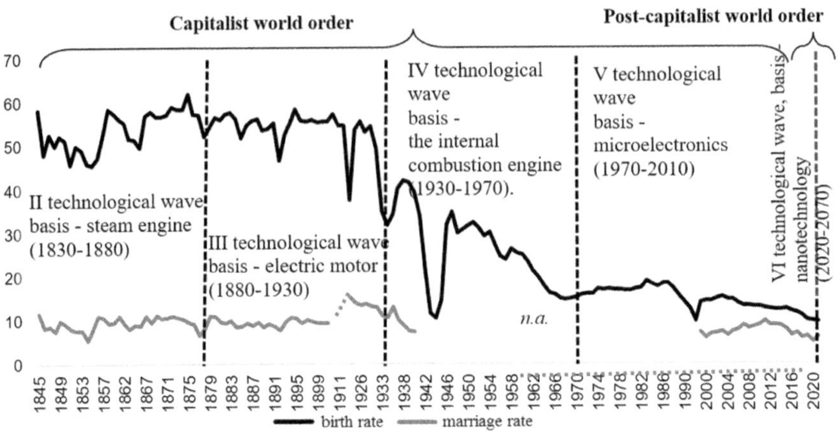

Source: compiled by the authors based on Kuz'min [14] for the period from 1845 to 1990 and population data (arithmetic mean value) from Rosstat for the constituent entities of the Greater Urals for the period from 1990 to 2020.

Fig. 1. Dynamics of changes in the behavior of marriage and fertility indicators in the Urals in 1845–2020.

figure was 72 children [17]. At the same time, the period of the IV technological wave is also characterized by a sharp decline in the birth rate as a reaction of the family institution to the most difficult period of the country - the Second World War. The consequences of the demographic and intellectual losses are still being felt today.

The need for skilled labor, the development of the industrial complex, and the improvement of the quality of life in the Urals contributed to the further development of the family institution, the change in attitudes towards the age of marriage, and the change in the nature and appearance of families (Table 1). At the beginning of the V-technological wave, the Urals family became not only a medium-sized family, but also a small family, and one child in the family became the norm. At the end of the 1980s the process of de-industrialization began in the Urals as well as in the whole country, and the demand for labor occupations decreased, people with a high level of human capital were no longer needed in the simplified model of economic development [18].

The reproductive function, which underpins the family institution, is intricately connected to the socio-economic development of society. The reproduction and adaptation of existing social institutions and patterns to changing conditions ensures the transmission and continuity of cultural traditions.

However, this process has been disrupted and today another negative consequence of de-industrialisation is the intergenerational gap in the transmission of knowledge and cultural traditions. This process is characterised by the fact that the older generation does not pass on knowledge to the subsequent one due to the fact that working specialties have lost their prestige, and therefore the cultural canons developed in Soviet times are rejected by the modern generation.

In light of these developments, the older generation has been unable to adapt to the demands of the digital age, despite the necessity of acquiring new skills in the context of a rapidly evolving economic landscape. Consequently, the current state of affairs can be described as follows: the younger generation is largely unaware of older technologies, while the older generation has limited familiarity with new technologies.

The intergenerational gap caused by the change of technological and economic socialist system in the country has led to a decrease in the level of human capital due to the simplification of the economic model in modern Russia and the Urals as an integral part of it. According to the UN data, the Human Development Index (HDI) of the USSR in 1990 was 0.92 points [19], placing it 26th in the world. It was in the first league along with Japan, Switzerland, Germany and other developed countries. However, by 2015, this indicator had decreased to 0.824 points, with Russia moving to the second league of countries to the 52nd place [20].

In light of the aforementioned, we can conclude that the historical trajectory of economic transformation in Russia, from socialist to capitalist, has resulted in a significant imbalance between productive forces and production relations. This has not only led to a shift in the economic model towards a more simplified structure, but has also contributed to the decline in the quality of human capital. These changes have contributed to the transformation of the family institution in the Urals, which will inevitably have an impact on economic development in the long term.

For many years Russia has been a catching-up country (with the exception of the 50–70s of the 20th century) in the technological race, which allowed it to preserve the traditional model of the family institution for a long time. However, the catching-up type of economic development has long-term negative consequences for the country's economy as a whole.

The catching-up type of economic development is characterized not just by lagging behind in the technological race, as the country always receives technologies one or two generations older. More importantly, this model is characterized by growing imbalances between productive forces and production relations. A. Shkolnikov in his work demonstrated the model of catch-up development on the example of China's economy [21]. Taking his scheme as a basis and adapting it to the Russian economy, as well as supplementing it with technological modes, we can see the following picture: the 5th wave's technologies coming to the country with the catching-up model of economic development form the scale and type of economy (Fig. 2).

At the same time, new technologies based on the old technological base with the use of imported raw materials and import of cheap labor, contribute to the formation of family income corresponding to the previous technological wave. Moreover, while receiving incomes corresponding to the previous wave, the consumption of households in this case corresponds to an even lower technological level. As a result, in a country with the catching-up type of economic development, multilevelism takes root and the process of accumulation of old technologies takes place, which leads to the strengthening of macroeconomic imbalance and further inhibition of technological development.

This situation is typical both for the country as a whole and for the Urals. Today the Urals territory is characterized by a multi-structured economy, where along with the technologies of the 5th wave there are technologies of the 4th and even the 3rd waves. This situation is representative of the country as a whole and the Urals region. The Urals region is currently characterized by a multi-structured economy, which incorporates

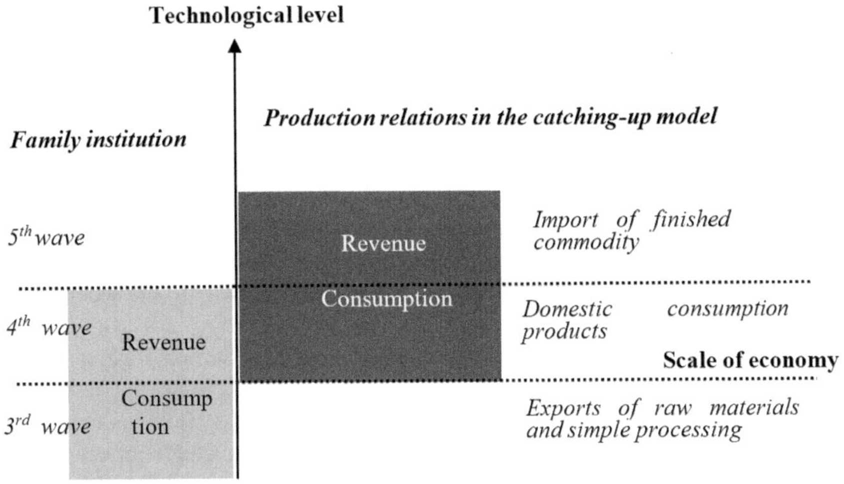

Source: compiled by the authors based on Shkolnikov [22].

Fig. 2. Imbalances between production relations and the institution of the family in the model of catching-up economic development.

technologies of the V mode, in addition to those of the IV and even III modes. This is also the reason why the growth of the population's income is artificially constrained, resulting in a significant proportion of household consumption being allocated to subsistence farming.

Due to the fact that Russia has always used the catch-up type of development model, the need for self-survival of the population was ensured at the expense of land plots, which is why dachas and gardens are so popular in the Urals. Ultimately, the imbalances caused by the catching-up type of economic development affect the decline in the level of human capital, as families have a narrower corridor of opportunities in access to good medicine, education, improvement of the quality of life, etc. Indeed, if we analyze the employed population in terms of sectors, we will find that the majority of the employed population in the Urals work in old waves.

To demonstrate the existing multilevelism in the Urals, we have performed some calculations. Taking the structure of the employed by types of economic activity as a basis for calculation and summing them up for all subjects of the Greater Urals, we have correlated the obtained values of working people according to their belonging to technological waves. For instance, all kinds of extractive industries and the majority of the manufacturing sector, as well as construction and transport, are classified within the 4th wave, as the technologies employed therein represent the core of this technological paradigm.

The exception in the manufacturing industry is the industry related to microelectronics and computers, which is the core of the 5th mode. Space-related industries, military-industrial complex, public administration and communications were also included in the same wave. Trade and all industries related to the service sector were excluded from the analysis, as they practically do not use technology. Agriculture was assigned to the 3rd technological wave.

Thus, the obtained structure of working people in connection with technological waves allowed us to obtain their distribution and analyze them in order to understand the formation of the population's income in the Urals.

The analysis of the structure of the employed population of the Urals territory in dynamics over five years (2017–2021) revealed a distribution that was almost identical to that obtained by Bashina [23]. The majority of the employed population of the Urals is concentrated in the fourth technological wave. Concurrently, there has been an improvement in the situation and a slight increase in the number of employees in the 5th technological wave in 2021 compared to 2017 (Fig. 3).

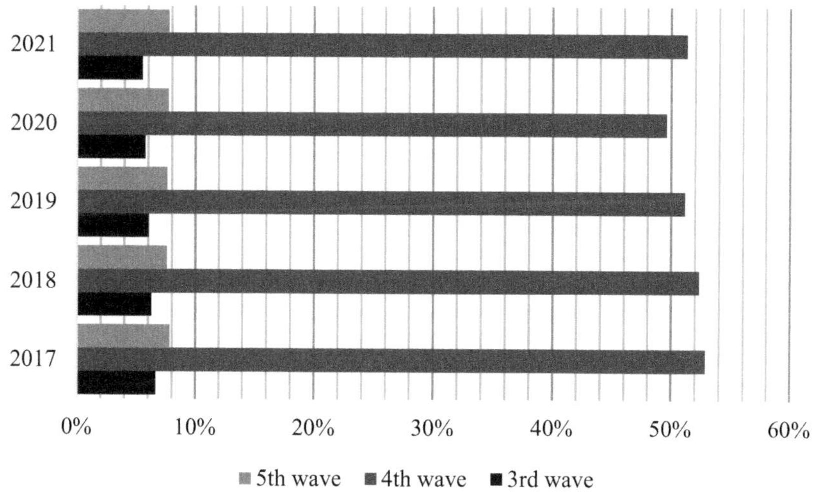

Fig. 3. Distribution of the employed population in the technological waves of the Urals.

It is noteworthy that Sverdlovsk Oblast stands out from other regions of the Urals, where a greater proportion of the population is employed in the fifth technological wave. This is due to the region's specific characteristics and the location of numerous factories belonging to the military-industrial complex.

The data presented in Fig. 3 allows us to conclude that the catching-up model of economic development in Russia, as exemplified by the Urals, does not contribute to the formation of a decent level of remuneration for labor. As a consequence of the growing imbalance, it will become a source of numerous negative socio-economic consequences, including the strengthening of regional disproportion in technological development. Conversely, the coexistence of traditional and modern lifestyles facilitates the preservation of the family institution as the foundation of Russian civilization. In such a hard situation, it is important to resolve this contradiction by preserving the role of the institution of the family in economic development and possibly strengthening its role in technological development.

5 Conclusion

The increasing complexity of the socio-economic sphere in the new technological wave presupposes the formation of a new economic model, which should correspond to the new world economic order. The advancement of science and technology, or the advent of new industrialization, invariably gives rise to a novel structure of division of labor, wherein the skills of those who specialize in the utilization of outdated technological patterns will become increasingly obsolete. Consequently, these individuals and geographical areas will be excluded from the scope of the new economic model.

In fact, a significant part of the rural population may sink into archaism, since high-tech products are produced in industrialized cities, where there is a concentration of educated people capable of complex labor. At the same time, it is important to understand that the rural population has always been the backbone of Russia's development - it is an inflow of healthy labor force and highly institutionalized relations between people, where the role of the family institution is much higher than in cities. In other words, the rural population in Russia preserves the socio-cultural canon that is its basis.

In this context, it is necessary to consider the question of how to address the regions and people who do not fit into this new economic model. The Urals territory is comprised of various regions, including those with agricultural regional specifics. On the one hand, the rural population has historically constituted a significant source of human resources for urban areas. On the other hand, this resource is not infinite.

If we continue to adhere to the concept of the industrial vector of development, without proper attention of state institutions to the problem of the family institution, then in this case there is a threat of its further transformation and the growth of families with the position of "child free". In this regard, it is extremely important to think through the state concept, where the basis of technological development will be socio-cultural meanings that are basic for the country.

The results have revealed the devastating impact of uneven technological development on the regional gap of Russian regions. The current situation can be viewed through the prism of the processes that took place in the United States, where technological states and lagging behind predominantly southern states with agricultural orientation have already formed. Another example is technological China with its ghost towns and aging population, which is expected to shrink significantly in the next decade due to the earlier "one family-one child" reforms.

In this regard, we believe that technological development is important and necessary, but it should not have a destructive impact neither on the regions, nor on the country and the world as a whole, but also on the family institution.

Acknowledgements. The article has been prepared in the framework of the state task to the Institute of Economics of the Ural Branch of RAS for 2024-2025.

References

1. Glazyev, S.: Theory of long-term technical and economic development. VlaDar, Moscow (1993)

2. Yakovets, Y.: Epochal innovations of the XXI century. Ekonomika Publ, Moscow (2004)
3. Sboichakova, Ye. V.: Structural shifts in technology as a way of innovative development in Russia. Industry: Economics. Manag. Technol. **5**, 57–61 (2010)
4. Lukina, N.P., Sazonova, P.V.: Transformation of family relations within the technological structure of the information society. Bulletin of Tomsk State University. Philosophy. Sociology. Political Science **47**, 158–167 (2019). https://doi.org/10.17223/1998863x/47/17
5. Chesley, N.: Families in a high-tech age: Technology usage patterns, work and family correlates, and gender. J. Fam. Issues **27**(6), 850–881 (2006). https://doi.org/10.1177/0192513X05285296
6. Sadovnikov, S.V.: Technological sovereignty and demographic growth as key elements of state security in the current geopolitical reality. Humanities. Bulletin of the Financial University **13**(2), 26–37 (2023). https://doi.org/10.26794/2226-7867-2023-13-2-26-37
7. Perkin, H.: The origins of modern English society. Routledge (2003). https://doi.org/10.4324/9780203412701
8. Aksoy, Y., Basso, H.S., Smith, R.P., Grasl, T.: Demographic structure and macroeconomic trends. American Econ. J. Macroecon. Forthcom. **11**(1), 193–222 (2018). https://doi.org/10.1257/mac.20170114
9. Feyrer, J.: Demographics and productivity. Rev. Econ. Stat. **89**(1), 100–109 (2007). https://doi.org/10.1162/rest.89.1.100
10. Feyrer, J.: The U.S. productivity slowdown, the baby boom, and management quality. J. Populat. Econ. **24**(1), 267–284 (2011). https://doi.org/10.1007/s00148-009-0294-z
11. Gordon, R.J.: Is U.S. economic growth over? Faltering innovation confronts the six headwinds. NBER Working Paper 18315 (2012). https://doi.org/10.3386/w18315
12. Gagnon, E., Johannsen, B.K., Lopez-Salido, J.D.: Understanding the new normal: the role of demographics. Finance and Economics Discussion Series 2016–080. Board of Governors of the Federal Reserve System (2016). https://doi.org/10.17016/FEDS.2016.080
13. Vishnevsky, A.G.: Evolution of a Russian family. Ecology and Life **7**, 8–13 (2008)
14. Kuz'min, A.I.: Family in the Urals: Demographic aspects of life choice. Nauka, Yekaterinburg (1993)
15. Glazyev, S.Yu.: Global transformations from the perspective of technological and economic world order change. AlterEconomics **19**(1), 93–115 (2022). https://doi.org/10.31063/AlterEconomics/2022.19-1.6
16. Kabaeva, Y.G.: Patriarchal family as an object of research in the history of everyday life. Actual Problems of Humanities and Natural Sciences **7**(3), 73–75 (2015)
17. Kornilov, G.E.: Evolution of infant mortality in the Ural during the first half of the 20th century. Ural Historical Journal **3**(44), 80–89 (2014)
18. Gimpelson, V.: Does the Russian economy need human capital? Ten doubts. Voprosy Ekonomiki **10**, 129–143 (2016). https://doi.org/10.32609/0042-8736-2016-10-129-143
19. United Nations Development Programme: Human development report. Oxford University Press, New York (1992). https://www.un-ilibrary.org/content/books/9789210576536
20. United Nations Development Programme: Human development report 2021/2022. Oxford University Press, New York (2022). https://www.un-ilibrary.org/content/books/9789210016407
21. Grinin, L.E., Grinin, A.L.: Cybernetic revolution and the sixth technological wave. Historical Psychology and Sociology of History **1**, 172–197 (2015)
22. Shkolnikov, A.Y.: National strategies: Geostrategic view of the future of the world and Russia. St. Petersburg: Corvus (2020)
23. Bashina, O.E.: Tasks of statistical education in the period of transition from the fifth to the sixth technological wave. Federal State Statistics Service (Rosstat) (2023). https://www.gks.ru/publish/konferenc/bashina.pdf

The Specifics of Labor Pendulum Migration in Agglomeration Centers and Satellite Cities

Natalia M. Logacheva[1], Anna Uskova[2](✉), and Julia Salomatova[2]

[1] Chelyabinsk Branch of Institute of Economics of the Ural Branch of the Russian Academy of Sciences, 155/1 Svobody Street, 454091 Chelyabinsk, Russia
logacheva.nm@uiec.ru

[2] Institute of Economics of the Ural Branch of the Russian Academy of Sciences, 29 Moskovskaya Street, 620014 Ekaterinburg, Russia
{uskova.ay,salomatova.jv}@uiec.ru

Abstract. Labor intraregional migration is based on different strategies in different periods of a person's life, and as a phenomenon in the labor market it has a significant impact on the quantity and quality of able-bodied population located in the territory. This article is a continuation of the research devoted to the analysis of the possibilities of social networks in identifying the peculiarities of labor intraregional migration of cities with millions of people in the Russian Federation. Official statistical data do not allow us to estimate the magnitude of labor intraregional migration in terms of gender and age. The purpose of this article is to evaluate the possibilities of social network data in the analysis of the gender and age structure of labor intraregional migration on the example of two cities with millions of inhabitants (Yekaterinburg and Chelyabinsk) and their satellite cities. The main research methods were social network analytics, comparative analysis, statistical methods and data visualization. The empirical data were anonymized data of VKontakte social network users and Rosstat data. The analysis revealed the scale, directions and specific features of the gender and age structure of labor intraregional migration of the cities under study. It was found that the main share of labor intraregional migrants from satellite cities to agglomeration centers are people aged 29–43, with women being more active at the age of 29–38 and men at the age of 29–43, the share of women is generally lower than men. The high share of women leaving for work in another city, which exceeds not only the corresponding indicator in satellite cities, but is also higher than the share of men (51% for Yekaterinburg and 65% for Chelyabinsk), is a peculiarity of labor intraregional migration of residents of cities with a million inhabitants. The results of the study can contribute to the targeted management of migration flows, be used in the development of regional and municipal strategies of socio-economic development, the formation of programs to support employment of the population of certain age groups, as well as planning the location of transport infrastructure facilities. Further research by the authors will be aimed at expanding the range of cities and clarifying the regularity of labor migrants' trips using additional tools - analysis of cellular operators' data.

Keywords: Intraregional migration · Pendulum migration · Labour migration · Spatial development · Social networks

E. Kuzmin et al. (Eds.): EASET 2024, SPBE, pp. 246–259, 2025.
https://doi.org/10.1007/978-3-031-91159-0_16

JEL Classifications: J6 · R1 · R23

1 Introduction

In studies of different years, for example in the article of Lukić, V. and in the article of Dimitrios Tsiotas, Konstantinos Raptopoulos, it is shown that cities with high population attract large amounts of switching activity [1], and there is also a general trend in which pendulum migrants choose settlements with larger population than in their place of residence [2].

Cities with a million inhabitants, which are the main centers of attraction for internal Russian migrants, draw the population not only from the peripheral territories, but also from the suburbs [3]. At the same time, at the regional level, the overall positive dynamics of socio-economic development can be observed in parallel with increasing polarization between municipalities due to the significant impact on the number of able-bodied population.

Migration processes are age-selective, and gender differences are also one of factors influencing variability of scale and directions of comutting [4], which in the context of the implementation of socio-economic policy at the municipal level (in terms of its impact on the labor market), poses the task to depart from typical programs and focus on the preservation of the population of certain age and gender groups that are more inclined to seek employment outside the city of residence.

Strong polarization of labor market between centers of agglomerations and satellite cities initiates large-scale return labor and permanent migration [3], while often with labor pendulum migration, "full migration begins", in this case a person is not just looking for a place of work that provides an opportunity to receive a higher level of salary, but is also looking at a new city as a potential for final relocation. Such an algorithm of actions can lead to demographic changes both in the "receiving" its population city and in the "losing one". In this regard, intraregional migration requires special attention of municipal authorities to manage migration processes [5]. For this purpose, data are needed to assess the scale, direction and peculiarities of intraregional migration of a particular territory. Possibilities of obtaining these data are quite limited, since Russia does not keep official records of pendulum migrants, which creates the need to search for tools that allow tracking migration flows, especially information base at municipal level needs to be clarified [6].

Purpose of the article: to show that social network data allow us to obtain prompt, relevant information on intraregional labor migration at the municipal level for the development of measures to regulate the local labor market, taking into account the gender and age specifics of migration.

2 Reviewing Previous Research

Researchers agree that there is no standardized, generally accepted definition of intraregional (pendulum) migration, as the process has its own peculiarities [7, 8]. This is due to the fact that depending on its duration and the territories in which the movement takes place, there are significant features that lead to the use of different terms, although the phenomenon of intraregional migration itself means repeated migration processes involving more than one movement (migration) and return. In this article, term "migration" is used in the broadest sense of the word, that is, it is not supposed to change the place of permanent residence.

Thus, the labor pendulum migration that occurs between countries (circular migration), which is positioned as a "triple win" solution for labor markets (meaning that it solves the problems of two countries and the worker), although it involves a return type of movement, implies a longer stay of a person in the territory, and therefore more often refers to temporary migration [9].

The next option is migration between regions (internal migration), often associated with shift work, relocation to regions with special working conditions [10]. In contrast, intraregional migration, which in its direction can be through urban to urban or rural to urban displacement (rural-urban circular migration), involves more closely spaced areas and may be shorter in duration. The scale of such migration can be very substantial. In China, the flow of migrants in internal migration over short distances (short-distance migrant workers) increased from 159 million people in 2011 to 171.9 million in 2022 [11]. The most active type of labor intraregional migration is daily recursive migration (the day-to-day recursive), requiring from the employee to be ready to spend time daily to move from the place of residence to work and back, which actualizes the demand for a high level of transport connectivity of territories. Meanwhile, Begoña Guirao, Juan Luis Campa, Natalia Casado-Sanz in their study showed (in the case of the Madrid functional area) that station location was cited as a key indicator that is even more important than the actual availability of commuter transportation services [12].

Labor intraregional migration has a significant impact both on the people involved in it and on the territories with which this process is associated. "Internal migration processes taking place on the territory of Russia, due to serious regional disproportions in the level of socio-economic development, have become a factor in the growth of uneven distribution of the population across the territory of the country" [13].

Sometimes labor migration from less developed areas can become "excessive, leading to underinvestment in vacancies and therefore in production" [14]. However, the "siphon effect" of easier commuting is not always harmful, and it can also help reduce labor wastage [15]. Given that labor migration, including intraregional migration, can be spontaneous/voluntary (unregulated) and purposeful (regulated), i.e. arising as a result of adopted programs, strategic documents, in the field of labor and employment, it becomes obvious to request a study of the gender and age structure of migrants. This understanding is necessary to identify opportunities to preserve labor resources in the territory or to regulate this process in accordance with the goals of socio-economic development and demographic situation.

Obviously, there are fundamental differences in attitudes and motivations across gender and age groups [16], as well as regional peculiarities of population migration (in particular, for elderly migrants, established in the study of Karachurina, Ivanova [17]. Pointing out that "commuting migration becomes an important factor in the realization of labor potential of the population, allowing to find a place of employment outside the locality of primary residence", researchers study a wide range of age groups, analyzing school, student, labor intraregional migration [18].

The most difficult to analyze is labor intraregional migration, since official statistical data that allow to study it are extremely limited. At the same time, the fact that intraregional migration "pulls away" labor resources, reducing opportunities for solving regional and municipal socio-economic problems, moreover, aggravating local problems of the territory, "the intensity of migration processes at the in-country level requires a targeted approach to migration management" [16]. At the same time, the developed employment support programs (both at the regional and municipal levels) are very general and do not take into account local specifics, in particular, the gender and age of migrants due to the inability to promptly assess the structure of migrants.

Studies of intraregional (circular) migration in some regions confirm that local labor markets have their own specifics. For example, a sample survey of intraregional migration of rural population in Nizhny Novgorod Oblast revealed that the share of women is 57% and among intraregional migrants, both men and women, the predominance of young people compared to other workers (17–30 years old) is characteristic [19]. In contrast to the peculiarities of "circular migration" of the rural population, the results of a questionnaire survey of the population of six cities of the Urals Federal District in the Sverdlovsk, Tyumen and Kurgan Oblasts showed that among intraregional labor migrants the share of women is 48%, while among young people aged 20–29 the share of women is significantly lower (only 29%) and with increasing age the share of women grows to 43–46% [20].

Study of pendulum migration based on data from the VKontakte social network, conducted on the example of Russian cities with millions of people, showed that VKontakte data have high geographical detail and breadth of coverage of the research object and, taking into account assumptions, can be used to assess imbalance in labor market of a particular city [21].

At the same time, there are not many studies on socio-demographic characteristics of intraregional labor migrants due to the limited statistical records of this category of population, and the main source of information in this area are sociological surveys and interviews [22], whereas the possibilities of new data sources, such as social networks [23], data from mobile operators [24] allow us to take a new approach to the analysis of labor intraregional migration, providing not only gender and age detail, but also geographical detail.

Given the importance of labor intraregional migration for the territories, in our view, it is necessary to deepen the analysis of intraregional migration, which will make it possible to develop specific measures to support the local labor market. In this sense, the gender and age structure of migrants is important because it not only influences the structure of the able-bodied population, but also generally affects the demographic processes of the territory.

3 Materials and Methods

The empirical base of the study was the impersonal database of users of the VKontakte social network formed by authors in March-April 2023, whose place of residence is one of the cities selected for the study – Russian cities with millions of people (with exception of federal cities of Moscow and St. Petersburg), or one of 97 settlements included in the agglomeration zones of these million-plus cities. In total, the database included information about 9.165 million users of VKontakte social network aged 14 to 74 years (the computer program was used "Obtaining data on labor migration based on VKontakte user profiles (certificate number: RU 2023619437 [25]), written in Python programming language). At the first stage, user accounts that have been blocked or inactive since the beginning of 2022 were excluded from the search in order not to take into account irrelevant data. When uploading data for further aggregation, all users have such characteristics as: gender, age, employment (school or university, job (city of work)).

At the second stage, based on the set research goal - to form a demographic portrait of labor intraregional migrant, 396 thousand VKontakte users who indicated their place of work were selected from the prepared database. Then, based on the classification of World Health Organization from 2016, they were grouped by gender and age (females and males in 12 age groups each (14–18 years, 19–23 years, 24–28, 29–33 years, 34–38 years, 39–43 years, 44–48 years, 49–53 years, 54–58 years, 54–58 years, 59–63 years, 64–68 years, and 69–73 years). In general, the share of VKontakte users who indicated their place of work was 2.7% of the number of residents of the analyzed cities in the given age period (14–74 years old). At the same time, Rosstat sample surveys cover 0.24% of the total number of households (the sample is over 130 thousand households). For other federal statistical observations on socio-demographic issues the sample is 60–100 thousand households.

In order to determine the peculiarities of labor intraregional migration depending on gender and age, data on Yekaterinburg and 11 of its satellites, Chelyabinsk and 8 of its satellites were analyzed for the gender and age distribution of users with the specified locality of work. Taking into account the proximity of cities, the study assumes that people who indicated another city as their place of work migrate daily (recursive). Cities with an extremely small number of objects for the study (Uralsky settlement of the Sverdlovsk Oblast) were excluded from the analysis.

4 Results and Discussion

The obtained data show (Fig. 1) that the main share of labor intraregional migrants from satellite cities to agglomeration centers are people aged 29–43 years - 64%, another 15% are people aged 19–28 years and almost 13% are people aged 44–53 years. Both men and women are more active at the age of 29–38 years, significant differences appear after 38 years (men remain highly active until the age of 43). The share of women in general is lower than men and amounts to 45%. This result is confirmed by research conducted through population surveys [20], which indicates the comparability of the VKontakte social network data.

However, for certain ages (29–33 years and 34–38 years), the share of women is higher - 50.8% and 51.3%, respectively, which is in line with migration trends in general [26].

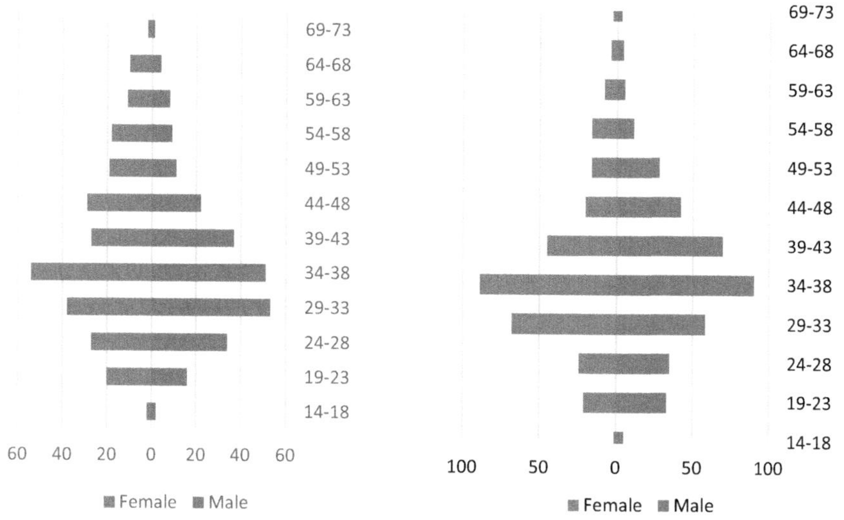

a) from Yekaterinburg to satellite cities b) from satellite cities to Yekaterinburg

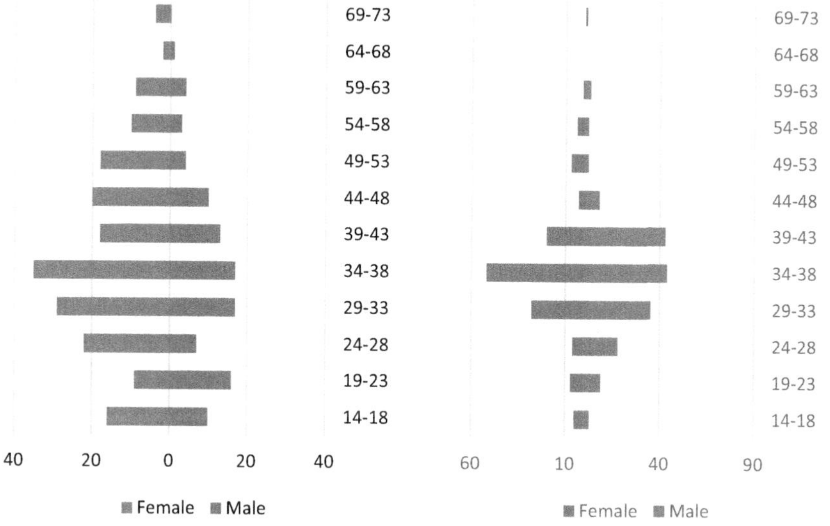

a) from Chelyabinsk to satellite cities b) from satellite cities to Chelyabinsk

Fig. 1. Gender and age structure of intraregional labor migration from satellite cities to the center of agglomeration in the Sverdlovsk and Chelyabinsk Oblasts, people.

In contrast to satellite cities, intraregional labor migration of residents of cities with a million inhabitants is distinguished by a number of peculiarities (Figs. 1, 2). First, the share of women traveling to work in another city is much higher than in satellite cities, and even higher than that of men. For example, from Yekaterinburg the share of women in labor migrants leaving for work in satellite cities is 51%, and from Chelyabinsk - 65%.

Secondly, a high proportion of intraregional labor migrants are aged 24–28 and 44–48.

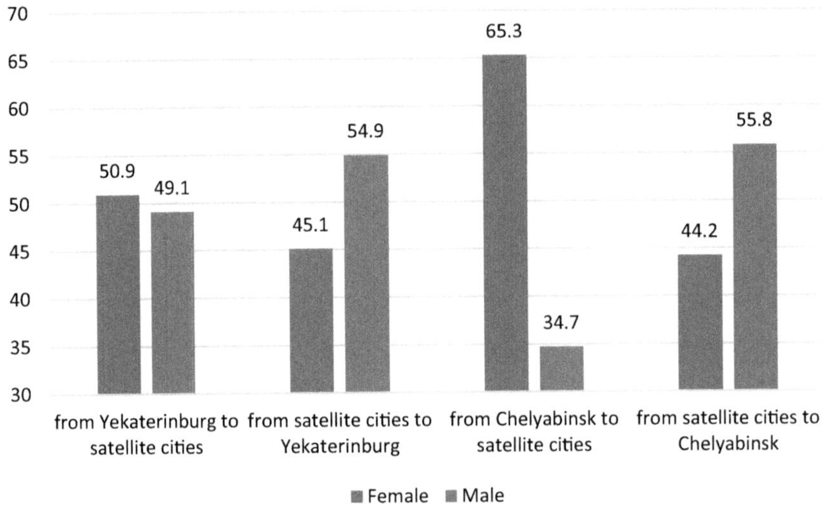

Fig. 2. Ratio of women to men among labor migrants of the Yekaterinburg and Chelyabinsk agglomerations.

Taking into account the values close to zero for the age groups of 14–18, 64–68, 69–73 years, in further conclusions these age groups are excluded from the analysis.

In the satellite cities of Yekaterinburg, the gender and age structure of labor intraregional migration is represented to a greater extent by men and women aged 34–38, while in general for all ages the share of male intraregional migrants is higher than that of women (Tables 1, 2).

Taking into account the activity (the presence of maximum values of the share of migrants in the age group) 3 groups, including people aged 29 to 43 years old, constitute the “core” of the migration process of Yekaterinburg satellite cities.

Table 1. Share of women living in satellite cities of Yekaterinburg involved in labor intraregional migration, % of the total number of VKontakte users of the respective city who indicated their place of work Yekaterinburg.

Age group, years	19-23	24-28	29-33	34-38	39-43	44-48	49-53	54-58	59-63	Share of persons from the total number of VK users of the city who indicated Yekaterinburg as their place of work
Sredneuralsk	9.1	0.0	9.1	**15.2**	3.0	3.0	0.0	3.0	3.0	45.5
Verkhnyaya Pyshma	3.1	5.0	8.8	**13.8**	5.6	1.3	1.9	2.5	0.0	41.9
Zarechny	0.0	5.3	7.9	**15.8**	7.9	2.6	7.9	2.6	0.0	**50.6**
Pervouralsk	3.7	2.2	**11.8**	9.6	4.4	2.2	3.7	2.2	0.0	39.7
Berezovsky	4.0	3.0	**11.0**	12.0	6.0	4.0	0.0	3.0	3.0	46.0
Sysert	6.7	3.3	3.3	**23.3**	0.0	0.0	0.0	3.3	0.0	40.0
Aramil	0.0	9.5	7.1	**21.4**	9.5	4.8	4.8	2.4	2.4	**61.9**
Degtyarsk	0.0	0.0	5.6	11.1	**16.7**	5.6	0.0	5.6	0.0	44.4
Polevskoy	1.6	4.7	6.3	9.4	**10.9**	4.7	1.6	0.0	1.6	40.6
Revda	1.4	0.0	**14.3**	10.0	7.1	4.3	2.9	0.0	2.9	42.9
Verkhneye Dubrovo	0.0	0.0	**20.0**	0.0	**20.0**	0.0	0.0	**20.0**	0.0	**60.0**
Total:	3.0	3.4	9.7	**12.8**	6.4	2.9	2.3	2.3	1.1	44.0

Note: gray fill is plotted in age groups with zero share, maximum shares of migrants in the corresponding satellite city are shown in bold. In the cities of Sredneuralsk, Verkhnyaya Pyshma, Zarechny, Pervouralsk, and Berezovsky there were single cases of migration in older age groups (64–73 years), not specified in the table.
Data source: compiled by the authors based on the results of their own research.

In Aramil, Verkhneye Dubrovo and Zarechny, the share of women included in the process of labor intraregional migration exceeds the share of men and 50% of those who indicated Yekaterinburg as their place of work.

Of all the analyzed groups, both among women and men, the highest share of migrants was recorded in Sysert (23.3%). Analysis of the gender and age structure of intraregional migration among men revealed the only city (Verkhnyaya Pyshma), where men of all age groups under study are involved in the migration process.

The peculiarities of the sex and age structure of Chelyabinsk satellite cities are presented in Tables 3 and 4. The most active age group among both women and men are labor migrants aged 34–38.

The share of women included in the labor migration process exceeds the share of men and 50% of those who indicated Chelyabinsk as their place of work in Argayash and Dolgoderevenskoye. At the same time, the maximum shares of migrants among women

Table 2. Share of men living in satellite cities of Yekaterinburg involved in labor intraregional migration, % of the total number of VKontakte users of the respective city who indicated their place of work Yekaterinburg.

Age group, years	19-23	24-28	29-33	34-38	39-43	44-48	49-53	54-58	59-63	Share of persons from the total number of VK users of the city who indicated Yekaterinburg as their place of work
Sredneuralsk	0.0	6.1	**18.2**	3.0	6.1	12.1	0.0	3.0	3.0	51.5
Verkhnyaya	5.6	6.3	7.5	**12.5**	11.3	5.0	3.1	0.6	0.6	57.5
Age group, years	19-23	24-28	29-33	34-38	39-43	44-48	49-53	54-58	59-63	Share of persons from the total number of VK users of the city who indicated Yekaterinburg as their place of work
Pyshma										
Zarechny	2.6	2.6	**10.5**	7.9	7.9	5.3	5.3	2.6	0.0	47.4
Pervouralsk	7.4	5.9	5.1	**15.4**	11.0	7.4	4.4	0.7	0.0	58.1
Berezovsky	5.0	5.0	8.0	**15.0**	6.0	5.0	6.0	2.0	0.0	52.0
Sysert	6.7	0.0	10.0	**23.3**	13.3	3.3	0.0	0.0	3.3	**60.0**
Aramil	2.4	2.4	4.8	4.8	**7.1**	**7.1**	4.8	2.4	0.0	38.1
Degtyarsk	11.1	5.6	5.6	**11.1**	**11.1**	0.0	5.6	0.0	5.6	55.6
Polevskoy	3.1	3.1	9.4	14.1	**15.6**	6.3	4.7	1.6	0.0	59.4
Revda	1.4	5.7	**12.9**	**12.9**	8.6	5.7	4.3	4.3	1.4	57.1
Verkhneye Dubrovo	0.0	**20.0**	0.0	**20.0**	0.0	0.0	0.0	0.0	0.0	40.0
Total:	4.7	5.0	8.3	**12.9**	9.9	6.0	4.0	1.6	0.7	54.9

Note: gray fill is plotted in age groups with zero share, maximum shares of migrants in the corresponding satellite city are shown in bold. In the cities of Verkhnyaya Pyshma, Zarechny, Pervouralsk, Aramil there were single cases of migration in older age groups (64–73 years), not specified in the table.

Data source: compiled by the authors based on the results of their own research.

are recorded in the age group 29–33 years in Argayash (25%), and among men - in the villages of Yetkul and Kunashak (33.3%).

Table 3. Share of women living in Chelyabinsk satellite cities involved in labor intraregional migration, % of the total number of VKontakte users of the respective city who indicated their place of work Chelyabinsk.

Age group, years	19-23	24-28	29-33	34-38	39-43	44-48	49-53	54-58	59-63	Share of persons from the total number of VK users of the city who indicated Chelyabinsk as their place of work
Yemangelinsk	0.0	0.0	4.3	17.0	6.4	4.3	6.4	2.1	0.0	40.4
Kopeysk	2.6	2.2	11.2	18.1	7.8	0.0	0.0	0.0	0.0	41.8
Korkino	3.9	5.2	7.8	11.7	3.9	1.3	5.2	1.3	0.0	40.3
Argayash	0.0	0.0	25.0	8.3	8.3	0.0	0.0	16.7	0.0	58.3
Dolgoderevenskoe	0.0	0.0	10.0	20.0	20.0	0.0	10.0	0.0	0.0	60.0
Yetkul	0.0	0.0	0.0	0.0	16.7	0.0	16.7	0.0	0.0	33.3
Kunashak	0.0	0.0	16.7	16.7	0.0	0.0	0.0	0.0	0.0	33.3
Miasskoye	7.1	0.0	0.0	21.4	7.1	0.0	0.0	7.1	7.1	50.0
Total:	2.5	2.2	9.7	16.3	7.2	0.7	2.2	1.2	0.2	42.3

Note: gray fill is plotted in age groups with zero share, maximum shares of migrants in the corresponding satellite city are shown in bold.
Data source: compiled by the authors based on the results of their own research.

Taking into account the activity (the presence of maximum values of the share of migrants in the age group) among women 3 groups including people aged 29 to 43 years, and among men 4 groups: from 24 to 43 years make up the "core" of the migration process of Chelyabinsk satellite cities.

At the same time, in these age groups, the share of persons from the total number of VKontakte users living in Chelyabinsk satellite cities who indicated their place of work as Chelyabinsk is greater than in the corresponding groups in Yekaterinburg. Also, unlike Yekaterinburg, there are no VKontakte users among men in almost all satellite cities of Chelyabinsk in the age groups over 44 years old who would indicate their place of work in the city with a million inhabitants, which may indicate a lower social and labor mobility of representatives of these age groups.

Table 4. Share of men living in Chelyabinsk satellite cities involved in labor intraregional migration, % of the total number of VKontakte users of the respective city who indicated their place of work Chelyabinsk.

Age group, years	19-23	24-28	29-33	34-38	39-43	44-48	49-53	54-58	59-63	Share of persons from the total number of VK users of the city who indicated Chelyabinsk as their place of work
Yemangelinsk	8.5	2.1	6.4	2.1	14.9	4.3	4.3	2.1	2.1	46.8
Kopeysk	3.9	8.6	12.9	17.2	13.4	0.0	0.0	0.0	0.0	56.0
Korkino	2.6	2.6	10.4	16.9	13.0	7.8	1.3	2.6	1.3	58.4
Argayash	0.0	25.0	0.0	8.3	0.0	8.3	0.0	0.0	0.0	41.7
Age group, years	19-23	24-28	29-33	34-38	39-43	44-48	49-53	54-58	59-63	Share of persons from the total number of VK users of the city who indicated Chelyabinsk as their place of work
Dolgoderevenskoe	0.0	0.0	0.0	10.0	30.0	0.0	0.0	0.0	0.0	40.0
Yetkul	0.0	33.3	0.0	16.7	0.0	0.0	0.0	0.0	0.0	50.0
Kunashak	0.0	0.0	33.3	0.0	16.7	0.0	0.0	0.0	0.0	50.0
Miasskoye	0.0	0.0	14.3	7.1	21.4	0.0	0.0	0.0	7.1	50.0
Total:	3.7	6.9	11.1	14.4	13.6	2.2	0.7	0.7	0.7	54.2

Note: gray fill is plotted in age groups with zero share, maximum shares of migrants in the corresponding satellite city are shown in bold.
Data source: compiled by the authors based on the results of their own research.

5 Conclusion

The study of migration flows of cities with a million inhabitants and satellite cities included in two regions of the Russian Federation has shown that the gender and age structure of intraregional labor migration has significant regional specifics.

Taking into account the fact that according to the survey results the most active group of both sexes are labor migrants at the age of 34–38 years - the optimal age for the creation and growth of a family and raising young children, we can conclude that most likely the decision on such a labor strategy is a forced necessity to find additional sources of income to support the family, both men and women, and especially for the last ones, considering the divorce statistics, the number of single-parent families and demographic processes.

Given that labor migration often leads to a change of residence and move to the city where the job is located, it becomes especially relevant for small towns to expand the local labor market in order to maintain the size of the permanent population.

At the same time, the role of intraregional migration processes in socio-economic development is not always taken into account in the development of municipal development strategies, programs aimed at supporting employment that affect people of a certain age, which is due to the lack of understanding of the municipal specifics of migration processes. Under such conditions, social network data analytics becomes a new tool for economic research in areas where other classical tools are limited in their use.

The practical significance of the study is that peculiarities of the gender and age structure of labor intraregional migration, identified in the framework of the study, can contribute to the targeted management of migration flows, the formation or adjustment of programs in the field of employment support for certain age groups.

The results obtained are correct, but taking into account the limitations of these social networks, in particular, they do not allow us to identify reasons that encourage population to work outside the city of residence, since the methods of social media analytics (SMA) used by the authors do not imply direct contact with population.

The proposed approach can be applied to study of other regions. A further direction of research could be to clarify the regularity of trips based on a deeper study of migration processes using data from cellular operators and additional research tools.

Acknowledgements. The article has been prepared in accordance with the research plan of the Institute of Economics of the Ural Branch of Russian Academy of Sciences for 2024–2026.

References

1. Tsiotas, D., Raptopoulos, K.: The Commuting Phenomenon as a Complex Network: The Case of Greece (2020). ArXiv Preprint. https://doi.org/10.48550/arxiv.2003.08096
2. Lukić, V.: Commuting in the settlement system of Serbia. Stanovništvo (2011). Retrieved from http://iriss.idn.org.rs/640/
3. Antonov, E.V., Kurichev, N.K., Treivish, A.I.: Studies of the urban system and agglomerations in Russia. Izvestiya Rossiiskoi Akademii Nauk. Seriya Geograficheskaya **86**(3), 310–331 (2022). https://doi.org/10.31857/S2587556622030037
4. Lukić, V.: Sex differences in commuting in Serbia. Glasnik Srpskog Geografskog Društva **87**(2), 67–77 (2007). https://doi.org/10.2298/GSGD0702067L
5. Mu, X., Yeh, A.G.-O.: Regional delineation of China based on commuting flows. Environ. Plan. A Econ. Space **52**(3), 478–482 (2019). https://doi.org/10.1177/0308518x19873006
6. Karachurina, L.B., Mkrtchyan, N.V., Savoskul, M.S.: New data and traditional approaches: How Russian geographers study population migration (2010–2021). Izvestiya Rossiiskoi Akademii Nauk. Seriya Geograficheskaya **86**(3), 353–373 (2022)

7. Sokolova, A.A., Kalachikova, O.N.: Circular migration: conceptual measurement problems. Econ. North-West Prob. Prospects Dev. **1**(68), 52–66 (2022). https://doi.org/10.52897/2411-4588-2022-1-52-66
8. Gregson, N.: Work, labour and mobility: Opening up a dialogue between mobilities and political economy through mobile work. Mobilities **18**(6), 888–902 (2023). https://doi.org/10.1080/17450101.2022.2158041
9. Wickramasekara, P.: Circular migration: A triple win or a dead end. Global Union Research Network Discussion Paper No 15 (2011). https://doi.org/10.2139/ssrn.1834762
10. Radovanović, S., Delibašić, B., Suknović, M., Vukanović, S.: Can we identify what are the causes and effects of internal migrations? The case of Serbia. Procedia Comput. Sci. **221**, 1329–1336 (2023). https://doi.org/10.1016/j.procs.2023.08.122
11. China Labour Bulletin: Migrant Workers and Their Children (2023). Retrieved from https://clb.org.hk/en/content/migrant-workers-and-their-children
12. Guirao, B., Campa, J.L., Casado-Sanz, N.: Labour mobility between cities and metropolitan integration: the role of high-speed rail commuting in Spain. Cities **78**, 140–154 (2018). https://doi.org/10.1016/j.cities.2018.02.008
13. Kozlova, O.A., Tukhtarova, E.: Socio-economic inequality as a factor of formation of migration flows. Narodonaselenie [Population] **4**, 78–90 (2017). (in Russ.)
14. Marchiori, L., Pascal, J., Pierrard, O.: (In)efficient commuting and migration choices: theory and policy in an urban search model. Reg. Sci. Urban Econ. **102**, 103936 (2023). https://doi.org/10.1016/j.regsciurbeco.2023.103936
15. Hu, Y., Deng, T., Zhang, J.: Can commuting facilitation relieve spatial misallocation of labor? Habitat Int. **106**, 102136 (2020). https://doi.org/10.1016/j.habitatint.2020.102136
16. Leonidova, G.V., Vyacheslavov, V.N.: Gender specifics of intraregional migration. Issues Territ. Dev. **2**(32), 4 (2016)
17. Karachurina, L.B., Ivanova, K.A.: Migration of the elderly population in Russia (according to the 2010 population census). Reg. Res. Russ. **9**, 164–172 (2019). https://doi.org/10.1134/s2079970519020059
18. Bedrina, E.B., Kozlova, O.A., Ishukov, A.A.: Methodology aspects in estimating commuting of the population. Ars Administrandi **10**(4), 631–648 (2018). https://doi.org/10.17072/2218-9173-2018-4-631-648
19. Shevchenko, I.A., Davydova, Y.V., Zamashkina, O.V., Zarubina, N.V., Lyabina, A.N., Bikmayeva, A.V.: The study of demographic aspects of circular migration of the population of Nizhny Novgorod region. Adv. Curr. Nat. Sci. **1**, 70–75 (2020). https://doi.org/10.17513/use.37323
20. Zakharchenko, A.A., Pit, V.V.: Regional features of circular labor migration in the Ural Federal District (using the example of a pilot study). Bull. Perm Univ. Philos. Psychol. Sociol. **4**, 594–603 (2018). https://doi.org/10.17072/2078-7898/2018-4-594-603
21. Uskova, A.Y., Logacheva, N.M., Salomatova, J.V., Salomatov, N.I.: The use of social media to study the features of commuting in Russian million-plus cities. Econ. Regions **19**(4), 1121–1134 (2023). https://doi.org/10.17059/ekon.reg.2023-4-13
22. Gavrilyuk, T.V., Bocharov, VYu.: The readiness assessment regarding labor migration of the new working-class youth. Semiotic Stud. **1**(2), 83–90 (2021). https://doi.org/10.18287/2782-2966-2021-1-2-83-90
23. Zamyatina, N.: Studying youth migrations through social networks data: Tomsk State University as a 'centre that produces and distributes' human capital (based on VKontakte social network data). Reg. Res. **36**(2), 15–28 (2012). (in Russ.)
24. Yumaguzin, V.V.: Opportunities and limitations of mobile operators' data in the study of population migration. In: Proceedings of the 2nd All-Russian Demographic Forum with International Participation, pp. 4–5 (2020). FCTAS RAS

25. Mkrtchyan, N.V.: Sex imbalances in long-term migration flows in Russia. Demogr. Rev. **8**(3), 6–19 (2021). https://doi.org/10.17323/demreview.v8i3.13264
26. Salomatova, Y.V., Salomatov, N.I.: Obtaining data on labor migration based on VKontakte user profiles [Computer program]. Certificate number: RU 2023619437 (2023)

New Trends in the Theory of Monetary Economics and Finance

Hypothesis on the Essence of Money as a Universal Equivalent of Stock of Negentropy in Economy

Vadim F. Islamutdinov(✉)

Urgench State University, 14 Kh.Alimdjan Street, Urgench 220100, Uzbekistan
isvad74@gmail.com

Abstract. The paper puts forward the hypothesis that money is a universal equivalent of stock of negentropy in the economy. The relevance of the research topic is underscored by the indispensable role of money in modern society. The paper generalizes the existing theoretical concepts of money, shows the way they solve the questions of whether money has intrinsic value, and what is the source of trust in money. We introduce the concepts of negentropy, source of negentropy, stock of negentropy and universal impersonal trust as a methodological basis of the negentropic approach to the substantiation of the essence of money in the economy. The importance of universal impersonal trust for ensuring the universality of money as an equivalent of stock of negentropy is shown. The essence of money as a universal equivalent of stock of negentropy is revealed. The laws of monetary circulation are explained from the point of view of the negentropic approach. We give an explanation of the functions of money in terms of the negentropic approach. Similarities and differences of the author's hypothesis with already existing alternative theories of money essence are shown. The advantages and disadvantages of the negentropic approach to the substantiation of the essence of money are discussed, possible areas of practical application of the hypothesis are outlined. The conclusion gives recommendations and prospects for using the hypothesis of the essence of money as a universal equivalent of the stock of negentropy in the economy.

Keywords: Money · Negentropy · Economic entropy

JEL Classifications: E42 · E49

1 Introduction

The concept of money has long captured the interest of economic scientists, starting with the works of mercantilists. Which is only natural, since a modern market economy cannot function without a robust monetary system. Money is such an important economic institution that many people call it the blood of economy, emphasizing its importance for the normal functioning of the market mechanism [1]. Even non-market economic systems cannot do without money yet, which was well demonstrated by the history of

E. Kuzmin et al. (Eds.): EASET 2024, SPBE, pp. 263–282, 2025.
https://doi.org/10.1007/978-3-031-91159-0_17

monetary circulation in the USSR, which could partially do without money inside the country, but had to organize a full-fledged monetary system for the needs of foreign trade [2], as well as by the history of the development of African monetary systems, including in the pre-colonial period and in traditional societies with non-market economies [3].

Although attempts to build a society of social harmony without money have been made quite a few times and on different theoretical and methodological basis, for example [4], and [5]. In practice, an economically developed, partially cashless society only really exists in Amish communities [6], who provide most services to each other in the form of barter. However, the Amish are forced to use money to interact with the outside world, also economic differentiation is increasing among the Amish due to the accumulation of land and other non-monetary forms of wealth. This is indicative of the fact that these attempts have not achieved complete success, which once again emphasizes the utopianism of the very idea of building a developed economic system without the use of money or at least some of its substitutes or analogues.

However, despite the fact that the phenomenon of money is so important for economic science and economic practice, most contemporary economic scholars refrain from delving into the fundamental essence of money. One of the reasons for this position of researchers is the point of view inherited from the authorities of neoclassical economic theory, who recognize the fact of existence of money as self-evident and not requiring an explanation of its in-depth essence.

Most modern researchers study various narrow aspects of the money circulation system, individual problems or phenomena in this system, leaving the whole picture out of focus. At the same time, there are many papers that summarize and comprehend the accumulated experience and current problems of the organization of monetary circulation. For example, one can note the works by Stephanie Kelton, one of the leading researchers of modern monetary theory [7], L. Randall Wray, a specialist in monetary theory and the history of money [8], Warren Mosler, one of the founders of modern monetary theory who studies the functioning of sovereign currencies [9], Bill Mitchell, an economics professor known for his work on modern monetary theory and macroeconomic policy [10], Scott Fullwiler, who studies the operational aspects of the monetary system and the interaction between central banks and commercial banks [11].

However, the existence of a large number of theories of money [12–15], many of them poorly consistent with each other [16], and often performing as poorly in practice [17], allows us to conclude that the essence of money has not yet been fully revealed. In addition, the emergence of new quasi-money phenomena, such as crypto-assets and cryptocurrencies, makes it necessary to take a new look at the essence of money and try to find a more solid theoretical basis to explain its essence [18]. The hypothesis of negentropic essence of money can serve as such a theoretical basis.

The author's hypothesis of negentropic essence of money, which is an evolutionary development of the entropic approach in economic research, can serve as such a theoretical basis. The essence of this hypothesis is that money is a universal equivalent of stock of negentropy in the economy.

Hence, the aim of this paper is to articulate the hypothesis of the negentropic essence of money, structured around several key objectives. Firstly, it examines existing theoretical frameworks regarding the essence of money. Subsequently, it introduces and refines the core terminology underpinning the negentropic approach, including concepts such as negentropy, sources of negentropy, stock of negentropy, and universal impersonal trust. Building upon these foundations, the hypothesis of the negentropic essence of money is substantiated. The hypothesis further provides explanations for the laws governing monetary circulation and the functional roles of money through the lens of the negentropic perspective.

The paper's structure is aligned with these objectives, beginning with a literature review that surveys theoretical contributions to the understanding of money's essence and explores prior applications of the entropic framework. The methodological section establishes definitions for critical concepts such as negentropy and universal trust, forming the theoretical backbone of the analysis. The results section elucidates the comparative nuances of economic behavior versus physical systems, formulates the hypothesis, and applies it to interpret monetary laws and functions. In the discussion, the advantages and limitations of adopting a negentropic approach to money are critically assessed. The conclusion synthesizes the findings and outlines the broader implications of this perspective for monetary theory and practice.

2 Literature Review

There are many theories of money, which in one way or another claim to reveal the essence of money, its role in economy and functions it performs. One can mention several works in which the authors try to summarize the existing multitude of monetary theories.

The paper [14] investigates the evolution of theoretical approaches to explaining the essence of money beginning with the classics of economic science and up to the present day. Also, the paper attempts to identify the relationship between the existing approaches to the rationale of the essence of money. The paper [15] also reviews the existing theories of money, compares these theories with each other, and identifies their advantages and disadvantages. However, the most interesting are the works trying to take a new view of the concept of money in economy and to find ways of its further development. Thus, the paper [19] shows the paradigm limitations of existing approaches to the formation of monetary theories and proposes an understanding of money as an institutional variable to characterize the amount of useful work performed and the corresponding part of GDP.

To understand the diversity of theoretical approaches to the theory of money, we can put them together (Table 1).

As can be seen from the table, most modern theoretical concepts of money tend to believe that the source of trust in money is both the market and the state. When answering the question of whether money has any intrinsic value, there is no consensus among representatives of different theories. Most likely, in fact, money has a dual nature, that is, it has its own value and also acts as an intermediary in exchange.

Even more interesting are works that attempt to provide a theoretical rationale for money on a new theoretical and methodological basis. One such rapidly developing approach is the entropic approach. The reason why economists are turning to the entropic approach to substantiate the essence of money is that existing theories of money cannot cope with the new challenges of modern economy. One such challenge is that the modern

Table 1. Diversity of theoretical approaches to the substantiation of the essence of money.

Theoretical Approach Name	Core idea	Intrinsic money value presumption	Source of trust in money
Evolutionary (metallic) theory	The amount of a particular precious metal reflects the purchasing power of money	Recognized	Market only
Nominalist theory	The purchasing power of money is determined by the money unit's face value, not by its material substance	Not recognized	State only
State theory (chartalism)	The purchasing power of money is determined not in the market, but by a directive, and by the one who carries out its issue	Not recognized	State only
Theory of money as a technical medium of exchange	The role of money is only one - to fulfill the function of the means of exchange (circulation)	Not recognized	Market only
Capital-creative theory of credit (money)	Money, issued in credit form, contributes to the formation of capital, first in the form of loan capital and then real capital	Recognized	Market only
Social class approach to understanding money	Money plays an important role in the process of formation and appropriation of surplus value by capitalists (exploitation of the working class)	Not recognized	Market and state together

(*continued*)

Table 1. (*continued*)

Theoretical Approach Name	Core idea	Intrinsic money value presumption	Source of trust in money
Quantitative theory	Comparing the amount of money in circulation with the amount of goods produced in the economy	Recognized	Market only
Keynesian theory	In the short term, by "giving away money" it is possible to stimulate demand and thereby overcome economic crisis	Recognized	State only
Neo-Keynesian theory	The need to take inflation expectations into account when stimulating demand	Recognized	State only
Post-Keynesian theory	The formation of money supply is considered as an endogenous process, as a result of the activity of all economic agents in the economy	Recognized	Market and state together
Monetarist theory	It is necessary to gradually increase the supply of money in accordance with the growth of the supply of goods	Recognized	Market and state together
Neo-Austrian private/parallel money theory	The government is not the only issuer of money in the economy	Recognized	Market only
Free (neutral) money theory	Forming a monetary system that is free of interest and credit by imposing a special tax/fee that devalues money over time	Not recognized	State only

(*continued*)

Table 1. (*continued*)

Theoretical Approach Name	Core idea	Intrinsic money value presumption	Source of trust in money
Institutional theory	Money is considered as one of the economic institutions that form the "rules of the game" in the economy	Recognized	Market and state together
Neo-institutional theory	Money is considered as a tool for ensuring transactions, reducing transaction costs of economic actors	Recognized	Market and state together
Behavioral finance theory	There is a distortion of the use value of money by economic actors due to cognitive errors	Recognized	Market and state together
Information theory of money by K. Waltuch	The use value of money corresponds to the amount of information that money adds to the economic system	Not recognized	Market and state together
Theories of Islamic finance	The need for interest waivers is justified from a religious rather than a scientific perspective	Not recognized	State only

Note: compiled by the author based on [12–15]

monetary system is in almost no way adapted to take into account the environmental consequences of people's economic activities. For example, in this dissertation [20], Camargo attempts to propose a monetary innovation, the entropic money rate, with which environmental behavior can be incentivized. The entropic money rate is essentially a development of the theory of free (neutral) money [21] but differs in that the rate of money depreciation is not constant, but floating and depends on the pace of deterioration (i.e. entropy growth) in the environment. According to the idea of this dissertation, this situation should make all people think about the deterioration of environmental conditions and change their behavior to a more environmentally friendly one.

It is worth noting that the use of the term *entropy* as applied to money has been developed for a relatively long time in the works of representatives of the information theory of value [22], the essence of which is that money is a carrier of information in economy and thus reduces its entropy. The concept of entropy is also used in the thermodynamic approach to the theory of money [23]. The point is that the existing monetary systems contradict the second law of thermodynamics on the increase of entropy, as money can multiply indefinitely, while all other objects and subjects in economy are subject to the second law of thermodynamics, and this leads to the emergence of gaps between the amount of money and the amount of real economic benefits.

The paper [24] identifies five main areas of research related to the use of entropy in the context of business and economy, emphasizing that traditional economic thought does not take into account the tendency of systems to chaos and disorder expressed by the second law of thermodynamics. The exponential growth of publications in this area is observed, and new promising research areas are outlined, including the application of entropy to the analysis of cryptocurrency markets and the assessment of sustainable development in business.

We have already presented the entropic approach to the substantiation of the value of economic benefits in the paper "Prerequisites for the formation of a comprehensive theory of value based on the entropic approach" [25]. This paper shows that the gap between the real cost (value) of benefits and their price is explained by the fact that people lack a special sensory receptor to assess the objective level and dynamics of their personal entropy, as well as the impact of benefits on the entropy of society and the environment. As a result, people have to rely on subjective feeling of entropy level and dynamics when making economic decisions. So, it is money that serves as this subjective measure of how much negative entropy or negentropy, allowing to reduce personal entropy, is contained in certain economic benefits. Therefore, the hypothesis is put forward that the essence of money is that it is a universal equivalent of stock of negentropy in economy.

Despite the attractiveness of the entropy approach, there are certain limitations to its application in economy. In particular, Ruth [26] points out such limitations:

- computational complexity: calculating entropy for complex systems such as economy is difficult because of the need for detailed information on material and energy flows;
- limited applicability: most studies using thermodynamics for economic analysis are based on equilibrium thermodynamics, which does not fully reflect the dynamic nature of the economy and ecosystem;
- analogy problem: the use of entropy in economy is often based on analogies with physical systems, which can lead to misinterpretations, e.g. equilibrium in the economic sense is not equivalent to thermodynamic equilibrium.
- insufficient predictive power: although the concept of entropy helps to understand the limitations of economic growth and the importance of sustainable development, it does not offer particular solutions or predictions.

The application of the entropy approach in economic research has also attracted more serious criticism. For example, the paper [27] criticizes the basic concept of Georgescu-Roegen with regard to the application of entropy in economy, stating that although he has proved the evolutionary nature of the economic process at the physical level, he has failed to relate this to the necessity of qualitative changes at the economic level. Modern approaches to the use of entropy in economic research are criticized in the paper [28]. Yatsky points out that entropy is an extra-historical physical process, while economic value is a historically determined construct. That is, entropy affects the economy as a parameter of the external environment, not as an internal factor determining value. In conclusion, S.A. Yatsky expresses his concern that the reduction of economic theory to physics can lead to the loss of its specificity as a science.

3 Materials and Methods

To formulate the hypothesis of money as a universal equivalent of stock of negentropy, it is necessary to define the concepts of *negentropy*, *negentropy source* and *stock of negentropy*.

Most often negentropy is understood as the inverse of entropy. In this case, negentropy is equated with the amount of information that is added to the system as it becomes more ordered [22]. However, it should be kept in mind that the increase of information (order) in the system does not occur by itself, but it requires work. Any work, according to the laws of physics, involves the expenditure (dissipation) of energy. In addition, it requires the exchange of matter with the environment, because very often energy has an embodied form (food, fuel), and information, for that matter, exists on some material carrier.

We believe that the concept of negentropy is most correctly used in the framework of general systems theory in relation to biological evolution. The specificity of biological evolution is that only living systems can resist the action of the second law of thermodynamics on the constant growth of entropy. Of course, entropy reduction occurs locally and temporarily, as well as by accelerating the rate of entropy growth in the rest of the universe. For local entropy reduction, living systems require a constant inflow of matter, energy, and information from the environment, which is called *negentropy* or *negative entropy* [29].

Thus, for the purposes of this study, negentropy is understood as energy or information embodied in the form of goods, works and services that can be used by economic entities to regulate (most often reduce) their own entropy or the entropy level of the economic systems they manage.

Another important point for understanding the essence of money is what the source of negentropy is in economic systems. According to [30], the source of negentropy in physical systems is presented by differences (gradients) in energy potentials of various forms: chemo-heat, nuclear, hydraulic, gravitational, and electromagnetic. Accordingly, any of them can be used as a source of negentropy to reduce entropy in a living system. Economy is a kind of living systems, so in economy the source of negentropy is also differences in socio-economic potentials: between countries, between regions, between colony and metropolis, between city and village, between household and business, etc.

The tangible form of energy and information movement in economy results in the possibility of the stock of negentropy formation. Actually, the stock of negentropy tended to appear even in primitive living systems - as reserves of fat and other nutrients. However, only in economy the accumulation of the stock of negentropy has reached a new level and acquired gigantic scales. It is the material nature of the stock of negentropy that allows to alienate it in the form of economic benefits, first of all, goods. That is, goods are essentially materialized and alienated stock of negentropy.

Economic theory widely applies models using the concepts of flow and stock. For example, this paper [31] presents the structure of a stock-flow consistency model using matrices that incorporate transactions between different agents (flows) and the corresponding changes in balance sheets (stocks). The concept of capital corresponds most precisely to the stock of negentropy in economy. Capital in the economy also exists in two forms, as a flow and as a stock. Capital flow is investment, capital stock is fixed and current assets. In macroeconomic modeling, it is important to take into account the stock-flow relationship in order to build consistent models that incorporate the dynamics of economic processes. Models that take this relationship into account are called stock-flow consistent models [32].

As for the category of trust, Economic science identifies two types of trust: personalized (interpersonal) and depersonalized (impersonal, institutional) [33]. The first type of trust is rather subjective, as it requires trusting people based on some subjective feelings. Impersonal trust is the trust provided not by the characteristics of a particular person, but by something objective that exists separately from the person and that can be measured [34]. The higher the trust, the lower the transaction costs [35]. In essence, transaction costs are economic entropy. Trust is provided by accurate information, which reduces entropy. Hence, universal impersonal trust is the trust of any economic entity provided by the objective characteristics of money as a universal equivalent of the stock of negentropy.

4 Results

4.1 Nuances of Economic Behavior Versus Physical Systems

There are two approaches to comparing economic behavior with physical systems in the literature. The first approach assumes an analogy between economic and physical systems. For example, the paper [36], proposes a model based on the use of both classical and quantum mechanics to describe the behavior of economic agents (buyers and sellers) in the price space. The model describes the dynamics of prices, demand and supply, as well as the influence of the external environment on the economic system. The paper [37] also draws an analogy between economic systems and thermodynamics. Saslow develops the concepts of economic temperature and entropy, identifying correspondences between economic quantities (utility, wealth, surplus) and thermodynamic parameters (energy, entropy, free energy).

The second approach emphasizes that the main difference between the economic behavior of subjects in the economy and the behavior of objects in a physical system is the anti-entropic orientation. Objects in a physical system cannot resist the action of the second law of thermodynamics, i.e. entropy always grows in such systems. Subjects in the economic system are a kind of living systems, and as any living systems, have a target function of survival, reproduction. That is, they are able, albeit locally and temporarily, to reduce their own entropy by means of energy, substance and information from the environment [38].

4.2 Hypothesis of Negentropic Essence of Money

Based on the negentropic approach, we can formulate the hypothesis on the negentropic nature of money as follows:

Money is the universal equivalent of the stock of negentropy in economy. Accordingly, the material content of money does not matter for the functioning of the economy, because money is just a reflection of the stock of negentropy produced and accumulated in the economy. Actually, the whole value of money, its user value, consists precisely in the fact that it serves as a universal equivalent of the society's stock of negentropy. In fact, it shows how much personal and/or social entropy the economy can regulate with the available resources and technologies.

4.3 Universal Impersonal Trust as the Basis for the Universality of Money as Stock of Negentropy

The key point to clarify in order to understand the essence of money is the concept of economic actors' trust in money.

In terms of the negentropy approach, there is no big difference between different negentropy supplies. The main thing is that this stock of negentropy should be sufficiently effective in regulating the level of current entropy of an individual or a society. However, the existence of many goods as negentropy supplies allowed people to start exchanging these supplies. This, in turn, posed the problem: which of these goods to choose as the universal equivalent of the stock of negentropy. The need for a universal equivalent was driven by expanding trade and exchange. But in order to become a universal equivalent, a commodity had to possess such a property as universal trust. It was the absence of universal trust that automatically deprived any other commodity claiming to fulfill the functions of money of the universality property.

For the universal equivalent of the stock of negentropy, the importance of universal trust is associated with the fact that, unlike ordinary goods with the stock of negentropy suitable mainly for regulating the current level of personal entropy, the stock of negentropy expressed in the universal equivalent could regulate not only personal entropy, but also public entropy; not only current entropy, but also future entropy. And to regulate public entropy, it is the public recognition of the universality of the stock of negentropy equivalent that is needed, manifested in universal trust. Just as the regulation of future entropy requires trust that in the future this universal equivalent of negentropy will not lose its filling, will not cease to be the equivalent.

Most of modern theoretical concepts of money are biased towards the fact that both the market (society) and the government serve as a source of trust in money [39]. In the market, trust was initially ensured through personal contacts of counterparties with each other, through joining special clans or castes. But with the expansion of trade and exchange operations, personal trust became insufficient, and impersonal trust mechanisms were needed, which were realized in the form of confidence in the material carrier of metallic money – precious metals, and then in the form of trust to the owner of these metals. At the national level, trust was also initially provided by personal qualities of the ruler, but over time there was also a transition to impersonal trust in national institutions ensuring the functioning of the monetary and banking system of the country.

Thus, one can say that it is due to universal impersonal trust that money has become the universal equivalent of the stock of negentropy in the economy. This has led to a radical change in the way economic actors regulate the entropy level, and, accordingly, to a radical reorganization of the very economic structure.

4.4 Explanation of Monetary Laws in Terms of Negentropic Approach

The negentropic hypothesis on the essence of money can be tested by using it to explain the point of monetary laws, such as the Law of the Quantity of Money in Circulation and Gresham's Law.

The law of the quantity of money in circulation is usually expressed by the Fisher equation [15, p. 2]:

$$M \times V = P \times Q \tag{1}$$

where M is amount of money in circulation; V is rate of circulation; P is prices of goods; Q is quantity of goods.

As an example, we can consider an empirical study of the quantitative theory of money based on the case of Romania from 2008 to 2013 [40]. Pătuţi&Tătulescu test the hypothesis that the change in the consumer price index (CPI) is explained by the change in the money supply (M2). They use regression analysis to analyze it, showing a high correlation between CPI and M2 ($R^2 \approx 0.95$). Based on the results obtained, Pătuţi & Tătulescu conclude that the quantitative theory of money is confirmed and suggest maintaining the stability of the money supply to control inflation.

The left part of this equation includes the amount of money and the velocity of its circulation. In terms of the negentropy approach, the whole left part is actually a mathematical expression of the universal equivalent of the stock of negentropy. In this regard, the total amount of such equivalent is in inverse dependence on the rate of money circulation in economy. That is, the faster the processes of reproduction of negentropy in economy are, the higher the rate of money circulation is, the less the universal equivalent is required for exchange.

The right side of the equation includes the quantity of goods multiplied by their prices. The quantity of goods in natural terms is actually the stock of negentropy, money being its universal equivalent. Then prices express individual proportions in which each of the goods correlates with the universal equivalent of negentropy, that is, prices express the content of negentropy in the goods, measured by money.

Thus, we can modify Fisher's equation by replacing money with a universal equivalent of negentropy and goods with the stock of negentropy:

$$UEN \times V = \sum P \times NS, \tag{2}$$

where UEN is universal equivalent of negentropy; V is rate of circulation of the universal equivalent = rate of reproduction of the stocks of negentropy; P is prices of goods; NS is stocks of negentropy accumulated in goods.

That is, the amount of the universal equivalent of negentropy in money is balanced with the stocks of negentropy in goods due to two proportional coefficients: commodity prices and the velocity of money circulation. Commodity prices serve to bring the specific stocks of negentropy contained in commodities to the universal equivalent of negentropy expressed in money. The velocity of money circulation corresponds to the speed of production and consumption of the stocks of negentropy contained in goods. The faster the reproduction cycle of negentropy, the faster the speed of circulation of the universal equivalent, and the less it is needed to serve the needs of the economy.

The Copernicus-Gresham law states: "The worst money drives the best money out of circulation" [14, p. 9]. That is, if there are two monetary currencies, coins or other material carriers of money in circulation at the same time, the one that is worse at the function of accumulation and formation of treasures remains in circulation, while the other one is gradually withdrawn from circulation and settles in these very treasures.

In terms of the negentropy approach, treasures are large and time-invariant negentropy supplies. It is natural that those monetary units that are least likely to lose their negentropic content over time are best suited to form treasures.

Accordingly, such monetary units are withdrawn from circulation. Meanwhile, economic agents promptly get rid of those monetary units that quickly lose their negentropic content, so they remain in circulation.

The paper [41] studies the operation of Gresham's law of money circulation, the Sparavigna's approach is based on the assumption of asymmetry of information about the value of coins, creating a problem similar to that of Akerlof's market for "lemons". Similarly, commodity money has always suffered from information asymmetry problems because the intrinsic value of coins, and especially their proof, could only be verified at relatively high costs. Sparavigna argues that asymmetric information about the value of coins between trading partners has contributed to the operation of Gresham's Law in some cases. The paper also discusses the role of the relative, rather than absolute, value people attribute to coins in the functioning of monetary circulation.

From the point of view of the hypothesis of negentropic essence of money, the relative value of coins (currencies) is determined by comparing the rate of loss of the negentropic content of monetary units. That is, the faster the monetary units lose their negentropic content, and the higher the asymmetry of information about the real negentropic content, the lower the relative value of this monetary unit, and the faster it is discarded.

4.5 Functions of Money in the Light of Negentropic Approach

Usually, economic theory textbooks and scientific papers emphasize five functions of money [14, 42, 43]. Using the negentropic hypothesis on the essence of money we can try to explain why money performs these particular functions.

1) *A measure of value of various goods.* Goods contain a stock of negentropy, i.e. consumption of goods allows economic agents to regulate the level of their personal entropy. There is also the industrial consumption of goods, i.e. the use of the stock of negentropy contained in them to create a new stock of negentropy. As a result, the value of goods is manifested through the change in entropy level [25], be it current entropy or future entropy, personal entropy or social entropy. However, people do not know how to estimate the level and dynamics of entropy directly, because we lack a special sensory receptor for this purpose. Therefore, we have to make such an assessment indirectly, and for this purpose we need some universal equivalent of stock of negentropy, using which we can express the cost of goods indirectly, i.e. through prices.
2) *Means of circulation (exchange).* The function of the means of circulation follows from the first function of money. Thanks to the emergence of a universal meter of stock of negentropy, it becomes possible to compare goods among themselves and

to identify the proportions of exchange. In addition, the use of money significantly reduces transaction costs in the process of exchange, making this exchange faster and less costly for economic actors. And this, in turn, makes it economically and entropically profitable to increase the scale of production of goods for exchange. That is, money, performing the function of means of circulation, in essence reduces entropy in the economy, i.e. acts as negentropy at the macro level of economy.

3) *Means of accumulating and forming treasures.* This function is directly related to the level of trust in money, since it is pointless to accumulate any equivalent of stock of negentropy if trust in it may disappear over time, or if only a part of society trusts this equivalent. It should be taken into account that money itself is also subject to entropy, i.e. loss of its negentropic content over time as a result of inflation and/or devaluation processes. Creation of treasures is possible only if the stock of negentropy, for which money can be exchanged at any moment, remains unchanged. The advent of a universal equivalent has led to the possibility of creating virtually unlimited negentropy supplies. Since the stock of negentropy nominated in money has turned out to be almost immune to deterioration over time, this, on the one hand, has increased the ability of nations to regulate the level of social entropy, and on the other hand, has led to the emergence of a class of bourgeoisie and capitalists, increasing the stratification in society, and hence the level of social entropy.
4) *Means of payment (credit).* This function of money appeared due to the fact that it allowed linking the present and future of economic actors, in fact, adding a new way to reduce current entropy. Before the appearance of money, individuals had only two ways to regulate the level of current entropy: creating and consuming negentropy supplies through their own labor or through the exploitation of other people's labor. Thanks to money it became possible to borrow from oneself from the future. That is, in the absence of stock of negentropy, in order to adjust the current entropy, it became possible to borrow the equivalent of stock of negentropy, adjust the current negentropy, restore the ability to work and by means of this repay the debt. It is therefore more correct to call this function a means of credit rather than a means of payment. But this, in turn, led to the emergence of a new relatively easy way to create a stock of negentropy - by receiving interest and commissions for money transactions. That is, a new stratum of society appeared - money changers and moneylenders, which again increased stratification in society and social entropy.
5) *Function of world money.* As mentioned above, the basic condition for the universality of money as a stock of negentropy is universal trust. However, the transition to credit money and the abandonment of the gold content of currencies has caused a crisis of trust in all currencies. Theoretically, none of the currencies of individual countries can have universal trust outside the territory of that country. However, countries need to trade with each other, and with globalization the scale of world trade has increased manifold. That is, there is a need for such a universal equivalent of negentropy, which would have really universal trust on the scale of planet Earth. In modern conditions such an equivalent is gold, which is accepted for payment in international transactions. But the amount of gold is limited, and it quickly settles down in treasures, as well as is spent in industry. Therefore, the functions of world money have begun to be performed by highly convertible reserve currencies, which are accepted almost anywhere in the world. The secret of reserve currencies is that, on the one hand, the nations that issue

them have powerful economies and strong political weight in the world, and on the other hand, the governments of these countries conduct a balanced and reasonable monetary policy, not allowing a sharp depreciation of their currencies. All this adds to the certainty that there will always be an opportunity to exchange these universal equivalents for real negentropy supplies.

4.6 Comparison to Alternative Approaches

In order to understand how productive the hypothesis of negentropic essence of money is, it is necessary to compare this hypothesis with the existing theoretical approaches (Table 2).

Table 2. Comparison of the hypothesis of negentropic essence of money with existing theoretical approaches.

Theoretical Approach Name	Similarities	Distinctions
Evolutionary (metallic) theory	Metals contain a stock of negentropy, so they can serve as a measure of other stocks of negentropy, and form treasure	Money has other functions besides the function of accumulation and treasure formation
Nominalist theory	Money is merely the equivalent of the negentropy contained in commodities	It is necessary to take into account subjective manifestations of entropy of money itself - inflation and expectations
State theory (Chartalism)	The quantity of money as an equivalent of the stocks of negentropy in commodities is relevant	The ratio between the stocks of negentropy in commodities and in money cannot be set prescriptively
Theory of money as a technical medium of exchange	Money can be used to compare the amount of negentropy contained in different goods and to find the correct proportion of exchange	Money has other functions besides that of a means of circulation (exchange)
Capital-creative theory of credit (money)	The value of money arises from its ability to link the current and future entropy of an economic actor	Money also has functions other than that of credit (payment)
Social class approach to understanding money	Capital owners allocate a volume of negentropy to workers to regulate only the current level of entropy, while they themselves can regulate the future entropy	Equalization of the amount of money in the economy through redistribution from the rich to the poor will lead to an increase in entropy and the cessation of economic development
Quantitative theory	Commodity prices are the proportion in which the total stock of negentropy accumulated in commodities relates to the total stock of negentropy denominated in money	The effect of money on the level of entropy in the economy is more complex than a simple equilibrium of stocks of negentropy. In addition, some of the money is deposited in treasuries

(*continued*)

Thus, the hypothesis of negentropic essence of money coincides in some aspects with all alternative theoretical approaches to the substantiation of the essence of money, but at the same time provides a much broader view of the essence of money, revealing the shortcomings and limitations of each of the existing approaches.

Table 2. (*continued*)

Theoretical Approach Name	Similarities	Distinctions
Keynesian theory Neo-Keynesian theory Post-Keynesian theory	In order to serve economic growth, more and more equivalent of negentropy in the form of money is required. By giving away money at the current moment, society borrows a stock of negentropy from itself from the future	Long-term consequences (entropy growth) of "giving away money", including social and subjective ones, should also be taken into account
Monetarist theory	The supply of money is ensured by the instruments of monetary policy, which avoids most of the consequences of the entropy of money itself	The influence of subjective factors and institutional conditions (level of perceived entropy) is taken into account, due to which monetary policy instruments work well only in developed democracies
Neo-Austrian private/parallel money theory	In conditions of weakness of the state monetary system there are processes of self-organization and emergence of alternative universal equivalents of negentropy	For self-organization and emergence of private money, certain institutional conditions are necessary, i.e. a certain level of orderliness ("negentropy") in the economy
Free (neutral) money theory	The penalty for the ability to borrow a stock of negentropy from oneself from the future by means of credit, increases the production of negentropy in the present	In addition to the function of the means of circulation, money must fulfill other functions, such as that of credit. Otherwise, investments will start to decline
Institutional theory	Money is a tool for social organization, for reducing social entropy	Money is not only a tool or an economic institution, but also an equivalent of real stocks of negentropy
Neo-institutional theory	The reduction in transaction costs due to money is a reduction in the entropy of economic actors	Money not only reduces transaction costs in the economy, but also creates additional costs (entropy) in the form of inflation, inequality, etc
Behavioral finance theory	A person cannot objectively measure the negentropy amount in money or goods, which leads to behavioral errors	Behavioral errors can be explained and predicted through the introduction of the concept of "subjective entropy", i.e. the perception of the level and dynamics of entropy with the help of the senses
Information theory of money by K. Waltuch	Money is a carrier of information, so by using it, uncertainty is reduced, hence entropy is reduced	In addition to information, stocks of negentropy contain embodied energy, which is needed to reduce entropy
Theories of Islamic finance	A complex system of social norms and rules based on the prescriptions of the Shariah can reduce the negative social consequences (entropy) from the use of money	In addition to the social consequences of using money, there are purely economic consequences that must also be considered, such as inflation

5 Discussion

Based on the above, we can conclude that the hypothesis of the essence of money as a universal equivalent of stock of negentropy provides certain bonuses for understanding the essence of money and its management.

First, the use of negentropic approach will finally allow the theory of money to get rid of accusations in subjectivism, bringing under the theory of money a powerful natural-scientific base.

Second, the negentropic approach has a significant explanatory power, i.e. it allows to explain the functions of money, many phenomena and monetary laws.

Third, the use of negentropic approach to understanding the essence of money opens up opportunities for more simple and understandable involvement in economic calculations of negative externalities associated with environmental pollution and exhaustion of mineral resources.

Fourth, the negentropic hypothesis of the essence of money provides a precise and definitive answer to the question of whether it is possible in principle to abandon money in the economy. The answer is yes, it is possible, since the level and dynamics of entropy can be regulated without a universal equivalent in the form of money. There are many examples of this in traditional societies and in the administrative-command system. However, any such moneyless system will be many times less efficient both in terms of the rate of circulation of goods and in terms of saving transaction costs. The only exception is if we humans somehow learn to accurately measure the content of stock of negentropy in goods directly rather than indirectly.

Fifth, the importance of universal impersonal trust for the universality of money as an equivalent stock of negentropy challenges ideas that cryptocurrencies displace "old" money from circulation [44]. In essence, cryptocurrencies do not solve the problem of trust, they only change the way that trust is secured. Instead of the mechanisms of the market or the bureaucracy, we propose a new way of ensuring trust - algorithmic. Of course, this way of ensuring trust is the most impersonal trust among the existing ones. However, it does not solve the problem of losing the content of the stock of negentropy, because cryptocurrencies and crypto assets are also subject to rate hikes.

Cryptocurrencies fit quite well within the hypothesis of the negentropic nature of money. Cryptocurrencies are based on blockchain technology, the essence of which is to encrypt all previous transactions in each new block. So, in essence, blockchain provides incremental information about how cryptocurrency is used in economic circulation. And any increase in information about a system reduces the entropy of the system. That is, it turns out that cryptocurrencies not only serve as a universal equivalent of the stock of negentropy, but also contain a certain amount of negentropy themselves.

Nevertheless, cryptocurrencies at the same time increase the entropy of the economic system. For example, the paper [45] explores the application of complexity theory and nonlinear dynamics methods to analyze the cryptocurrency market, in particular bitcoin. The authors analyze various methods for quantifying complexity, including entropy, Lyapunov exponents, and recurrent network analysis. The results show that some of the measures considered can serve as indicators of impending crisis events in the bitcoin market, which indicates an increase in entropy in the economy.

However, the application of the negentropic approach in the theory of money faces some problems. For example, the lack of reliable methods of measuring the stock of negentropy contained in goods does not provide a sufficiently objective comparison of the amount of negentropy in goods and in their monetary equivalent. This leads to the preservation of subjectivity in measuring the user value of money. Perhaps in the future, with the widespread use of the Internet of Things, mankind will finally learn to objectively assess the negentropy supplies produced by society.

In addition, the presence of subjective entropy expressed in behavioral errors and effects will still distort the perception of the objective consumer value of the stock of negentropy contained in the monetary equivalent, which leaves wide opportunities for various speculations and manipulations. Perhaps, the use of strong artificial intelligence as an advisor in making economic decisions will somehow smooth out behavioral errors, but this is still only in the realm of assumptions.

The most interesting is the practical application of the hypothesis about the negentropic essence of money. For example, it is possible to propose a solution to the question of admissibility of money emission for solving economic problems based on the way the emission affects the stocks of negentropy in individual economic agents and in the economy as a whole. If additional emission allows increasing the total stocks of negentropy and sustainable rates of production of negentropy, then it is justified.

The second field of practical use can be the determination of admissibility of money surrogates and their share in the economy. If money surrogates lead to the growth of real stocks of negentropy, then their use is justified. Also, the hypothesis of negentropic essence of money allows us to formulate the rules of regulation of monetary surrogates: they should provide impersonal trust and have universality as an equivalent of stocks of negentropy.

The third field of action may be to address the issue of sources of funding for green projects. The creation of stocks of negentropy in the economy is associated with the growth of entropy in the environment. Accordingly, in the green economy it is justified to use only such sources of financing that allow creating new stocks of negentropy with a minimum increase in entropy in the environment.

The fourth, most interesting field of practical application may be the regulation of the circulation of cryptocurrencies as an additional universal equivalent of stocks of negentropy in the economy, but based on a new way of ensuring universal impersonal trust - the algorithmic one.

6 Conclusion

Thus, the influence of money on the level and dynamics of entropy in the economy is ambiguous. On the one hand, money has been an effective tool to regulate the level of personal entropy of economic actors. Also, with the help of money, transaction costs in the economy have significantly decreased, and so has the social entropy. On the other hand, money has led to the emergence of stratification and imbalances in society, increased chaotic economic development, increased super-exploitation of natural resources and human beings, thereby increasing both personal entropy of individual actors and social entropy as a whole.

Thus, the hypothesis of the essence of money as a universal equivalent of negentropy in economy is confirmed. Commodities are negentropy supplies in the economy. And since money is also a commodity, money is a stock of negentropy. But money is a specific commodity and its specificity consists in the fact that it is a universal equivalent of stock of negentropy, and as a result it can serve as an equivalent of value of any goods.

In addition, the hypothesis of negentropic essence of money provides a logical explanation of monetary laws. Such as Gresham's Law and the Law of the Quantity of Money in Circulation. Also, with the help of this hypothesis, all the functions of money can be explained in a fairly consistent way.

Using the hypothesis of the essence of money as a universal equivalent of stock of negentropy gives a new perspective of the phenomenon of money, and based on it one can formulate recommendations for the formation of a truly universal monetary unit and a more efficient monetary system.

As a recommendation for the use of the hypothesis of the negentropic essence of money, we can offer a study of the misfits and failures of monetary policy in developing countries. Probably, the reason for failures is that traditional monetary policy instruments are not able to reliably regulate the stocks of negentropy, their dynamics and distribution in developing economic systems.

We can also recommend further development of the Internet of Things to increase the amount of information about the creation and movement of stocks of negentropy in the economy, and based on this more accurate determination of the required amount of the universal equivalent of negentropy (money and quasi-money instruments) in the economy.

A very promising field is the use of the hypothesis in the development and assessment of the effectiveness of sources of green finance and, in general, the formation of a coherent and consistent methodological basis for the green economy.

Also, one of the distant prospects is the formation of a truly "global" reserve currency based on the negentropic approach to the substantiation of the essence of money, which does not depend on the condition of national economy and actions of the central bank of a particular country.

References

1. Akhmetshin, E.M., Vasilev, V.L., Gapsalamov, A.R., Pavlyuk, A.V., Sharipov, R.R., Gatin, R.G.: Formation of institutional arrangement of economic security improvement of Russia: task definition. In: Proceedings of the 31st International Business Information Management Association Conference, IBIMA 2018: Innovation Management and Education Excellence through Vision 2020, pp. 6395–6401 (2018)
2. Yasushi, N.: Soviet foreign trade and the money supply. BOFIT Discussion Papers, 30 (2013). https://nbn-resolving.de/urn:nbn:fi:bof-201408072191
3. Guyer, J.I., Pallaver, K.: Money and currency in African history. In: Spear, T. (ed.) Oxford Research Encyclopaedia of African History, pp. 1–28. Oxford University Press, New York (2018). https://doi.org/10.1093/acrefore/9780190277734.013.144
4. Nelson, A., Timmerman, F.: Life Without Money: Building Fair and Sustainable Economies. Pluto Press (2011)
5. Subhendu, D.: Moneyless economy. Bus. Rev. Camb. **20**(1), 1–9 (2012)
6. Amyaz, M., McConnell, D., Sugars, S., Connor, B.: Amish economic transformations: new forms of income and wealth distribution in a traditionally 'flat' community. J. Amish Plain Anabapt. Stud. **2**(1), 1–22 (2014). https://doi.org/10.18061/1811/59692
7. Kelton, S.: The Deficit Myth: Modern Monetary Theory and the Birth of the People's Economy. PublicAffairs, New York (2020)

8. Wray, L.R.: Modern Money Theory: A Primer on Macroeconomics for Sovereign Monetary Systems. Palgrave Macmillan, New York (2012)
9. Mosler, W.: The Seven Deadly Innocent Frauds of Economic Policy. Valance Co. (2010)
10. Mitchell, W., Fazi, T.: Reclaiming the State: A Progressive Vision of Sovereignty for a Post-Neoliberal World. Pluto Press, London (2017). https://doi.org/10.2307/j.ctt1v2xvvp
11. Fullwiler, S.T.: Modern monetary theory – a debate. Real-World Econ. Rev. **89**, 57–69 (2019)
12. Durani, F., Qureshi, I.: A historical analysis of the theories of money. Int. J. Bus. Econ. Dev. **4**(1), 71–84 (2016)
13. Lawlor, M.S.: Equilibrium, interest, and money: three essays in the history of economic theory. Retrospective Theses and Dissertations (1986). https://lib.manaraa.com/books/Equilibrium%20interest%20and%20money-%20three%20essays%20in%20the%20history%20of%20economic%20theory.pdf
14. Malkina, M.: Evolution of the theory of money in economic science. Financ. Credit **48**(384), 8–16 (2009). (in Russian)
15. Petrosov, A.S., Popkov, A.A.: Retrospective analysis of the theoretical concept of money. Naucnye Issledovania **3**(14), 21–24 (2017). (in Russian)
16. Kalb, D.: Two theories of money: on the historical anthropology of the state-finance nexus. Focaal J. Glob. Hist. Anthropol. **95**, 92–112 (2023). https://doi.org/10.3167/fcl.2023.950102
17. Hasse, R., Ekstedt, E.: Intrinsic contradictions of the money concept: from real bill to monetarism and back again. Chin. Bus. Rev. **16**(4), 170–192 (2017). https://doi.org/10.17265/1537-1506/2017.04.002
18. Peretolchin, A.P.: Genesis and prospects of development of legal regulation of digital financial assets in the Russian Federation. J. Digit. Technol. Law **1**(3), 752–774 (2023). https://doi.org/10.21202/jdtl.2023.33
19. Biryukov, V.V.: Alternative institutional strategies for developing monetary theories. AlterEconomics **19**(2), 262–282 (2022). https://doi.org/10.31063/AlterEconomics/2022.19-2.4. (in Russian)
20. Camargo, F.J.: Sustainable monetary system: Entropic contribution from the ecological economy. (Thesis Dr. Econ. Sciences). National University of La Matanza, Buenos Aires (2020). https://repositoriocyt.unlam.edu.ar/bitstream/123456789/1908/1/DCE-E-Camargo.pdf
21. Kennedy, M.: Money without interest and inflation: How to create a medium of exchange that serves everyone (Translated from English by L. Culmer). IPK "Moskovskaya Pravda", Moscow (1993). https://www.kennedy-bibliothek.info/cx-content/uploads/bibliothek/GeldbuchRussisch.pdf (in Russian)
22. Valtukh, K.K.: Information Theory of Value. Nauka, Novosibirsk (1996). (in Russian)
23. Karakatsanis, G.A.: Thermodynamic theory of money. In: 12th Biennial ISEE Conference "Ecological Economics and Rio+20", pp. 1–10 (2012). https://www.isecoeco.org/conferences/isee2012-versao3/pdf/354.pdf
24. Abad-Segura, E., González-Zamar, M.-D., Squillante, M.: Examining the research on business information-entropy correlation in the accounting process of organizations. Entropy **23**, 1493 (2021). https://doi.org/10.3390/e23111493
25. Islamutdinov, V.F.: Prerequisites for the formation of a complex theory of value based on the entropy approach. Sib. Financ. Sch. **3**(151), 104–117 (2023). https://doi.org/10.34020/1993-4386-2023-3-104-117. (in Russian)
26. Ruth, M.: Entropy, Economics, and Policy. Artec-paper **140**, 1–19 (2007)
27. Heinzel, C.: Schumpeter and Georgescu-Roegen on the foundations of an evolutionary analysis: the problem of qualitative change, its methodical implications and analytical treatment. Dresden Discuss. Pap. Ser. Econ. **10**(06), 1–30 (2006)
28. Yatsky, S.A.: On the issue of the entropic nature of value. Vektor Econ. 5 (2024). http://vectoreconomy.ru/images/publications/2024/5/economic-theory/Yatsky.pdf (In Russian)

29. Bertalanffy, L.: General System Theory: Foundations, Development, Applications. George Braziller, New York (1969)
30. Krehm, W.: The entropy concept as a tool of economic analysis. Econ. Appl. **30**(1), 65–83 (1977). https://doi.org/10.3406/ecoap.1977.4196
31. Caldentey, E.P., Rodríguez, L.R.: A stock-flow approach to investment requirements within balance-of-payments constrained growth. Economic Commission for Latin America and the Caribbean (ECLAC). Printed at United Nations, Santiago (2020)
32. Godley, W., Lavoie, M.: Monetary Economics: An Integrated Approach to credit, Money, Income, Production, and Wealth. Palgrave Macmillan, Houndmills, Basingstoke, Hampshire (2007). https://doi.org/10.1057/9780230626546
33. Hassan, M., Semerciöz, F.: Trust in personal and impersonal forms: its antecedents and consequences – a conceptual analysis within organizational context. Int. J. Manag. Inf. Syst. **14**(2), 67–84 (2010). https://doi.org/10.19030/ijmis.v14i2.832
34. Vanhala, M., Puumalainen, K., Blomqvist, K.: Impersonal trust: the development of the construct and the scale. Pers. Rev. **40**(4), 485–513 (2011). https://doi.org/10.1108/00483481111133354
35. Gull, I.A., Wani, A.A., Khan, A.: Impersonal trust: a review of literature. Int. J. Manag. Technol. Eng. **9**(1), 2115–2118 (2019)
36. Kondratenko, A.V.: Physical Modeling of Economic Systems: Classical and Quantum Economies. Nauka, Novosibirsk (2005)
37. Saslow, W.M.: An economic analogy to thermodynamics. Am. J. Phys. **67**(12), 1239–1247 (1999). https://doi.org/10.1119/1.19110
38. Islamutdinov, V.F., Kurikov, V.M.: On the application of the entropy approach in economic research on the management of economic systems. Sib. Financ. Sch. **2**(146), 168–178 (2022). https://doi.org/10.34020/1993-4386-2022-2-168-178. (in Russian)
39. Khusainova, A.I.: Institutional Foundations for the Formation of Trust in Money. (Thesis Cand. Econ. Sciences). Ufa: Ufa State Aviation Technical University (2021). (in Russian)
40. Pătuţi, A., Tătulescu, A.: Empirical evidence for the quantity theory of money: Romania – a case study. Rom. Stat. Rev. **11**, 12–19 (2013)
41. Sparavigna, A.C.: Some notes on the Gresham's law of money circulation. Int. J. Sci. **3**(2), 80–91 (2014). https://doi.org/10.18483/ijSci.417
42. Bazulin, Yu.V.: Origin and Nature of Money: Financial Aspect. (Thesis Dr. Econ. Sciences). St. Petersburg: St. Petersburg State University (2009). (in Russian)
43. Martin, F.: Money: An Unofficial Biography of Money (Translated from English). Sinbad Publishing House, Moscow (2016). (in Russian)
44. Iarutin, I.K., Gulyaeva, E.E.: International and Russian legal regulation of the turnover of crypto-assets: conceptual-terminological correlation. J. Digit. Technol. Law **1**(3), 725–751 (2023). https://doi.org/10.21202/jdtl.2023.32
45. Bielinskyi, A., Serdyuk, O., Semerikov, S., Soloviev, V.: Econophysics of cryptocurrency crashes: an overview. SHS Web Conf. **107**, 03001 (2021). https://doi.org/10.1051/shsconf/202110703001

Interest Rate Derivatives Market: Peculiarities, Problems and Prospects for Russia

Eldar Karov, Pavel Yu. Soloviev, and Konstantin V. Krinichansky(✉)

Financial University, 49/2 Leningradsky Prospekt, 125167 Moscow, Russia
psoloviev@fa.ru, kkrin@ya.ru

Abstract. Interest rate risk is the main market risk with regard to fixed income instruments on the capital market. Interest rate risk is inherently non-diversifiable. It requires the use of specific methods and financial management tools. Hedging remains the primary mechanism by which market participants manage interest rate risk on capital market. This study highlights the critical features of the derivatives application for hedging interest rate risk on the capital market. The authors explain that when forming long-term interest rate futures as the main exchange derivatives, it is crucially important to consider the features of the local market for underlying assets, including the volume and number of bond issues; the number of bonds used as underlying assets for futures contracts; trading volume and liquidity characteristics of the secondary bond market. Based on the analysis of the development of long-term interest rate futures and studying the structure and specification of derivatives traded at the biggest exchanges the authors highlight features of basic groups of current long-term interest rate futures, classify experience of the launch of these derivatives, postulating that the structure of the futures contract must correspond to the peculiarities of the local market of underlying assets. The authors critically examine the experience of forming the interest rate derivatives market in Russia. They find that the lack of demand for interest rate derivatives traded on the Moscow Exchange from 2011 to 2022 was caused by problems when designing these agreements, particularly by the fact that the specialists who develop them did not fully take into account the specific features of the Russian government bond market.

Keywords: Interest Rate Risk · Debt Market · Bonds · Derivatives · Futures · Hedging

JEL Classifications: D47 · E43 · G13

1 Introduction

One of the components of market risk in the capital market is the interest rate risk related with the fixed income financial products [1]. Interest rate risk arises when an investor incurs financial losses as a result of an unfavorable change in the average level of interest rates or a parallel shift in the yield curve, a change in the slope or shape of the yield curve [2, 3]. Interest rate risk factors also include interest rate volatility and changes in

E. Kuzmin et al. (Eds.): EASET 2024, SPBE, pp. 283–298, 2025.
https://doi.org/10.1007/978-3-031-91159-0_18

correlations between different interest rates [4]. Its consequences are manifested, when the structure of cash flows on debt instruments changes. The central risks for investors are the risks of losses on their balance sheets, regardless of changes in the direction of interest rates.

The retail component of the bond market has been actively developing in recent years, and size of lots are splitting. Issuers place low face value bonds de-signed for retail investors. Such a model of the fixed income market is typical for Russia, where demand from the retail investors is developing, and collective investment mechanism is not dominant.

Currently, Russia is experiencing a steady growth of the bond market. The interest rate risk on the part of the market participants is growing along with this process. However, at the moment, the Russian exchange market has not been able to offer a successful tool for managing the growing interest rate risk.

Thus, an urgent issue is the lack of access to effective instruments for hedging interest rate risk in Russia [5]. The Moscow Exchange made attempts to launch interest rate futures, however this experience turned out to be a failure. An analysis of the reasons for these failures, as well as recommendations for correcting the mistakes of developers of interest rate futures on the Moscow Exchange, constitutes the main motivation of this study.

Implicit here is the hypothesis that the success of the formation of the interest rate futures market depends on whether certain characteristics of the underlying asset market, on the basis of which the delivery baskets are formed, are fully taken into account when launching contracts in question.

The novelty of our study is finding the link between futures contracts' characteristics arising from the peculiarities of the local futures market, their specifications and the liquidity of the interest rate futures market. We also show the impact of the structure of long-term futures contracts on interest rates on the demand for these derivatives. In addition, we show that the structure and features of local markets for underlying assets are also important.

2 Literature Review

In publications by Choudhry [1], De Jong and Fabozzi [3], Chisholm [6], Hull [7], Kolb and Overdahl [8], Panda and Thiripalraju [9], Sundaram and Das [10], Tuckman and Serrat [11] deliverable US Treasury Bond futures considered as a tool to manage interest rate risk. With varying degrees of detail, these papers show the contract specification, highlight the key parameters of the contract, describe the feature of the underlying asset, namely deliverable bonds basket with the possibility of choosing one of the bond for delivery. The papers discuss the rules of choosing a "cheapest to deliver" (CTD) issue taking into account the ratio of underlying bonds' prices and the corresponding conversion factor.

The regularity of designation of the CTD bond depending on the position of the benchmark yield relative to the market values of the yield to maturity of the underlying bonds is shown in De Pooter [12]. The authors also show the features of forward pricing of bond futures, taking into account the put option of the futures contract and the features of hedging the interest rate risk of the bond portfolio, including the calculation of the hedging ratio. The authors consider these most famous and widely used futures contracts as a given, but do not describe the prerequisites for the setting up such contracts by exchanges, they do not study the advantage of bond futures for the market and its participants [13]. The previous literature, moreover, does not focus on the obstacles preventing the launch of trading and the task of developing alternative exchange-traded instruments.

The studies of individual authors devoted to the local and regional markets of derivatives are of interest, since they contain the description of some futures contracts, features of the markets of underlying assets, as well as historical aspects of the establishment of derivatives markets in a particular jurisdiction or sectors [14]. Interesting studies address to the features of the exchange-traded contracts leading in the world ranking in terms of trading volume, such as futures for European and Japanese government bonds. These are publications by Ahn, Cai and Cheung [15], Batten, Fetherston and Szilagyi [2, 16]. These works describe the features of the markets of underlying assets, the characteristics of futures contracts, their parameters and strategies for using them. In general, these futures contracts, as we note earlier, are very similar to the US Treasury bond futures, with the exception of certain parameters, such as "the calculation of the conversion factor, due to the specifics of the underlying asset market conventions" [17].

Along with other markets, it is of interest to study the experience of Australia and India. Frino, William, and Lepone [18], as well as Cheung [19], analyzed the pricing characteristics of cash-settled derivatives on long-term interest rates in the Australian market, including their parameters and methods of execution. The authors highlight the key approaches to the formation of settlement baskets of bonds and methods for calculating final settlement price. The features of derivatives on long-term interest rates in India were revealed in the works of Alrawashdeh [20], Ankur and Madhurjya [21], Bansal [22], Divya and Shashi [23], Korivi and James [24], Manish [25], Panda and Thiripalraju [9]. Taking into account the peculiarities of local markets for underlying assets, futures for long-term rates in India have been restarted several times. In particular, Bansal [22] revealed the pricing mechanism of a futures contract based on the values of the zero-coupon yield curve, indicating its advantage over deliverable futures contracts for bond baskets common in world practice and academic literature. However, the shortcomings and potential risks that influenced the subsequent lack of demand for these derivatives were not revealed in Bansal's paper. A more detailed analysis of the characteristics and parameters of derivatives for long-term interest rates in the Indian market was carried out by Alrawashdeh [20]. In his study, the causes of the failures of both the initially launched long-term derivatives and deliverable futures for the bonds baskets in India were revealed, and the optimal structure of the cash-settled derivative was suggested, the characteristics of which take into account the characteristics of the local bond market.

Overall, the literature review reveals that several types of long-term interest rate futures are being discussed. The main one is the deliverable futures on baskets of bonds, which are widely used on key exchanges in the world's leading economies. The use of other types of interest rate derivatives is presumably the result of certain features of local underlying asset markets that hinder the construction of deliverable futures on baskets of bonds.

3 Material and Methods

Interest rate risk, as the main market risk for bonds, is non-diversifiable and requires the use of special management techniques. The most common way to manage interest rate risk in the capital market is hedging with derivatives, or transferring interest rate risk from one participant (hedger) to another participant in a transaction. On a worldwide scale, the demand for derivatives hedging interest rate risk is confirmed by reported open interest both in the exchange-traded and OTC derivatives markets (Fig. 1).

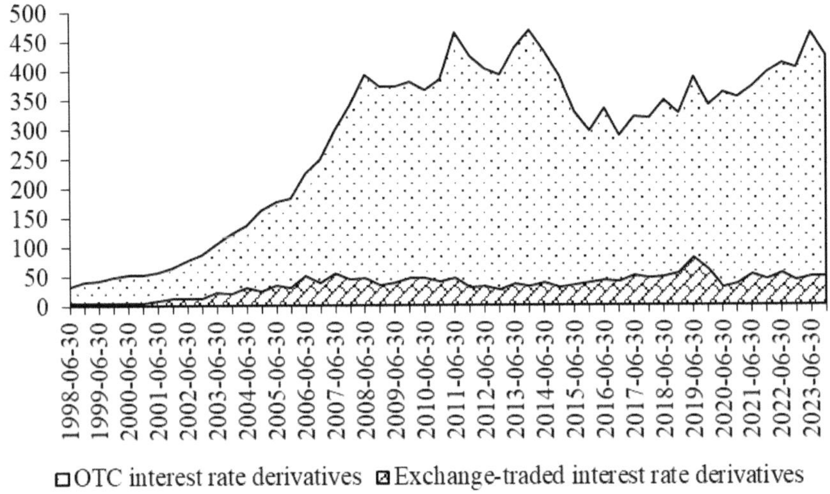

Source: BIS statistics. URL: https://data.bis.org/

Fig. 1. Interest rate derivatives open interest in the world.

The underlying assets for OTC interest rate derivatives are predominantly indicators of money market interest rates, much less often – price indices of short-term debt securities. As Karov writes, "In the exchange-traded market, the segment of derivatives with underlying assets represented by bonds, and with price quotation based on the price/yield of bonds or the corresponding index, is much wider comparing to OTC. The standardization and liquidity of trading in such instruments provides opportunities for dynamic adjustment of derivatives positions to reflect changes in the structure of underlying securities portfolios" [17].

Even though OTC derivatives can be more adaptive and more accurate when taking into account the specifics of hedging, exchange-traded instruments remain prefera-ble due to their advantages. In the exchange market the central counterparty assumes credit risks, while in an OTC transaction, the counterparty's risk is assumed by the participant, or, if they are the source of this risk themselves, they have to pay a high rate for hedging. The exchange market provides the participant with free and open access to open a position without prior assessment of credit risk and the opportunity of early closure at no additional cost.

In the exchange-traded market LTIR derivatives represented by futures and options. The correct setting of the underlying asset for exchange-traded derivatives is of critical importance, since it directly affects, due to the standardization of the terms of exchange-traded contracts, the presence and magnitude of the basis risk, that is, the risk of deviation of the price dynamics of derivatives from the price dynamics of the underlying assets that are the subject of hedging. The underlying asset of futures on long-term interest rates can be particular bond issues (very rarely), bond baskets, yield curve indicators, bond indices.

Futures contract on a separate bond issues is a direct analogue of forward, but at the same time, due to the potential concentration of trading activity, it is subject to manipulation, regardless of the type of execution (delivery or settlement). Futures on separate bonds could exist as an exchange-traded derivative when particular bond issues are acceptable in terms of their trading volumes and liquidity.

The futures on baskets of bonds became a solution to the problem of low liquidity of separate issues leading to the price manipulation. The underlying asset in this case is a basket of issues of the same issuer, with a similar cash flow structure and duration within a given range. The seller of such a futures contract has the right to choose the issue of bonds, which is delivered upon the execution of the contract. Due to this mechanism, the risk of a corner/squeeze is minimized, since if one issue of bonds is not available, it is replaced for the purposes of delivery with another one from those included in the basket. The requirement of presence in the market of a number of bonds of the same type, similar in terms, is the reason of an obstacle for the diversity of such contracts: the predominant type of such derivatives is a futures contract on baskets of government bonds. A variety of contracts on baskets of bonds are the cash-settled derivatives.

Bond index futures and futures on a section of the yield curve are cash-settled futures. In fact, these are index-based instruments, the difference lies in the calculation method. Bond indices are calculated according to the relevant calculation base (government, municipal, corporate, high-yield bonds) with the respective maturities. A section on the yield curve is an alternative way to calculate the indicator for the bond market. It is the value of the zero-coupon yield curve formed based on transaction prices and quotations for the conforming bonds, for a specific maturity. Using a bond index or yield curve section as an underlying asset eliminates the risk of price manipulation and allows liquidity to be concentrated on a limited number of instruments, but includes such critical drawbacks as high basis risk when working with separate bond issues and custom (non-index) bond portfolio structures and, as a result, a high error of spot-futures arbitrage operations.

Table 1 presents a comparison of these types of underlying assets.

Deliverable futures contracts on government bonds baskets are considered as the normal type of futures on long-term interest rates in the world. There are several reasons for spreading this type of contract.

Firstly, governments are the largest issuers, placing many issues with large volumes outstanding. Despite the use of government securities by institutional investors as a usual component of diversified portfolios and, as a result, an insignificant free-float quantity of bonds, this portion is sufficient to maintain liquidity of these debt instruments in

Table 1. Futures on long-term interest rates classification based on the underlying asset and the type of execution.

Type of underlying asset	Advantages	Disadvantages	Execution mode	
			Physical delivery	Cash settlement
Separate bond issue	Ease of delivery and settlement	High risks of price manipulation	yes	yes
	Clarity of Arbitrage Operations	The representative price problem for a cash-settlement contract		
	Minimal basis risk	Liquidity dilution		
Bond basket	Liquidity concentration	Complication of pricing (put option)	yes	yes
	Low risks of price manipulation	Significant basis risk		
	Clarity of arbitrage transactions with deliverable futures	Limited issuers of the underlying asset		
Bond index	Representativeness of the underlying index, protection against manipulation	Index of Bonds of Different "Quality"	no	yes
	Liquidity concentration	High basis risk for individual assets		
	Different issuers of the underlying asset	High arbitrage error		
Yield curve section	Universal instrument for a variety of bond types	Significant basis risk	no	yes
	Low risks of price manipulation	Limited issuers of the underlying asset		
	Liquidity concentration	High arbitrage error		

the market. All of these things create the basis for effective pricing and avoiding price manipulations.

Secondly, there is practically no credit risk on government bonds. This allows you to allocate interest rate risk in its pure form (excluding credit risk).

Thirdly, the government places its bonds on a regular basis, in most cases in the same type, by reference issues. Most often, these are fixed-coupon bonds, they include identical frequency of payments, they do not include amortization and offers. Although, exotic options are not excluded in the market. Issues of government bonds not only constitute a large amount outstanding, but also cover the long distance of the yield curve, allowing the formation of hedging instruments along its entire term.

As a result, the majority of futures contracts on long-term interest rate in the Futures Industry Association (FIA's) Top 40 by trading volume of futures and options are futures on baskets of government bonds.

For the introduction of deliverable futures on bond baskets, in order to prevent the creation of corners/squeezes using them, the market of underlying asset must meet a number of requirements. First of all, there should be a sufficient number of outstanding bond issues to compose baskets, which have a significant issue volume and typical characteristics, which ensures that the seller of the futures contract can choose the most affordable issue for delivery.

With an insufficient number of outstanding bond issues included in delivery baskets, there is a risk of price manipulations, and cash-settled futures on a bond basket becomes more effective contract. Such a contract may be based on a small number of underlying bonds. However, the cash settlement method of execution reduces the effectiveness of arbitrage operations, constraining the potential liquidity of instruments. It should be noted that ignoring the local features of bond markets and introducing a deliverable futures on a basket of bonds with an insufficiently capacious and liquid underlying market, in the absence of a sufficient number of reference issues outstanding, can cause systematic manipulative risks and, as a result, a lack of demand from market participants for these instruments. The shortcomings inherent in local markets make cash-settled futures on baskets of bonds in demand. Such instruments are also found in the FIA's TOP-40 interest-bearing contracts.

The underlying asset of a futures contract for a basket of government bonds is a set of real issues included in the delivery basket, with individual maturities, coupon rates, in some cases the frequency of payments and the market yield. Due to the choice of one issue from the basket for delivery under the terms of the specification, the pricing of the contract is carried out in relation to a notional bond, the coupon rate and maturity of which are set in the specification [25]. A conversion factor (ratio) is used to bring underlying physical bond in line with a notional bond. Conversion factor is calculated for each bond included in the supply baskets in relation to each futures series in circulation. This is the theoretical price of the bond on the day of the futures execution, which is calculated taking into account the yield set by the exchange in the contract specification.

The minimum value of the calculated theoretical bond prices adjusted for the corresponding conversion factor is taken for the "cheapest to delivery" issue (CTD). This implies the greatest cost-effectiveness of delivery (least lost profits, or least arbitration opportunity) for the seller of the futures. Notional bond has hypothetical terms so the pricing of the futures on the basket of bonds is based on the forward price of the underlying CTD bond divided by the conversion ratio of that issue for the corresponding futures series.

The mechanism for reduction of the risk of price manipulations is contained in the right of the futures seller to replace an issue of bonds that is not available for delivery with another issue from the delivery basket. The more representative the supply basket is, the lower the risk of price manipulations is included in this contract.

The yield, on the basis of which the conversion ratio is calculated, is set by the exchange and is fixed, as a rule, for all series of the futures considered. This yield corresponds to the size of the coupon rate of the notional bond of the futures.

In order to ensure transparency and predictability of futures pricing for long-term hedging strategies, an exchange can adjust the value of the benchmark yield, which is done very rarely [13]. In recent work, we found that "a significant divergence between the benchmark yield level and the current market values allows, in the allows clearly highlight as CTD:

- the minimum duration bond – if the benchmark yield is higher than the market yields of the bonds included in the delivery basket;
- the maximum duration bond – if the benchmark yield is lower than the market yields of the bonds included in the delivery basket" [17].

If the benchmark yield is close to market yield, there are frequent changes of the CTD bond. This creates excess volatility in the theoretical price of the futures con-tract that occurs when the CTD bond changes.

Futures on long-term interest rates began to be introduced in the second half of the 1970s on the American exchange-traded market. Long-term futures were initially launched on the Chicago Board of Trade (CBOT).

Futures contracts on US Treasury bonds and notes have the structure of deliverable futures on baskets of bonds. US municipal bond futures are derivatives on the bond index.

Following the US, bond futures were launched on the LIFFE. Most of the originally launched contracts have either undergone significant specification changes over time or have been delisted. The launch of futures contracts for government bonds, including foreign governments (offshore futures contracts), testified to the intention of LIFFE to be the leader in the financial futures segment in Europe.

Among the offshore contracts, the most popular futures contract for US Treasury bonds, the launch of which had a positive impact on the volume of trading in US bonds in the European market.

The largest trading activity on LIFFE was generated by a futures contract on British long-term bonds. The causes of the growth in demand were the arrival in the 1980s foreign participants in the UK debt market and the volatility of interest rates that existed at that time.

Later interest rate derivatives were launched in the Asian region. The most popular interest rate futures were launched on the Japanese and Singapore markets. Futures on 10-year Japanese government bonds were launched in 1985. The contract was introduced due to the lack of other mechanisms for hedging interest rate risk, which was of particular interest to money market participants who faced restrictions on short sales of bonds.

Today, futures contracts on long-term interest rates are traded at many exchanges in the world. Since the launch of the first interest rate derivatives the leading positions remain with the US market, where the main share of trading falls on the CME Group (including CBOT). Futures contracts on long-term rates in the USA contain the maximum number (7) of types of futures traded simultaneously, located along the entire yield curve. The key parameters of these financial instruments are shown in Table 2.

Table 2. Futures contracts on long-term interest rates in the United States.

Bond Futures	Bonds maturity, year	Face value, USD	Benchmark yield
2-Year T-Note Futures	1 year and 9 months–2 years	$200,000	6%
3-Year T-Note Futures	2 years and 9 months–3 years	$200,000	
5-Year T-Note Futures	4 years and 2 months–5 years and 3 months	$100,000	
10-Year T-Note Futures	6.5 years–10 years	$100,000	
Ultra 10-Year T-Note Futures	9 years 5 months–10 years	$100,000	
T-Bond Futures	15–25 years	$100,000	

Source: CME group. Understand Treasuries Contract Specifications. – URL: https://www.cmegroup.com

American contracts are a classic version of deliverable futures on baskets of government bonds. A feature of these contracts is the delivery period, which is the entire delivery month. If a short futures position to make delivery, sellers set the delivery date and the class of the asset underlying physical bond satisfying the contract specification and its own financial interests. Delivery can be made on any business day of the delivery month, which is similar to an American-style option. The delivery process under futures contracts takes 3 days (three-day delivery process): intention day, notice day and delivery day.

The segment of interest rate derivatives on LTIR is represented here by futures contracts on baskets of bonds of Germany, Italy, France, Spain and Switzerland (Table 3).

The benchmark yield for the three main contracts is 6%, for the Buxl Futures contract it equal 4%. These levels significantly exceed the near-zero yields that were observed on the European market for a long period of time after 2012.

In general, futures contracts of other countries traded at EUREX are identical to the German contracts. The difference concerns only the number of contracts and the length of maturity of the underlying bonds. The expiration date for all contracts falls on the same day - the delivery day.

The number of contracts and bonds' term to maturity of in their delivery baskets are presented in Table 3. The wider limits for basic issues of futures contract on Swiss government bonds are explained by the smaller number of outstanding bond issues, which is an important factor in the formation of delivery baskets.

The benchmark yield of a notional bond for all contracts of the considered groups is 6%. Euro-Buxl Futures is an exception and these contracts have a benchmark yield of 4%.

Table 3. Futures contracts on long-term rates at EUREX.

Futures contracts	Remaining terms in years	Face value	Benchmark yield
Germany			
Euro Schatz Futures	1.75–2.25	100 000 EUR	
Euro Bobl Futures	4.5–5.5	100 000 EUR	6%
Euro Bund Futures	8.5–10.5	100 000 EUR	
Euro Buxl® Futures	24–35	100 000 EUR	4%
Italy			
Short-Term Euro-BTP Futures	2.0–3.25	100 000 EUR	
Mid-Term Euro-BTP Futures	4.5–6.0	100 000 EUR	
Long-Term Euro-BTP Futures	8.5–11.0	100 000 EUR	6%
France			
Mid-Term Euro-OAT Futures	4.5–5.5	100 000 EUR	
Euro-OAT Futures	8.5–10.5	100 000 EUR	6%
Spain			
Euro-Bono-Futures	8.5–10.5	100 000 EUR	6%
Swiss Confederation			
CONF Futures	8.0–13.0	100 000 CHF	6%

Source: Eurex. Fixed Income Futures. – URL: https://www.eurex.com/ex-en/markets/int/fix/government-bonds

EUREX uses an additional qualification for underlying bond issues to enable them to be included in the delivery baskets. This is the bonds' placement volume, which should not be less than the value set by the exchange. For baskets containing German debt securities, the two nearest contracts by expiration date must meet a minimum issue volume of 5 billion EUR, and the farthest contract, the third quoted contract by date of expiration, must be 4 billion EUR. The minimum volume of issues for debt securities of Italy, France and Spain to be recognized as suitable for delivery should be 5 billion EUR. In Italy and Spain, there is an additional criterion: this issue volume of 5 billion EUR must be established no later than 10 business days before the last trading day of the next settlement month. For futures contracts with Swiss bonds as the underlying asset, the basket must have a minimum issuance of 500 million Swiss francs. These requirements allow to minimize market manipulation risks, providing sufficient volume of supply and liquidity for market players.

In addition to EUREX, the Intercontinental Exchange (ICE Futures Europe), which absorbed the pan-European EURONEXT, occupies a leading position in the segment of interest rate derivatives in the European derivatives market. Contemporary derivatives trading on long-term interest rates on ICE Futures Europe is represented by 16 contracts from 5 countries, focused on various terms, starting from 1 year. In terms of the number of contracts, this exchange surpasses EUREX, however, in terms of trading volumes and liquidity of contracts on long-term interest rates, it is much inferior to the latter.

Contracts traded at ICE Futures Europe complement those traded at EUREX, expanding the overall range of futures on LTIR. At the same time, the contracts of the German and Italian bond futures traded at ICE Futures Europe fully correspond to the contracts traded on EUREX. Of the differences, it should be noted that at ICE Futures Europe, the Swiss bond futures, in addition to the 10-year bond futures, also includes the 5-year bond contract; the Spanish bond futures, in addition to the futures, identical to those traded at Eurex on 10-year bonds, includes contracts on 2-year and 5-year bonds. Also quoted here are contracts on British government bonds, which make up the main turnover of futures on long-term interest rates and include three main contracts with maturities of underlying bonds up to 12 years and a futures contract on ultra-long-term 30-year bonds, which has significantly less liquidity.

The difference between contracts on British bonds and other contracts on European countries' bonds is the delivery period, which, similar American contracts, lasts the entire delivery month.

Australian settled futures are based on a bonds basket and are priced on a notional bond. Cash-settlement contracts on the ASX include at least three bonds with the corresponding maturity. Based on the real prices of the underlying bonds included in the settlement basket, an average indicative yield is formed. This value determines the quoted price of the futures contract and the corresponding price of the notional bond. The use of a basket of bonds as the underlying asset allows for more objective pricing by limiting excessive influence on the futures price of an individual bond issue.

As we wrote earlier, "although the benchmark yield for Australian futures contracts varies, it remains fixed and does not change for subsequent calendar series of the respective futures. Another feature of Australian futures contracts on long-term interest rates is their quotation, which is carried out as a difference of 100 and indicative yield" [17].

One of the most important aspects to consider when structuring derivatives is the choice of their underlying assets. Baskets of futures contracts are formed from underlying bonds, that is, issues with a constant coupon and par value, without early redemption (amortization and offers), with a typical payment frequency. The selection of bond issues of the same type simplifies the composition of bond baskets, which is carried out by maturity, which is generally identical to the duration restriction for such issues, as a result of which bonds with a comparable interest rate risk are included in the baskets. The statistics regarding the share of benchmark yield in the total number/volume of government bonds issues in the jurisdictions under consideration, for the bonds of which futures contracts are traded, are important to assess the potential for the development of trading in such contracts.

The share of reference bond issues that are potentially suitable for addition in the delivery and settlement baskets of futures contracts exceeds 60% in terms of number of issues and 80% by volume of issues in all the jurisdictions considered.

Another factor for assessing the quality of bonds as an underlying asset is the volume of the market, that is, the total volume of placed bond issues at a particular moment, and its dynamics.

4 Results and Discussion

Previously, we examined the Russian experience in introducing interest rate derivatives and notes that it "differs from the world one due to the fact that in different periods there were attempts to launch futures with a different structure. The largest number of varieties of futures contracts was launched by the Russian Trading System (RTS) in the period from 2004 to 2011" [17].

The underlying asset of these futures contracts was separate bond issues, which created potential risks of price manipulation before the expiration date. For this reason, such a structure is not common in the world. However, in Russian market, such instruments were traded, meeting the local demand of market participants, due to the lack of sufficient capacity of the government or other bonds market, which would allow forming contracts of the generally accepted basket structure.

In 2011, RTS launched long-term interest rates futures. It was the futures on baskets of Russian federal bonds OFZ. The structure of these contracts corresponded to the generally accepted in international practice structure, however, a number of parameters of these instruments had notable differences, which could lead to limited demand. Ultimately, these futures contracts were delisted.

The trend in the total amount of outstanding OFZ, the market for futures on OFZ baskets steadily declined since its peak in 2013, as a result of which trading in them was terminated in July 2022. It should be noted that the share of OFZ issues potentially suitable for inclusion in the settlement baskets, is currently significantly lower than foreign indicators and amounts to less than 60 percent (bearing in mind the trend towards an increase in the share of floaters).

To test the hypothesis stated at the beginning of our study, we analyzed the model of a futures contract on a basket of bonds used in Russia. We also compared this model with those that are typical for foreign exchanges. It was found that this model of LTIR futures had built-in shortcomings that caused the futures low liquidity in the market and, ultimately, led to the removal of these contracts from trading.

Let us show where we saw the identified shortcomings.

Firstly, when launching futures on OFZ baskets, the trading volume and the number of bonds that can be included in the deliverable basket of the contract were not taken into account. Despite the fact that the Russian government bond market is inferior to foreign markets in terms of these indicators (Fig. 2), the Russian market of futures contracts on long-term interest rates had an excessive number of baskets (equals 5), which significantly diluted liquidity without providing additional risk management opportunities (Table 4). As our analysis showed, 1 contract is enough to hedge a parallel shift in the yield curve, 2 contracts are enough to hedge a change in the yield curve angle, and 3 contracts are enough to hedge a change in the yield curve shape.

Secondly, the futures specification on OFZ baskets at the Moscow Exchange did not imply a fixed value of the benchmark yield. The composition of the baskets and

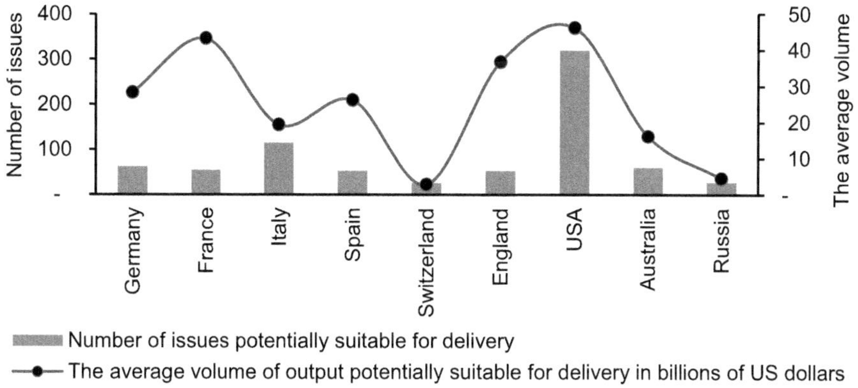

Source: authors' calculations based on Bloomberg data. https://www.bloomberg.com/professional/solution/bloomberg-terminal/

Fig. 2. Total number and average volume of potentially deliverable bond basket futures, April 2021.

Table 4. Number of futures contracts on the settlement basket of government bonds (by countries).

Country	Number of contracts	Country	Number of contracts	Country	Number of contracts
USA	7	France	2	Switzerland	2
Great Britain	4	Italy	3	Australia	4
Germany	4	Spain	3	Russia	5

Source: authors' calculations based on Bloomberg data. https://www.bloomberg.com/professional/solution/bloomberg-terminal/

the value of the benchmark yield were set by the Moscow Exchange when the next series of futures were launched based on the current market conditions. The instability of benchmark yield on these contracts, that was observed, had two negative effects:

- reduced predictability of futures pricing over a long planning horizon, as the benchmark yield of following series of futures is currently unknown;
- because the Moscow Exchange set the benchmark yield on the basis of the current market yields of the bonds included in the delivery basket at the time the futures series was launched, the CTD bond issue on the basis of which the theoretical price of the futures was calculated, changed frequently during the life of the contract. This made the calculation of the hedge ratio very difficult and reduced the effectiveness of arbitrage trading.

Together with the delisting of all deliverable futures contracts on OFZ baskets, in early 2022 the Moscow Exchange prepared and launched a new instrument that has no successful analogues in world practice at the moment - a settlement futures contract on the government bond index (RGBI). Unlike the above example of the futures on the

US municipal bond index, this index does not contain the mentioned shortcomings, in particular, its calculation base is homogeneous, because includes only government bonds. The lack of positive dynamics of trading volume and open interest for this instrument demonstrates insufficient demand from market participants, which may be associated with the inefficiency of the structure of this contract proposed for the financial market players for hedging and arbitrage operations.

The restraint of this instrument in terms of hedging is the underlying asset itself. RGBI is an index, the calculation base of which includes the most liquid Russian federal loan bonds with a duration of more than one year. This index combines issues of various durations, which complicates the calculation of the hedging ratio for a portfolio that does not correspond to the index structure, and makes it impossible to hedge changes in the slope and shape of the yield curve.

The restraining factors for the formation of demand for the RGBI index futures in terms of arbitrage trading are the settlement procedure stipulated in the contract and the underlying asset in the form of a bond index. To build an arbitrage strategy of the cash-and-carry type, which includes holding two opposite positions at the same time - in the future and in the underlying asset, it is necessary to observe the structure of the underlying asset in the cash position as accurately as possible, as well as to conclude a transaction with the underlying asset at the lowest possible costs. The bond market is not completely liquid, which creates increased transaction costs, and also limits the possibility of simultaneously concluding transactions across the entire structure of the index.

The Russian government bond market has been steadily growing in recent years, which means that interest rate risk in the economy is becoming more substantial. This determines the potential demand for a hedging instrument for this type of risk in the capital market. However, an interest rate risk hedging instrument is still missing in the Russian market.

We consider it relevant to continue a detailed analysis of the accumulated Russian and foreign experience in order to develop interest rate derivatives with a clear, calculated utility not only for speculators, but mainly for arbitrageurs (since arbitrageurs begin the formation of initial liquidity in the market), and hedgers, as the main consumers of derivatives as target products.

5 Conclusion

The emergence of a developed market for long-term interest rate derivatives was the result of a direct demand for interest rate risk hedging instruments in the capital market. The world market shows a close relationship between the indicators of the underlying asset market and the derivatives market.

The experience of some countries and the largest world exchanges allows us to single out deliverable futures contracts on baskets of government bonds as a key type of instrument for hedging the long-term interest rates risk. However, when bond futures are launched it is important to consider underlying asset market and to design contract parameters with a clear understanding of the procedure for their use by all categories of market participants. The lack of transparent formation of internal parameters of the futures contract' structure fully comply with world practice, may lead to a lack of actual demand for these derivatives, which could be observed in the market of futures on OFZ baskets at the Moscow Exchange.

At the same time, our analysis did not consider another feature: the change in the structure of the government bond market towards a significant increase in the share of floaters. As of mid-2024, this share, according to the Ministry of Finance of the Russian Federation, was more than 40%. Such a structural transformation of the bond market makes the formation of delivery baskets for LTIR futures a more challenging task. Thus, some limitations arise with respect to the conclusions formulated above.

The presented study made it possible to systematize the classification of types of futures contracts on long-term interest rates, highlight the key strengths and weaknesses of the varieties of these derivatives, show the relationship between the development of the main type of contracts on long-term interest rates – futures on baskets of government bonds – with quantitative indicators of the underlying government bond market, as well as highlight a successful example of taking into account the specifics of the local bond market when forming a contract that is different from the typical type, namely, a settlement futures on a basket of bonds. In addition, the study showed the ratio of the number of futures for government bonds in individual markets in comparison with the number of benchmark bond issues of government bonds underlying such futures and their volume – which is important when predicting the potential liquidity of contracts when they are put into circulation, as well as the dynamics of the benchmark yield set by exchanges and its relationship with real yields to maturity in the bond market - which reflects the systematic establishment and change of the benchmark yield by exchanges to ensure greater transparency in futures pricing and predictability of hedging operations over the long horizon. Thus, the study made it possible to present the problems of futures on long-term interest rates on the part of the stock exchange as the organizer of the market for such financial instruments.

References

1. Choudhry, M.: The Bond and Money Markets: Strategy, Trading, Analysis. Butterworth-Heinemann, Oxford (2001). https://doi.org/10.1016/B978-075064677-2.50041-3
2. Batten, J.A., Fetherston, T.A., Szilagyi, P.G.: European Fixed Income Markets: Money, Bond and Interest Rate Derivatives. Wiley, England (2004)
3. De Jong, M., Fabozzi, F.J.: The market risk of corporate bonds. J. Portf. Manag. **46**(2), 92–105 (2019). https://doi.org/10.3905/jpm.2019.1.120
4. Patashkova, Y., Niyazbekova, S., Kerimkhulle, S., Serikova, M., Troyanskaya, M.: Dynamics of Bitcoin trading on the Binance cryptocurrency exchange. Econ. Ann.-XXI **187**(1–2), 177–188 (2021). https://doi.org/10.21003/ea.v187-17
5. Krinichansky, K.V., Annenskaya, N.E.: Financial development: the concept and prospects. Vopr. Ekon. **10**, 20–36 (2022). https://doi.org/10.3209/0042-8736-2022-10-20-36. (in Russian)
6. Chisholm, A.M.: Derivatives Demystified: A Step-by-Step Guide to Forwards, Futures, Swaps and Options, 2nd edn. Wiley (2010)
7. Hull, J.C.: Options, Futures, and Other Derivatives, 11th edn. Pearson (2021)
8. Kolb, R.W., Overdahl, J.A.: Financial Derivatives: Pricing and Risk Management (2010). https://doi.org/10.2139/ssrn.1568206

9. Panda, P., Thiripalraju, M.: Rise and fall of interest rate futures in Indian derivative market. Int. J. Financ. Manag. (2015). https://doi.org/10.21863/ijfm/2015.5.1.006
10. Sundaram, R., Das, S.: Derivatives, 2nd edn. McGraw Hill (2015)
11. Tuckman, B., Serrat, A.: Fixed Income Securities: Tools for Today's Markets. John Wiley & Sons, Hoboken (2022). https://doi.org/10.1002/9781119835622
12. De Pooter, M.: Examining the Nelson-Siegel class of term structure models. Tinbergen Institute Discussion Paper, 07-043/4. Tinbergen Institute (2007). https://www.econstor.eu/bitstream/10419/86575/1/07-043.pdf
13. Oviedo, R.: Improving the design of Treasury bond futures. J. Bus. **79**(3), 1293–1315 (2006). https://doi.org/10.1086/500677
14. Cusatis, P.J.: An analysis of the failed municipal bond and note futures contracts. J. Futur. Mark. **28**(7), 656–679 (2008). https://doi.org/10.1002/fut.20312
15. Ahn, H.J., Cai, J., Cheung, Y.-L.: What moves German Bund futures contracts on the Eurex? J. Futur. Mark. **22**(7), 679–696 (2002). https://doi.org/10.1002/fut.10027
16. Batten, J.A., Fetherston, T.A., Szilagyi, P.G.: Japanese Fixed Income Markets: Money, Bond and Interest Rate Derivatives. Elsevier, England (2006)
17. Karov, E.K.: Bond Futures Contracts as an Interest Rate Risk Hedging Tool: Foreign and Russian practice (Doctoral dissertation). Moscow (2022)
18. Frino, A., William, P.H., Lepone, A.: The pricing and efficiency of Australian Treasury Bond futures. Aust. Acc. Bus. Financ. J. **8**(2), 3–14 (2014). https://doi.org/10.14453/aabfj.v8i2.2
19. Cheung, B.: Trading in Treasury Bond Futures Contracts and Bonds in Australia. Reserve Bank of Australia Bulletin, September, 47–52 (2014)
20. Alrawashdeh, N.H., Alrawashdeh, N.H.: Hedging of interest rate risk with interest rate futures. Int. J. Geol. Agric. Environ. Sci. **3**(2), 8–23 (2015)
21. Ankur, P., Madhurjya, D.: Interest Rate Futures Market in India. Indian Institute of Management, Bangalore (2009)
22. Bansal, R.: Long-run risks and financial markets. NBER Working Paper No. 13196 (2007). https://ssrn.com/abstract=997552
23. Divya, S., Shashi, S.: Success and failure of interest rate futures in India. Adv. Manag. **6**, 56–59 (2013)
24. Korivi, S.R., James, E.: Interest rate futures and market structure in India. Res. Bull. **42**(1), 129–137 (2016)
25. Manish, S.: The impact of interest rate futures on the underlying interest rate markets in India. Dev. Country Stud. **11**(2), 101–111 (2012)

Author Index

E. Kuzmin et al. (Eds.): EASET 2024, SPBE, pp. 299–300, 2025.
https://doi.org/10.1007/978-3-031-91159-0

GPSR Compliance

The European Union's (EU) General Product Safety Regulation (GPSR) is a set of rules that requires consumer products to be safe and our obligations to ensure this.

If you have any concerns about our products, you can contact us on ProductSafety@springernature.com

In case Publisher is established outside the EU, the EU authorized representative is:

Springer Nature Customer Service Center GmbH
Europaplatz 3
69115 Heidelberg, Germany

Batch number: 08545060

Printed by Printforce, the Netherlands